The Neurobiology of
Learning and Memory

The Neurobiology of Learning and Memory

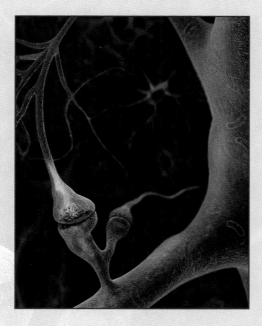

JERRY W. RUDY
University of Colorado, Boulder

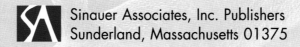
Sinauer Associates, Inc. Publishers
Sunderland, Massachusetts 01375

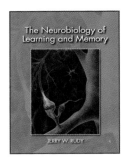

The Cover

Deep inside the brain, a neuron prepares to transmit a signal to its target. To capture that fleeting moment, Graham Johnson based this elegant drawing on ultra-thin micrographs of sequential brain slices. After scanning a sketch into 3D modeling software, he colored the image and added texture and glowing lighting reminiscent of a scanning electron micrograph. (Image created by Graham Johnson of www.fiVth.com for the Howard Hughes Medical Institute/HHMI Bulletin © 2004.)

The Neurobiology of Learning and Memory
Copyright © 2008 by Sinauer Associates, Inc.

Address inquiries and orders to
Sinauer Associates, Inc.
23 Plumtree Road
Sunderland, MA 01375 U.S.A.

www.sinauer.com
FAX: 413-549-1118
orders@sinauer.com
publish@sinauer.com

Library of Congress Cataloging-in-Publication Data

Rudy, Jerry W., 1942-
  The neurobiology of learning and memory / Jerry W. Rudy.
      p. cm.
  Includes bibliographical references and index.
  ISBN 978-0-87893-669-4 (alk. paper)
  1. Memory—Textbooks. 2. Learning—Textbooks. 3.
Neurobiology—Textbooks. I. Title.

QP406.R83 2008
612.8—dc22

                              2007050489

Printed in China
5 4 3 2 1

Preface

The scientific study of learning and memory, originally the domain of psychologists, now is shared by scientists trained in a variety of disciplines that include biochemistry, cellular–molecular biology, electrophysiology, neuroanatomy, and neuropsychology. The work of hundreds of scientists from these diverse fields has produced an explosion of knowledge about learning and memory that almost defies comprehension.

This book represents my attempt to integrate some of what we have learned from this interdisciplinary approach into a coherent framework that can be understood by students who have a rudimentary background in psychology and neuroscience and also by the wider scientific community. The challenge was how to compress such an enormous and diverse field into a manageable end product.

As I began this task, it became clear that I could tell three large, interrelated, and fascinating stories, a choice that prompted me to organize the book into three major sections. This organization results in telling the tale from the bottom up: it progresses from neurons, synapses, and molecules that provide the basic infrastructure of memories, to the neural systems that capture the rich content of our experience.

After a brief conceptual and historical introduction to the field presented in Chapter 1, the first story (Part 1) is organized around the central idea that synapses are elementary storage units that can be modified by experience. Chapter 2 introduces the general problem of identifying synapses that might store memories and a basic methodology for studying how synapses can be modified. Chapters 3–6 describe some of the fundamental processes that are engaged by synaptic activity and alter synaptic strength—modifications and interactions among existing proteins, the trafficking of AMPA receptors, the transcription of new genes and their translation into useful protein, the role of calcium, and structural and functional changes in dendritic spines.

The second story (Part 2) begins with a discussion in Chapter 7 of the basic conceptual issues researchers face in trying to relate cellular processes and molecules to memory and describes some of the behavioral and neurobiological methods that are used to make this connection. Chapters 8 and 9 build on the foundation provided in Part 1 to show how cellular and molecular processes identified from studies of synaptic plasticity also participate in making memories of behavioral experiences. Chapter 10 introduces the concept of memory modulation systems, and Chapter 11 discusses the fate of retrieved memories and how they can be modified.

The third story (Part 3) is organized around what is sometimes called the multiple memory systems view—that different neural systems have evolved to capture the various content contained in our experiences. Three neural systems are discussed. Chapters 12 and 13 introduce the multiple memory systems concept and focus on how the medial temporal hippocampal system supports a category of memory called episodic memory. Chapter 14 describes the relationship of the medial temporal hippocampal system to theories of systems consolidation that attempt to explain Ribot's law—that old memories are more resistant to disruption than newly formed memories. Chapter 15 describes the cortical-striatal system that supports our ability to learn instrumental behaviors, called actions and habits, which enable us to successfully drive cars and play sports and musical instruments. Chapter 16 describes a neural system that stores the emotional content of aversive experiences and how these emotional memories might be extinguished.

In writing this book, I tried to provide a broad context in which to introduce the key concepts and facts that are central to a particular topic. I made no attempt to be comprehensive in the material I covered. Instead, I tried to maintain a level of description and discussion that was sufficient to ensure a basic understanding of the relevant principles and processes, without getting to a level of detail that would be tedious. If this approach was successful, then I will have provided the reader with a foundation to continue an in-depth exploration of this field, while presenting some of the remarkable achievements of many wonderful researchers who have made this field one of the great scientific adventures of our time.

Acknowledgments

Writing this book was the most exciting intellectual endeavor of my career. I am most grateful to the many wonderful scientists who have created the field this book represents. I owe a special debt to three individuals, Allan R. Wagner, Robert J. Sutherland, and Randall C. O'Reilly, who played a major role in the development of my research interests and my career. Without their timely appearance at different stages of my career, this book would never have been written.

Several individuals provided thoughtful comments on specific chapters, and I thank them for their helpful suggestions: Hisham E. Atallah, MIT; Heidi Day, University of Colorado, Boulder; Stephen Maren, University of Michigan; James L. McGaugh, University of California, Irvine; and Robert J. Sutherland, University of Lethbridge. I especially thank Timothy J. Teyler, University of Idaho, for his comments on the chapters about synaptic plasticity.

The preparation of this book benefited greatly from the staff at Sinauer Associates. I thank Graig Donini, the editor for the project; Chris Small, Joanne Delphia, and Elizabeth Morales for their talented design ideas, book layout, and artwork; and especially Sydney Carroll, who made the arduous task of writing a textbook a relatively painless process.

As I approached the completion of the book, Sinauer Associates agreed to allow my wife, Julia A. Rudy, to assume major editorial responsibility for the final product. At this point the book truly became a joint effort. Without Julie's involvement, I cannot imagine how this project would have been completed. Her editorial skills and commitment to excellence are directly responsible for the book's organizational clarity and readability.

Jerry W. Rudy
Professor of Psychology
University of Colorado, Boulder

About the Author

Jerry W. Rudy

Jerry W. Rudy is a professor in the Department of Psychology and Center for Neuroscience at the University of Colorado, Boulder. He served as chair of the psychology department for eight years and was interim Associate Dean of Sciences. He has taught undergraduate and graduate courses in learning, learning theory, and the neurobiology of learning theory for more than 25 years. He has served as the editor of *Developmental Psychobiology* and is currently on the editorial board of *Learning and Memory, Behavioral Neuroscience*, and *Neuroscience and Biobehavioral Reviews*. He has also served as president of the Society for Developmental Psychobiology. Rudy is noted for his work on the development of memory systems and the role of the hippocampus in episodic memory. The National Science Foundation and the National Institute of Mental Health have supported his research. Outside of his academic pursuits he has been extensively engaged as a tennis player and coach and in honing his skills as a guitarist, including a two-year stint as the rhythm guitarist in a local gypsy jazz band called Deco Django that performs in the Boulder–Denver area. He is also currently president of Imagine!, a non-profit center for developmental disabilities located in Boulder County.

Table of Contents

CHAPTER 16
Learning about Danger: The Neurobiology of Fear Memories 325

Introduction: Fundamental Concepts and Historical Foundations

Our uniqueness as human beings derives in large part from evolutionary adaptations that permit experience to modify connections linking networks of neurons in the brain. Information conveyed into the brain by our sensory channels can leave a lasting impression on neural circuits. These networks not only can be modified, the information contained in the modifications can be preserved and later retrieved to influence our behavior. Our individual experiences act on these networks to make us who we are. We have the ability to learn a vast array of skills. We can become musicians, athletes, artisans, skilled craftsmen, or cooks. Experience tunes our emotions to our environments. We acquire food preferences and aversions. Incredibly, without intention, we also lay down an autobiographical record of the events, times, and places in which our experiences occur. We are connected with our past and can talk about it. We learn and we remember.

Historically, the study of learning and memory has been the domain of philosophers and psychologists who have defined the relevant phenomena and many of the important variables that influence them. Only recently have brain scientists seriously weighed in on this topic. Armed with sophisticated methods to measure and manipulate brain processes and conceptual frameworks to guide their application, neurobiologists have now made enormous inroads into the mystery of how experience modifies the brain.

Consequently, an important field now exists called the **neurobiology of learning and memory**. Scientists working in this field want to know how the brain stores and retrieves information about our experiences. The goal of this book is to present a coherent account of some of the major accomplishments of this field and to provide a background that will enable you to understand many of the issues and central assumptions that drive research in this field.

Learning and Memory Described

The terms learning and memory are often used as if they are directly observable entities, but they are not. *Learning and memory are theoretical concepts used to explain the fact that experience influences behavior* (Figure 1.1). A familiar example will suffice to make the point.

You have an exam tomorrow. So, over the next few hours you closet yourself with your books and class notes. You take the test and answer the questions to the best of your knowledge. Later you receive your grade, 90%. Assuming that your grade would have been 50% if you had not studied, then a reasonable person (the professor) would assume that you learned and remembered the information needed to pass the test. The key phrase here is "would assume." Learning and memory were never directly observed. The only directly observable events in this example are that (a) you spent time with

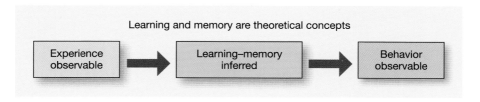

FIGURE 1.1
Learning and memory are unobservable, inferred processes used to explain the fact that our past experience influences our behavior.

your notes and books, and (b) you took the test and performed well. That you learned and remembered is inferred from your test performance and the professor's knowledge that you studied.

Larry Squire (1987) has provided a useful definition of the terms learning and memory: "Learning is the process of acquiring new information, while memory refers to the persistence of learning in a state that can be revealed at a later time" (p. 3). Other, more restrictive definitions have been proposed. They usually also stipulate what learning and memory are not. For example, a restricted definition would appropriately exclude fatigue, maturation, and injury that might result from or be associated with experience.

Although learning and memory are theoretical concepts, neurobiologists are motivated by the belief that they have a physical basis in the brain. A slight modification of Squire's definition provides a useful definition of the field: The goal of neurobiologists working in this field is to understand how the brain acquires, stores, and maintains representations of experience in a state that permits the information contained in the representation to be retrieved and influence behavior.

Psychological and Neurobiological Approaches

The study of learning and memory is the domain of both psychology and neurobiology. It is useful to point out some fundamental differences between the two approaches.

Psychological Approach

The general goal of psychology is to (a) derive a set of empirical principles that describe how variation in experience influences behavior, and (b) provide a theoretical account that can explain the observed facts. The study of memory became a science when Hermann Ebbinghaus developed the first methods for assessing the acquisition and retention of a controlled experience. He recognized that to study "pure memory" required a methodology that could separate what the subject already has learned from what the subject is now being asked to remember (Ebbinghaus, 1913). To do this, he invented what are called **nonsense syllables**. A nonsense syllable consists of a vowel placed between two consonants, such as *nuh*, *vag*, or *boc*. These syllables

Hermann Ebbinghaus

were designed to be meaningless so they would have to be learned without the benefit of prior knowledge. Thus, for example, *dog*, *cat*, or *cup* would be excluded. Ebbinghaus made up hundreds of nonsense syllables and used them to produce lists that were to be learned and remembered. Among the task variables he manipulated were factors such as the number of times a given list was presented during the memorization phase and the interval between the learning and the test phase.

Ebbinghaus worked alone and was the only subject of his experiments. He found that his test performance increased the more he practiced a given list. He also documented the fact that retention performance was better when he spaced the repetition of a given list than when the list was repeated without inserting a break between the learning trials. He also documented the first "forgetting curve." As is illustrated in Figure 1.2, retention was excellent when the test was given shortly after the learning trial, but it fell off dramatically within the first hour. Remarkably, the curve stabilized thereafter.

Empirical principles such as those produced by Ebbinghaus's experiments led to theoretical questions about the underlying structure of the memory (Figure 1.3). Consider Ebbinghaus's forgetting curve. One could imagine that this behavioral function is direct reflection of the property of a single memory trace, the strength of which declines monotonically as a function of the retention interval. In essence, the behavioral function directly represents the decay properties of the memory trace. Another theorist looking at the same data might be struck by the fact that although the rate of forgetting is initially rapid there is very little change after the first hour. This theorist might propose that the forgetting curve is a product of two memory traces with different decay rates: A short-term memory trace that decays relatively rapidly and a

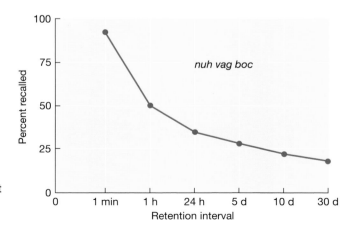

FIGURE 1.2
Ebbinghaus documented the first forgetting curve. Note that substantial forgetting occurs in the first hour after learning, but thereafter recall is fairly stable.

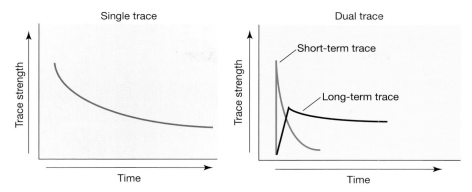

FIGURE 1.3
The single-trace theory explains Ebbinghaus's forgetting curve by assuming that the strength of a single memory trace declines monotonically as a function of time between learning and the retention test. The dual-trace theory explains that the forgetting curve results from two memory traces whose strength decays at different rates.

long-term memory trace that has much slower decay rate. Note in both cases hypotheses are put forth that point to properties—memory strength and memory traces with different decay rates—that defy direct observation.

A fundamental feature of the psychological approach is that a single methodology is used to collect the data and to test theory. Psychologists do not directly manipulate or measure brain function. They vary only the nature of experience and measure only behavior (Figure 1.4). Thus the psychological approach can be described as operating at a single level of analysis. Psychological research has identified critical phenomenon and concepts that provide the starting point for neurobiological investigation.

Neurobiological Approach

The goal of neurobiology is to relate the basic facts of learning and memory to events happening in the brain. If, in the above example, the dual-trace theory was established as valid by psychological experiments, the neurobiologist would want to know what are the properties of the brain that support two different memory traces. This goal requires a multi-level approach. In addition to using the behavioral methods of psychology that reveal how task variables such as trial spacing and repetition influence learning and retention, the neurobiological approach requires methods for:

- determining the regions of the brain that make up the brain system supporting the memory;

FIGURE 1.4
Psychologists study only the relationship between experience and behavior. Neurobiologists study how experience influences memory-dependent behavior by its influences on brain systems, synapses, and molecules.

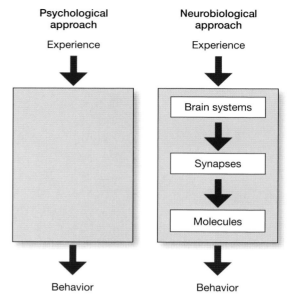

- determining how synapses that are potential storage mechanisms are altered by experience; and
- manipulating and measuring molecules in neurons that ultimately support the memory.

Thus the neurobiological approach is an interdisciplinary, multi-level approach. It combines the behavioral methods of psychology with the methods of anatomy, electrophysiology, pharmacology, biochemistry, and genetics. Because the methodologies of each discipline are complex and require specialized training to learn, different scientists often combine their individual skills to attack the problem.

Historical Influences: The Golden Age

The full-scale application of neurobiological methods to the study of learning and memory is a relatively new development. However, many of the important phenomena, concepts, insights, and methods that drive the field emerged over 100 years ago. Thirty years ago, in his comprehensive review of the psychobiology of memory, Paul Rozin (1976) described the last decade of the nineteenth century as the Golden Age of Memory because many of the basic phenomena and ideas emerged during that period.

Phenomena and Ideas

It was at the beginning of that decade that the French psychologist Théodule Ribot published his classic *Diseases of Memory* (1890). He was motivated by the belief that the study of brain pathology could provide insights into the normal organization of memory. His studies of many clinical cases led him to believe that the dissolution of memory accompanying pathology or injury followed an orderly temporal progression. He proposed that recent memories are the first to be lost, followed by autobiographical or personal memories that also have a temporal gradient. He believed that habits and emotional memories were the most resistant to dissolution.

Théodule Ribot

The idea that there is a temporal progression to memory loss—that old memories are more resistant to disruption than new ones—is often referred to as Ribot's Law (Figure 1.5). This generalization begs the question, what is it about old memories that makes them resistant to disruption? This question remains at the center of contemporary research and is the source of both excitement and controversy.

It was also during this period that Serge Korsakoff (1897) described the amnesic syndrome that now bears his name. Patients with this syndrome display what would now be called a severe, **anterograde amnesia**. They are not able to remember events experienced after the onset of the syndrome. However, early in the disease, memories established before the onset of the

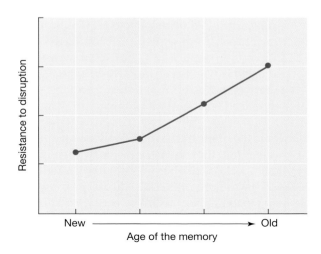

FIGURE 1.5
Ribot proposed that older memories are more resistant to disruption by traumatic events than newer memories. This hypothesis is called Ribot's Law.

Serge Korsakoff

William James

syndrome are generally preserved. Thus they initially display very little **retrograde amnesia**.

Korsakoff believed that the primary defect was an inability to form new memories. His interpretation of the deficit included two ideas. One idea was that the pathology impaired the physiological processes needed to establish and retain the memory. Today one might say that the mechanisms of memory storage or consolidation are impaired. The second idea was that the pathology in some way weakened the associative network that contained the memory or, in modern terms, produced a retrieval deficit, that is, the core memory trace is established but cannot be accessed. Korsakoff believed both factors contributed to the syndrome. Whether memory impairment is the result of a storage or retrieval failure can still be the source of heated debate in the contemporary literature.

One can only marvel at the insights contained in William James's *Principles of Psychology* (1890). An often noted contribution was his conception of memory as a sequence of processes initiated by an experience that begins with a briefly lasting sensation he called **after images**, then to the stage he called **primary memory**, and to the final stage he called **secondary memory** or **memory proper** (Figure 1.6).

Primary memory was viewed as the persisting representation of the experience that forms part of a stream of consciousness. Secondary memory contained the vast record of experiences that had receded from the stream of consciousness but could be later retrieved or recollected: "It is brought back, fished up, so to speak, from a reservoir in which, with countless other objects, it lay buried and lost from view" (James, 1890, p. 646). An object in primary memory is not brought back: it was never lost. Thus, we have the roots of the modern distinction between short-term memory and long-term memory that remain central to modern investigations of the neurobiological bases of memory.

James devoted an entire chapter to the brain. However, the absence of any relevant information precluded an attempt to directly relate memory phenomena to any specific regions of the brain or mechanisms. Nevertheless, he strongly believed that the retention of experience was not a mysterious mental property but that "it was a purely physical phenomenon, a morphological feature . . ." (p. 655). He even provided a connectionist model of the memory trace to bolster his belief. In at least two places he used the term **plasticity** to describe the property of

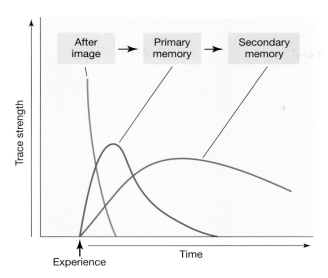

FIGURE 1.6
William James proposed that memories emerge in stages. The after image is supported by a short-lasting trace, then replaced by the primary memory trace. Secondary memory is viewed as the reservoir of enduring memory traces.

the brain that allows it to be modified by experience. For example, in his discussion of memory he wrote, "What happens in the nerve-tissue is but an example of that plasticity or of semi-inertness, yielding to change . . ." (p. 655). Thus, modern developments would come as no surprise to him.

During this period, the Spanish neuroanatomist Santiago Ramón y Cajal formulated what is known as the **neuron doctrine**—the idea that the brain is made up of discrete cells called nerve cells or neurons that are the elemental signal units of the brain (Ramón y Cajal, 1894–1904, translated by Swanson and Swanson, 1990). He also understood that neurons communicate at contact points called **synapses** and proposed that synapses can be modified by neural activity. This hypothesis is known as the **synaptic plasticity hypothesis**: "the strength of synaptic connections—the ease with which an action potential in one cell excites (or inhibits) its target cell—is not fixed but is plastic and modifiable" (Squire and Kandel, 1999, p. 35). Moreover, Ramón y Cajal believed that the plastic property of synapses could provide a means by which

Santiago Ramón y Cajal

experience could produce the persistent changes in the brain needed to support memories. The idea that the synapse is the basic information storage unit remains at the very heart of contemporary investigations of the mechanisms of memory storage.

Methods

The Golden Age documented important clinical phenomenon that provided initial insights into memory organization and produced ideas that remain fundamental to contemporary investigations. Remarkably, this period also produced some of the essential behavioral methods that in one form or another continue to be used to study how the brain supports learning and memory. Ebbinghaus's contribution already has been discussed. His work provided the basis for the scientific study of human memory.

Neurobiologists, however, want to understand how the brain supports learning and memory. Studies of normal people and patients with brain damage can identify interesting phenomenon that can provide some insight into the organization of memory. However, there are obvious major ethical concerns that constrain the direct manipulation of the human brain. Thus, to directly manipulate and measure brain events, neurobiologists have relied extensively on methods that allow the study of learning and memory with nonhuman animals. During the Golden Age, Ivan Pavlov and Edward L. Thorndike developed methodologies that remain essential to contemporary researchers who study the learning and memory processes of animals.

Pavlov (1927) began his career shift from studying digestive physiology to investigating the integrative activity of the brain. In doing so, he developed the fundamental paradigm for studying associative learning and memory in animals (Figure 1.7). The essence of this methodology, called classical or Pavlovian conditioning, is that a neutral stimulus such as the ringing of a bell (called the conditioned stimulus or CS) was paired with a biologically significant event such as food (called the unconditioned stimulus or US). The US caused the dog to salivate; this response is called the unconditioned response or UR. As a consequence of the several pairings of the bell (CS) and food (US), simply ringing the bell caused the dog to salivate. The response to the CS is called the conditioned response or CR. The ability of the CS to evoke the CR is believed to be the result of the brain associating the occurrence of the CS and US (Figure 1.8). Today no one uses dogs or measures the salivary response to study learning and memory in nonverbal animals. However, many neurobiologists still use variations of the Pavlovian conditioning methodology to study learning and memory in other nonhuman animals.

It was also at this time that Thorndike (1898) published his dissertation on animal intelligence in which he provided a methodology that permitted an

FIGURE 1.7
Pavlov in his laboratory.

objective investigation of how animals learned the consequences of their action. He invented what is referred to as Thorndike's puzzle box (Figure 1.9). An animal such as a cat or chicken would be placed in a wooden crate and to escape it had to learn to depress a lever to open an escape door. Thorndike's experiments provided the foundation for study of what is now called instrumental learning or Thorndikian conditioning. Variations of his methods continue to be extensively employed to reveal the systems of the brain involved in how animals learn to adapt their behavior based on the consequences of their actions.

FIGURE 1.8
In the Pavlovian conditioning method, two events called the CS and US are presented together. Subsequently, the CS evokes the response called the CR. Psychologists assume that the CS evokes the CR because the CS gets associated with the US. Psychologists and neurobiologists continue to use this method to study associative learning in animals.

FIGURE 1.9
Edward L. Thorndike invented the methodology for studying what is now called instrumental learning or Thorndikian conditioning. Cats, dogs, and chickens were placed into his puzzle box and had to learn how to manipulate levers to escape.

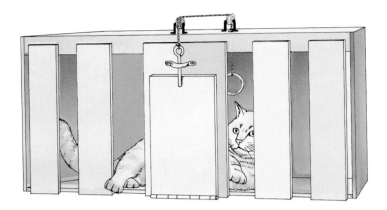

Edward L. Thorndike

Thorndike also proposed a theory of learning called the **Law of Effect** to explain the behavioral changes that he observed. The essence of this theory was that the correct behavior was learned because the consequences of successful outcome (a satisfying state) strengthened connections between the stimulus (S) and correct response (R) and the consequence of unsuccessful responses (annoying state) weakened the competing and wrong S–R connections. This theory continues to influence contemporary neurobiological investigations.

Core Themes

Scientists from a wide range of disciplines have been intrigued by questions about how the brain supports learning and memory. Their efforts have generated an enormous literature that even seasoned researchers find overwhelming. No single book can begin to do justice to the current state of knowledge. However, it may be possible to provide a road map for appreciating some of the major accomplishments of this field and provide a foundation for future study. To achieve this more modest goal, this book is organized around three large themes that represent much of the field: synaptic plasticity, molecules and memory, and memory systems.

Synaptic Plasticity

Contemporary neuroscientists believe that the synapse is the fundamental unit of memory storage. For synapses to support memory they have to be plastic or modifiable. The last 30 years have yielded remarkable insights into some of the basic mechanisms that support changes in the strength of synapses. Thus, a considerable portion of this book has the goal of providing a coherent introduction to the important ideas that have been generated by this field.

Molecules and Memory

Memories result from behavioral experiences. The past 30 years also have witnessed the development of many useful behavioral procedures for studying memory formation in nonverbal animals. Armed with these behavior methods, researchers have been emboldened to determine if memories are a product of some of the same cellular–molecular events that alter the strength of synaptic connections. Bringing ideas from the study of synaptic plasticity to the study of memory formation is one of the most dynamic and exciting adventures in brain–behavioral sciences. Thus, another section of this book is concerned with providing a basic introduction to the central findings and ideas that have emerged from this enterprise.

Memory Systems

The content of our experience matters to the brain. One of the important achievements of the modern era has been the realization that the brain has evolved neural systems that are specialized to capture and store the varied content generated by our experiences. This idea is generally represented by the term **multiple memory systems**. For example, different systems have been identified that enable us to keep track of the episodes that make up our personal history and to record emotionally charged events to protect us from danger. These stand apart from other brain systems that enable us to learn the consequences of our actions and acquire the routine and not so routine skills and habits that enable us to interact successfully with our environment. The last section of this book provides an introduction to some of the important developments in this domain.

Summary

In this chapter a number of fundamental concepts were presented that provide a background needed to go forward. Some of the historical foundation for the field was also described. Many of the core phenomena, concepts, and behavioral methods that are central to the neurobiology of learning and memory emerged in what Rozin called the Golden Age of Memory, the last decade of the nineteenth century. These ideas are intimately linked to individuals

(Ebbinghaus, James, Korsakoff, Pavlov, Ramón y Cajal, Ribot, and Thorndike) who have provided a context from which the central themes that guide contemporary research emerged.

References

Ebbinghaus, H. (1913). *Uber das Gedachtnis: Untersuchungen zur experimentellen Psychologie.* Leipzig: Dunke and Humboldt. Trans. by H. A. Ruger and C. E. Byssennine as *Memory: A contribution to experimental psychology.* New York: Dover.

James, W. (1890). *Principles of psychology.* New York: Holt.

Korsakoff, S. S. (1987). Disturbance of psychic function in alcoholic paralysis and its relation to the disturbance of the psychic sphere in multiple neuritis of nonalchoholic origins. *Vesin. Psychiatrii 4*: fascicle 2.

Pavlov, I. P. (1927). *Conditioned reflexes.* London: Oxford University Press.

Ramón y Cajal, S. (1894–1904). *Textura del sistema nervioso del hombre y de los vertebrados.* Trans. by N. Swanson and L. W. Swanson as *New ideas on the structure of the nervous system in man and vertebrates.* Cambridge, MA: MIT Press, 1990.

Ribot, T. (1890). *Diseases of Memory.* New York: Appleton and Company.

Rozin, P. (1976). The psychobiology of memory. In M. R. Rosenzweig and E. L. Bennett (Eds.), *Neural mechanisms of learning and memory* (pp. 3–46). Cambridge, MA: The MIT Press.

Squire, L. R. (1987). *Memory and brain.* New York: Oxford University Press.

Squire, L. R. and Kandel, E. R. (1999). *Memory from mind to molecules.* New York: W. J. Freeman and Company.

Thorndike, E. L. (1898). Animal intelligence: an experimental study of the associative processes in animals. *Psychological Review*, Monograph Supplement 2, no. 8.

PART ONE

Synaptic Basis of Memories

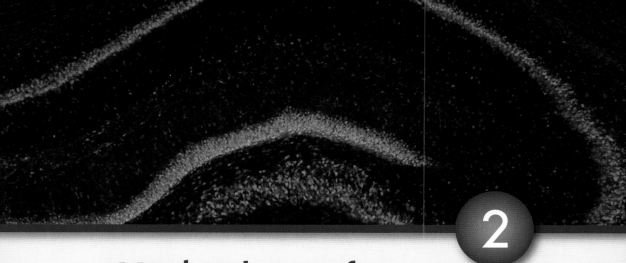

Mechanisms of Synaptic Plasticity: Introduction

What properties of the brain allow it to acquire and maintain information generated by our experiences? Conventional wisdom is that memories are stored in large networks of interconnected neurons and that experience leaves its impact by modifying the connections between those neurons (Teyler, 1999). Thus, neurobiologists are motivated by the belief that the information content of our various experiences persists in a retrievable form because the synapses (points of contact between neurons) can be modified by experience. The strength of an existing connection can be increased or decreased by experience. This synaptic property is known as "plasticity." This was Ramón y Cajal's (1894–1904) big idea, that synapses are plastic.

No one believes that a synapse or a neuron is the fundamental unit of memory, but many neurobiologists believe that changes in synaptic strength among groups of neurons can represent experience. This belief has attracted a large number of scientists to the study of synaptic plasticity and generated an enormous and complex literature. The work of these scientists has yielded some important clues about how the brain acquires and stores memories.

The goals of this chapter and several that follow are (1) to present some of the fundamental concepts and methodologies needed to understand how synapses are modified and (2) to highlight some of the important findings that provide the clues to how synapses might store memories. You will learn that insights about the mechanisms of synaptic plasticity can often come from studies of neurons completely isolated from the organism. Such artificial preparations have proven to be invaluable to understanding how synapses are modified. However, as you approach this topic, keep in mind that any clues derived from the study of synaptic plasticity must be tested in behavioral experiments before a claim can be made that a synaptic mechanism supports a memory. Specifically, we must show that this mechanism operates in an intact animal to support the effect an experience has on a behavior that depends on learning and memory.

Two Approaches to Studying Synapses that Support Memory

In an ideal world we would like to study how experience actually modifies the synapses of a collection of interconnected neurons that support a memory. This turns out to be a daunting task. It requires that we locate the memory trace (also called the **engram**) in the brain and its natural sensory inputs.

Karl Lashley (1950) is generally credited with mounting the first serious attempt to locate the memory trace. His attempt was unsuccessful and discouraging. Workable approaches to this problem, however, began to emerge in the late 1960s. One of these, sometimes called the **simple system approach**, emerged from a deliberated strategy, while another emerged from a discovery called **long-term potentiation** in a region of the brain called the hippocampus. These approaches are described below.

Simple System: The Gill Withdrawal Reflex

Biologists believe that the answer to a big question often can be found by reducing the problem to its most elementary form. If you believe that a memory trace is created when experience modifies some synaptic connections, then you want to find an animal with the simplest nervous system that can support a modifiable behavior. In this case you would be willing to sacrifice the complexities of the human brain and the richness of the memories it can support to gain other important advantages. Specifically, with the right animal it might be possible to locate the neural circuit that supported the memory and study the synaptic connections in this circuit that are modified by experience.

In the late 1960s, Eric Kandel (1976) followed this strategy to initiate a research program that focused on an invertebrate named *Aplysia Californica*, a large sea slug. This animal has several important properties.

Eric Kandel

- It has a behavior called the gill withdrawal reflex that can be modified by experience.

- It has a relatively simple brain, located in its abdomen and called the abdominal ganglion, which has far fewer neurons than any vertebrate brain.

- The cell bodies of these neurons are very large, almost visible with no magnification.

- The location of individual neurons is consistent from one animal to another.

The gill of the sea slug is the principle organ for extracting oxygen. The **gill withdrawal reflex** is a defensive behavior the animal displays when its skin is stimulated. See Figure 2.1A for an illustration of the gill in its normal state and when a tactile stimulus is applied to its siphon. Note that the gill contracts when the siphon is touched. This simple behavior can be modified by experience. If the siphon is tapped every few seconds, the amplitude of the response decreases. This change in behavior is called **habituation**: *the magnitude of the response decreases with repeated stimulation*. After the response has diminished, if there is a significant pause between taps, the response to the next tap will increase. This is called **spontaneous recovery**: *with the passage of time between stimulus presentations the response to that stimulus can recover*. The phenomenon of habituation coupled with spontaneous recovery is referred to as **short-term habituation**. If the experiment is repeated over several days, the amount of spontaneous recovery greatly diminishes. This is called **long-term habituation**. The gill withdrawal reflex also can be sensitized by strongly stimulating (shocking) the animal's tail. Thus, a strong stimulus to the tail greatly enhances the gill withdrawal response to the relatively weak stimulus applied to the siphon (Figure 2.1B).

The set of phenomena just described is not unique to sea slugs. Reflexive responses elicited in other animals, including people, also habituate, show spontaneous recovery, and can be sensitized by strong stimulation. So, although habituation is a simple behavioral adaptation, it is quite general. Behavioral habituation clearly meets our definition of learning and memory. In some way, information contained in the tap persists in a form that can influence behavior.

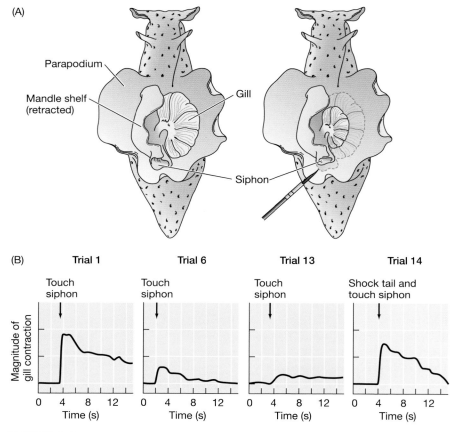

FIGURE 2.1

(A) An illustration of the gill of *Aplysia Californica* in a relaxed state (left) and its withdrawal when the siphon is touched (right). (B) The gill withdrawal reflex habituates. Note that on Trial 1 a touch to the siphon produces vigorous withdrawal but that by trial 13 the same stimulus fails to elicit a response. Sensitization is illustrated on trial 14 where a strong shock applied to the tail restores the response.

Figure 2.2 illustrates the *Aplysia* abdominal ganglion structure and the locations of the large cell bodies of its neurons. Remarkably, the abdominal ganglion can be isolated from the body of the animal while still connected to the sensory neurons that respond to the siphon taps and to the motor neurons that, when activated, cause the gill to retract. This feature makes it possible to identify the exact connections that participate in the gill withdrawal reflex, that is, to map out the circuit of neurons that support the behavior. Once the part of the neural circuit that is modified by repeated taps is discovered

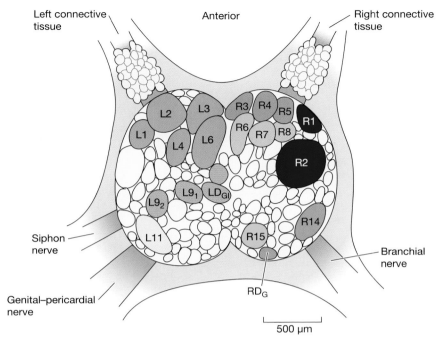

Left connective tissue

Anterior

Right connective tissue

Siphon nerve

Branchial nerve

Genital–pericardial nerve

RD$_G$

500 µm

FIGURE 2.2
The abdominal ganglion of *Aplysia Californica*. The cell bodies are large and identifiable from one animal to another.

(Figure 2.3), we are then in a position to study synaptic mechanisms that allow experience (repeated taps) to modify the gill withdrawal behavior.

Kandel and his colleagues were able to locate the site of the memory trace—the set of synapses connecting sensory neurons from the siphon to the motor neurons that controlled the gill withdrawal reflex. The part of the circuit that was modified was the synapse. Repeated tapping caused changes that weakened the strength of the synapses connecting the sensory and motor neurons.

The story of just what happens when the gill withdrawal reflex habituates is about discovering synaptic mechanisms that participate in this change. Much of this has been described in Kandel's papers, including one based on his Nobel Prize address (2001). The goal of this discussion, however, is only to introduce the logic behind the simple system approach. By trading complexity for simplicity, researchers who have employed the simple system approach have made important contributions to our understanding of how experience modifies synapses and have provided important clues to how memories are made.

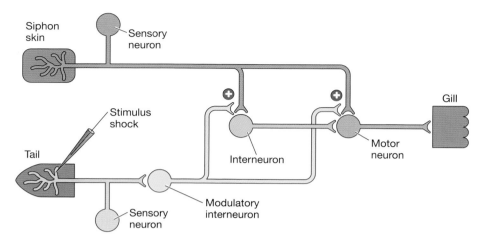

FIGURE 2.3

A diagram of the neural circuit that supports the gill withdrawal reflex and sensitization. Stimulation of the siphon activates a sensory neuron that synapses onto an interneuron and a motor neuron that produce the contraction of the gill. Habituation occurs because repeated taps to the siphon weakens the synaptic connections between the sensory and motor neurons. Note that the circuit activated by tail shock connects to the sensory neuron. Stimulating the tail enhances the size of the gill withdrawal reflex elicited by the siphon. This is called sensitization.

Long-Term Potentiation in the Hippocampus

No one would seriously imagine that the information contained in the modified sensory–motor synapses of a sea slug remotely resembles that which is contained in the modified synapses that would let you recall where you went to lunch yesterday and who was with you. This kind of information requires memory traces that are far more complex and integrated. It is not currently possible to isolate the specific circuits that contain such complex traces. However, there is good reason to believe that a structure in the brain called the hippocampus may contain modifiable synapses that can maintain this kind of information (see Chapters 13 and 14). Moreover, the anatomical organization of the hippocampus is well known.

Indeed, the hippocampus has a very interesting anatomical organization— a so-called trisynaptic circuit—that attracted neurophysiologists who were interested in studying neuron-to-neuron communication. This circuit is shown in outline form in Figure 2.4. The three components of the circuit are:

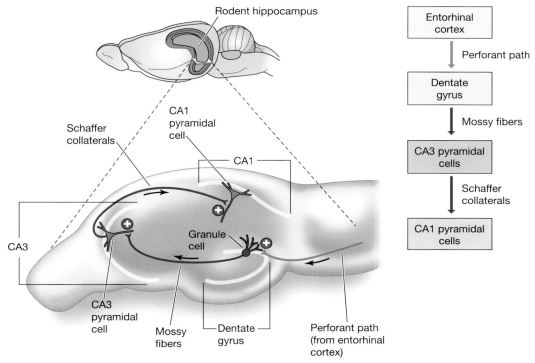

FIGURE 2.4
The hippocampus has a very interesting anatomical organization. This schematic representation of the rodent hippocampus shows the direction of the flow of information.

1. Neurons in the entorhinal cortex connect to a region in the hippocampus called the **dentate gyrus** by what is called the **perforant path**.
2. Neurons in the dentate gyrus connect to the **CA3** region by what are called **mossy fibers**.
3. Neurons in CA3 connect to neurons in the **CA1** region by what are called **Schaffer collateral fibers**.

Although it is not possible to study specific neuron-to-neuron connections in the intact hippocampus, the organization of the hippocampus makes it possible to study connections between neurons in one region or subfield with neurons in another subfield. The specific methods are described in a later section. The basic strategy is simple: you stimulate a set of fibers known to synapse onto neurons in a particular subfield and record what happens in that region

(A)

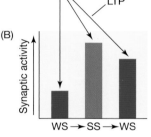

FIGURE 2.5
(A) Bliss and Lomo discovered LTP by stimulating (S) the perforant path and recording (R) in the dentate gyrus. (B) They first applied a weak stimulus (WS) to the perforant path and measured synaptic activity. They then applied a strong stimulus to the perforant path. It evoked more synaptic activity than the initial weak stimulus. In addition, however, the strong stimulus (SS) produced an enduring increase in the synaptic response to the WS. This enhanced response is called long-term potentiation (LTP). SE = stimulating electrode; RE = recording electrode.

when the impulse arrives. If the fibers connect to cells near the recording electrode, you will detect a response in those neurons.

Working in Per Anderson's laboratory, Timothy Bliss and Terje Lomo (1973) took advantage of the anatomy of the hippocampus in a living rabbit to determine if it was possible to modify the strength of synapses. They stimulated the fibers in the perforant path and recorded synaptic activity that occurred in the dentate gyrus (Figure 2.5). Their experiment was simple:

Timothy Bliss

1. They established that a weak stimulus applied to the perforant path would evoke some synaptic activity in the dentate gyrus.
2. They next delivered a stronger stimulus to the same perforant path fibers, which evoked a bigger synaptic response.

3. They then repeatedly presented the weak stimulus and found that it now evoked a bigger response.

Terje Lomo

Thus, the strong stimulus potentiated the response to the weak stimulus. The potentiated response lasted a relatively long time (several hours). This phenomenon is called **long-term potentiation (LTP)**. As noted, neurobiologists believe that experience is stored in the brain because it modifies the strength of synapses connecting networks of neurons. Thus, Bliss and Lomo's discovery of LTP was greeted with great enthusiasm because it provided a way to study how synaptic strength can be modified by experience. Hundreds of researchers have dedicated their scientific careers to the study of LTP as a model system for discovering the synaptic mechanisms that produce lasting changes in synaptic strength. The work of these scientists has greatly increased our understanding of these mechanisms and identified a number of important molecules and processes that are likely to be involved in making memories. To appreciate their discoveries, it is necessary to have a detailed understanding of the methodology used to study LTP and its conceptual basis.

The Conceptual Basis and Methodology of LTP

Although Bliss and Lomo discovered LTP in the hippocampus of a living rabbit, the most widely employed basic procedure for studying LTP centers on what is called an in vitro preparation (Figure 2.6A,B). It requires dissecting a very thin slice of tissue from the hippocampus and placing it into a special chamber that contains a cocktail of chemicals in a solution that will keep the slice of tissue functional for several hours. A stimulating electrode is then positioned to deliver electrical current to a chosen set of fibers and a recording electrode is placed in the region where these fibers terminate.

Bliss and Lomo (1973) stimulated the fibers in the perforant path and recorded the synaptic response in the dentate gyrus. Many researchers choose instead to stimulate the Schaffer collateral fibers and record the response of the pyramidal cells in the CA1 subfield (Figure 2.6C). The recording electrode is placed in the extracellular space among a population of pyramidal cells in CA1. It records the extracellular excitatory postsynaptic potential (EPSP) in a particular area and is referred to as the **field potential** (also called the **field EPSP** or **fEPSP**). The field potential is a critical concept because it is what is measured in an LTP experiment.

(A)

(B)

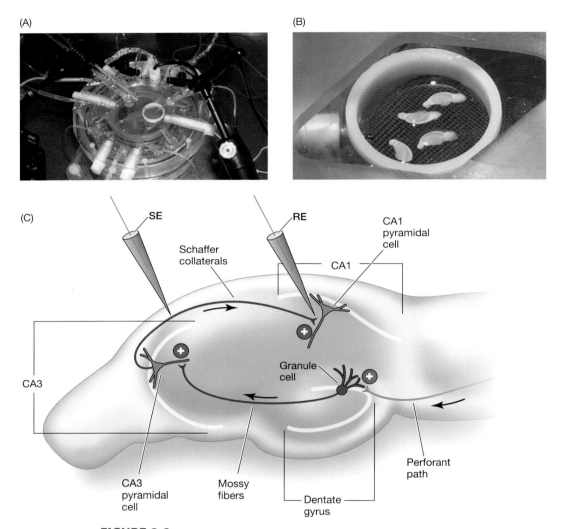

(C)

FIGURE 2.6

LTP can be studied in tissue slices taken from the hippocampus. This is called an in vitro preparation. (A) The recording apparatus consists of a large chamber that is filled with fluid needed to keep the slice viable, a small chamber that holds the slice being studied, the stimulating electrode used to induce LTP, and the recording electrode used to measure the field EPSP. (B) Prior to beginning the experiment, slices of hippocampal tissue are placed into the small recording chamber. (C) Many researchers use the in vitro methodology to study LTP induced in neurons in the CA1 region of the hippocampus. To do this they stimulate the Schaffer collateral fibers and record field potentials from a recording electrode placed in the CA1 region. SE = stimulating electrode; RE = recording electrode.

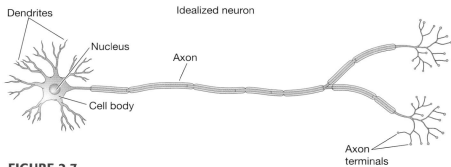

Idealized neuron

Dendrites

Nucleus

Axon

Cell body

Axon terminals

FIGURE 2.7
A neuron is composed of a cell body (which contains the nucleus), dendrites, an axon, and axon terminals.

Understanding the Field EPSP

To more fully understand the fEPSP requires a review of the basic structure and function of the neuron and how neurons communicate, as well as a discussion of membrane potential and depolarization.

STRUCTURE AND FUNCTIONS OF THE NEURON   An idealized neuron is presented in Figure 2.7, which shows that a neuron is composed of a cell body, dendrites, an axon, and axon terminals. Neurons are connected in networks and serve many functions. A neuron is:

- an input device that receives chemical and electrical messages from other neurons;
- an integrative device that combines messages received from multiple inputs;
- a conductive–output device that sends information to other neurons, muscles, and organs; and
- a representation device that stores information about past experiences as changes in synaptic strength (Figure 2.8A).

The function a particular neuron serves depends on whether it is a presynaptic "sending" neuron or a postsynaptic "receiving" neuron. The **synapse** (Figure 2.8B) is the point of contact between the sending and receiving neuron. It is where neurons communicate and information is thought to be stored. The basic components of the synapse are the **presynaptic terminal**, the **postsynaptic dendrite**, and the **synaptic cleft**, which is a small space between the terminal and the spine that contains structures that maintain the connection.

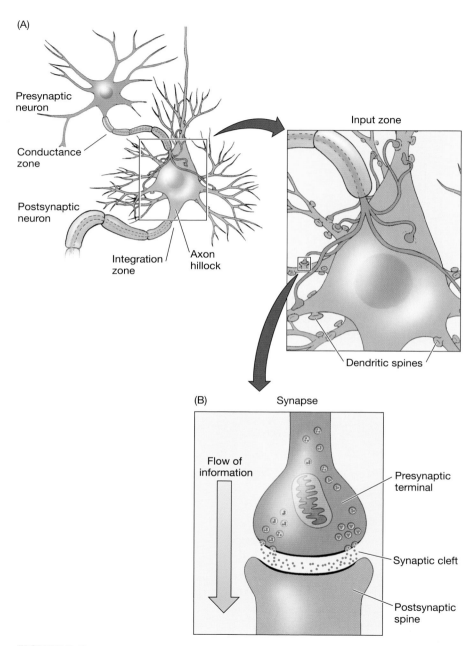

(A)

Presynaptic neuron

Conductance zone

Postsynaptic neuron

Integration zone

Axon hillock

Input zone

Dendritic spines

(B) Synapse

Flow of information

Presynaptic terminal

Synaptic cleft

Postsynaptic spine

FIGURE 2.8
(A) Neurons are connected in networks and serve many functions. (B) The basic components of a synapse are the presynaptic terminal, a synaptic cleft, and a postsynaptic dendrite. This figure shows a presynaptic neuron synapsing onto a dendritic spine.

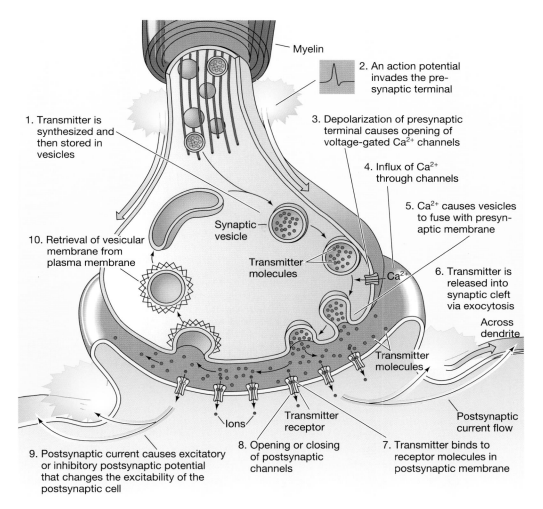

1. Transmitter is synthesized and then stored in vesicles

Myelin

2. An action potential invades the pre-synaptic terminal

3. Depolarization of presynaptic terminal causes opening of voltage-gated Ca^{2+} channels

4. Influx of Ca^{2+} through channels

5. Ca^{2+} causes vesicles to fuse with presyn-aptic membrane

10. Retrieval of vesicular membrane from plasma membrane

Synaptic vesicle

Transmitter molecules

Ca^{2+}

6. Transmitter is released into synaptic cleft via exocytosis

Across dendrite

Transmitter molecules

Transmitter receptor

Postsynaptic current flow

Ions

8. Opening or closing of postsynaptic channels

7. Transmitter binds to receptor molecules in postsynaptic membrane

9. Postsynaptic current causes excitatory or inhibitory postsynaptic potential that changes the excitability of the postsynaptic cell

FIGURE 2.9
When an action potential arrives in the presynaptic axon terminal, neurotransmitter molecules are released from synaptic vesicles into the synaptic cleft where they bind to specific receptors, causing a chemical or electrical signal in the postsynaptic cell.

NEURONAL COMMUNICATION   Information transmitted between neurons de-pends on a combination of electrical events that allow the presynaptic neuron to influence the postsynaptic neuron. Some of the important details of this process are shown in Figure 2.9. The general story, however, is that the termi-nal ending of the sending neuron contains packages of molecules called **neu-rotransmitters**, which are packaged in structures called **synaptic vesicles**. These molecules are called neurotransmitters because they are the primary

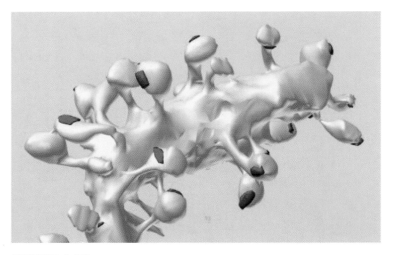

FIGURE 2.10
A three dimensional reconstruction of a section of a dendrite with spines of different shapes and sizes. Dendrites are extensively populated with structures called dendritic spines. A spine is a small (sub-micrometer) membranous extrusion that protrudes from a dendrite. Dendritic spines are of special interest because (a) key receptors involved in the regulation of synaptic plasticity are located in spines and (b) changes in the composition and architecture of the spine are altered by neural activity. (From Synapse Web, Kristen M. Harris, PI, http://synapse-web.org/.)

communication agent of the sending neuron. When **action potentials** (spikes of electrical activity that travel along the axon) are generated in the axon of the sending neuron, they can cause the neurotransmitters to be released into the synaptic cleft. The receiving neuron has specialized receptors, generally located on the **dendrites** (Figure 2.10), which are designed to receive the neurotransmitter signals emitted by the sending neuron. After the neurotransmitters are released, they can bind to receptors located on the dendrites of the receiving neuron.

When enough receptors are occupied, a brief electrical event called the **postsynaptic potential** is generated in the postsynaptic neuron. Postsynaptic potentials occur because activation of the synapse causes a brief change in the resting membrane potential of the postsynaptic neuron.

MEMBRANE POTENTIAL   There is fluid inside the neurons called intracellular fluid and neurons are surrounded by what is called extracellular fluid. The intracellular fluid is separated from the surrounding extracellular fluid by a cell membrane. Both the intracellular and extracellular fluids contain positively and negatively charged molecules called **ions**. The **membrane potential** is

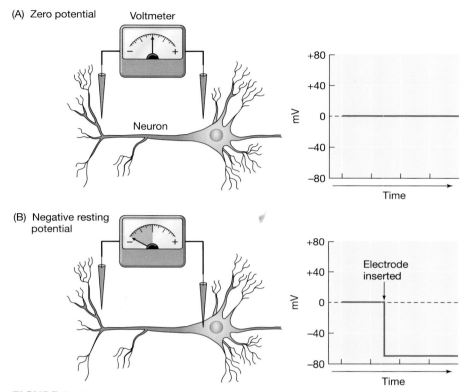

FIGURE 2.11
(A) When two recording electrodes are in the extracellular space surrounding neurons, there is zero potential between them. Likewise, the membrane potential would be zero if the ionic composition of the extracellular and intracellular fluids were exactly the same. (B) However, if one electrode is inserted into the neuron but the other electrode remains in the extracellular space, it would record the resting membrane potential as negative because in the inactive state there are more negatively charged ions in the intracellular fluid than in the extracellular fluid.

the difference in the electrical charge inside the neuron's cell body compared to the charge outside the cell body. If the ionic composition of the intracellular and extracellular fluids were exactly the same, the membrane potential would be zero. However, the composition is not the same. There are more negatively charged ions in the intracellular fluid than in the extracellular fluid. Thus, the membrane potential in the inactive state, that is, the **resting membrane potential**, is negatively charged with respect to the extracellular fluid. The electrical potential is measured in millivolts (mV); each millivolt is 1/1000 of a volt. The resting membrane potential is typically in the range of –50 to –80 mV where the – represents a negative potential (Figure 2.11).

FIGURE 2.12

The resting membrane potential is negative. Depolarization occurs when the ionic composition of the intracellular fluid becomes less negative. Hyperpolarization occurs when the ionic composition of the intracellular fluid becomes more negative.

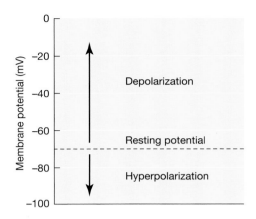

DEPOLARIZATION AND HYPERPOLARIZATION   The membrane potential is dynamic and can be driven to become either less negative or more negative. The term **depolarization** represents the case where the membrane potential becomes less negative. When depolarization occurs, the composition of the intracellular fluid becomes more like the composition of the extracellular fluid. The term **hyperpolarization** represents the case where the membrane potential becomes more negative. When hyperpolarization occurs, the composition of the intracellular fluid becomes less like the composition of the extracellular fluid. The process of depolarization drives the neuron *towards* generating action potentials, while the process of hyperpolarization drives the neuron *away* from generating action potentials (Figure 2.12).

The electrical stimulation used to produce LTP in the hippocampus generates action potentials in the axons of the sending neurons. As a result, many of the synapses on the postsynaptic neurons will depolarize, that is, positive ions will flow into those neurons. This is called **postsynaptic depolarization**. In principle, postsynaptic potentials can be recorded from either a very small intracellular electrode (an electrode that penetrates the neuron) or from a larger electrode placed in the extracellular fluid in the region where the stimulated axons synapse with the receiving neurons (Figure 2.13). The intracellular electrode would detect positive ions flowing into the neuron, indicating depolarization. However, the extracellular electrode will detect a change in the potential difference between the ionic composition of the extracellular fluid at the recording electrode and another, distant and inactive electrode called the ground electrode. Normally the potential difference between the extracellular recording electrode and ground is zero. As the positive ions flow into the postsynaptic membrane, however, they will flow away from the extracellular recording electrode. This means that the potential between the recording and

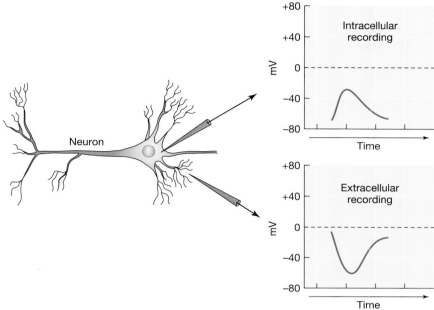

FIGURE 2.13
Postsynaptic potentials can be recorded from either an intracellular electrode that penetrates the neuron or an electrode placed in the extracellular fluid. The intracellular electrode detects positive ions flowing into the neuron, indicating depolarization. The extracellular electrode measures the electrical potential between the extracellular fluid and a ground electrode. When synapses depolarize, positive ions move away from the tip of the electrode into the neuron. This results in the electrical potential between the extracellular fluid and ground electrode becoming negative. Thus, the extracellular recording has a negative slope.

ground electrodes will become negative. Theoretically, as more synapses contribute to depolarization, the negative potential will increase because more positive ions will flow away from the extracellular recording electrode.

What is Synaptic Strength?

Now that you understand the dynamics of the resting membrane potential, you can appreciate what it means to say that a synapse has been strengthened and why the increase in the fEPSP is thought to represent an increase in synaptic strength. Simply put, in the context of the LTP experiment, synaptic strength is measured by how much postsynaptic depolarization is produced by the stimulus—how many positive ions flow into the neurons surrounding the extracellular recording electrode. The extracellular electrode reads this as the flow of positive ions away from its tip. Thus, the size of fEPSP recorded by the extracellular electrode is assumed to indirectly measure the strength of the synaptic connections linking the presynaptic and postsynaptic neuron. You are now in the position to begin to understand how LTP is induced and measured.

Inducing and Measuring LTP

Figure 2.14A illustrates the delivery of a high-frequency stimulus to Schaffer collateral axons or fibers that synapse onto the CA1 pyramidal neurons. An extracellular recording is positioned to measure the field potential that is produced when synapses located on pyramidal neurons depolarize. The waveform (Figure 2.14B) produced by the recording electrode is complex because the electrode detects several electrical events. One event is a stimulus artifact associated with simply triggering the current generator that produces the stimulus, another is the fiber volley (the action potentials generated by the electrical stimulus), and another is the critical field EPSP. The fiber volley represents the fact that the electrical stimulus applied to the fibers generated action potentials that arrived at the recording site. The field EPSP is detected as the downward slope of the waveform. The steepness of the slope is assumed to reflect the amount of postsynaptic depolarization that occurred. A quantitative representation of the results of a typical LTP experiment is provided in Figure 2.14C.

To understand Figure 2.14C it is necessary to describe the details of the LTP experiment. A good place to start is with a discussion of how the independent variable in the LTP experiment—the intensity of the electric current used to evoke the field potential—is determined.

The electrical current applied to the fibers is measured in what are called microamperes, μA. This unit of measure is very small. You would not detect this level of current if it were applied to your finger. Nevertheless, it will generate action potentials in the fibers to which it is applied. It is important to know that in an LTP experiment there are two stimuli: the test stimulus and the inducing stimulus. The **test stimulus** is relatively weak and thus evokes a small fEPSP. The **inducing stimulus** is much stronger and evokes a larger fEPSP.

The intensity of the test stimulus is usually arrived at by preliminary tests in which the intensity of the stimulus is varied, from about 2.5 to 45 μA (Sweat, 2003), and the experimenter measures the amplitude of the fiber volley and the slope of the fEPSP. The goal of this preliminary stage is to find a test stimulus that evokes an fEPSP that is about 35–50% of the maximum response (Figure 2.15).

(A)

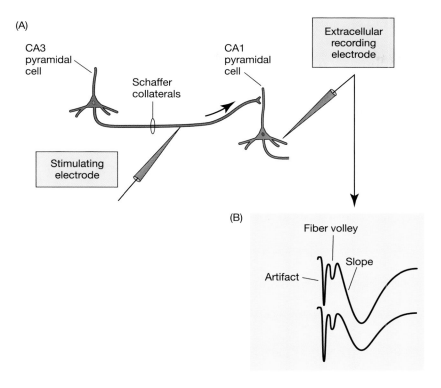

(B)

Fiber volley

Slope

Artifact

(C)

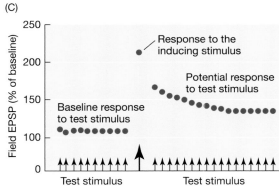

FIGURE 2.14

(A) A stimulating electrode delivers a small amount of electric current to Schaffer collateral fibers. (B) The extracellular recording electrode detects a population of depolarizing synapses in the CA1 region and generates a waveform. The steepness of the slope of the waveform represents the amount of synaptic depolarization around the recording electrode. Thus, more synaptic depolarization is recorded in the top waveform than in the bottom one. (C) A quantitative representation of the results of a typical LTP experiment.

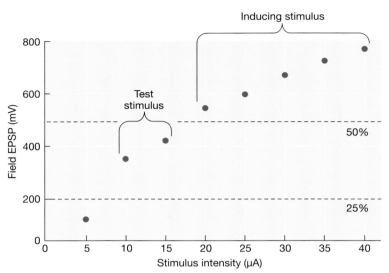

FIGURE 2.15
A hypothetical relationship between the slope of the field EPSP and the intensity of the stimulus. In this example, either the 10 or 15 μA stimuli might be selected to serve as the baseline–test stimulus and intensities from 20 μA to 40 μA might serve as the inducing stimulus.

The test stimulus has two functions. First, it is repeatedly presented to establish a baseline level of synaptic activity, that is, a baseline fEPSP. Once the baseline is established, the strong, inducing stimulus is presented. Its function is to change the strength of the synaptic connections between the stimulated fibers and the receiving neurons. The second function of the test stimulus is to act as a probe to determine if the inducing stimulus changed the strength of connections between the presynaptic fibers and the postsynaptic neurons. Thus, after the inducing stimulus is presented, the test stimulus is repeatedly presented (about every 20 seconds). If the experiment is successful, then the test stimulus will evoke a much larger fEPSP than it did during the baseline period (previously shown in Figure 2.14C).

The dependent variable shown in Figure 2.14C—field EPSP (% of baseline)—represents the difference between the fEPSP produced by the test stimulus during the baseline period prior to when the inducing stimulus is presented (T1), and the response to the test stimulus after the inducing stimulus is presented (T2). To calculate this value, simply divide the value of T2 by the value of T1 and multiply by 100:

$$\text{Field EPSP (\% of baseline)} = T2/T1 \times 100$$

For example, if the average baseline fEPSP (T1) was 350 mV and the fEPSP evoked by the test stimulus after the inducing stimulus was presented (T2) was 500 mV, then the field EPSP (% of baseline) value would be 143%. In order to conclude that the inducing stimulus strengthened the synaptic connections between axon fibers stimulated by the test stimulus and the postsynaptic neurons, that is, that it induced LTP, this value must exceed 100%. Note that the results presented in Figure 2.14C would lead to the conclusion that the strong inducing stimulus had produced LTP.

The inducing stimulus, which generates LTP, is stronger than the test stimulus. Its intensity is also determined from the preliminary tests (see Figure 2.15). If a weak induction protocol is desired, the stimulus might be set to evoke at least half the maximal fEPSP. In this protocol the stimulus would be presented at a high frequency (100 Hz = 100 times in a second) for 1 second. If a stronger protocol is desired, then the intensity of the inducing stimulus might be set to evoke the near maximal response. In the stronger protocol, the stimulus would be presented three times at 100 Hz. The three presentations would be separated by 20 seconds. Researchers often call the inducing stimulus the **high-frequency stimulus** (**HFS**).

The Chemical Basis of LTP

The induction of LTP is the product of many biochemical interactions, far more than can be described here. However, there are several basic interactions that, if understood, will provide a foundation for appreciating some of the complexities of LTP that are presented later. They involve glutamate, the ionotropic receptors to which it binds, and the consequence of this binding process.

The Glutamate Binding Process

The primary neurotransmitter in the LTP story is called **glutamate**. It is what is termed an excitatory amino acid. It is released from presynaptic axon terminals when an inducing (high-frequency) stimulus is applied to the axons of the sending neurons in the LTP experiment. Some receptors on the receiving dendritic spines are called **ionotropic receptors** or **ion-gated channels**. They are located in the cell membrane so that they protrude outside the cell as well as inside the cell. These receptors are constructed from four or five protein subunits that come together to form a potential channel or pore (Figure 2.16A).

(A)

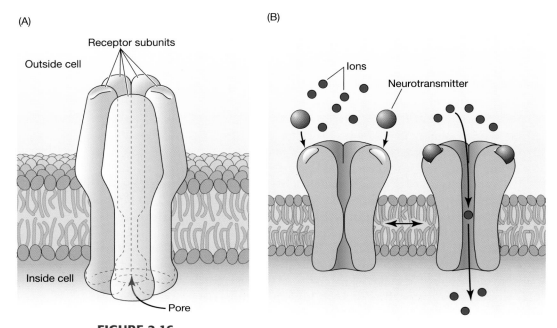

(B)

FIGURE 2.16
(A) Ionotropic receptors are located in the plasma membrane. (B) When a neuro-transmitter binds to the receptor, the channel or pore opens and allows ions such as Na^+ and Ca^{2+} to enter the cell.

These receptors are called ionotropic because, when the pores are open, ions such as Na^+ or Ca^{2+} can enter the cell. They are called gated channels because something has to open the pore. The significant event that opens the channel is the binding of the neurotransmitter glutamate to a site on the receptor. When this happens, the conformation or shape of the receptor is changed so that the channel is briefly open and ions can enter the cell (Figure 2.16B). If enough of the channels are concurrently open, then the receiving neuron may depolarize because positively charged ions will enter the cell.

AMPA and NMDA Receptors

As noted, glutamate is the primary excitatory neurotransmitter in the brain. Glutamate binds to three ionotropic receptors: (1) the α-amino-3-hydroxyl-5-methyl-4-isoxazole-propionate (AMPA) receptor, (2) the N-methyl-D-aspartate (NMDA) receptor, and (3) the kainate receptor (Figure 2.17). To understand how LTP is induced we only need to consider AMPA and NMDA

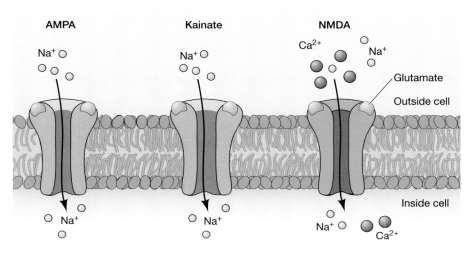

FIGURE 2.17
There are three types of glutamate receptors. AMPA and NMDA receptors are located in dendritic spines and play a major role in the induction and expression of LTP. When glutamate binds to these receptors their channels open and ions in the extracellular fluid (Na^+ and Ca^{2+}) enter the neuron.

receptors. AMPA receptors are the major contributor to whether or not the sending neuron will depolarize the receiving neuron. This is because gated AMPA receptors open and allow positively charged Na^+ ions to enter the cell. The NMDA receptor has somewhat different properties that will be discussed after its importance for LTP is established.

Our understanding of the induction of LTP took a giant step forward when Graham Collingridge (Collingridge, Kehl, and McLennan, 1983) applied a pharmacological agent to the brain called amino-phosphono-valeric acid (abbreviated as APV) that competitively antagonizes the NMDA receptor. Competitive receptor antagonists are molecules that have the property of occupying the receptor site so that the normal binding partner (in this case glutamate) cannot access the site (Figure 2.18). However, the antagonist doesn't fit the site well enough to change the conformation of the receptor. Instead, it acts like a shield.

Using this methodology, Collingridge made two important observations: (1) applying APV before presenting the high-frequency stimulus prevented the induction of LTP (Figure 2.19), but (2) if APV was applied after LTP had been induced, that is, during the test phase, the test stimulus still evoked a potentiated fEPSP.

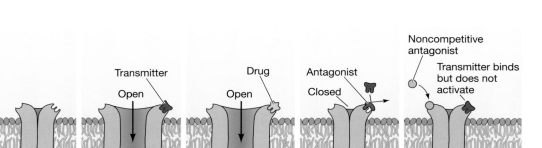

Noncompetitive antagonist

Transmitter binds but does not activate

Transmitter

Open

Drug

Open

Antagonist

Closed

| Unbound receptor. In this example, it is normally closed. | An endogenous ligand is a naturally occurring molecule, such as a transmitter, that binds to the receptor. An endogenous ligand usually activates its cognate receptor and is therefore classified as an **agonist**. | An exogenous ligand (that is, a drug or toxin) that resembles the endogenous ligand and is capable of binding to the receptor and activating it is classified as a **receptor agonist**. | Some substances bind to receptors but do not activate them, and simply block agonists from binding to the receptors. These are classified as **competitive antagonists**. | Some agonist or antagonist drugs may bind to target receptors at a site that is *different* from where the endogenous ligand binds; such drugs are known as **noncompetitive agonists or antagonists**. |

FIGURE 2.18
The agonistic and antagonistic actions of drugs.

These two observations indicate that the NMDA receptor plays a critical role in inducing LTP but is not necessary once LTP is established. Thus, glutamate must bind to the NMDA receptor to produce the changes in synaptic strength measured as LTP, but it does not have to bind to the NMDA receptor once LTP is established. Experts say that the NMDA receptor is necessary for the induction of LTP but is not necessary for the expression of LTP. The phrase "NMDA receptor-dependent LTP" is often used to denote the special importance of the NMDA receptor to the induction of LTP.

Why the NMDA Receptor Is Special

The NMDA receptor is an ion-gated channel that can conduct Na^+ into the cell. However, under the appropriate conditions, it also permits Ca^{2+} into the cell, and the influx of Ca^{2+} turns out to be critical for the induction of LTP. The NMDA receptor has two critical binding sites. One site binds to glutamate and

(A)

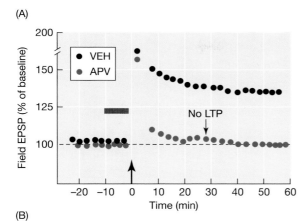

(B)

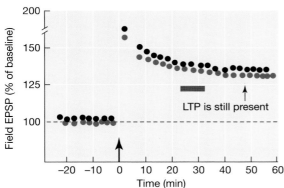

FIGURE 2.19
APV is an NMDA receptor antagonist. It prevents glutamate from binding to NMDA receptors. (A) If APV is applied to brain tissue prior to presenting the high-frequency stimulus (represented by the vertical arrow), LTP is not produced. (B) In contrast, if APV is administered after the high-frequency stimulus has produced LTP, the test stimulus continues to evoke the enhanced field potential. These results mean that NMDA receptors are critical for the production of LTP but not for its expression. The bar in each figure represents the application of the drug, that is, APV or the control vehicle (VEH).

the other site binds to magnesium, Mg^{2+} (Figure 2.20A). The binding site for Mg^{2+} is in the pore formed by the protein subunits that make up the receptor. Because Mg^{2+} binds to a site in the pore it is sometimes called the Mg^{2+} plug. Ca^{2+} cannot enter the cell unless Mg^{2+} is removed from the pore. The trick is how to pull the plug.

To pull the plug requires two events: (1) glutamate has to bind to the NMDA receptor, and (2) the cell has to depolarize (Figure 2.20B). Thus, the binding of glutamate to the NMDA receptor is a necessary but not a sufficient condition to remove the Mg^{2+} plug; the cell must also depolarize while glutamate is still bound to the receptor. When glutamate is released onto the dendrite it not only binds to the NMDA receptor, it also binds to AMPA receptors. It is the Na^+ influx through the gated AMPA receptors that is thought to depolarize the cells. The AMPA receptor Na^+ channel only requires one event to open—the binding of glutamate to that receptor.

FIGURE 2.20

(A) The NMDA receptor binds to glutamate. It also binds to Mg^{2+} (sometimes called the magnesium plug) because Mg^{2+} binds to the NMDA channel. (B) The opening of the NMDA receptor requires two events: glutamate must bind to the receptor and the cell must depolarize. When this happens, the Mg^+ plug is removed and Ca^{2+} can enter the cell.

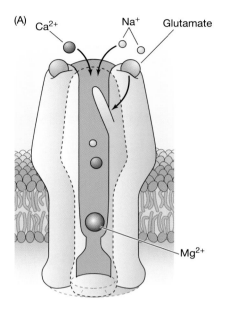

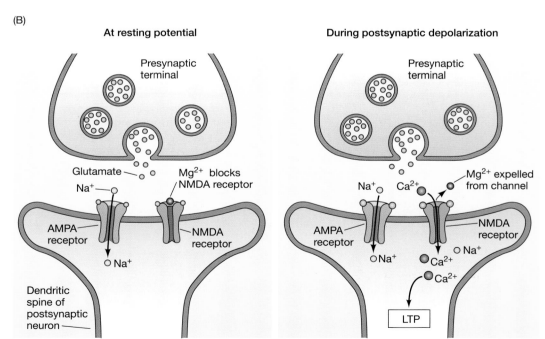

The NMDA Receptor and Associative Learning

The big event associated with opening the NMDA pore is the entry of Ca^{2+} into the cell. The significance of this event is discussed in detail later, but first it is useful to expand more fully on operating characteristics of the NMDA receptors and their relationship to memory.

Psychological accounts of learning and memory place a heavy theoretical burden on the concept of associative learning and its product—a strengthened association. An association is a theoretical concept used to represent the fact that if you experience two independent events, A and B, in temporal proximity, a later presentation of A will retrieve some representation of B. The co-occurrence of A and B produces a connection or association between them. As mentioned in Chapter 1, one reason why the Pavlovian conditioning methodology is so popular is because it provides an objective way to study the development of associations in animals. The two events are the conditioned stimulus (CS) and the unconditioned stimulus (US). The conditioned response (CR) is the behavioral measure of the acquired association between the CS and US.

Associative learning requires a biological mechanism for detecting co-occurring events. The operating rules for opening the NMDA Ca^{2+} channel (shown in Figure 2.20B) provide such a mechanism. The connection between the NMDA receptor and associative learning is described in the context of the Pavlovian conditioning experiment. Figure 2.21 illustrates connections among

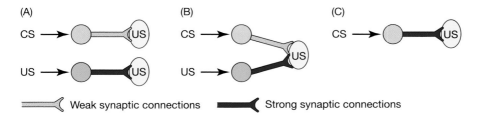

FIGURE 2.21
The properties of NMDA receptors provide a mechanism for associative learning such as occurs in Pavlovian conditioning. (A) Synaptic connections between the CS input and neurons representing the US are initially weak, but the US input connections to those neurons is strong. (B) If the CS and US inputs co-occur, the conditions for strengthening the CS-US synaptic connections will be met: (a) CS inputs will release glutamate that will bind to NMDA receptors on the postsynaptic sites of the neurons representing the US, (b) the US input will depolarize those neurons and the NMDA-receptor Ca^{2+} channels will open and initiate processes that strengthen these synapses. (C) These strong CS-US synaptic connections will allow the CS to activate the neurons representing the US.

neurons representing the CS and US. Note that the connections between the CS input and US representations are initially weak, but the connections between the US input and the US representation are strong (see Figure 2.21A). So activating the CS input might release glutamate onto postsynaptic receptors on neurons representing the US, but not enough to depolarize the cell. However, the US input would depolarize the neurons representing the US. Now imagine that the CS and US inputs coincided (see Figure 2.21B). This would mean that the US representation neurons would depolarize while glutamate was bound to NMDA receptors at synapses connecting the CS input to the US representation. According to the rules governing the opening of NMDA receptor channels, when this occurs Ca^{2+} will enter the dendritic spines of the these synapses and they will be strengthened (see Figure 2.21C). As a consequence of this change, one might say that the network has now stored information about the co-occurrence of CS and US. Thus, when the CS is presented alone, it will now activate (depolarize) the US representation neurons.

Long-Term Depression: The Polar Opposite of LTP

Although experience can strengthen synaptic connections, embedded in the concept of synaptic plasticity is the idea that experience can also weaken synaptic connections. Synaptic plasticity is in fact bidirectional. Depending on the nature of experience-produced synaptic activity, the synaptic connection can be either strengthened or weakened. The term **long-term depression (LTD)** is used to represent the case in which synaptic activity weakens the strength of the synaptic connections. The experimenter uses a high-frequency stimulus protocol to induce LTP. The protocol used to induce LTD, however, is much different (Bear, 2003; Dudek and Bear, 1992). For example, Dudek and Bear discovered that LTD in the hippocampus could be induced by applying 900 pulses of a low-frequency stimulus (1–3 Hz), which takes about 15 minutes. This reduced the field EPSP evoked by the test stimulus for at least an hour (Figure 2.22). Moreover, they also found that applying the NMDA receptor antagonist APV to the slice blocked the induction of LTD. Thus, not only can synapses in the hippocampus be both strengthened and weakened, the NMDA receptor is the gateway to both processes. LTD is of great interest to many researchers. However, because there are very few behavioral–memory experiments that draw directly on studies of LTD, this topic is not further explored.

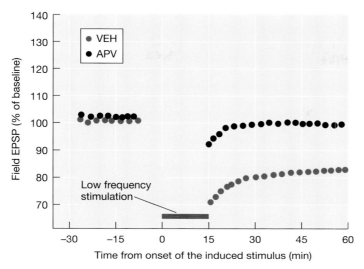

FIGURE 2.22
The delivery of a low-frequency stimulus to Schaffer collateral fibers for about 15 minutes produces a long-term depression in the dendritic field of CA1 neurons. Note that the slope of the field EPSP evoked by the test stimulus is markedly reduced. In addition, this effect is blocked when the NMDA receptor antagonist, APV, is applied to the slice. (After Dudek and Bear, 1993.)

Summary

The idea that experience can be stored by altering the strength of neuron-to-neuron connections is fundamental to the neurobiology of memory. Locating the synapse that contains a memory trace is a difficult task. Neurobiologists have used two general strategies: (a) the simple system approach and (b) a model of plasticity called long-term potentiation. LTP is produced by stimulating axon fibers and measuring the fEPSP evoked in the receiving neurons. A strong stimulus will potentiate the response to a weak stimulus.

Understanding how LTP is produced requires knowing how neurons communicate. One way neurons communicate is by what are called chemical synapses. The communication process involves both electrical and chemical actions. A key outcome in the process is the depolarization of the receiving neuron.

LTP requires the cooperation of two types of glutamate receptors, AMPA and NMDA receptors. The primary role of AMPA receptors is to depolarize the cell. Two events are required to open the NMDA channel: glutamate has to bind to the receptor and the cell must depolarize. Opening the NMDA channel allows Ca^{2+} to enter the cell.

Associative learning requires a mechanism for detecting co-occurring events. The NMDA receptor provides such a mechanism.

The strength of synapses can also be weakened by synaptic activity. This is called long-term depression and is produced by applying long-lasting, low-frequency stimulation. It is important to note that this form of synaptic plasticity also requires the participation of the NMDA receptor.

References

Bear, M. F. (2003). Bidirectional synaptic plasticity: from theory to reality. *Philosophical Transactions of the Royal Society of London Series B, 358,* 649–655.

Bliss, T. V. and Lomo, T. (1973). Long lasting potentiation of synaptic transmission in the dentate area of the anaesthetized rabbit following stimulation of the perforant path. *Journal of Physiology, 232,* 331–356.

Collingridge, G. L., Kehl, S. J., and McLennan, H. (1983). Excitatory amino acids in synaptic transmission in the Schaffer collateral–commissural pathway of the rat hippocampus. *Journal of Physiology, 34,* 334–345.

Dudek, S. M. and Bear, M. F. (1992). Homosynaptic long-term depression in area CA1 of hippocampus and effects of N-methyl-D-aspartate receptor blockade. *Proceedings of the National Academy of Sciences, 89,* 4363–4367.

Kandel, E. R. (1976). *Cellular basis of behavior: an introduction to behavioral neurobiology.* San Francisco: W. H. Freeman.

Kandel, E. R. (2001). The molecular biology of memory storage: a dialogue between genes and synapses. *Science, 29,* 1030–1038.

Lashley, K. S. (1950). In search of the engram. *Symp. Soc. Exp Biol., 4,* 454–482.

Ramón y Cajal, S. (1894–1904). *Textura del sistema nervioso del hombre y de los vertebrados.* Trans. by N. Swanson and L. W. Swanson as *New ideas on the structure of the nervous system in man and vertebrates.* Cambridge, MA: MIT Press, 1990.

Sweat, J. D. (2003). *Mechanisms of memory.* London: Academic Press.

Teyler, T. J. (1999). Use of brain slices to study long-term potentiation and depression as examples of synaptic plasticity. *Methods, 18,* 109–116.

Strengthening Synapses: Assembling Existing Parts

Several important events have been identified that are part of a biochemical sequence that can strengthen the synapses measured as LTP:

- Glutamate is released from the presynaptic or sending neuron.

- Glutamate binds to both AMPA and NMDA receptors.

- The cell is depolarized when enough Na^+ enters the cell through AMPA receptors.

- The combination of binding glutamate to the NMDA receptor and depolarizing the cell removes the Mg^+ plug from the NMDA channel.

- Calcium enters the dendritic spine through the NMDA channel.

Ca^{2+} influx into the spine is a significant event in the initiation of LTP. There is no doubt that LTP can be blocked or reduced by manipulations that should reduce the rise in Ca^{2+} associated with LTP induction. To understand how an increase in Ca^{2+} in the cell produces this effect, however, it is necessary to examine

- first and second messengers;
- functional endpoints produced when Ca^{2+} enters the postsynaptic neuron;
- AMPA receptor function and the expression of LTP;
- post-translation modification processes; and
- trafficking and regulation of AMPA receptors.

Messengers and Functional Endpoints

A **messenger** conveys information from a sending source to a receiving source. A **first messenger** carries information from one neuron to another neuron. Neurotransmitters are first messengers because they transmit information between cells. Thus, glutamate is a first messenger. **Second messengers** (also called intracellular second messengers) are molecules that relay the signal received by receptors located in the plasma membrane, such as NMDA and AMPA receptors, into the cells. They do this by initiating biochemical processes within the cell. The entry of Ca^{2+} into the cell is significant because it is a second messenger. Thus, Ca^{2+} has properties that allow it to initiate biochemical processes within the cell that can lead to LTP (Figure 3.1).

Biochemical processes initiated within the cell by synaptic activity are important for LTP because they ultimately change the composition of the synapses so that the sending neurons are more likely to depolarize the receiving neurons. The biochemical processes that change synaptic strength are many and complex. To understand how this works it is helpful to note two **functional end points** of the biochemical processes initiated by the second messenger Ca^{2+} (Figure 3.2).

First, the entry of Ca^{2+} into the cell through synaptic activity can initiate parallel biochemical processes that (1) *assemble or modify material that is already present* in the cell to strengthen synaptic connections or (2) *generate new material* that is necessary for this outcome.

Thus, synaptic activity that induces LTP initiates biochemical processes that work on the already existing parts to modify and assemble them to strengthen synaptic connections. If the activity is strong enough, it will also initiate processes needed to manufacture new parts. The processes involved in assembling or modifying existing parts are sometimes called **post-translation modifications** (discussed in greater detail in a section below). The processes needed to manufacture new parts are called **transcription** and **translation** processes (discussed in Chapter 4). It is generally believed that all of these processes—transcription, translation, and post-translation modifications—can contribute to strengthening synaptic connections.

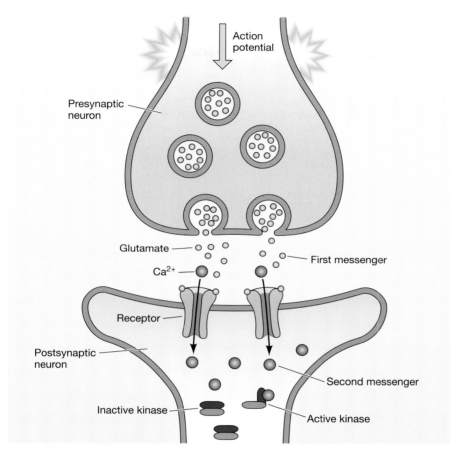

FIGURE 3.1

First messengers carry information between neurons, while second messengers carry the signal into the neuron. In this illustration an action potential causes the presynaptic neuron to release glutamate, which binds to sites on receptors in the postsynaptic membrane. This allows calcium to enter the cell where it can bind to a receptor site on a kinase and put it into an active state. Glutamate in this case is a first messenger because it communicates between the two neurons. Calcium is a second messenger because it relays the signal into the cell.

Second, an important functional consequence of the biochemical processes initiated by Ca^{2+} is that *the contribution of AMPA receptors to synaptic strength is enhanced.* It will be helpful to discuss the function of these receptors in a bit more detail before moving to a discussion of the post-translation modifications that alter their function.

FIGURE 3.2
When high-frequency stimulation generates synaptic activity, biochemical interactions are initiated that lead to several functional outcomes that are critical to the induction of LTP. Post-translation modification processes assemble and rearrange existing proteins. Transcription and translation processes generate new proteins. A major consequence of these processes is that the contribution of AMPA receptors to synaptic depolarization is enhanced, that is, synapses are strengthened.

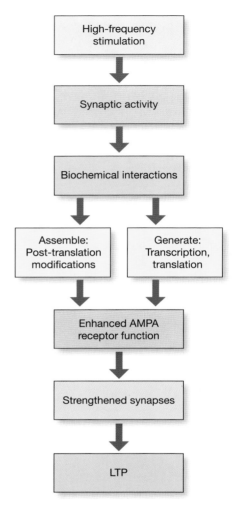

AMPA Receptor Function and the Expression of LTP

As you have previously learned, AMPA receptors play a major role in the post-synaptic response to glutamate. When glutamate binds to them, Na^+ enters the cell and moves the neuron in the direction of depolarizing. You have learned as well that AMPA receptors contribute to opening the NMDA Ca^{2+} channel by depolarizing the cell. It is also the case that enhancing the AMPA receptor function is a major determiner of the enhanced synaptic response to the test stimulus that is the expression of LTP.

Although many of the mysteries of synaptic plasticity remain, two prominent researchers, Robert Malenka and Mark Bear, concluded: "It now appears safe to state that a major mechanism for the expression of LTP involves increasing the number of AMPA receptors in the plasma membrane at synapses via activity-dependent changes in AMPA receptor trafficking" (Malenka and Bear, 2004, p. 7). Thus, a major outcome of the biochemical interactions that produce LTP is that they alter the contribution AMPA receptors make to synaptic depolarization.

Robert Malenka

As noted, an AMPA receptor is an ion channel positioned to span the cell membrane where it can bind to glutamate and allow Na⁺ to enter the cell. However, not all AMPA receptors occupy this position; some are found in the cytoplasm or inside the plasma membrane. AMPA receptors in the cytoplasm cannot respond to glutamate. The location of AMPA receptors, however, is far from static, as they are able to move in and out of the plasma membrane (Figure 3.3). This dynamic situation is captured by the concept called **AMPA trafficking**, described in detail in a later section of this chapter (Esteban, 2003; Malinow and Malenka, 2002; Derkach, Oh, Guire, and Soderling, 2007). In addition, some synapses do not contain AMPA recep-

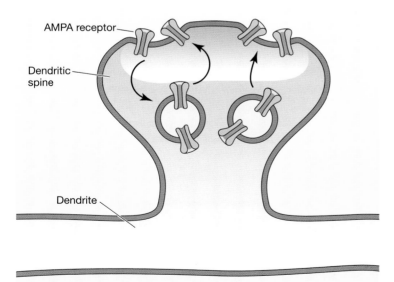

FIGURE 3.3
AMPA receptors traffic into and out of dendritic spines. AMPA trafficking is regulated constitutively (double arrows) and by synaptic activity (single arrow). Constitutive trafficking routinely cycles AMPA receptors into and out of dendritic spines, while synaptic activity is thought to deliver new AMPA receptors to them.

tors. When this is the case, even if glutamate is released these synapses cannot respond. Lynch and Baudry (1984) proposed the term **silent synapse** to represent this situation. Finally, not all AMPA receptors located in the cell membrane respond the same when glutamate binds to them.

The number of molecules and their interactions that influence the induction and maintenance of LTP is so large as to be bewildering (Sanes and Lichtman, 1999). The discussion of AMPA receptors provides an endpoint or organizing principle for understanding some of these complexities. *The principle is that in many cases the biochemical interactions that produce LTP do so by either directly or indirectly influencing the contribution of AMPA receptors to synaptic depolarization.* With these ideas in mind we can now consider some of the important biochemical interactions (generally called post-translation modifications) that Ca^{2+} initiates when it enters the dendritic spine.

Post-Translation Modification Processes

Many of the components needed to strengthen synapses, called **proteins**, are already present in dendrites at the moment Ca^{2+} enters the cell. Ca^{2+} initiates biochemical interactions that modify and rearrange these existing proteins and, as referenced above, these interactions constitute the post-translation modification process.

When Ca^{2+} enters the dendritic spine, it can bind to the receptor site of **calmodulin**, a calcium-binding protein that can regulate a number of protein targets. It is a surrogate second messenger for Ca^{2+}. When Ca^{2+} binds to it, calmodulin undergoes a conformational change, taking on a new shape (Figure 3.4). This new shape enables it to bind to some proteins that do not have Ca^{2+} binding sites.

One important protein influenced by calmodulin is a kinase called calcium-calmodulin-dependent protein kinase II (**CaMKII**). A **kinase** is an enzyme that can exist in both an inactive and active state. When a kinase is inactive it does very little. However, once activated it is able to change the conformation of other components in the cell. It does this by a process called **phosphorylation**, in which it attaches a phosphate to another protein and thereby alters the conformation and functional properties of that protein.

FIGURE 3.4
Calmodulin undergoes a conformational change when it binds to calcium. This new shape enables it to bind to other proteins that do not have Ca^{2+} binding sites.

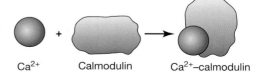

The Role of CaMKII and Autophosphorylation

CaMKII is one of the most important kinases involved in the induction of LTP. Its name is derived from the fact that it is activated by calmodulin. It has a large presence at synapses and is the main protein in the **postsynaptic density zone (PSDZ)**, a region at the tip of the dendritic spine (Lisman, Schulman, and Cline, 2002). It is in the right place to contribute to strengthening synapses and is critical for the induction of LTP. For example, LTP is prevented if activation of CaMKII is inhibited. LTP is also greatly reduced in hippocampal slices taken from mice who have been genetically altered so that CaMKII cannot stay active (Giese, Fedorov, Filipkowski, and Silva, 1998). Given that CaMKII has been strongly linked to LTP, it is important to know why this is the case. This requires some understanding of its basic structure (Lisman et al., 2002).

CaMKII is formed from 12 protein subunits or isoforms (proteins that have the same function). Technically it is called a **dodecameric holoenzyme**. The multi-subunit nature of the CaMKII complex is unique among protein kinases and is thought to be endowed with unusual properties. Like other kinases, each CaMKII subunit consists of two domains. One is called an **autoinhibitory** or **regulatory domain**, the other a **catalytic domain**. Together the two domains are conceptualized as forming a gate.

A subunit can be in two states. When the gate is closed the subunit is in an *inactive* state and cannot actively influence other molecules. When the gate is opened it becomes *active*. The gate opens when Ca^{2+}–calmodulin binds to a region on the autoinhibitory–regulatory domain. Now the catalytic domain is free to phosphorylate (that is, add a phosphate to) other proteins. In addition, when the gate is open a site on the autoinhibitory–regulatory domain called **Thr286** is exposed. When this site is exposed, it can be phosphorylated by a neighboring subunit that is also in the active state. Thus, Thr286 is referred to as a phosphorylation site (Figure 3.5).

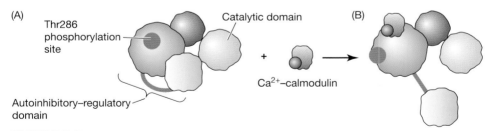

(A)

Thr286 phosphorylation site

Catalytic domain

(B)

+ Ca^{2+}–calmodulin

Autoinhibitory–regulatory domain

FIGURE 3.5
Like other kinases, CaMKII is composed of two domains, an autoinhibitory–regulatory domain and a catalytic domain. Like a switch, CaMKII can be in a closed state (A) or an open state (B). When Ca^{2+}–calmodulin binds to the autoinhibitory–regulatory domain, the switch opens and the catalytic domain can now phosphorylate other proteins. In the open state, a phosphorylation site on the regulatory domain called Thr286 is now exposed.

Ca²⁺–calmodulin will not stay bound to the autoinhibitory–regulatory domain and, because of the gate-like structure of the subunit, when Ca²⁺–calmodulin dissociates the gate will close and the subunit will return to the inactive state unless other events take place. The significance of the Thr286 site is that when it is phosphorylated the gate will stay open and the subunit will remain active even without Ca²⁺–calmodulin. The open state becomes independent of Ca²⁺–calmodulin. It is critical to understand that the catalytic domain of an active subunit can phosphorylate the Thr286 site of another active subunit. The process of active subunits phosphorylating each other is called **autophosphorylation**.

The subunits that form the holoenzyme come together in the shape of two stacked rings, which facilitate autophosphorylation. Imagine that enough Ca²⁺–calmodulin is available to bind to the autoinhibitory–regulatory domains of the subunits that make up the holoenzyme. Consequently, (1) all gates are open, (2) each subunit is in the active state, and (3) the Thr286 site on each autoinhibitory–regulatory domain is exposed (Figure 3.6). Through this process, CaMKII can persist in an active state without Ca²⁺–calmodulin. Not

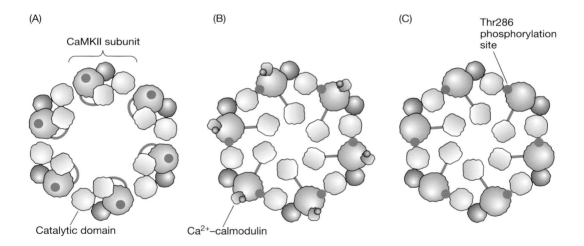

(A)

CaMKII subunit

Catalytic domain

(B)

Ca²⁺–calmodulin

(C)

Thr286 phosphorylation site

FIGURE 3.6
(A) The structure of CaMKII is complex. Subunits of the kinase assemble into a ring-like complex called a holoenzyme. (B) When Ca²⁺–calmodulin binds to the autoinhibitory–regulatory domain of all subunits, the subunits become active and the Thr286 phosphorylation site on the regulatory unit is exposed. (C) Because of the ring-like structure of the holoenzyme, a subunit can now phosphorylate its neighbor. This process of autophosphorylation enables the subunits to remain active even when Ca²⁺–calmodulin is no longer present. Thus, the holoenzyme can remain in a perpetually active state.

only does CaMKII persist, but some of this activity also occurs specifically at synapses.

Some Functional Consequences of CaMKII Activity

What does it mean to say a particular synapse or set of synapses has been strengthened? As you learned in Chapter 2, one answer is that the release of a fixed quantity of glutamate onto the postsynaptic cells now produces a larger postsynaptic field EPSP than it did before the synapses were strengthened.

If the enhanced synaptic response produced by LTP is mediated by CaMKII activity in the postsynaptic neurons, then one might expect that *the direct application of CaMKII onto these cells would also enhance the postsynaptic response to glutamate.* This result has occurred in many experiments, thus supporting the idea that CaMKII activity contributes to strengthening synapses by modifying the postsynaptic response to glutamate (see Lisman et al., 2002, for a thorough review of such experiments).

CaMKII and AMPA Receptors

What does CaMKII do that enhances the postsynaptic response to glutamate? Given the importance of AMPA receptors to LTP, it is not surprising that CaMKII activity in synapses contributes to an enhanced synaptic response by increasing AMPA receptor function (Lisman et al., 2002). The dynamic life of AMPA receptors reviewed earlier provides several possible ways for CaMKII to influence their contribution to the enhanced synaptic response to glutamate. CaMKII activity might:

- modify the conformation of AMPA receptors so that when glutamate binds they allow a large influx of Na^+;
- modify processes to prevent AMPA receptors from trafficking out of the membrane into the cytoplasm where they can no longer contribute to the synaptic response;
- initiate processes that move AMPA receptors from the cytoplasm to the cell membrane; and/or
- move AMPA receptors into silent synapse.

John Lisman

In theory, any combination of these possibilities would allow the same quantity of glutamate to produce a larger synaptic response. There is some evidence for each of these possibilities (Lisman et al., 2002).

CaMKII and the Persistence of LTP

The synaptic protein interactions involving CaMKII are necessary and sufficient to support the induction of LTP. Activated CaMKII might also contribute to the maintenance of established LTP. The ring shape structure of the CaMKII holoenzyme in principle provides a way to maintain information because, once placed in the active state, the subunits can phosphorylate each other. However, to do this requires that the enzyme stay in the active state in the face of other biochemical processes that might inactivate it. Specifically, there is another class of enzymes called **phosphatases** whose function is to *dephosphorylate* (remove phosphates from) proteins, thus returning them to their previous inactive state. They reverse the effect of kinases. The *opponent action* of kinases and phosphatases provides a mechanism for regulating the state of proteins.

In order for a CaMKII holoenzyme to remain in an active state, the rate of autophosphorylation has to be faster than the rate of dephosphorylation produced by the phosphatases (called **PP1** and **PP2**) that act on CaMKII. Theoretically, then, it is possible that CaMKII enzymes, once turned on, can stay on. This conclusion has provided a basis for pursuing the idea that CaMKII is a **molecular switch** that, when in the *on* state, can help support the maintenance of LTP once it is established.

The hypothesis that CaMKII contributes to the long-term maintenance of changes in synaptic strength has been tested by pharmacologically inhibiting CaMKII after LTP has been induced. If CaMKII is critical for the maintenance of the synaptic changes that support LTP, then inhibiting CaMKII should eliminate LTP. Until quite recently, no support has been provided for this hypothesis. However, Sanhueza, McIntyre, and Lisman (2007) report that the noncompetitive inhibitor of CaMKII (called **CaMKIINtide**) can in fact reverse LTP. Their data thus support the idea that persistently active CaMKII is not only involved in the induction of LTP, it is also involved in maintaining established changes in synaptic strength that underlie LTP (Figure 3.7).

CaMKII Autophosphorylation and PKA

Synaptic plasticity is also regulated by another kinase called **cyclic AMP-dependent protein kinase A** (**PKA**). It is called cyclic AMP-dependent because it is activated by the second messenger, cyclic adenosine monophosphate (cAMP), which can be activated by calcium. The role of PKA in synaptic plasticity is complex (Nguyen and Woo, 2003). However, some basic ideas have emerged. One hypothesis is that PKA influences LTP by its effect on the phosphatase PP1 and indirectly by its effect on CaMKII. Remember that phosphatases dephosphorylate proteins. Thus, if PP1 is active when CaMKII is activated, it could prevent CaMKII from autophosphorylating and achieving

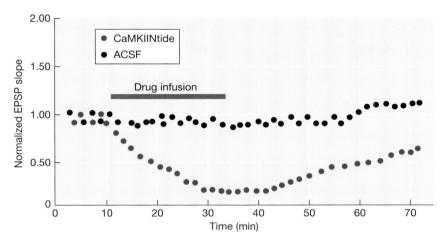

FIGURE 3.7
The persistent activation of CaMKII is necessary for maintaining LTP. In an experiment conducted by Sanhueza et al. (2007), LTP was induced in normal slices of hippocampus tissue. This figure shows that the application of a drug called CaMKIINtide (an antagonist that prevents CaMKII from remaining active) in the vehicle artificial cerebral spinal fluid (ACSF) reversed the LTP that had been induced. However, the application to control slices of the ACSF vehicle alone (without the CaMKIINtide) did not disrupt the maintenance of LTP. This means that CaMKII continues to be involved in the processes that maintain LTP once it is established. The bar represents application of the antagonist.

a persistent active state. So if PP1 is inhibited, it is more likely that CaMKII can achieve a state of persistent activation and thus influence AMPA receptor function. Robert Blitzer and his colleagues have provided evidence that PKA can influence LTP by initiating processes that ultimately inhibit PP1 (Blitzer, Wong, Nouranifar, Iyengar, and Landau, 1995; Blitzer et al., 1998).

AMPA Receptor Trafficking and Regulation

It is clear that many biochemical interactions influence LTP by altering the contribution of AMPA receptors to synaptic depolarization. An enormous amount of research has been directed at understanding processes that regulate AMPA-receptor function and trafficking. As illustrated previously in Figure 3.3, there are two general ways in which AMPA receptors traffic in and out of the plasma membrane: constitutive trafficking and synaptic-activity-regulated trafficking.

1. The concept of **constitutive trafficking** recognizes that on a routine basis AMPA receptors cycle in and out of dendritic spines. Constitutive trafficking is necessary because the proteins that make up the receptor become damaged and need to be replaced. The constitutive process serves to maintain synaptic strength.

2. The concept of **synaptic-activity-regulated trafficking** recognizes that AMPA receptors also are influenced by synaptic activity generated when the LTP-inducing stimulus causes the release of glutamate. Synaptic activity is thought to deliver new AMPA receptors to dendritic spines.

The Composition of AMPA Receptors

Technically, AMPA receptors are hetero-oligomeric molecules that are composed of different combinations of subunits called GluR1, GluR2, GluR3, and GluR4. The contribution an AMPA receptor makes to synaptic depolarization depends on its subunit composition (Figure 3.8). GluR1 AMPA receptors are designed to make a larger contribution to synaptic potentials than other types of AMPA receptors, such as GluR2 and GluR3. This is because when CaMKII phosphorylates GluR1 subunits, the channel conductance property of these receptors is enhanced—they are more likely to open when fully bound by glutamate and have a higher permeability to Ca^{2+}. A GluR2 subunit can also significantly alter the properties of the AMPA receptor and synaptic transmission. The presence of GluR2 prevents the enhanced conductance that

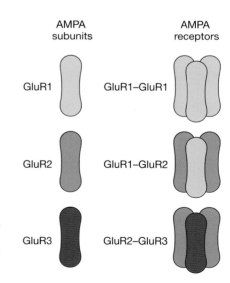

FIGURE 3.8
AMPA receptors are composed of subunits. The GluR1–GluR2 and GluR2–GluR3 receptors are constitutively trafficked into and out of the synapse. The trafficking of GluR1–GluR1 receptors is regulated by synaptic activity.

would normally accompany phosphorylation of the GluR1 subunit and thereby cools it down. Thus, you might think of GluR1 AMPA receptors as "hot" compared to AMPA receptors that contain GluR2 subunits.

Under basal conditions—prior to the induction of LTP—most membrane-spanning AMPA receptors in the hippocampus are composed of GluR2–GluR3 subunits that are constitutively cycled in and out of the dendritic spine. However, synaptic activity sufficient to generate LTP puts in motion events that lead to the preferential trafficking of AMPA receptors that *do not contain GluR2* subunits (e.g., GluR1–GluR1 AMPA receptors).

AMPA Receptor Trafficking into the Synapse

The regulation of GluR1 function and trafficking is complex. GluR1s have three phosphorylation sites, Ser 818 (P1), Ser 831 (P2), and Ser 845 (P3). Each site plays a different role in regulating GluR1 AMPA receptor trafficking and function, and each site is phosphorylated by a different kinase—CaMKII, PKA, and **protein kinase C (PKC)**. CaMKII phosphorylates the P2 site, PKA the P3 site, and PKC the P1 site. When CaMKII phosporylates the P2 site, the GluR1 channel conductance is increased, as noted. The functional effects associated with this and the other phosphorylation sites are summarized in Figure 3.9.

The process of inserting AMPA receptors into the plasma membrane is called **exocytosis**. The trafficking of GluR1 AMPA receptors into the synapse is thought to take place in two stages. First, the receptors are trafficked from the **cytosol**, the internal fluid of the neuron, to the extrasynaptic region of the dendrite, a region just outside of the dendritic spine head. They are then trafficked to the PSDZ of the dendritic spine. These two steps are regulated by the phosphorylation of the other sites, P3 and P1 (Figure 3.10).

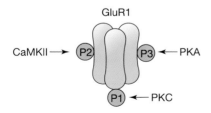

Regulatory function

(P1) Ser 818 anchors GluR1 to the PSDZ

(P2) Ser 831 changes GluR1 channel conductance

(P3) Ser 845 traffics GluR1 to extrasynaptic region

FIGURE 3.9
The GluR1 subunit has three phosphorylation sites represented as P1, P2, and P3. Each site is phosphorylated by a different kinase. The phosphorylation of each site regulates a different function.

FIGURE 3.10
GluR1 AMPA receptors are trafficked into dendritic spines in two stages. In Stage 1, PKA phosphorylation of the P3 (Ser 845) site moves GluR1 AMPA receptors to the extrasynaptic region. In Stage 2, the influx of Ca^{2+} via NMDA receptors activates PKC, which phosphorylates the P1 (Ser 818) site and helps to anchor the receptors in the PSDZ. (After Derkach et al., 2007.)

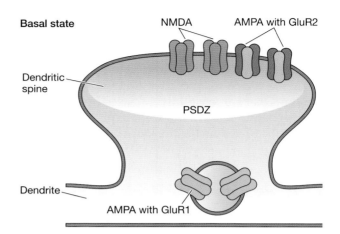

Basal state

NMDA   AMPA with GluR2

Dendritic spine

PSDZ

Dendrite

AMPA with GluR1

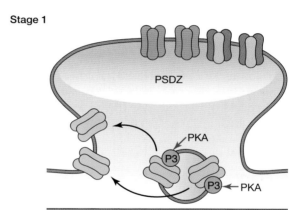

Stage 1

PSDZ

PKA

P3

P3 ← PKA

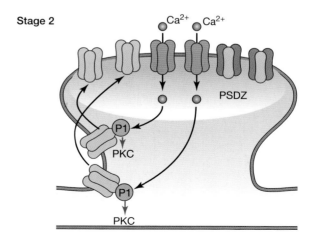

Stage 2

Ca^{2+} Ca^{2+}

PSDZ

P1

PKC

P1

PKC

In the first stage, processes set in motion by the release of another neurotransmitter called **dopamine** move the GluR1 AMPA receptors into the extrasynaptic region by activating the kinase PKA. This kinase mobilizes the insertion of AMPA receptors into the extrasynaptic space by phosphorylating the P3 site on GluR1. This process does not depend on the activation of the NMDA receptor.

These extrasynaptic GluR1s, however, do not contribute to synaptic depolarization. Before this can happen *they have to be moved to the synapses.* This happens in the second stage and is brought about by the influx of Ca^{2+} through the NMDA receptor. In this process the kinase is activated by Ca^{2+} and it phosphorylates the P1 site on GluR1 subunits. This process is thought to facilitate the anchoring of these GluR1 AMPA receptors in the PSDZ.

GluR1 AMPA receptors do not make a long-lasting contribution to LTP. Within about 30 minutes, they are trafficked out of the synapse and replaced by AMPA receptors containing GluR2 subunits. Nevertheless, the trafficking of GluR1 AMPA receptors into the dendritic spine lays a foundation for sustaining a more enduring LTP because *the insertion of GluR1s into the dendritic spine creates new slots for AMPA receptors.* Thus, even though constitutive trafficking processes replace GluR1s with AMPA receptors that contain GluR2 subunits, *the overall number of AMPA receptors is increased.* It is this overall increase in AMPA receptors that can provide a basis for a more enduring enhanced synaptic response (Figure 3.11).

Summary

In this chapter some of the important biochemical events initiated by an LTP-inducing stimulus have been described. The introduction of Ca^{2+} into dendritic spines initiates biochemical events that converge to persistently activate CaMKII, which cooperates with PKA and PKC to increase the contribution AMPA receptors make to synaptic depolarization. These processes (1) drive GluR1 AMPA receptors into the postsynaptic density zone and (2) phosphorylate these receptors, thereby enhancing their channel conductance properties. GluR1 AMPA receptors, however, only temporarily stay in the PSDZ. AMPA receptors containing GluR2 replace them. Overall, however, the number of AMPA receptors in the PSDZ is increased relative to the basal level prior to the induction of LTP.

These changes in AMPA receptor function provide a basis for the enhanced synaptic depolarization that is called LTP. Note that all of the processes that have been described only involve interactions among ions and the modification of existing proteins. These interactions are sufficient to initiate the induction of LTP but its long-term persistence requires transcription and translation processes that generate new products. These processes are discussed in the next chapter.

FIGURE 3.11

(A) In the basal state, before an LTP-inducing stimulus is presented, a dendritic spine has NMDA receptors and AMPA receptors with a GluR2 subunit in the plasma membrane, anchored in the PSDZ. (B) The induction stimulus causes GluR1 AMPA receptors to be trafficked into the plasma membrane and anchored in the PSDZ. Note there are now more AMPA receptors in the spine. (C) GluR1s are only temporarily anchored in the PSDZ. Within about 30 minutes constitutive trafficking processes replace them with AMPA receptors that contain GluR2 subunits. Note, however, that compared to the basal state, there are still more AMPA receptors present in the modified synapses than were present before LTP was induced. (After Derkach et al., 2007.)

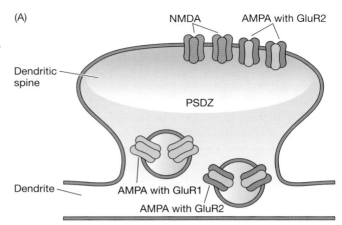

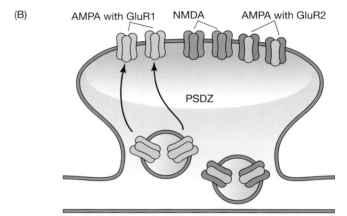

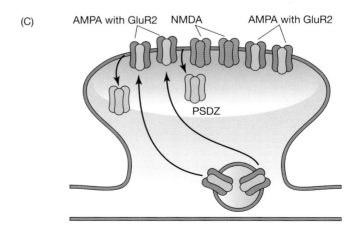

References

Blitzer, R. D., Connor, J. H., Brown, G. P., Wong, T., Shenolikar, S., Iyengar, R., and Landau, E. M. (1998). Gating of CaMKII by cAMP-regulated protein phosphatase activity during LTP. *Science, 280,* 1940–1942.

Blitzer, R. D., Wong T., Nouranifar, R., Iyengar, R., and Landau, E. M. (1995). Postsynaptic cAMP pathway gates early LTP in hippocampal CA1 region. *Neuron, 15,* 1403–1414.

Derkach, V. A., Oh, M. C., Guire, E. S., and Soderling, T. R. (2007). Regulatory mechanisms of AMPA receptors in synaptic plasticity. *Nature Reviews Neuroscience, 8,* 8101–8113.

Esteban, J. A. (2003). AMPA receptor trafficking: a roadmap for synaptic plasticity. *Molecular Intervention, 3,* 375–385.

Giese, K. P., Fedorov, N. B., Filipkowski, R. K., and Silva, A. J. (1998). Autophosphorylation at Thr286 of the alpha calcium-calmodulin kinase II in LTP and learning. *Science, 279,* 870–873.

Lisman, J. E., Schulman, H., and Cline, H. (2002). The molecular basis of CaMKII function in synaptic and behavioral memory. *Nature Reviews Neuroscience, 3,* 175–190.

Lynch, G. and Baudry, M. (1984). The biochemistry of memory: a new and specific hypothesis. *Science, 224,* 1057–1063.

Malenka, R. C. and Bear, M. F. (2004). LTP and LTD: an embarrassment of riches. *Neuron, 44,* 5–21.

Malinow, R. and Malenka, R. C. (2002). AMPA receptor trafficking and synaptic plasticity. *Annual Review of Neuroscience, 25,* 103–126.

Nguyen, P. V. and Woo, N. H. (2003). Regulation of hippocampal synaptic plasticity by cyclic AMP-dependent protein kinases. *Progress in Neurobiology, 71,* 401–437.

Sanhueza, M., McIntyre, C., and Lisman, J. E. (2007). Reversal of synaptic memory by Ca^{2+}–calmodulin-dependent protein kinase II inhibitor. *Journal of Neuroscience, 27,* 5190–5199.

Sanes, J. R. and Lichtman, J. W. (1999). Can molecules explain long-term potentiation? *Nature, 7,* 597–604.

Strengthening Synapses: Generating New Material

We have discussed LTP as if it were a single phenomenon. It is now appropriate to introduce a critical fact: *The duration of LTP depends on the stimulus parameters used to induce it* (Figure 4.1). Weak stimulation tends to induce LTP that has a limited duration. It decays within an hour or so after it has been induced. In contrast, if a strong stimulus protocol is used, LTP can last for the duration of the slice (over six hours). It can last for months in a living animal (Abraham, Logan, Greenwood, and Dragunow, 2002). These two types of LTP are often referred to as **short-lasting** (**S-LTP**) and **long-lasting** (**L-LTP**).

The relatively transient nature of S-LTP implies that the weak stimulus failed to initiate intracellular events needed to sustain the synaptic changes that were initially produced. It is now recognized that S-LTP is a product of the post-translation processes discussed in the previous chapter. These processes primarily involve modifications of existing proteins and protein–protein interactions. Thus, S-LTP does not depend on the production of new proteins. In contrast, L-LTP appears to depend on synaptic activity inducing additional

FIGURE 4.1
There are two types of LTP. Weak high-frequency stimulation (HFS) induces a relatively short-lasting LTP and strong stimulation induces a much longer-lasting LTP.

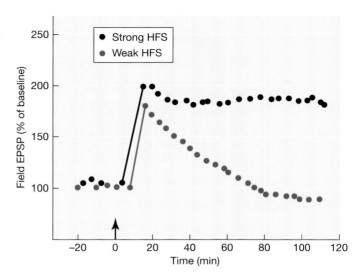

biochemical processes that do produce new proteins. Relevant genetic material must be available and the proteins must be synthesized.

The process of producing the relevant genetic material requires both **transcription** and **translation** mechanisms. Transcription is the process of converting genetic material from DNA to messenger RNA (mRNA), while translation is the process by which mRNA is converted to protein. This chain of events occurs when signaling molecules enter the nucleus and activate **transcription factors**, that is, proteins that interact with DNA to produce mRNA. The process of translating mRNA into protein is also called **protein synthesis**.

The goal of this chapter is to provide you with some basic understanding of how these processes contribute to L-LTP. We look first at two parallel processes induced by synaptic activity—**genomic signaling**, which produces new protein through transcription and translation, and **local protein synthesis**, which translates existing mRNAs. We end with an examination of **synaptic tagging theory**, which addresses the problem of how these new protein products get to the correct synapses.

Genomic Signaling

One common view of the general steps involved in producing enduring or L-LTP is called the genomic signaling hypothesis: *The delivery of a stimulus that produces L-LTP initiates signaling cascades that lead to the phosphorylation of transcription factors, which results in the production of mRNAs that subsequently are*

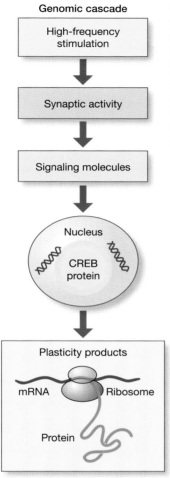

Genomic cascade

FIGURE 4.2
High-frequency stimulation generates synaptic activity that activates signaling molecules that translocate into the nucleus where they phosphorylate the transcription factor CREB protein. Messenger RNAs are transcribed and new proteins are translated that are thought to be essential to the construction of enduring changes in synaptic strength.

translated into new proteins needed to maintain strengthened synapses that support L-LTP.

L-LTP is thought to depend on the initiating stimulus inducing both the transcription of new gene products and their translation into protein. It should be understood that the maintenance of all parts of a cell depends on ongoing, constitutive transcription and translation processes. The distinguishing feature of the genomic signaling hypothesis is that it assumes that the relevant new proteins needed to sustain L-LTP are derived from *new* mRNAs, produced as a direct consequence of neural activity associated with the stimulus that induces LTP (Figure 4.2).

This idea gained support when Nguyen, Abel, and Kandel (1994) reported that inhibitors of transcription blocked the development of L-LTP when given immediately after the inducing stimulus but not when given much later. This temporal dependency suggested that L-LTP required that new mRNAs be produced in response to the inducing stimulus; mRNAs that were already available were not adequate.

The Role of CREB Protein in Transcription

The hypothesis that L-LTP depends on transcription also gained support when it became known that a transcription factor called **cAMP-responsive element-binding** (**CREB**) protein was implicated in both synaptic plasticity and behavioral memory. For example, Dash, Hochner, and Kandel (1990) found that preventing the translation of CREB protein prevented synaptic changes needed to enhance responding of the *Aplysia* gill-withdrawal reflex. Others reported that fruit flies with mutation of the CREB gene showed impaired memory (Tully, 1991). The importance of this transcription factor to persistent synaptic change was further implicated when it was reported that L-LTP could not be induced in slices taken from genetically engineered mice lacking the CREB gene. These slices, however, were able to support S-LTP (Bourtchuladze et al., 1994). A number of papers provide comprehensive reviews of the role CREB plays in synaptic plasticity and memory (Nguyen and Woo, 2003; Silva, Giese, Fedorov, Frankland, and Kogan, 1998; Yin and Tully, 1996).

The general conclusion from this work is that CREB protein transcribes mRNAs that are critical to the production of long-lasting changes in synaptic strength. These mRNAs are sometimes called **plasticity products** (**PPs**) because they are thought to be critical to long-term changes in synaptic strength.

In its unphosphorylated state, CREB protein has little effect on gene transcription. It is only when it is phosphorylated that it initiates the production of mRNAs that participate in producing long-lasting changes in synaptic strength. Because its function depends on whether it is in the active or inactive state, CREB protein is sometimes thought of as a **molecular memory switch** (Kandel, 2001). In the *on* state it initiates the production of memory-making mRNAs, but when it is in the *off* state these products are not transcribed.

CREB Protein Activation: Two Models

If the generation of plasticity-related mRNAs depends on the phosphorylation of CREB protein, then it is important to know how CREB protein is activated. Adams and Dudek (2005) have described two general models of how the signals reach the nucleus: **synapse-to-nucleus signaling** and **soma-to-nucleus signaling** (Figure 4.3).

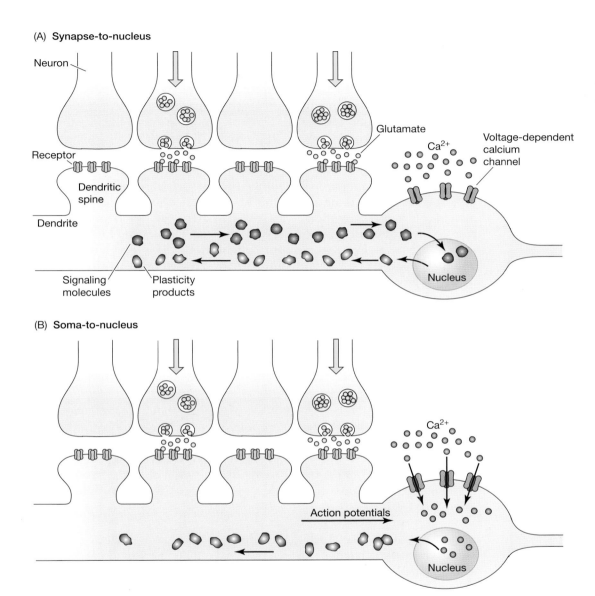

(A) **Synapse-to-nucleus**

Neuron

Receptor

Dendritic spine

Dendrite

Signaling molecules

Plasticity products

Glutamate

Ca^{2+}

Voltage-dependent calcium channel

Nucleus

(B) **Soma-to-nucleus**

Ca^{2+}

Action potentials

Nucleus

FIGURE 4.3
Synaptic activity can signal the nucleus in two ways. (A) The synapse-to-nucleus signaling model assumes that synaptic activity initiates a cascade that produces signaling molecules that eventually translocate to the nucleus to initiate transcription. (B) The soma-to-nucleus signaling model assumes that, as a result of action potentials produced by synaptic activity, Ca^{2+} enters the soma through voltage-dependent calcium channels (vdCCs) where it can more directly initiate transcription. Note that both of these hypotheses could be true.

SYNAPSE-TO-NUCLEUS SIGNALING   The details of the synapse-to-nucleus signaling model are complex. However, the general outline of the process is relatively simple. The stimulation of a postsynaptic neuron first activates second messengers that then activate protein kinases. Second messengers or their kinase targets translocate into the nucleus where they phosphorylate CREB protein and transcription is initiated. There are multiple intracellular pathways that converge to phosphorylate CREB protein (Figure 4.4). This convergence suggests that CREB protein activation will reflect the combined influence of several sources.

There is no need to discuss all of the possible signaling pathways. However, it is instructive to describe some key ones. One such signaling cascade also involves the activation of PKA. When activated by cAMP, PKA can translocate to the nucleus to phosphorylate CREB protein and initiate transcription. Moreover, PKA inhibitors can block the development of L-LTP, and the reduction in L-LTP is accompanied by a reduction in genes controlled by CREB protein (Nguygen and Woo, 2003).

Another signaling cascade involves the activation of the extracellular-regulated kinase (ERK)–mitogen-activated protein (MAP) kinase (**ERK–MAPK**). The activation of this signaling pathway is initiated by **neurotrophic factors**. Neurotrophins are a family of molecules that promote survival of neural tissues and play a critical role in neural development and differentiation. These factors bind to a class of plasma membrane receptors in the tyrosine kinase family called **trk receptors**.

When activated, both PKA and ERK–MAPK are thought to translocate to the nucleus where they engage transcription factors, including CREB protein, and induce transcription of plasticity-related mRNAs. Stimulation that leads to the induction of L-LTP induces the transcription of CREB-dependent mRNAs. Inhibitors of PKA and ERK–MAPK activation block the transcription of these mRNAs. Moreover, inhibitors of these kinases also block the development of L-LTP.

SOMA-TO-NUCLEUS SIGNALING   According to the soma-to-nucleus signaling model, the action potential produced when a cell depolarizes also can generate a signal. Repetitive action potentials are assumed to open what are called voltage-dependent calcium channels (vdCCs) that are located on the soma (cell body of the neuron). When action potentials are produced, these channels open and calcium enters the soma. Calmodulin already exists in the nucleus. Thus, when activated by Ca^{2+} it could induce the activation of nuclear enzymes such as CaMKIV that can phosphorylate CREB protein. Activated calmodulin outside of the nucleus also might translocate to the nucleus. This source of Ca^{2+} might also stimulate ERK to translocate to the nucleus to participate in the phosphorylation of CREB protein.

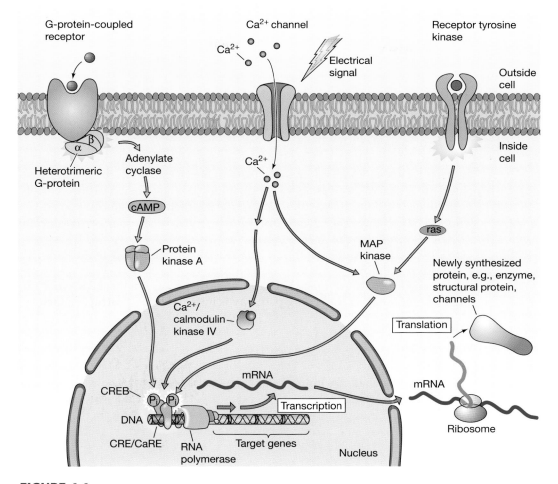

FIGURE 4.4
There are many synapse-to-nucleus signaling pathways that can lead to the phosphorylation of CREB protein and to the production of new mRNA and new proteins that are critical for L-LTP.

Two arguments support an action-potential model (Adams and Dudek, 2005). First, the amount of signal generated at single synapses that reaches the nucleus may not be enough to initiate transcription. Second, signaling molecules activated by synaptic processes have a long journey to reach the nucleus. So, the time it takes for them to translocate to the nucleus may be too long to allow them to participate in the immediate transcription of genes needed to support L-LTP.

There also is experimental support for the action-potential model. A strong prediction from this model is that *soma-to-nucleus signaling can substitute for synapse-to-nucleus signaling to produce L-LTP*. Dudek and Fields (2002) provided support for this prediction. Recall that a weak stimulus protocol will only generate S-LTP but that a strong stimulus will generate L-LTP. A strong stimulus is also very likely to repeatedly produce the action potentials needed to repeatedly open the calcium channels.

Dudek and Fields reasoned that if action potentials are the critical event for L-LTP, then it should be possible to convert S-LTP into L-LTP by initiating action potentials without strongly stimulating synapses. To do this they weakly stimulated Schaffer collateral input to CA1 and then initiated action potentials in the CA1 cells antidromically (stimulating from axon to soma in these cells). These action potentials were sufficient to prevent the decay of LTP normally produced by weak stimulation. The action potentials alone also were sufficient to phosphorylate ERK and CREB protein (Figure 4.5). This type of experiment is also an example of synaptic tagging, a concept that is discussed in detail later in this chapter.

Local Protein Synthesis

As we have learned, the induction of long-lasting changes in synaptic strength depends on the availability of relevant mRNAs. Unless these gene transcripts are translated into protein, however, they cannot participate in the intracellular biochemical interactions necessary to sustain an enduring change.

Transcription and Local Translation

As pointed out in the introduction to this chapter, the changes in synaptic strength that support S-LTP depend only on post-translation modifications, while changes in synaptic strength that support L-LTP may require both transcription and translation of new plasticity products. This dual requirement suggests that understanding how transcription is regulated is key to understanding how enduring changes in synaptic plasticity are produced. The implication of this idea is that transcription is the primary step in the induction of L-LTP and translation is just the obligatory consequence of the need for synthesizing newly available mRNAs (Kelleher, Govindarajan, and Tonegawa, 2004a).

By this scheme one would envision a sequence in which (1) neural activity would induce the genomic signaling cascade that transcribes genes into mRNAs, (2) these mRNAs would leave the nucleus, and (3) these mRNAs

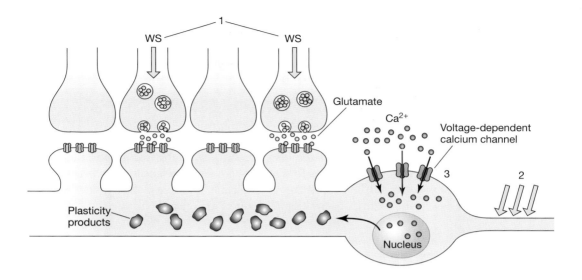

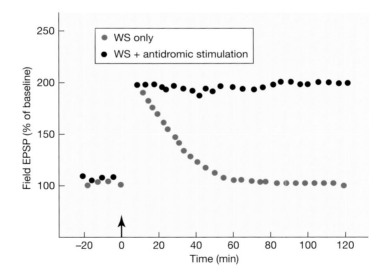

FIGURE 4.5

The top of this figure illustrates how Dudek and Fields (2002) tested the soma-to-nucleus signaling hypotheses. They applied a weak stimulus (WS) to the Schaffer collateral fiber pathway (1). In some slices this was followed by electrical stimulation applied to the axons (called antidromic stimulation) of the CA1 pyramidal cells (2) to produce action potentials in those neurons and allow the influx of Ca^{2+} into the soma and nucleus (3). The bottom of this figure shows that weak stimulation produced only a short-lasting LTP, but when it was followed by antidromic stimulation L-LTP was induced.

would then be translated into the protein needed to support L-LTP (illustrated earlier in Figure 4.2). However, this is not the case. Instead, *synaptic activity produced by a strong stimulus initiates protein synthesis (translation) almost immediately, well in advance of when new mRNAs resulting from the genomic cascade would become available for translation* (Kelleher et al., 2004a; Sutton and Schuman, 2005, 2006).

Kelleher and his colleagues provided a useful illustration of this point by comparing the effects of translation and transcription inhibitors on L-LTP (Kelleher, Govindarajan, Jung, Kang, and Tonegawa, 2004b). To do this they applied either the protein synthesis inhibitor anisomycin or the transcription inhibitor actinomycin D to the slice before applying a strong stimulus that would normally produce L-LTP. Both drugs dramatically shortened the duration of LTP. However, the critical observation illustrated in Figure 4.6 is that the *effect of inhibiting translation occurred well in advance of the effect of inhibiting transcription.*

This result is inconsistent with the sequence of events predicted by the genomic signaling cascade hypothesis because it predicts that the effect of in-

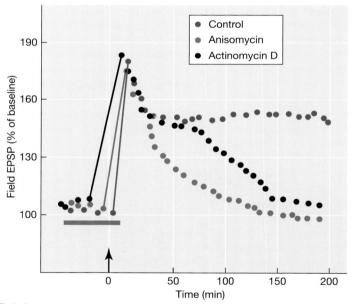

FIGURE 4.6
This figure compares the effects of the protein synthesis inhibitor anisomycin and the transcription inhibitor actinomycin D on the duration of L-LTP. Note that both of these drugs prevented L-LTP but the effect of anisomycin emerged earlier than the effect of actinomycin D. These results suggest that synaptic activity that produces L-LTP induces protein synthesis almost immediately, well before mRNA transcribed from a genomic cascade would be available for translation. Bar represents the drug infusion. (After Kelleher et al., 2004a, 2004b.)

hibiting transcription should be observed *before* the effect of inhibiting translation. The implication of this pattern of data is that *synaptic activity induces the
translation of mRNAs that were already present and not derived from the genomic
signaling cascade.* There is now strong evidence that this rapid translation of
new protein takes place *locally in the dendrites.*

Translation Machinery in Dendrites

The traditional view is that the primary site of translation is in the soma and
that synapses depend on proteins synthesized there to meet their requirements.
However, it is now recognized that **translation machinery** (such as endoplasmic reticulum, Golgi elements, ribosomal assemblies) is present in dendrites
(Figure 4.7). Remarkably, the elements are located within or near the dendritic spine neck and the shaft of the dendrite—the route through which current must flow when spine synapses are activated (Steward and Schuman,
2001). Moreover, a large number of mRNAs are also distributed within the dendrite as well as the soma (Miyashiro, Dichter, and Eberwine, 1994). They include mRNAs near dendritic spines destined to become proteins (CaMKII and
AMPA receptors) that are needed to induce LTP. These observations suggest
that dendritic protein synthesis provides a mechanism that permits local protein to rapidly change in response to neural activity (Steward and Worley, 2002).

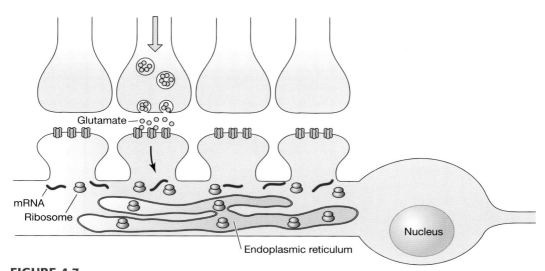

FIGURE 4.7
Protein translation machinery, such as endoplasmic reticulum (ER) and ribosomes,
is present in dendrites near spines. Synaptic activity can activate this machinery.

The Role of Local Protein Synthesis in L-LTP

Local protein synthesis (translation) not only occurs, it plays a role in establishing L-LTP (Sutton and Schuman, 2006). Two general strategies have been used to reveal this fact. The first involves separating CA1 dendrites in hippocampus slices from their cell bodies, making it impossible for proteins that have been newly synthesized in the soma from a genomic cascade to influence synaptic strength (Figure 4.8). Studies with this preparation have found that protein synthesis in the dendrite is sufficient to support L-LTP (Kang and Schuman, 1996). The second strategy involves applying protein synthesis inhibitors selectively to the soma and dendritic fields of CA1 pyramidal cells.

Bradshaw, Emptage, and Bliss (2003) used the second strategy (Figure 4.9). They took advantage of the fact that pyramidal neurons in CA1 have both api-

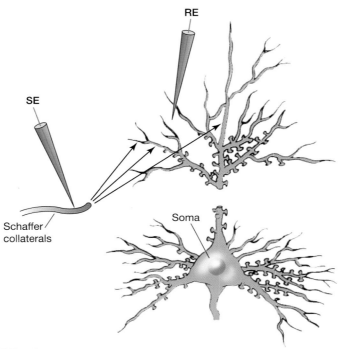

FIGURE 4.8
In the preparation shown here, the dendritic field is surgically separated from the soma. This prevents the delivery of new proteins that were the product of a genomic signaling cascade. Nevertheless, stimulation delivered to the Schaffer collateral fibers can produce a relatively long-lasting LTP and synthesize new proteins in the dendrites. SE = stimulating electrode; RE = recording electrode.

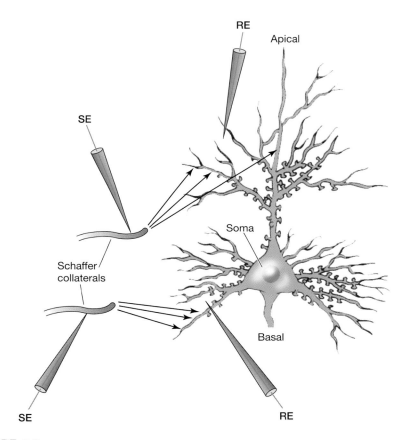

FIGURE 4.9
This figure illustrates the methodology Bradshaw et al. (2003) used to demonstrate the contribution local–dendritic protein synthesis makes to L-LTP. By stimulating one set of Schaffer collateral fibers they could produce L-LTP in synapses located on dendrites in the apical region of the neuron. By stimulating another set of Schaffer collaterals they could produce L-LTP in synapses located on dendrites in the basal region of the neuron. When the protein synthesis inhibitory emetine was applied to the entire slice, it prevented L-LTP in both dendritic fields. However, when emetine was applied to just the apical dendrites, it blocked L-LTP only in those dendrites, and when applied to just the basal dendrites, it blocked L-LTP only in the basal dendrites. It did not block L-LTP in either region of the dendrites when it was applied to just the soma. These results mean that L-LTP depended on proteins that were translated in the dendrites in response to the LTP-inducing stimulus. SE = stimulating electrode, RE = recording electrode.

cal and basal dendrites and receive input from different Schaffer collateral fibers. They first demonstrated that when the protein synthesis inhibitor emetine is applied to the hippocampal slice preparation, it prevented the induction of L-LTP by strong high-frequency stimulation of Schaffer collateral fibers. They then applied emetine selectively to the soma of these cells and found that it did not influence L-LTP. In contrast, the application of emetine to the apical dendrites blocked the development of L-LTP in those dendrites but did not block L-LTP in the basal dendrites, while selectively applying emetine to the basal dendrites blocked L-LTP in those dendrites but did not affect L-LTP in the apical dendrites. The combined observation that a dose of emetine selectively delivered to the soma did not influence LTP but did so when delivered to the dendritic fields strongly implicates a role for local protein synthesis in L-LTP. Based on such data it is reasonable to believe that the initial round of protein synthesis initiated by an L-LTP-inducing stimulus occurs in the dendrites.

BOX 4.1 Summary of Transcription and Translation

The fundamental points about the relationship between transcription and translation processes are summarized in Figure 4.10. Synaptic activity initiates two parallel processes:

- **Genomic Signaling Cascade.** Synaptic activity induces a signaling cascade, either synapse-to-nucleus or soma-to-nucleus, that results in the transcription of new plasticity products that make their way back to the activated synapses. This process is slow and requires at least 30–40 minutes.

- **Local Protein Synthesis.** Synaptic activity induces the translation of proteins locally in the dendritic region near the spines. This process occurs relatively fast, within minutes. Note that this implies that important plasticity-relevant mRNAs are already present in the dendritic region.

It is important to note that in principle there are two scenarios whereby strong high-frequency stimulation can result in the synthesis of new proteins that can be captured by weakly stimulated synapses. The strong stimulus can initiate both local protein synthesis in dendrites and a genomic signaling cascade that results in the delivery of proteins from the soma. This means that there may be *two waves of protein synthesis* that potentially contribute to producing L-LTP: (1) An early wave that results from the translation of mRNAs already present in the dendrites and (2) a late wave that results from the translation of the new mRNAs produced by activity-induced genomic signaling (Figure 4.11).

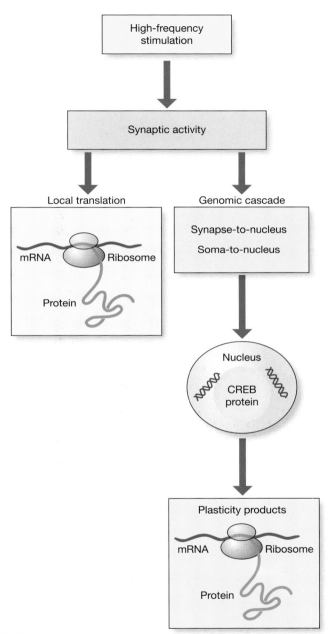

FIGURE 4.10
Long-lasting L-LTP depends on the parallel effects of synaptic activity. It induces both local translation and genomic signaling cascades (synapse-to-nucleus and soma-to-nucleus) that lead to transcription followed by translation.

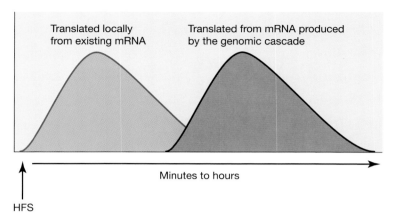

FIGURE 4.11
Strong high-frequency stimulation (HFS) can result in two waves of protein synthesis that may be important for L-LTP. The first wave occurs locally in the dendrites. The second wave occurs when new protein is synthesized from the new mRNA produced by the genomic cascade. These proteins could be synthesized in either the soma or dendritic regions.

Why Are New Proteins Critical?

All of the proteins used to construct a neuron are replaced on a continuing basis. So new mRNAs must constantly be transcribed and new proteins must regularly be synthesized to satisfy this need. Moreover, we know that the initial induction of LTP does not require that synaptic activity induce a new round of protein synthesis. All the relevant synaptic proteins such as calmodulin, CaMKII, glutamate receptors, and PKA are already present. Evidently, however, *these basal levels of protein and their constitutive replacements are not sufficient to provide recently activated synapses with the material needed to ensure that their recently enhanced strength will endure.*

Why must synaptic activity itself induce local protein synthesis to secure this enhancement? Is there something special about proteins synthesized in dendrites in response to synaptic activity that distinguishes them from proteins already present, or from proteins synthesized in the soma? Currently there is very little information available to answer such questions. However, some possibilities are worth noting. mRNAs needed for producing CaMKII are prominent in dendrites and, following the induction of LTP, rapid synthesis of this protein is known to occur in hippocampus neurons (Ouyang,

Rosenstein, Kreiman, Schuman, and Kennedy, 1999). We have already discussed the many ways this protein contributes to L-LTP. It may be that newly synthesized CaMKII is needed to support the functions that depended on the initial phosphorylation of this protein.

Malenka and his colleagues have reported that mRNAs needed to produce GluR1 and GluR2 subunits are also present in dendrites and that these mRNAs can be translated in dendrites isolated from the cell body (Ju et al., 2004). Given what is known about the relationship between AMPA receptor trafficking and LTP (see Chapter 3), one might speculate that AMPA receptors are synthesized locally in order to ensure that they are spatially proximal to recently potentiated synapses.

There is a special class of mRNAs that are needed to produce translation machinery proteins such as ribosomes and elongation factors. Blitzer, Iyengar, and Landau (2005) have proposed that one of these, called **eukaryotic elongation factor 1A (eEF1A)**, is synthesized locally in response to an L-LTP-inducing stimulus and gets incorporated into the spine. eEF1A is thought to facilitate the joining of ribosomes and mRNA and thereby boost the capacity to translate mRNAs in the vicinity of synapses activated by high-frequency stimulation (Blitzer et al., 2005). Tsokas and his colleagues have provided support for this general idea. They reported that (a) high-frequency stimulation that produced a protein-synthesis-dependent L-LTP increased the expression of eEF1A in dendrites, and (b) blocking the synthesis of these specific proteins prevented L-LTP (Tsokas et al., 2005). This appears to be a promising hypothesis.

Finding the Correct Synapses: Synaptic Tagging Theory

A given postsynaptic neuron has hundreds of dendrites, each supporting thousands of synaptic contacts. Yet, only those synapses that were activated by the delivery of high-frequency stimulation are strengthened. Thus, the stimulus input pattern specifies which synapses will be changed. However, according to the genomic signaling hypothesis, the long-term changes in synaptic strength depend on transcription processes that occur far removed in space from the strengthened synapses. As described earlier, all mRNAs are produced in the nucleus. If they are to be used to modify synaptic strength, they have to make their way from the nucleus to the relevant synapses activated by the high-frequency stimulus. This scenario raises a fundamental question. How do the plasticity products initially transcribed in the nucleus in response to neural activity find the appropriate synapses to strengthen?

Tagging Synapses and Capturing Plasticity Products

To answer this question, Frey and Morris (1997, 1998) proposed what is called the **synaptic tagging** hypothesis. They assumed that a stimulus that can induce L-LTP initiates two independent processes: (1) processes within dendritic spines that generate a biological **tag** that marks the spines as having been stimulated, and (2) a genomic cascade that produces new mRNAs and proteins (plasticity products). Weak stimulation that only produces S-LTP is sufficient to tag synapses but not sufficient to initiate the genomic cascade. Frey and Morris (1998) also assumed that new plasticity products are promiscuous—once produced they can be used to strengthen any synapses that have been recently tagged. Only tagged synapses have the capacity to capture new plasticity products; untagged synapses do not. Both the tag and the plasticity products, however, have a limited duration and they must overlap if L-LTP is to be induced (Figure 4.12).

Frey and Morris (1997) provided the initial experimental basis for the synaptic tagging hypothesis. They developed a methodology that allowed them to stimulate two different sets of Schaffer collateral fibers that formed synapses on the same population of CA1 cells and to record field EPSP associated with each stimulus. The stimuli used to induce LTP are identified as S1 and S2 pathways (Figure 4.13). By controlling the intensity of the stimulus delivered to separate Schaffer collateral fibers, they could generate either S-LTP or L-LTP on different sets of synapses belonging to the same neurons. Remember that a strong stimulus should both tag synapses and generate the genomic cascade, but a weak stimulus should only tag synapses. Using this two-stimulus protocol, they discovered that:

- S-LTP produced by weak S1 stimulation could be converted into L-LTP if a strong S2 stimulus was delivered either before or after S1. However, there was a time-dependent requirement: As the interval separating S1 and S2 increased, the ability of the strong S2 stimulus to convert S-LTP into L-LTP decreased.

FIGURE 4.12

(A) Synaptic tagging theory is based on three assumptions. (B) A strong stimulus (SS) both tags a synapse and generates a genomic signaling cascade that leads to transcription and translation of proteins (plasticity products or PPs) used to support L-LTP. The function of the tag is to capture the protein. A weak stimulus (WS) will not generate a genomic signaling cascade. However, it can tag synapses and thus capture PPs produced by a strong stimulus providing the timing is correct. Note that untagged synapses do not capture PPs.

(A)

Weak stimulation only tags synapses. Strong stimulation tags synapses and generates PPs. Both tags and PPs are transient.

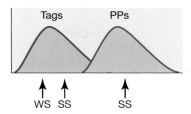

The order in which the tag and PPs are produced does not matter.

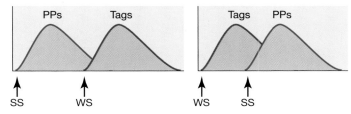

Tags and PPs must overlap to produce L-LTP.

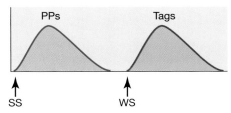

(B)

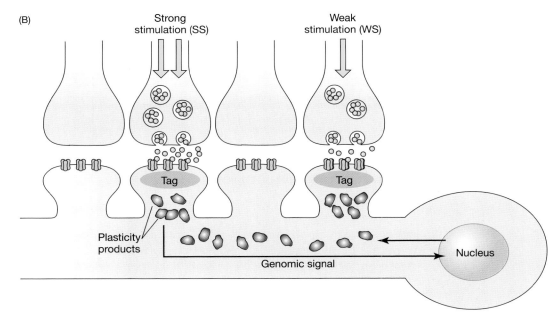

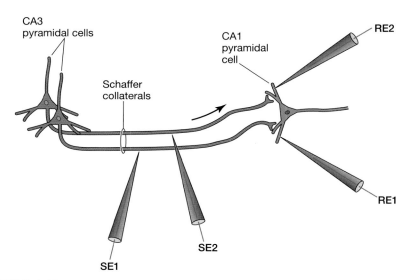

FIGURE 4.13
This schematic illustrates the procedure Frey and Morris (1997,1998) used to test synaptic tagging theory. It shows that separate sets of Schaffer collateral fibers can synapse on dendrites belonging to the same CA1 neurons. Stimulating electrodes (SE1 and SE2) can generate field EPSPs in the dendritic fields that can be recorded by the extracellular recording electrodes (RE1 and RE2). By controlling the intensity of the stimulation delivered by the stimulating electrodes, it is possible to generate either L-LTP or S-LTP.

- Blocking protein synthesis prior to the delivery of strong S2 stimulation eliminated the ability of S2 to convert S-LTP produced by weak S1 into L-LTP.

These results, of course, are consistent with the basic premises of synaptic tagging theory (Figure 4.14).

Tagging and Local Protein Synthesis

Given that protein synthesis is rapidly induced near dendritic spines, the problem addressed by the synaptic tagging hypothesis—how gene products from the nucleus get directed to the synapses that should be strengthened—may not be as severe as once imagined. Blitzer and his colleagues (2005) have proposed that the proteins captured by the tagging operation are local proteins translated from mRNAs already present in the dendrites. Their idea is that the local proteins that were synthesized by strongly stimulating one set of synapses on a dendrite can also be captured by neighbor synapses that have been tagged

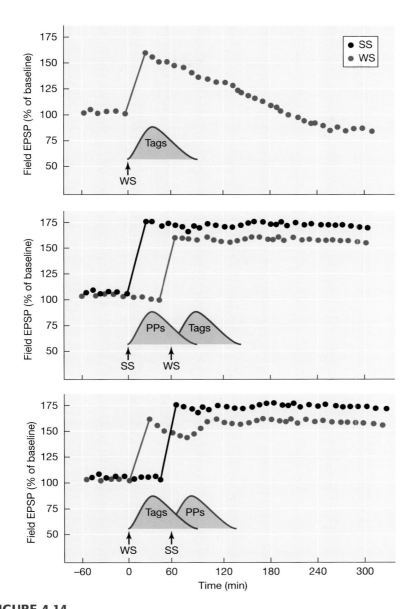

FIGURE 4.14

Some of the important results supporting synaptic tagging theory are presented in this figure. Top: A weak inducing stimulus normally only generates S-LTP. Theoretically, it only tags synapses. Middle and Bottom: If the weak stimulus (WS) is given either before or after the strong stimulus (SS), it will now produce L-LTP. Theoretically, this happens because the synaptic tags produced by the weak stimulus will capture plasticity products (PPs) generated by the strong stimulus.

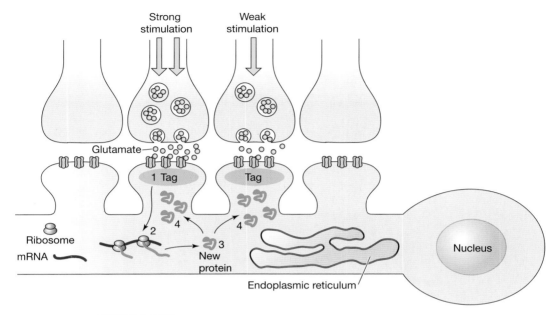

FIGURE 4.15

This figure represents a modification of the original synaptic tagging hypothesis. In this scheme, mRNA is already present in the dendrites. Weak stimulation only tags the synapse. Strong stimulation tags the synapse (1) and initiates the local synthesis of new protein (2). This new protein (3) can be captured by tags on both strongly stimulated spines and tags on weakly stimulated spines (4). By this modified account, tagged synapses capture protein that has been translated locally rather than protein that is the end product of a genomic cascade. (After Blitzer et al., 2005.)

with weak stimulation. By this account, the mRNAs that are translated are not the product of a genomic cascade initiated by a strong stimulus. Rather, they have been delivered as a consequence of ongoing basal transcription processes (Figure 4.15).

Summary

In this chapter two types of LTP were discussed. S-LTP has a relatively short duration but L-LTP is much more persistent. S-LTP is a product of post-translation processes; it does not depend on the translation of new proteins. In contrast, L-LTP appears to depend on synaptic activity inducing two parallel processes, local protein synthesis and a genomic signaling cascade that produces new mRNAs and proteins. Two genomic signaling cascades, synapse-to-nucleus and soma-to-nucleus, were described.

Protein translation machinery is present in dendrites near spines, and there is evidence that this machinery is activated by strong high-frequency stimulation because protein synthesis in dendrites has been demonstrated. These locally synthesized proteins include CaMKII, GluR1 and GluR2, and proteins that facilitate the translation of other proteins, such as eEF1A. These locally translated proteins support L-LTP.

The concept of synaptic tagging was introduced to explain how plasticity products make it from the nucleus to the relevant synapses. The key idea is that weak synaptic activity can mark or tag synapses in some way that enables them to capture proteins produced in response to a strong high-frequency stimulus. This idea can also be applied to the capture of proteins translated locally.

References

Abraham, W. C., Logan, B., Greenwood, J. M., and Dragunow, M. (2002). Induction and experience-dependent consolidation of stable long-term potentiation lasting months in the hippocampus. *Journal of Neuroscience, 22,* 9626–9634.

Adams, J. P. and Dudek, S. M. (2005). Late-phase long-term potentiation: getting to the nucleus. *Nature Reviews Neuroscience, 6,* 737–743.

Blitzer, R. D, Iyengar, R., and Landau, E. M. (2005). Postsynaptic signaling networks: cellular cogwheels underlying long-term plasticity. *Biological Psychiatry, 57,* 113–119.

Bourtchuladze, R., Frenguelli, B., Blendy, J., Cioffi, D., Schutz, G., and Silva, A. J. (1994). Deficient long-term memory in mice with a targeted mutation of the cAMP-responsive element-binding protein. *Cell, 79,* 59–68.

Bradshaw, K. D., Emptage, N. J., and Bliss, T. V. P. (2003). A role for dendritic protein synthesis in hippocampal late LTP. *European Journal of Neuroscience, 18,* 3150–3152.

Dash, P. K., Hochner, B., and Kandel, E. R. (1990). Injection of the cAMP-responsive element into the nucleus of *Aplysia* sensory neurons blocks long-term facilitation. *Nature, 345,* 718–721.

Dudek, S. M. and Fields, R. D. (2002). Somatic action potentials are sufficient for late-phase LTP-related cell signaling. *Proceedings of the National Academy of Science, 99,* 3962–3967

Frey, U. and Morris, R. G. (1997). Synaptic tagging and long-term potentiation, *Nature, 385*, 533–536.

Frey, U. and Morris, R. G. (1998). Synaptic tagging: implications for late maintenance of hippocampal long-term potentiation. *Trends in Neurosciences, 21*, 181–188.

Ju, W., Morishita, W., Tsui, J., Gaietta, G., Deerinck, T. J., Adams, S. R., Garner, C. C., Tsien, R. Y., Ellisman, M. H., and Malenka, R. C. (2004). Activity-dependent regulation of dendritic synthesis and trafficking of AMPA receptors. *Nature Neuroscience, 7*, 244–253.

Kandel, E. R. (2001). The molecular biology of memory storage: a dialogue between genes and synapses. *Science, 29*, 1030–1038.

Kang, H. and Schuman, E. M. (1996). A requirement for local protein synthesis in neurotrophin-induced hippocampal synaptic plasticity. *Science, 273*, 1402–1406.

Kelleher, R. J., Govindarajan, A., and Tonegawa, S. (2004a). Translational regulatory mechanisms in persistent forms of synaptic plasticity. *Neuron, 44*, 59–73.

Kelleher, R. J., Govindarajan, A., Jung, H. Y., Kang, H., and Tonegawa, S. (2004b). Translational control by MAPK signaling in long-term synaptic plasticity and memory. *Cell, 116*, 467–479.

Miyashiro, K., Dichter, M., and Eberwine, J. (1994). On the nature and differential distribution of mRNAs in hippocampal neurites: implications for neuronal functioning. *Proceedings of* the *National Academy of Science, 91*, 10800–10804.

Nguyen, P. V., Abel, T., and Kandel, E. R. (1994). Requirement of a critical period of transcription for induction of a late phase of LTP. *Science, 265*, 1104–1107.

Nguyen, P. V. and Woo, N. H. (2003). Regulation of hippocampal synaptic plasticity by cyclic AMP-dependent protein kinases. *Progress in Neurobiology, 71*, 401–437.

Ouyang, Y., Rosenstein, A., Kreiman, G., Schuman, E. M., and Kennedy, M. B. (1999). Tetanic stimulation leads to increased accumulation of Ca^{2+}/calmodulin-dependent protein kinase II via dendritic protein synthesis in hippocampal neurons. *Journal of Neuroscience, 19*, 7823–7833.

Silva, A. J., Giese, K. P., Fedorov, N. B., Frankland, P. W., and Kogan, J. H. (1998). Molecular, cellular, and neuroanatomical substrates of place learning. *Neurobiology of Learning and Memory, 70*, 44–61.

Steward, O. and Schuman, E. M. (2001). Protein synthesis at synaptic sites on dendrites. *Annual Review of Neuroscience, 24*, 299–325.

Steward, O. and Worley, P. (2002). Local synthesis of proteins at synaptic sites on dendrites: role in synaptic plasticity and memory consolidation. *Neurobiology of Learning and Memory, 78,* 508–527.

Sutton, M. A. and Schuman, E. M. (2005). Local translational control in dendrites and its role in long-term synaptic plasticity. *Journal of Neurobiology, 64,* 116–131.

Sutton, M. A. and Schuman, E. M. (2006). Dendritic protein synthesis, synaptic plasticity, and memory. *Cell, 127,* 49–58.

Tsokas, P., Grace, E. A., Chan, P. M., Sealfon, S. C., Iyengar, R., Landau, E. M., and Blitzer, R. D. (2005). Local protein synthesis mediates a rapid increase in dendritic elongation factor 1A after induction of late long-term potentiation. *Journal of Neuroscience, 25,* 5843–5843.

Tully, T. (1991). Physiology of mutations affecting learning and memory in *Drosophila*—the missing link between gene product and behavior. *Trends in Neurosciences, 5,* 163–164.

Yin, J. and Tully, T. (1996). CREB and the formation of long-term memory. *Current Opinion in Neurobiology, 2,* 264–268.

Calcium:
The Master
Plasticity Molecule

You are now familiar with some of the fundamental theories on how synapses are strengthened and LTP is induced. Of special importance in this process is the influx of extracellular calcium into the dendritic spine through the NMDA receptor. The NMDA receptor, however, is by no means the only avenue for this source of Ca^{2+}. Moreover, the Ca^{2+} entering through the NMDA receptor may not be sufficient to induce LTP (Sabatini, Maravall, and Svoboda, 2001; Morgan and Teyler, 1999; Raymond and Redman, 2006). It appears that this extracellular source of calcium needs to be amplified by additional Ca^{2+} in order to mount the other intracellular cascades needed to produce LTP. The purpose of this chapter is to provide a more complete understanding of the complexities associated with the role of Ca^{2+} in the generation of LTP. We begin with a discussion of the different sources of Ca^{2+} and how they are activated. New forms of LTP are introduced and experiments that reveal the relationship between these forms of LTP and the various sources of calcium are described. Finally, the potential role of calcium in local protein synthesis is discussed.

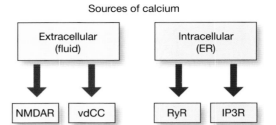

Sources of calcium

FIGURE 5.1
There are two general sources of calcium that influence LTP. One source is the Ca²⁺ in the extracellular fluid surrounding the neuron. This Ca²⁺ enters the dendritic spines through NMDA receptors and enters the soma through vdCCs. The other calcium source is intracellular. Ca²⁺ is stored in the ER. It can be released when it binds to the RyRs located on the ER in the spine or when IP3 binds to IP3Rs located on ER in the dendrite.

Extracellular and Intracellular Sources of Calcium

Two sources of calcium, one extracellular and one intracellular, can influence the induction and duration of LTP (Figure 5.1). The *extracellular* source is the fluid that surrounds the neuron. You have already learned that extracellular Ca²⁺ can enter the neuron through ionotropic NMDA receptors. This happens when glutamate binds to the NMDA receptors and the neuron depolarizes. You have also learned that extracellular Ca²⁺ can enter the neuron through the voltage-dependent calcium channels (vdCCs) located on the plasma membrane that defines the soma. They are called voltage dependent calcium channels because they open and close in response to depolarizing stimuli, such as action potentials. When they are open, they allow extracellular Ca²⁺ to enter the neuron, thus producing a transient increase in intracellular Ca²⁺ in the soma.

Intracellular Ca²⁺ resides in the neuron, stored in what is called the **endoplasmic reticulum (ER)**. Briefly mentioned in Chapter 4 as one of the elements of translation machinery (and shown in Figures 4.7 and 4.15), the ER is part of the endomembrane system, similar in composition to the plasma membrane. For some time, the ER has been recognized as extremely important to Ca²⁺ signaling (Berridge, 1998). The ER network extends continuously throughout the neuron (Droz, Rambourt, and Koenig, 1975; Terasaki, Slater, Fein, Schmidek, and Reese, 1994), even extending into the dendritic spines (Figure 5.2). Because it is continuous within the neuron and responds to signaling events in the cytosol, Berridge has characterized the ER network as *the neuron within the neuron*. He has proposed that these two membranes, the plasma membrane and the ER, work together to regulate many neuronal processes such as transmit-

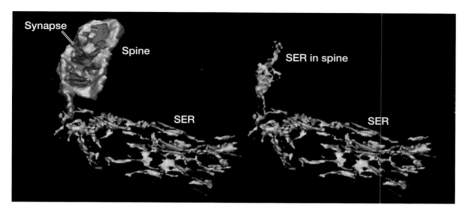

FIGURE 5.2

The three-dimensional reconstruction of the endoplasmic reticulum (purple) in a rat hippocampal CA1 dendritic segment. The membrane of the dendrite is not visible, but in the left side of the figure the membrane of the attached spine is present. Note that the ER in the dendrite is contiguous with the ER entering the thin neck of a large dendritic spine (gray). Berridge (1998) has called ER the "neuron within the neuron" because it is contiguous with the neuron and responds to signaling molecules. (From Synapse Web, Kristen M. Harris, http://synapse-weborg/)

ter release, synaptic plasticity, and gene regulation. The ER is important in the context of synaptic plasticity because (1) it is a *calcium sink* that can rapidly sequester or store free Ca^{2+}, and (2) it is a *calcium source* that can release Ca^{2+} in response to second messengers.

The release of Ca^{2+} from the intracellular ER source is regulated by two second messengers. Ironically, one of these is the extracellular Ca^{2+} that enters the dendritic spine through the NMDA receptor. The other second messenger, **inositol 1,4,5-triphosphate (IP3)**, becomes activated when glutamate binds to a subtype of metabotropic receptor, located in the plasma membrane near dendritic spines, called **metabotropic glutamate receptor 1 (mGluR1)**. (This receptor is discussed in greater detail later in this chapter.) In order for these second messengers to cause the ER to release Ca^{2+}, they must bind to receptors that are located on the ER.

There are two types of ER receptors that bind to second messengers. One type, called the **ryanodine receptor (RyR)**, is most abundant in the ER that extends into the dendritic spine. RyRs bind to the second messenger calcium. They are responsible for what is called **calcium-induced calcium release (CICR)**. CICR is thought to occur when a small amount of extracellular Ca^{2+} enters the spine through the NMDA receptor and binds to RyRs, causing a release of Ca^{2+} from the ER (Berridge, 1998). Note that this process—the bind-

(A) Compartments of the neuron

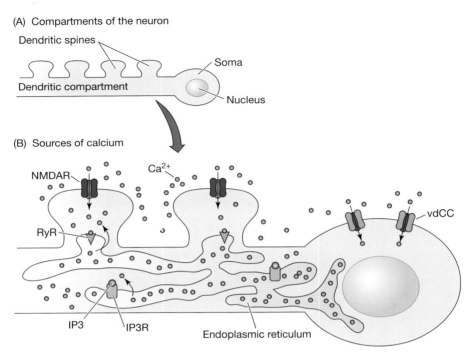

FIGURE 5.3
(A) The view of a neuron as consisting of three compartments: the soma, the dendritic compartment, and dendritic spines. (B) Calcium is present in the extracellular fluid as well as stored intracellularly in the ER. Ca^{2+} levels can increase in each of the three distinct compartments of the neuron. Extracellular Ca^{2+} can enter a dendritic spine through NMDA receptors and can enter the soma through vdCCs. Intracellular Ca^{2+} stored on the ER can be released into dendritic spines when Ca^{2+} binds to RyRs located in dendritic spines or can be released into the dendritic compartment when IP3 binds to IP3Rs located in the dendrite.

ing of calcium to RyRs—can be viewed as a way to increase the Ca^{2+} level in the spine. This triggers some of the post-translation modifications (discussed in Chapter 3) that are necessary to induce LTP. The second type of receptor located on the ER is called the **inositol 1,4,5-triphosphate receptor (IP3R)**. As you might expect, IP3Rs bind to the second messenger IP3. IP3Rs are located in the dendritic compartment near the spines. When IP3 binds to them, ER calcium is released in this area. As depicted in Figure 5.3, it is useful to conceptualize the neuron as being made up of three distinct compartments—the soma or cell body, the dendritic compartment, and dendritic spines—to best appreciate the major points of this discussion.

Multiple Forms of LTP and Calcium Sources

You are already familiar with the idea that different levels of high-frequency stimulation produce LTP of different durations, called S-LTP and L-LTP. To understand the multiple effects of Ca^{2+} it is necessary to describe a somewhat different stimulus protocol for inducing LTP and the forms of LTP it induces. This protocol is called **theta-burst stimulation (TBS)**. TBS is modeled after an increased rate of pyramidal neuronal firing that occurs when a rodent is exploring a novel environment. Pyramidal neurons fire bursts of action potentials at about 5 bursts per second.

One TBS stimulus protocol used to induce LTP consists of trains of 10 × 100-Hz bursts (5 pulses per burst) with a 200-millisecond interval between bursts. The experimenter can thus vary the number of TBS trains. When the TBS protocol is varied, at least three distinct types of LTP have been reported that can be differentiated by their decay times (Abraham and Otani, 1991; Racine, Milgram, and Hafner, 1983). For example, Raymond and Redman (2002) varied the number of TBS trains (1, 4, or 8) and found that they produced LTP functions with distinct decay rates: The duration of LTP increased as a function of the number of TBS trains (Figure 5.4). These different types

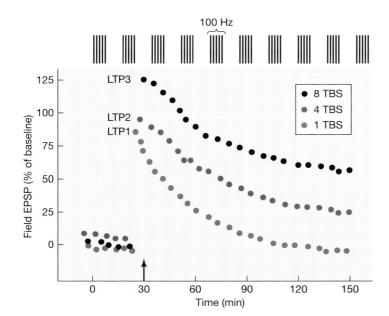

FIGURE 5.4
The top of the figure illustrates 1 train of theta-burst stimulation (TBS). Note that as the number of trains of TBS increases, the resulting LTP is larger and persists for a longer duration. The three durations of LTP are called LTP1, LTP2, and LTP3. (After Raymond and Redman, 2002.)

of LTP are called LTP1, LTP2, and LTP3, with each higher number indicating a longer-lasting LTP. Different sources of Ca^{2+} regulate these different types of LTP.

Raymond and Redman (2002, 2006) have described a set of experiments that reveal a remarkable relationship between calcium sources and the induction of LTP. Their experiments were motivated by the hypothesis that different types of LTP depend on Ca^{2+} in different compartments of the neuron. To understand these experiments you have to remember that (1) ER calcium stores can be released when a second messenger binds to either RyRs or IP3Rs, and (2) when the neuron depolarizes, extracellular Ca^{2+} enters the neuron through vdCCs. To test their hypothesis, these researchers (2002) used pharmacological agents that selectively antagonized three of the regulators of these different potential Ca^{2+} sources. They examined the effect of each antagonist on the three types of LTP associated with different levels of TBS. LTP was measured in the CA1 pyramidal cell region.

To inhibit the CICR regulated by RyRs, they applied an antagonist called ryanodine. It reduced short-lasting LTP1 normally produced by a 1-train TBS but had no effect on either LTP2 or LTP3. To antagonize the IP3Rs, they applied an antagonist called xestospongin C. It reduced LTP2 without affecting either LTP1 or LTP3. Finally, they found that nifedipine, an agent that selectively antagonized vdCCs, reduced LTP3 without influencing LTP1 or LTP2. The results of these experiments (illustrated in Figure 5.5) revealed:

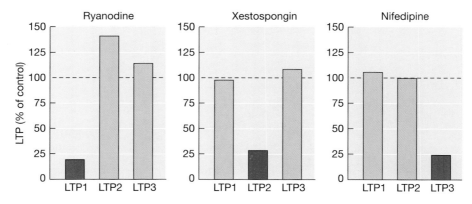

FIGURE 5.5
Selective antagonists reveal that direct sources are critical for three types of LTP. Ryanodine, which blocks the RyRs, selectively reduces LTP1. Xestospongin, which selectively blocks IP3Rs, reduces LTP2. Nifedipine, which blocks vdCCs, reduces LTP3. The red bars highlight which type of LTP was affected by the antagonists. (After Raymond and Redman, 2002.)

- Three sources of calcium contribute to LTP. ER provides two sources: one source is released when RyRs are occupied and the other is released when the IP3Rs are occupied. The vdCCs provide a third source.

- The threshold for recruiting these sources is different. The weakest protocol (1-train TBS) activated the RyR-dependent source; the moderate protocol (2-train TBS) activated the IP3R-dependent source; and the strongest protocol (4-train TBS) activated the vdCC source.

Clarke Raymond

- The importance of each Ca^{2+} source in LTP induction diminished as the number of TBS trains increased.

Recall that RyRs are prominent in dendritic spines of CA1 pyramidal cells but are virtually absent in the dendritic compartment (Raymond and Redman, 2002; Sharp et al., 1993). In contrast, IP3Rs are predominantly located in the dendritic compartment and vdCCs are predominantly located on the soma (Westenbroek, Ahlijanian, and Catterall, 1990). The spatial location of these receptors motivated Raymond and Redman (2006) to measure precisely where the calcium was being released in response to the different levels of TBS.

Steve Redman

In these experiments they again used the three levels of TBS to produce LTP of different durations. They also used additional methods that allowed them to *visualize Ca^{2+} activation* in the different compartments of the neuron (Figure 5.6). In addition to using selective antagonists to block RyRs, IP3Rs, and vdCCs, they also used APV to antagonize NMDA receptors. These experiments revealed that:

- The weak 1-train TBS triggered release of Ca^{2+} *in the dendritic spine* but did not induce the release of Ca^{2+} in the dendritic compartment or soma. This effect was prevented by the RyR antagonist and the NMDA-receptor antagonist but not by the IP3R or vdCC antagonists.

- The moderate 4-train TBS triggered the release of Ca^{2+} *in the dendritic compartment*. This effect was blocked by the IP3R and NMDA-receptor antagonists but not by either the RyR antagonist or the vdCC antagonist.

- The strong 8-train TBS triggered Ca^{2+} activity *in the soma* that was blocked by the vdCC antagonist but unaffected by either the RyR or IP3R antagonists. It was also relatively unaffected by the NMDA-receptor antagonist.

(A)

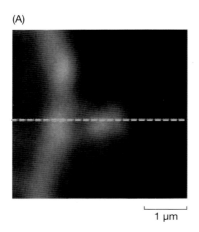

(B)

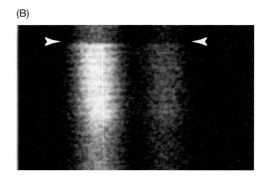

1 μm

(C)

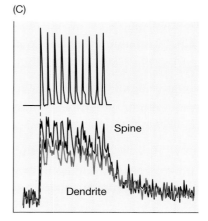

FIGURE 5.6
(A) A section of the dendrite of a CA1 pyramidal neuron filled with a calcium-sensitive indicator showing the positioning of line scanning through a spine. (B) Example of changes in Ca^{2+} concentration in the indicator during a 1-train TBS. Note the scan begins at the arrowheads and time is vertical; thus the intensity of the scan is initially bright but dims after the stimulus ceases. (C) The change in membrane voltage evoked by the TBS is aligned with the mean relative change in Ca^{2+} in the spine and the dendrite. (Courtesy of Clarke Raymond; after Raymond and Redman, 2006.)

ER Calcium Release and Local Protein Synthesis

You learned in Chapter 4 that glutamate released by high-frequency stimulation can initiate an intracellular cascade that leads to local protein synthesis. Because IP3Rs are located on the ER in the dendritic compartment near spines, it is possible that the calcium released by these receptors is responsible for initiating local protein synthesis. Although direct evidence is lacking, there is indirect support for this general idea.

As noted earlier, the second messenger IP3 is activated when glutamate binds to mGluR1s. Ionotropic receptors such as NMDA and AMPA respond quickly and are responsible for rapid synaptic transmission. Metabotropic receptors such as mGluR1s, however, respond more slowly and have different operating characteristics. They do not have channels or pores. When gluta-mate binds to an mGluR1, the receptor does not open a channel. Instead, the conformational change produced by glutamate binding activates what are called guanine nucleotide binding proteins (**G proteins**) in the plasma mem-brane. G proteins can then act either by gating some other ion channel or by stimulating or inhibiting other enzymes that are involved in the synthesis or breakdown of second-messenger molecules (Figure 5.7). In the case under dis-cussion, the activation of mGluR1s initiates the processes that stimulate the synthesis of IP3.

Raymond, Thompson, Tate, and Abraham (2000) provided evidence that den-dritic protein synthesis may depend on glutamate binding to mGluR1s and caus-ing the IP3Rs to release Ca^{2+} (Figure 5.8). They did this by using a strategy similar to that used by Frey and Morris (1998) to study the synaptic tagging hy-pothesis discussed in Chapter 4. They stimulated Schaffer collateral fibers with a weak inducing stimulus that produced only a short-lasting LTP in the CA1 neurons (see Figure 5.8A). In their protocol, instead of presenting a strong stim-ulus to generate plasticity products that could be captured by the weakly stim-ulated synapses, they applied an mGluR1 agonist called (**R,S)-3,5-dihydroxy-phenylglycine** (**DHPG**) to the slice before the weak stimulus was presented. This drug acts like glutamate when it binds to mGluR1s. Thus, theoretically, when DPHG binds to mGluR1s, the second messenger IP3 would be produced and it would bind to the IP3Rs. Consequently, Ca^{2+} stored in the ER would be released in the dendritic compartment, which could initiate local protein syn-thesis. The synapses tagged by the weak stimulus could then capture these pro-teins and a long-lasting LTP would then be produced at the weakly stimulated synapses. As also shown in Figure 5.8A, treating the slice with DHPG before the weak stimulus was presented indeed enhanced the duration of LTP that would normally be produced by the weak stimulus.

The next step in this strategy was to determine whether the new proteins were synthesized locally from mRNAs already present in dendrites or from new mRNAs that were transcribed as a result of a genomic signaling cascade initiated by DHPG. To address this question, in another experiment, Raymond and his colleagues (2000) examined three conditions. In each condition DPHG was applied before the weak stimulus was presented. However, in two of the conditions either emetine, a protein synthesis inhibitor, or actinomycin D, a transcription inhibitor, was also applied to the slice prior to the weak stim-ulus. They reasoned that if the proteins produced by DPHG were translated from mRNAs resulting from a genomic signaling cascade, then *both* emetine and actinomycin D should prevent DPHG from enhancing the duration of LTP produced by the weak stimulus. However, if the proteins were synthesized from mRNAs that were already locally available, then only emetine should block the enhancing effect of DHPG.

(A)

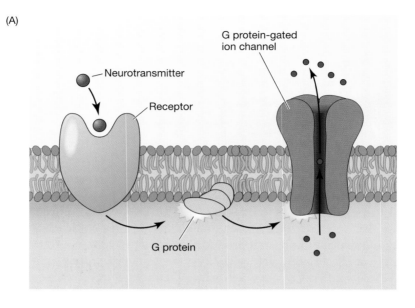

(B)

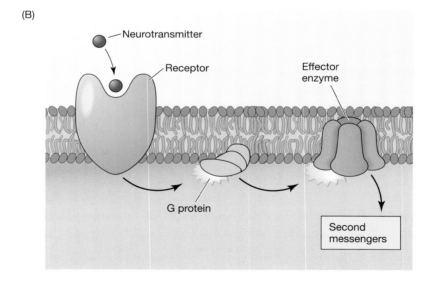

FIGURE 5.7
Metabotropic receptors activate G proteins in the plasma membrane, which may either alter the opening of a G-protein-gated ion channel (A) or stimulate an effector enzyme that either synthesizes or breaks down a second messenger (B).

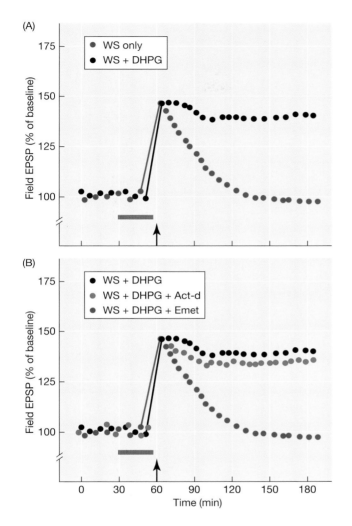

FIGURE 5.8
(A) A weak inducing stimulus (WS) normally produces a very short-lasting LTP. However, applying the mGluR1 agonist DHPG prior to delivering the WS results in a much-longer-lasting LTP. (B) The effect of DHPG is blocked when the protein synthesis inhibitor emetine (Emet) is applied to the slice but is not blocked by the transcription inhibitor actinomycin D (Act-d).

As illustrated in Figure 5.8B, only emetine blocked the effect of DHPG. Raymond and his colleagues concluded that DHPG initiated a signaling cascade in the dendrites that resulted in local protein synthesis. Since this cascade involved IP3, one can infer that Ca^{2+} released from ER in the dendritic compartment was critically involved in local protein synthesis. Given that logically the strategy used by Raymond and his colleagues is the same as the strategy used in synaptic tagging experiments, these results also support the hypothesis of Blitzer, Iyengar, and Landau (2005) that tagged synapses capture locally translated proteins.

Implications of These Experiments

The results of the Raymond et al. (2000) and Raymond and Redman (2002, 2006) experiments have a number of important implications in understanding how enduring changes in synaptic strength might occur. To appreciate them it is useful to remember that the duration of LTP varies. Initially we learned that different intensities of high-frequency stimulation produce either S-LTP or L-LTP. We now know that different TBS trains can reveal at least three forms of LTP with different durations.

The most important implication of these experiments is that the duration of LTP is orchestrated by the activity of Ca^{2+} in different compartments of the neuron.

- LTP1 depends primarily on Ca^{2+} activation in the dendritic spine. One might speculate that the combination of NMDA-dependent Ca^{2+} and the Ca^{2+} released from the ER in the spine is sufficient to initiate the post-translation processes that initially establish LTP.

- LTP-2 depends primarily on the release of Ca^{2+} in the dendritic compartment. Given what we have learned about the dependency of long-lasting LTP on local translation, one might speculate that this increase of Ca^{2+} in the dendrite that occurs when IP3Rs are occupied, is a critical event for the initiation of local protein synthesis. This hypothesis may be correct. The mGluR1s control the activation of the second messenger IP3, which binds to the IP3Rs. Activating these mGluR1s with DHPG results in local protein synthesis (Raymond et al., 2000).

- LTP3 depends primarily on Ca^{2+} entering via vdCCs into the soma. Note that this finding is consistent with the action-potential, soma-to-nucleus model of genomic signaling (Adams and Dudek, 2005). Recall that in support of the soma-to-nucleus model, Adams and Dudek showed that generating action potentials by stimulating the axons belonging to CA1 neurons was sufficient to convert an S-LTP normally produced by a weak inducing stimulus into L-LTP.

These experiments also provide new insights into the contribution NMDA receptors make in inducing LTP. The most novel implication is that *the influx into the dendrite of Ca^{2+} dependent on the NMDA receptor is a critical but not a sufficient condition for the induction of LTP*. In the 2006 Raymond and Redman experiments, antagonizing this receptor greatly impaired the induction of LTP1 and LTP2. LTP1 also depended on the release of RyR-dependent Ca^{2+} from ER stores in the spine, and LTP2 depended on IP3R-dependent calcium released from the ER in the dendritic compartment. Thus, for NMDA-associated Ca^{2+} to induce LTP it must be amplified with the addition of calcium released from the ER.

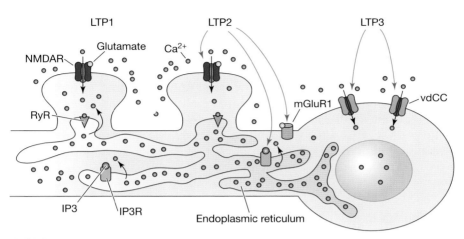

FIGURE 5.9
Illustration of how different sources of Ca^{2+} contribute to different forms of LTP.
LTP1 is induced when glutamate produced by a weak stimulus (1-train TBS) binds
to the NMDA receptor (NMDAR). This results in a modest influx of Ca^{2+} into the
spine. Acting as a second messenger, Ca^{2+} binds to the RyRs and causes the ER
to release additional Ca^{2+} into the spine. LTP2 is induced when glutamate resulting
from stronger stimulation (4-train TBS) binds both to NMDA receptors and to
mGluR1s and results in local protein synthesis. LTP3 is produced when the
strongest stimulation (8-train TBS) repeatedly opens the vdCCs, and the level of
Ca^{2+} in the soma is increased to the point where it can translocate to the nucleus
to initiate transcription of genes necessary for the expression of LTP3.

Summary

There are two general sources of calcium that can influence LTP. Extracellular calcium enters the spine through NMDA receptors and the soma through
vdCCs. Intracellular calcium stored in the ER is released into the dendritic
spine when Ca^{2+} binds to RyRs and is released into the dendritic compartment
when IP3 binds to IP3Rs.

Varying the number of TBS trains (1, 4, or 8) can produce three different
types of LTP—LTP1, LTP2, and LTP3—with each ascending number indicating a longer-lasting LTP. Experiments show that the duration of LTP depends
on the level of calcium in the different compartments of the neuron:

- LTP1 requires an increase in calcium in the spine compartment, mediated by the NMDA receptors and RyRs.
- LTP2 requires an increase in calcium in the dendritic compartment, mediated by NMDA receptors and IP3Rs.

- LTP3 requires an increase in calcium in the soma, which enters through vdCCS.

Calcium provided through the opening of the NMDA channel is necessary but may not be sufficient to induce LTP. The effect of this extracellular calcium source needs to be amplified by Ca^{2+} released from the internal source, the ER. A summary of the many ways Ca^{2+} regulates the induction and persistence of LTP is presented in Figure 5.9.

Regardless of its source, it is difficult to deny that calcium is the most essential second messenger in the production of changes in synaptic plasticity. It appears to be the master plasticity molecule.

References

Abraham, W. C. and Otani, S. (1991). Macromolecules and the maintenance of long-term potentiation. In F. Morrell (Ed.), *Kindling and synaptic plasticity. The legacy of Graham Goddard* (pp. 92–109). Boston, MA: Birkhauser.

Adams, J. P. and Dudek, S. M. (2005). Late-phase long-term potentiation: getting to the nucleus. *Nature Reviews Neuroscience, 6,* 737–743.

Berridge, M. J. (1998). Neuronal calcium signaling. *Neuron, 21,* 13–26.

Blitzer, R. D., Iyengar, R., and Landau, E. M. (2005). Postsynaptic signaling networks: cellular cogwheels underlying long-term plasticity. *Biological Psychiatry, 57,* 113–119.

Droz, B., Rambourt, A., and Koenig, H. L. (1975). The smooth endoplasmic reticulum: structure and role in the renewal of axonal membrane and synaptic vesicles by fast axonal transport. *Brain Research, 93,* 1–13.

Frey, U. and Morris, R. G. (1998). Synaptic tagging: implications for late maintenance of hippocampal long-term potentiation. *Trends in Neurosciences, 21,* 181–188.

Morgan, S. L. and Teyler, T. J. (1999). VDCCs and NMDARs underlie two forms of LTP in CA1 hippocampus in vivo. *Journal of Neurophysiology, 82,* 736–740.

Racine, R. J., Milgram, N. W., and Hafner, S. (1983). Long-term potentiation phenomena in the rat limbic forebrain. *Brain Research, 260,* 217–231.

Raymond, C. R. and Redman, S. J. (2002). Different calcium sources are narrowly tuned to the induction of different forms of LTP. *Journal of Neurophysiology, 88,* 249–255.

Raymond, C. R. and Redman, S. J. (2006). Spatial segregation of neuronal calcium signals encodes different forms of LTP in rat hippocampus. *Journal of Physiology, 570,* 97–111.

Raymond, C. R., Thompson, V. L., Tate, W. P., and Abraham, W. C. (2000). Metabotropic glutamate receptors trigger homosynaptic protein synthesis to prolong long-term potentiation. *Journal of Neuroscience, 20,* 969–976.

Sabatini, B. L., Maravall, M., and Svoboda, K. (2001). Ca^{2+} signaling in dendritic spines. *Current Opinion Neurobiology, 11,* 349–356.

Sharp, A. H., McPherson, P. S., Dawson, T. M., Aoki, C., Campbell, K. P., and Snyder, S. H. (1993). Differential immunohistochemical localization of inositol 1,4,5-trisphosphate- and ryanodine-sensitive Ca^{2+} release channels in rat brain. *Journal of Neuroscience, 13,* 3051–3063.

Terasaki, M., Slater, N. T., Fein, A., Schmidek, A., and Reese, T. S. (1994). Continuous network of endoplasmic reticulum in cerebellar Purkinje neurons. *Proceedings of the National Academy of Science, 91,* 7510–7514.

Westenbroek, R. E., Ahlijanian, M. K., and Catterall, W. A. (1990). Clustering of L-type Ca^{2+} channels at the base of major dendrites in hippocampal pyramidal neurons. *Nature, 347,* 281–284.

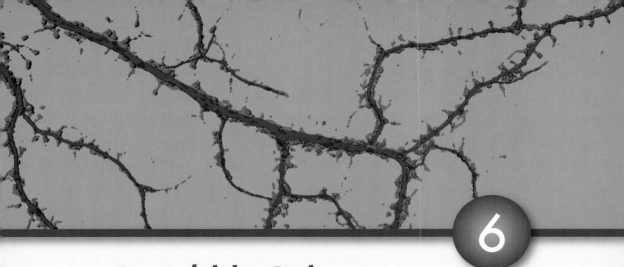

Dendritic Spines: The Dynamic Relationship between Structure and Function

An LTP-inducing stimulus initiates a variety of processes that can bring about changes in synaptic strength. Previous chapters discussed one important part of the general story of how this happens, that is, the contribution AMPA receptors make to changes in synaptic potentials. You learned that an LTP-inducing stimulus causes additional AMPA receptors to traffic into dendritic spines. Consequently, the postsynaptic neuron is more likely to depolarize in response to the same amount of glutamate released by the presynaptic neuron.

There is, however, a second part to the story. The LTP-inducing stimulus initiates another set of parallel processes that *significantly alter the structure (morphology) of dendritic spines and their connection with their presynaptic partners*. These changes in the spine are believed to play a critical role in the spine's stability and consequently its ability to hold information (Figure 6.1).

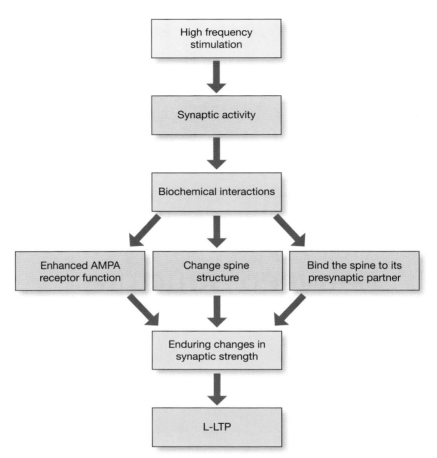

FIGURE 6.1

High-frequency stimulation initiates a set of parallel biochemical interactions that enhance AMPA receptor function, change the structure of the spine, and strengthen the bond between the dendritic spine and its presynaptic partner.

Thus, in order to more fully appreciate how enduring changes in synaptic strength are produced, it is important to understand how an LTP-inducing stimulus alters the structure and functional properties of dendritic spines. The goal of this chapter is to provide you with some understanding of the processes that bring about these changes and their functional consequences for understanding LTP and memory. To accomplish this goal, this chapter addresses:

- The role of actin (a cytoskeleton protein) in determining the structure of spines and how that structure contributes to their function.

- The essential contribution of actin modification to LTP.
- The binding of the presynaptic and postsynaptic elements of the synapse by the neural cell adhesion molecule cadherin.
- The relationship between synaptic plasticity, spine stability, and memory.

Actin Regulates Spine Shape and Size

There are thousands of minute spiny-like protrusions on the dendrites of pyramidal cells and each is thought to represent excitatory synapses. As illustrated in Figure 6.2, dendritic spines come in many sizes and shapes (Kasai, Matsuzaki, Noguchi, Yasumatsu, and Nakahara, 2003; Matus, 2000; Dillon and Goda, 2005). The basic morphology of a spine consists of an expanded head connected to the dendritic compartment by a narrow neck; it looks like a mushroom. But there are also "stubby" spines that lack necks as well as spines that appear to be headless. Headless spines are especially abundant during brain development (Matus, 2000; Dillon and Goda, 2005). Spines not only come in a variety of sizes and shapes, they are inherently dynamic. They are said to be motile, that is, the size, shape, and function of spines can change over

(A)

(B)

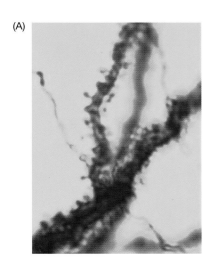
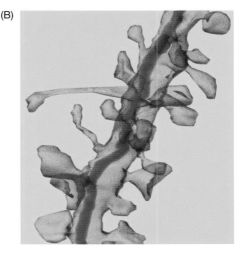

FIGURE 6.2
(A) Dendrites with spines. (B) A high-resolution reconstruction of a small region of the dendrite of a hippocampal pyramidal neuron with spines of different shapes and sizes. (From Synapse Web, Kristen M. Harris, http://synapse-web.org/)

Andrew Matus

time. Specifically, they can expand and contract, extending from and retracting into the dendritic compartment.

With regard to size, Kasai et al. (2003) organized spines into two categories, small and large. It is possible to observe specific dendrites and their spines in the cortex of living adult rodents in imaging studies. Such studies have revealed that small spines change their form rapidly and either disappear or grow into large spines (Figure 6.3). In contrast, large spines are very stable and survive for up to eight months (Grutzendler, Kasthuri, and Gan, 2002; Trachtenberg et al., 2002; Holtmaat et al., 2005). This observation implies that the size of a spine determines its stability, that is, a large spine has a better chance of persisting than a small spine. The significance of this property is elaborated in the discussion below on regulating spine stability.

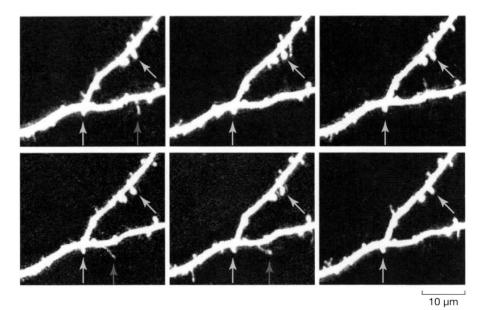

10 μm

FIGURE 6.3
Images of a dendritic branch in a living mouse, captured over six consecutive days. Note the persistent spines are large (yellow arrows) and the transient spines are small (blue arrows). (Image provided by Karel Svoboda; after Holtmaat et al., 2005.)

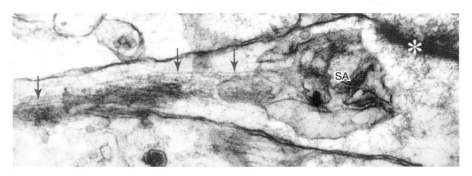

FIGURE 6.4
Red arrows point to microfilaments of actin running in parallel in the dendritic spine neck. SA = spine apparatus. (From Synapse Web, Kristen M. Harris, http://synapse-web.org/)

In the nervous system, the cytoskeleton provides the cell's cytoplasm with structure and shape. It plays a major role in the formation of axons and dendrites and helps in the wiring of neural circuitry by driving both the guidance of neuronal processes and synaptic formation (Matus, 2005; Dillon and Goda, 2005). The cytoskeleton network is composed of three types of **cytoskeleton protein filaments**: actin, microtubules, and intermediate filaments. The shape and size of a dendritic spine depend particularly on the cytoskeleton filament **actin** (Figure 6.4).

The Dynamics of Actin

Actin exists in two states: globular actin (**G-actin**) and filament actin (**F-actin**). G-actin are individual subunits of actin that serve as monomer building blocks and assemble into F-actin, a two-stranded helical polymer. A polymer is a large organic molecule formed by combining many smaller molecules (monomers); this process is called **polymerization**. F-actin is in a continuous state of turnover, with new subunits added to the barbed end of the strand and older units being removed from the pointed end. You may think of the addition and subtraction of the subunits as similar to the action of a treadmill (Figure 6.5). Because F-actin can be rapidly assembled and disassembled, the balance between F- and G-actin is often in a state of flux (Dillon and Goda, 2005).

Given that the morphology of the spine depends on the state of actin, spines can rapidly change their shape as the balance between F- and G-actin shifts. Time-lapsed photography in fact has revealed rapid motility of dendritic spines on cultured hippocampal neurons (Halpain, 2000). This action has been referred to as "dancing" or "morphing."

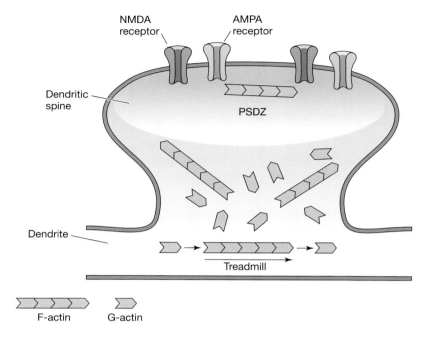

F-actin   G-actin

FIGURE 6.5
Actin exists in two states. Single arrow tips represent the monomer state, G-actin. Strings of arrows represent filament actin (F-actin), its polymer state. Actin is in a continuous state of turnover similar to a treadmill. Old units are removed from the pointed end and new units are added to the barbed end.

The instability of actin and its effect on spine motility has important implications for memory. If the dendritic spine is a basic unit of information storage, then the spine's ability to spontaneously extend and retract has to be constrained because if a spine retracts when F-actin disassembles, then it follows that the information that the spine contains can be lost. Fortunately, as illustrated in Figure 6.6, the stability of F-actin—and thus actin-based spine motility—can be regulated by synaptic activity produced by high-frequency stimulation that induces LTP (Carlisle and Kennedy, 2005; Colicos, Collins, Sailor, and Goda, 2001).

Regulation of Spine Stability

The regulation of actin-based spine motility begins with the release of glutamate from the presynaptic neuron. Studies with cultured neurons indicate that when glutamate binds to AMPA receptors, it produces a rapid blockage of

(A)   (B)   (C)

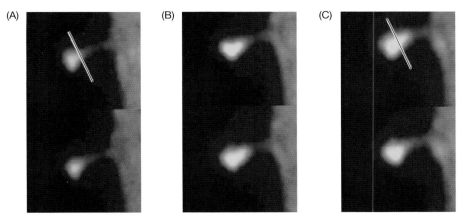

FIGURE 6.6
Synaptic activity can regulate F-actin. (A) shows fluorescent F-actin in a spine, captured 1 minute apart, prior to the application of a single stimulation. (B) and (C) show F-actin in the same spine captured 1, 2, 4, and 6 minutes after the stimulation. The diagonal line allows a comparison of the position of actin prior to stimulation and 4 minutes after stimulation. (After Colicos et al., 2001.)

spine motility. Viewed through time-lapsed recordings, spines appear to freeze immediately when this binding occurs (Oetner and Matus, 2005). This effect is transient because motility resumes when glutamate is no longer present. The influx of Ca^{2+} through the NMDA receptor, however, blocks spine motility in cultured neurons for hours (Ackermann and Matus, 2003). Glutamate activation of NMDA receptors and calmodulin produces another effect: It increases *spine volume*, that is, the spine appears to swell.

Recall that large spines are very stable and survive much longer than small spines, implying that the structure of the spine determines its stability. This is important for several possible reasons (Fukazawa et al., 2003).

- Morphological changes in the spine itself that accompany actin-remodeling, such as spine extension towards presynaptic terminals and the formation of such terminals on spines, could directly contribute to supporting increased synaptic strength.
- Spine morphology is strongly related to the distribution of AMPA receptors within the spine.
- Actin filaments within the spine may influence membrane trafficking. In Chapter 3, you learned that AMPA receptors traffic in and out of the membrane. One way to enhance synaptic strength is by restricting AMPA receptor movement out of the membrane. F-actin may be critical to this process because disrupting F-actin is accompanied by internalization of AMPA receptors (Zhou, Xiao, and Nicoll, 2001).

- Newly synthesized proteins are critical to the creation of a persistent increase in synaptic strength. Some of these proteins must be delivered to the postsynaptic density zone if they are to support increased synaptic strength. F-actin in this region might support the trafficking of these proteins to the correct location.

- F-actin in the postsynaptic density zone might also act as a scaffold on which other key proteins such as AMPA receptors and CaMKII are anchored.

An important implication of the above discussion is that a large, well-formed spine head will contain more AMPA receptors and be more sensitive to glutamate than a less-well-formed one. Matsuzaki et al. (2003) have been able to test this hypothesis in dendrites of CA1 pyramidal neurons in slices taken from the rat hippocampus. They found that the size of the spine head strongly correlated with the spine's response to glutamate; spines with large heads displayed a much more robust response than spines with small heads.

In contrast to the increase in AMPA receptors associated with spine size, the number of NMDA receptors in a spine head is only weakly correlated with spine head size. Moreover, as you learned in Chapter 3, the number of NMDA receptors in a spine head does not appear to be influenced as a consequence of the induction of LTP.

Thus, the emerging picture is that enduring forms of LTP may depend on increased numbers of AMPA receptors in the postsynaptic density zone of the spine accompanied by the morphological changes that are supported by stabilizing F-actin. NMDA occupancy is not significantly changed.

Actin Modification Is Critical to LTP Induction

Not only is F-actin modified by glutamate activation of NMDA receptors, its modification is critical to the induction of LTP (Kim and Lisman, 1999; Krucker, Siggins, and Halpain, 2000). Kim and Lisman were the first to report a functional role for F-actin in LTP. They applied two actin polymerizer inhibitors, latrunculin B and cytochalasin D (drugs that interfere with the assemblage of G-actin into F-Actin), to a slice preparation and found that each inhibitor prevented the induction of LTP and also slowly reduced the contribution of AMPA receptors to synaptic transmission.

The induction of LTP in an awake, normally functioning rat is called *in vivo* LTP. When Fukazawa et al. (2003) induced in vivo LTP in the dentate gyrus by stimulating the perforant pathway, F-actin levels were increased in dendritic spines of the synaptic layers where LTP was induced. Moreover, this increase lasted for at least five weeks and the level of F-actin correlated with the duration of LTP. LTP-induced F-actin not only persisted, it was critical to the long-term maintenance of in vivo LTP. When latrunculin A was infused into the hippocampus, it prevented the development of persistent L-LTP, but had no effect on the shorter-lasting S-LTP.

Interfering with the processes that stimulate actin polymerization reduces LTP. There are also molecules that directly contribute to the disassemblage of F-actin. One member of this class is called the **actin-depolymerization factor/cofilin** family of proteins (abbreviated as **ADF/cofilin**). As its name implies, in its normal state ADF/cofilin actively depolymerizes F-actin. However, ADF/cofilin has a single phosphorylated site called **Ser-3** that regulates its ability to depolymerize F-actin. When this site is phosphorylated ADF/cofilin's depolymerizing properties are turned off and F-actin becomes less likely to disassemble (Fukazawa et al., 2003). A kinase called **LIMK1** is thought to phosphorylate this site.

These ideas suggest that one way in which an LTP-inducing stimulation might stabilize F-actin is by phosphorylating ADF/cofilin. Consistent with this hypothesis, when LTP is induced, the level of phosphorylated ADF/cofilin is increased in the region where LTP is measured. Moreover, one might expect that if the Ser-3 phosphorylation site is pharmacologically blocked, then this would prevent the induction of LTP by high-frequency stimulation because the depolymerizing properties of ADF/cofilin would remain intact. Fukazawa et al. (2003) tested this hypothesis and reported that a competitive antagonist designed to block the Ser-3 site impaired the ability of the inducing stimulus to produce L-LTP (Figure 6.7).

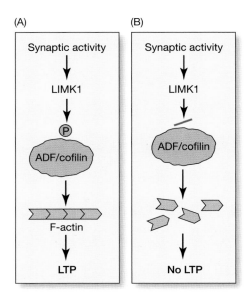

FIGURE 6.7

(A) If synaptic activity results in LIMK1 phosphorylating ADF/cofilin, the depolymerization of F-actin by ADF/cofilin will be inhibited and LTP can occur. (B) If a molecule, represented as the slanted line, blocks the ability of LIMK1 to phosphorylate ADF/cofilin, depolymerization will occur and prevent LTP.

Cadherins Bind Modified Spines to Presynaptic Neurons

As you know, LTP reflects an increase in the strength of synaptic connections so that the same amount of glutamate released from the presynaptic neuron results in increased depolarization of the postsynaptic neuron. Modifying the size and shape of spines is important for providing the space for additional AMPA receptors and thereby increasing the spine's response to glutamate. However, as you also know, the spine is only one component of the synapse. Unless modified spines are connected to their presynaptic partners, they will not be positioned to maximally receive the glutamate released in response to the high-frequency stimulus. The binding of modified spines to their presynaptic partners is another way in which synaptic strength is increased and maintained. This binding is the function of a class of **adhesion molecules** called neural cadherins.

Adhesion molecules are proteins located on the cell's surface that bind cells together. For example, the cells that make up your skin are held together by adhesion molecules. **Neural cadherins** are calcium-dependent cell adhesion molecules; they are strands of proteins held together by Ca^{2+} ions. Cadherins are anchored in the plasma membrane of both the presynaptic terminals and postsynaptic spines. They can exist as either monomers or *cis*-stranded dimers (Figure 6.8). The monomer form is weakly adhesive but the *cis*-stranded or bonded dimers are strongly adhesive. Thus, when a dimer from the presynaptic domain contacts an identical dimer from the postsynaptic domain they form what is sometimes called an "adhesive zipper" that couples the two domains into a stable relationship (Huntley, Gil, and Bozdagi, 2002).

Neural cadherins also respond dynamically to high-frequency stimulation that can strengthen synapses. Although the details are not completely understood, based on results with cultured hippocampus neurons (Tanaka et al., 2000), it is believed that a strong depolarizing stimulus causes cadherin monomers to dimerize. Moreover, this process also appears to depend on Ca^{2+} entering the spine through NMDA receptors because it is blocked if an NMDA receptor antagonist is present. An enhanced adhesive state is also associated with the induction of L-LTP in the hippocampus (Bozdagi, Shan, Tanaka, Benson, and Huntley, 2000).

More tightly coupling the presynaptic and modified postsynaptic components of the synapse could have several effects. This process could ensure that glutamate released by the presynaptic neuron would be optimally positioned to be received by receptors on dendritic spines. It could also help to ensure that AMPA receptors on the spine are maximally positioned to bind to released glutamate. Thus, this alignment would help to increase the likelihood that the postsynaptic neuron would depolarize in response to a fixed amount of glu-

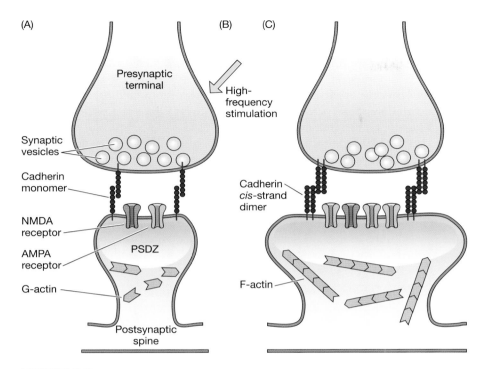

(A)

Presynaptic
terminal

High-
frequency
stimulation

(B)   (C)

Synaptic
vesicles

Cadherin
monomer

NMDA
receptor

AMPA
receptor

PSDZ

G-actin

Postsynaptic
spine

Cadherin
cis-strand
dimer

F-actin

FIGURE 6.8
Cadherins are reorganized by an LTP-inducing stimulus. (A) Illustration of an unpo-
tentiated synapse with the presynaptic terminal and postsynaptic spine weakly
bonded by cadherin monomers. (B) A high-frequency stimulation is delivered to this
synapse to induce LTP. (C) The high-frequency stimulus promotes cadherin dimer-
ization so the now-enlarged spine containing additional AMPA receptors is tightly
coupled to the presynaptic terminal and well positioned to receive glutamate
released from the presynaptic terminal. (After Huntley et al., 2002.)

tamate released by the presynaptic neuron. This coupling could also contribute
to increasing the durability of the synapse.

Synaptic Plasticity, Spine Stability, and Memory

Memory is a psychological concept. Information extracted from our experience can persist and be retrieved. We all agree that memories are stored in the
brain. Moreover, as you know, since Ramón y Cajal put forth the synaptic plasticity hypothesis (see Chapter 1), many neurobiologists believe that the synapse

is the fundamental information storage element in the brain. Information storage devices should have two important properties: they should be modifiable and the resulting modification should be stable. The synapse meets the modifiability criterion because experience can alter its strength. It is plastic. This property, however, is essentially just the opposite of the stability requirement. If a modified synapse is to maintain the information it represents, then it should be resistant to change. It should be stable.

It is certainly the case that information about our past experiences can be lost. We call this phenomenon forgetting and this may in part be due to the weakening of the synaptic connections that represent the information. However, we also have to be impressed with the durability of our memories. Thus, once changed, synapses that support memories must become less plastic and more difficult to modify. In this sense, synaptic plasticity is the enemy of memory stability. In this last section, ideas are presented about how changes in the morphology of the spine that accompany LTP make them resistant to change and thus able to store information for long periods of time.

Spine Morphology and Synaptic Stability

As you have so far learned in this chapter, the shape of dendritic spines can change dramatically in response to the high-frequency stimulus that produces LTP. A general feature of potentiated spines is that they have broader heads and shorter necks. Moreover, large spines are more stable than small ones. Some researchers have proposed that this altered structure changes the spine's functional properties so that it becomes resistant to further modification (Kasai et al., 2003; Matsuzaki et al., 2001; Hayashi and Majewska, 2005). Thus, stability might be preserved because the structure of the spine is also modified by synaptic activity. How might this happen?

You know that the amount of Ca^{2+} that accumulates in the spine is critical to the initiation of biochemical processes that change synaptic strength; once the morphology of the spine is changed, the regulation of Ca^{2+} is altered. Specifically, the new spine morphology—broad head and short neck—allows the spine to more rapidly diffuse or eliminate the increased Ca^{2+} resulting from NMDA receptor activation (Noguchi, Matsuzaki, Ellis-Davies, and Kasai, 2005; Hayashi and Majewska, 2005). Thus, even though these spines would contribute to exciting the neuron (because they allow more Na^+ to enter it), they would be resistant to modification by Ca^{2+}-induced plasticity processes (Figure 6.9). Thus, the stability of the spine is to some extent an additional benefit that results because high-frequency stimulation changes its morphology.

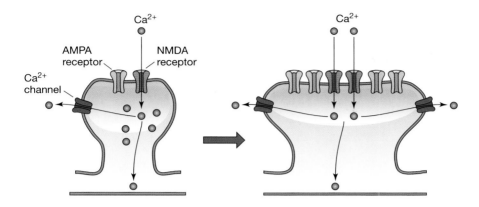

FIGURE 6.9
A spine's structure determines its stability and resistance to modification. High-frequency stimulation induces a cascade of biochemical processes that change the morphology of the spine by broadening its head and results in the insertion of disproportionately more AMPA than NMDA receptors. The changes in the spine structure are thought to make it resistant to future changes that might occur in response to glutamate by increasing the capacity of the spine to diffuse Ca^{2+} out of the head into extracellular space and into the dendrites. Thus, in the smaller spine on the left, Ca^{2+} accumulates in the head in sufficient quantity to initiate the biochemical cascades required to alter synaptic strength. However, on the right, the potentiated spine with a broader head and wider neck allows Ca^{2+} to rapidly efflux out of the head without initiating these cascades. (After Hayashi and Majewska, 2005.)

Dendritic Spines and the Storage Saturation Problem

The picture you should have in mind as you reflect on the material covered in this chapter is that spines are dynamic and in many cases quite unstable. They can come and go. However, synaptic activity can alter this basic state and create a spine structure that greatly enhances its survival. These spines, as you now know, are often large and mushroom-shaped.

It is possible that such spines hold information about our past experiences that can subsequently be retrieved. However, as just discussed, such modified spines, in some sense, *are no longer eligible to be modified*. They are not very plastic. In principle, one could imagine that eventually all spines might become large and stable and the brain would lose its capacity to store new information. Dendrites would become *saturated* with spines that are no longer plastic and new information could not be stored.

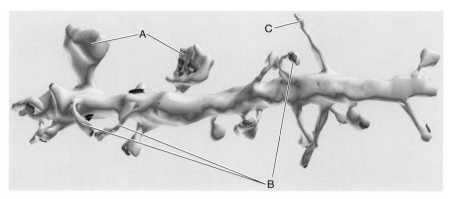

FIGURE 6.10
A three-dimensional reconstruction of a dendritic section of a CA1 pyramidal cell.
(A) Large spines may no longer be plastic and modifiable. (B) Small spines may be
plastic and modifiable. (C) Small filopodium-like spines are unstable and withdraw
within about three days unless they synapse with a presynaptic partner. The constant generation of new spines may be the dendrite's solution to maintaining storage capacity. (From Synapse Web, Kristen M. Harris, http://synapse-web.org/)

Karel Svoboda

It appears, however, that some neurons have
evolved a strategy to counter the saturation problem.
Evidently, processes are operating in dendrites to constantly generate new spines that can become eligible
for modification provided that they find a proper
presynaptic partner to pair up with. Karel Svoboda
and his colleagues (Knott, Holtmaat, Wilbrecht, Welker, and Svoboda, 2006) have directly monitored this
process in the cortex of mice and found that spine-like
filopodia are continuously growing out of dendrites
and may be looking to pair with presynaptic elements.
If within two to three days they do not form a synapse
with a presynaptic element they disappear. However,
if they do pair up with a presynaptic element, a new weakly connected synapse
becomes available. One might speculate that *these new synapses are quite plastic and if properly stimulated their strength could be modified and thus they would be
able to store new information.* From this perspective, the dendrite counters the
saturation problem by constantly making new spines that have the capacity
to store information (Figure 6.10). One might also speculate that over time we
become less able to generate new spines, and this might contribute to the decrease in memory capacity that occurs as we age.

Summary

In addition to influencing AMPA receptor function, high-frequency stimulation initiates processes that alter the morphology of the spine and its connection with a presynaptic partner. This chapter described some of the mechanisms that produce these changes and their consequences for spine stability and function and memory storage.

Dendritic spines exist in different shapes and sizes and come and go. The motility of spines in part reflects the dynamic properties of actin. Actin is regulated by some of the same molecules that regulate AMPA receptor trafficking, such as the influx of Ca^{2+} through NMDA receptors, which causes actin to polymerize. This process increases the size and shape of the spine. The resulting large spines are more stable than small spines. This regulation of actin in response to the high-frequency stimulus is essential to the induction of LTP because blocking actin polymerization prevents LTP.

High-frequency stimulation also initiates processes that bind the modified spine to its presynaptic partner. This is accomplished by its effect on cadherin, a neural cell adhesion molecule. High-frequency stimulation causes monomer strands of cadherin molecules located in both the presynaptic neuron and postsynaptic spine to bond into much more adhesive dimers. These dimers form what is called an "adhesion zipper," which connects the presynaptic terminals and postsynaptic spines. This helps to insure that the synapse will be stable.

These structural changes have several functional effects. They produce a synapse that is much more efficient, so that the same amount of glutamate released from the presynaptic process will produce a larger postsynaptic response. They also increase the stability of the spine. Large, mushroom-shaped spines endure longer than long, thin spines because large spines can more quickly diffuse Ca^{2+} and thereby blunt its ability to initiate other biochemical interactions that would alter the spine. That large spines may be resistant to modification by additional synaptic activity has encouraged some theorists to propose that they are suitable memory storage devices.

Dendrites are continuously sprouting spine-like filopodia. The fate of such protrusions appears to depend on whether they form a synapse with a presynaptic partner. If these spine-like filopodia do not form a synapse, they retract back into the dendritic compartment. Spines that form a synapse endure much longer. Because the postsynaptic spines of these new synapses are small, they are thought to be eligible for modification and available to store new memories. Thus, even though large synapses are no longer eligible for modification, there is now speculation that new synaptic storage units are constantly becoming available to represent our experiences.

References

Ackermann, M. and Matus, A. (2003). Activity-induced targeting of profilin and stabilization of dendritic spine morphology. *Nature Neuroscience, 6,* 1194–2000.

Bozdagi, O., Shan, W. S, Tanaka, H., Benson, D. L., and Huntley, G. W. (2000). Increasing numbers of synaptic puncta during late-phase LTP: N-cadherin is synthesized, recruited to synaptic sites, and required for potentiation. *Neuron, 28,* 245–259.

Carlisle, H. J. and Kennedy, M. B. (2005). Spine architecture and synaptic plasticity. *Trends in Neurosciences, 28,* 182–187.

Colicos, M. A., Collins, B. E., Sailor, M. J., and Goda, Y. (2001). Remodeling of synaptic actin induced by photoconductive stimulation. *Cell, 107,* 605–616.

Dillon, C. and Goda, Y. (2005). The actin cytoskeleton: integrating form and function at the synapse. *Annual Review of Neuroscience, 28,* 25–55.

Fukazawa, Y., Saitoh, Y., Ozawa, F., Ohta, Y., Mizuno, K., and Inokuchi, K. (2003). Hippocampal LTP is accompanied by enhanced F-actin content within the dendritic spine that is essential for late LTP maintenance in vivo. *Neuron, 38,* 447–60.

Grutzendler, J., Kasthuri, N., and Gan, W. B. (2002). Long-term dendritic spine stability in the adult cortex. *Nature, 420,* 812–816.

Halpain, S. (2000). Actin and the agile spine: how and why do dendritic spines dance? *Trends in Neurosciences, 23,* 141–146.

Hayashi, Y. and Majewska, A. K. (2005). Dendritic spine geometry: functional implication and regulation. *Neuron, 46,* 529–532.

Holtmaat, A. J., Trachtenberg, J. T., Wilbrecht, L., Shepherd, G. M., Zhang, X., Knott, G. W., and Svoboda, K. (2005). Transient and persistent dendritic spines in the neocortex in vivo. *Neuron, 20,* 279–291.

Huntley, G. W., Gil, O., and Bozdagi, O. (2002). The cadherin family of cell adhesion molecules: multiple roles in synaptic plasticity. *Neuroscientist, 8,* 221–233.

Kasai, H., Matsuzaki, M., Noguchi, J., Yasumatsu, N., and Nakahara, H. (2003). Structure-stability-function relationships of dendritic spines. *Trends in Neurosciences, 26,* 360–368.

Kim, C. H. and Lisman, J. E. (1999). A role of actin filament in synaptic transmission and long-term potentiation. *Journal of Neuroscience, 19,* 4314–4324.

Knott G. W., Holtmaat, A., Wilbrecht, L., Welker, E., and Svoboda, K. (2006). Spine growth precedes synapse formation in the adult neocortex in vivo. *Nature Neuroscience, 9,* 1117–1124.

Krucker, T., Siggins, G. R., and Halpain, S. (2000). Dynamic actin filaments are required for stable long-term potentiation (LTP) in area CA1 of the hippocampus. *Proceedings of the National Academy of Sciences, 97,* 6856–6861.

Matsuzaki, M., Ellis-Davies, G. C., Nemoto, T., Miyashita, Y., Iino, M., and Kasai, H. (2001). Dendritic spine geometry is critical for AMPA receptor expression in hippocampal CA1 pyramidal neurons. *Nature Neuroscience, 4,* 1086–1092.

Matus, A. (2000). Actin-based plasticity in dendritic spines. *Science, 290,* 754–758.

Noguchi, J., Matsuzaki, M., Ellis-Davies, G. C., and Kasai, H. (2005). Spine-neck geometry determines NMDA receptor-dependent Ca^{2+} signaling in dendrites. *Neuron, 46,* 609–622.

Oertner, T. G. and Matus, A. (2005). Calcium regulation of actin dynamics in dendritic spines. *Cell Calcium, 37,* 477–482.

Tanaka, H., Shan, W., Phillips, G. R., Arndt, K., Bozdagi, O., Shapiro, L., Huntley, G. W., Benson, D. L., and Colman, D. R. (2000). Molecular modification of N-cadherin in response to synaptic activity. *Neuron, 25,* 93–107.

Trachtenberg, J. T., Chen, B. E., Knott, G. W., Feng, G., Sanes, J. R., Welker, E., and Svoboda, K. (2002). Long-term in vivo imaging of experience-dependent synaptic plasticity in adult cortex. *Nature, 420,* 788–794.

Zhou, Q., Xiao, M., and Nicoll, R. A. (2001). Contribution of cytoskeleton to the internalization of AMPA receptors. *Proceedings of the National Academy of Sciences, 98,* 1261–1266.

PART TWO

Molecules and Memories

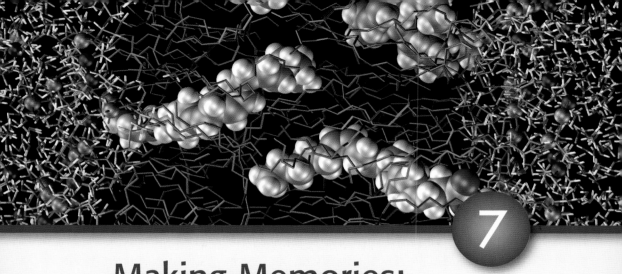

Making Memories: Conceptual Issues and Methodologies

A fundamental question for many students of memory is *how is information contained in a behavioral experience stored in the brain?* Many researchers believe that the synapse is the basic information storage unit, and previous chapters have described some of the essential findings and ideas about how synapses can be modified. We are now going to use this foundation to explore how memories might be made.

In studies of synaptic plasticity, the stimulus that modified synapses was high-frequency electrical stimulation. Memories, however, are established as a result of a **behavioral experience**, that is, a behaving organism interacting with its environment. This experience is assumed to produce changes in synaptic strength in regions of the brain that store the experience. Memory researchers are thus in the difficult position of connecting the mechanisms of synaptic plasticity to behavioral experience. To do this the researcher has to navigate a number of difficult conceptual and interpretive issues and the research requires behavioral and brain methodologies that we have not yet discussed. Thus, the goal of this chapter is to provide you with an understanding of some of these issues and methodologies.

LTP and Memory

If the synapse is the fundamental storage unit in the brain, and if studies of LTP had produced a complete understanding of how synapses are modified (which they have not), then one might argue that we already know how memories are made. The problem with this argument is that the information acquired by studying LTP comes from a highly artificial preparation.

First, the experience used to induce LTP is a low-intensity, high-frequency electrical event that bypasses all the sensory inputs that normally bring environmental information into the brain. No one has any firm idea about how the pattern of electrical stimulation used to produce LTP corresponds to the pattern of neural activity generated by normal sensory stimulation that initiates the formation of a **memory trace** in a behaving organism. It should be appreciated that a slightly more intense inducing stimulus would generate seizure activity in a normal brain. Moreover, the modified synapses typically are in slices of brain tissue that are maintained in a chemical cocktail to keep them functional. There are huge consequences associated with the removal of the tissue that require a number of preparatory steps just to get a functional preparation. In short, to produce LTP, an unnatural stimulus is often delivered to an abnormal neural preparation. So in principle, *all the results and ideas that we have discussed might have no relevance to how a normal brain stores the information contained in natural experiences.*

Fortunately, even though there are enormous differences between the sensory consequences of a behavioral experience arriving into an intact brain and the electrical stimulation arriving into a population of neurons, studies of LTP have yielded important ideas about how memories are formed. Thus, although the synaptic changes that are recorded as LTP do not constitute a memory, *studies of synaptic plasticity are the fundamental source of hypotheses about how the brain makes memories.* Thus, much of what we already have learned will serve us well as we try to understand the molecules that make memories.

Behavior and Memory

Memories are the product of behaving organisms interacting with their environments. In the first chapter, we made the point that memory is a concept offered to explain why our behavioral experiences can influence our subsequent

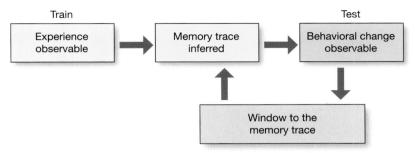

FIGURE 7.1
All experimental investigations of memory require a training phase to establish a
memory and a test phase to detect the memory. The existence of a memory trace
is inferred when the training experience influences behavior. Thus, test behavior
can be thought of as the window to the memory trace.

behavioral responses to the environment. No one has ever directly observed
a memory. This state of affairs has important implications for trying to understand the biological basis of memory. In reality, the effort requires trying
to link some physical properties of the brain to an abstract, unobservable concept. To approach this endeavor requires some discussion about the relationship between memory and behavior.

To start the discussion, let us consider the basic paradigm used in all studies of learning and memory (Figure 7.1). The inference that a memory has been
established requires that the subject in the experiment have a particular experience and then be tested with some component of that experience. If the
experience influences the behavioral test, then one might infer that a memory
has been established. Recall, for example, that Ebbinghaus trained himself
on lists of nonsense syllables and then tested himself to see if he remembered them.

Test Behavior: The Window to the Memory Trace

Given that Ebbinghaus recalled the nonsense syllables, we might infer that a
memory was established. However, this was because his past behavioral experience influenced his test behavior. The memory was not observed. What
was observed was that studying the lists influenced his recall of the nonsense syllables. Note that without a measurable behavioral test response, there
would be no evidence that his studying produced a memory trace. Thus, one
might conclude that *test behavior is the window to the memory trace.* Unless the
researcher can demonstrate that experience alters test behavior, there is no basis to say it established a memory.

FIGURE 7.2
An organism's behavioral response is determined by the interaction of many different component processes. Thus, before one can conclude that some biological manipulation influenced some aspect of memory, one has to be sure that it did not influence some other component that influences behavior.

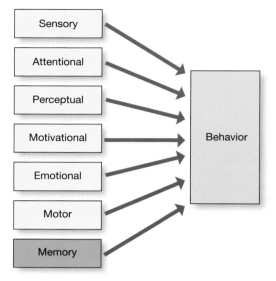

If memory were the only thing that influenced behavior, the study of the biological basis of learning and memory would still be difficult, but far simpler. Unfortunately, this is not the case; *a measurable behavior is the final product of many different component processes* (Figure 7.2). To list just a few, there are:

- sensory, attention, and perceptual processes that determine what the subject experiences at the time of training and testing;
- motivational processes that determine the subject's willingness to initiate a response;
- emotional processes that can interfere with the subject's ability to access stored information;
- motor systems that provide the basis for the behavioral response to be expressed; and
- a memory system that stores the experience.

Let's consider the implications of this state of affairs. In studying the biological basis of memory, neurobiologists use a variety of methods to influence brain function. They include:

- experimentally damaging a particular region of the brain;
- injecting drugs into the brain that are designed to influence some aspect of neural function; and
- genetic engineering to increase or decrease the expression of some potential memory molecule.

These methods are discussed in greater detail later in this chapter.

Now imagine that you have a hypothesis that a specific region of the brain stores the memory for some particular experience. So you damage this region of the brain and then conduct an experiment in which you provide the subjects with a learning experience and then test them. Your results are stunningly clear: compared to control subjects that had no brain damage, your subjects with brain damage displayed no behavioral evidence that they ever had the training experience. They behaved as if they had no memory for the experience. If you think that you demonstrated that the damaged region of the brain was essential to storing the memory, you are wrong.

The Learning–Performance Distinction

The proper conclusion in the above example would be simply that your data are consistent with your hypothesis. Unfortunately, the *results are also consistent with other explanations.* Before anyone would believe that the damaged region was critical to memory formation, you would have to conduct additional experiments to rule out alternative explanations of your results. The lesion might have impaired (1) sensory–attention or perceptual processes, (2) motivation or emotional processes, or (3) motor processes. Thus, your work has just begun and you may need to figure out additional behavioral tests that could be used to rule out these alternative explanations. *This caveat applies to the interpretation of any manipulation of brain processes that alters the behavioral measure of memory.*

Successful inroads into understanding the biological basis of memory depend on researchers establishing a strong basis for their conclusions. They must be able to show that the brain manipulation in their experiment influenced behavior by selectively influencing the unobservable memory component and *not* by affecting some other component process. Psychologists call this problem the **learning–performance distinction**. It just means that we want to be sure that our manipulation exerted its influence on the memory component and not some other component process that could also influence performance. To rule out the possibility that the brain manipulation did not influence other component processes is a daunting task. However, as we will see, in spite of these complexities memory researchers have made significant advances in this area.

Dimensions of Memory Traces

At least since William James's treatise on psychology, some memory researchers have believed that behavioral experience produces a succession of memory traces in the brain. How many traces are created is a matter of debate that we do not need to consider here. However, most researchers who study the biological basis of memory agree that experience initiates at least two mem-

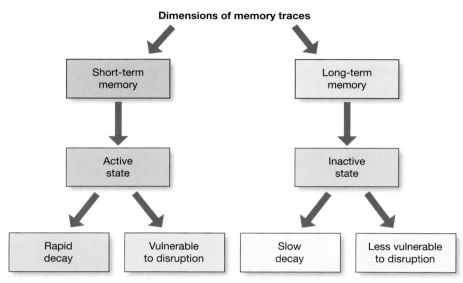

FIGURE 7.3
Memory traces can differ on at least three dimensions: duration, state, and vulnerability to disruption.

ory traces: a **short-term memory trace** that decays relatively quickly and a more stable, **long-term memory trace** that has a much slower decay rate. Because this distinction is so important to neurobiological memory research, it will be useful to discuss it more fully.

The idea that short-term and long-term memory traces have different decay rates is important. This *duration* distinction also is tied to two other dimensions: the *state* of the memory trace (active versus inactive) and its *vulnerability to disruption* (Figure 7.3). For example, a football player who receives a blow to the head may not recall any events he experienced several minutes prior to the blow but he may have full recall of everything that happened in the locker room before the game started. The blow to the head produced a very time-limited **retrograde amnesia** (a failure to remember an experience that happened prior to the occurrence of the disrupting event). Not all memories were lost; the amnesia was limited only to events that occurred just before the causal event, that is, the blow to the head. One explanation for the limited retrograde amnesia is that the blow only affected the memory traces in the *active state*. Memories that had achieved long-term memory status and were not in the active state at the time of the trauma were not lost. This point is illustrated in Figure 7.4.

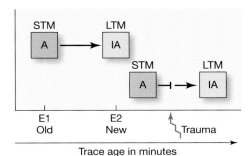

FIGURE 7.4
A football player has two sets of experiences. E1 represents the locker room experiences prior to the game. E2 represents experiences just prior to the head trauma. Thus, the E1 memories are older than the E2 memories. The trauma only produces amnesia for the newer E2 memories because they are still in an active state at the time the trauma occurs. The E1 memories are not affected because they had achieved the inactive, long-term memory state. STM = short-term memory; LTM = long-term memory; A = active state; IA = inactive state; E1 = experience 1; E2 = experience 2.

The Concept of Memory Consolidation

Following a learning experience, the memory trace is vulnerable to disruption. With the passage of time, the trace becomes more stable and resistant to memory disruption. This outcome is attributed to a process called **memory consolidation** (Figure 7.5). Two German researchers, Georg Müeller and Alfons Pilzecker (1900), are credited as the first to propose the concept of consolidation. They used Ebbinghaus's methodology and required subjects to learn two lists of nonsense syllables. They varied the amount of time separating the learning of the two lists and later asked subjects to recall nonsense syllables from the first list. They reported that more items were recalled when the interval separating the two lists was long than when it was short. To ac-

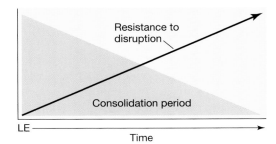

FIGURE 7.5
The concept of memory consolidation. Following a learning experience (LE), a memory trace is vulnerable to disruption. With the passage of time, resistance to memory disruption increases and the trace becomes more stable. The term memory consolidation is used to describe this change from vulnerable to less vulnerable. The term consolidation processes is used to designate processes that stabilize the memory trace. The term consolidation period refers to the time it takes to stabilize the memory trace.

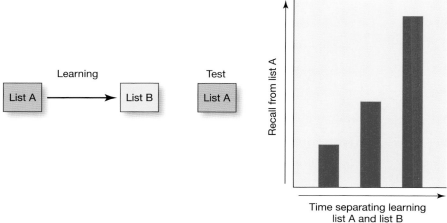

FIGURE 7.6
The design and results of the Müeller and Pilzecker experiment that led to their concept of memory consolidation. Note that as the time between studying the two lists increased, the subjects recalled more items from the first list.

count for why time was important, they proposed that memory traces for the items in the first list were fragile and were disrupted when the subjects learned the second list. With time, however, these traces stabilized and so were less vulnerable to disruption (Figure 7.6).

Electroconvulsive Shock and Memory Disruption

As noted, it was more than a hundred years ago that Müeller and Pilzecker introduced the idea that the memory trace is initially fragile and requires time to stabilize. Experimental investigations of memory disruption associated with brain trauma, however, did not emerge until nearly half a century later. (See McGaugh [2003] for a review of the history of this development.)

In the late 1930s, two Italian physicians, Ugo Cerletti and Lucio Bini, began to use **electroconvulsive shock (ECS)** to treat psychiatric disorders. Clinical observations indicated that patients treated with ECS often did not recall their experiences in the time period leading up to the treatment. A decade later, Carl Duncan (1949) recognized that ECS might be a useful tool for experimentally producing amnesia in animals. He trained rats and administered ECS within a minute or so of training, or an hour later. Rats that received ECS shortly after training displayed a memory impairment. Dozens of experiments were subsequently conducted that used the ECS methodology. Unfortunately, however, this research did not answer any fundamental questions about memory consolidation (McGaugh, 2003). In essence, based on clinical examples, we already knew that brain trauma can disrupt recently established memories and the ECS methodology did not advance our understanding beyond this point.

Memory Disruption:
A Storage or Retrieval Failure?

In the preceding discussion, the term memory disruption was used to describe the vulnerability of newly established memory traces. You may recall from Chapter 1 that in his analysis of the memory problems produced by the syndrome named after him, Serge Korsakoff (1897) recognized that memory can be disrupted for two reasons (Figure 7.7):

- The impairment is a **storage failure**. According to this hypothesis, the agent that produces amnesia, for example a blow to the head, interferes with the processes responsible for storing the memory. The implication of this idea is that events experienced prior to the trauma will never be remembered. A memory not stored can never be recovered.

- The impairment is a **retrieval failure**. According to this hypothesis the memory is stored but cannot be accessed. The agent that produces amnesia in some way disrupts the neural pathways that enable the memory to be retrieved. The implication of this idea is that the memory loss

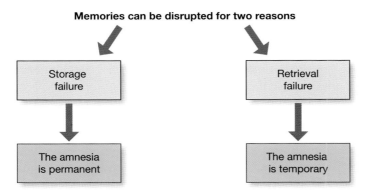

FIGURE 7.7
A disrupting event can interfere with the storage of the memory trace or it can interfere with processes involved in retrieval.

is temporary. Even without trauma, we often have retrieval failures. For example, consider how often you have said that you can't remember something such as where you put a book or a coffee cup, only later to remember the location. In this case the information had been stored but for some reason could not be accessed.

The ECS methodology did not contribute anything substantive to our understanding of how memories are formed. However, it sensitized researchers to the idea that memory failures produced by brain trauma can be either a storage failure or retrieval failure. For a time, research on memory consolidation stalled because researchers using this methodology could not resolve the question of whether or not an event that produces a memory impairment interfered with storage or retrieval. *The possibility that a memory impairment can be due to retrieval failures must always be considered when someone claims that their brain manipulation interferes with the consolidation processes that store the memory.* The retrieval hypothesis is diabolical because it is impossible to completely disprove. You can never prove that a memory will not recover with time. The question is, how much time must you allow before you can conclude the impairment is due to a storage failure: a day, a week, a month? There is no good answer to this question except that longer is better.

Some Behavioral Test Methods for Studying Memory

Memory researchers use a wide variety of behavioral test methods to study the biological basis of memory. It would be impossible to cover even a small fraction of what is known in this area, so choices have to be made. Much of what we know about the biological basis of memory can be illustrated by initially focusing on results and ideas that have emerged from three extensively used methods: (1) inhibitory avoidance conditioning, (2) fear conditioning, and (3) spatial learning in a water-escape task. This section describes these methods and some of the advantages they have for memory research. Other methods are described in subsequent sections.

Inhibitory Avoidance Conditioning

An illustration of the apparatus used to study inhibitory avoidance conditioning is shown in Figure 7.8. The basic procedure is simple. A rodent (rat or mouse) is placed in the bright side of the apparatus. Rodents generally prefer to be in dimmer environments, so within 10 seconds or so, it will cross over to the dark side. When this occurs, a brief electrical shock is applied to its feet and the subject is removed. Some time later the rodent is again placed in

(A)

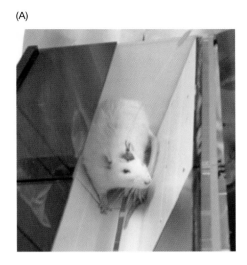

(B)

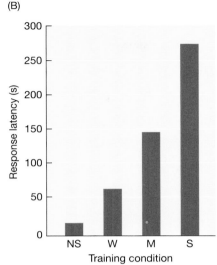

FIGURE 7.8

(A) A photograph of an apparatus used to study inhibitory avoidance learning. The rat is placed in the bright end of the apparatus. When it crosses to the dark side, it receives an electric shock across its feet. To assess the memory for this experience, the rat is placed again in the bright end and the time it takes to cross to the dark side (crossover latency) is measured. (B) The graph illustrates the effect of increasing shock intensity on response latency. Note that as shock intensity increases, so does response latency. NS = no shock; W = weak shock; M = moderate shock; S = strong shock. (A courtesy of James L. McGaugh.)

the bright side of the apparatus, and the experimenter measures the time it takes the rodent to enter the dark side of the compartment. The expectation is that if the rodent remembers that it was shocked in the dark side, it will be reluctant to cross over. So the latency to cross over to the dark side should increase. This methodology is called inhibitory avoidance because the rodent has to inhibit its tendency to cross over and thus avoid the place where it was shocked. Note that in using this task, the researcher assumes that the strength of the memory trace is reflected in the response latency, that is, longer latencies reflect a stronger memory trace.

Inhibitory avoidance conditioning has two important attributes. First, only one training trial is required to produce a memory for the experience, although more trials can be given. Second, the rodent's crossover latency is quite sensitive to the intensity of the shock. As shock intensity is increased, the latency to cross over also increases.

You will learn later that there are drug treatments that can increase or decrease the strength of the memory. So, if you are studying a drug or some other manipulation that you think will strengthen a memory trace, you would use a low-intensity shock because if a strong shock is used, the rodent's crossover latency would be so long that you could not observe the effect of the drug. This outcome is called a **ceiling effect** because if the response measure is at the maximum (ceiling), there is no way you can see the influence of some other manipulation.

In contrast, if you think that your drug impairs the memory processes that produce avoidance behavior, then you would use a somewhat higher level of shock that produces a long latency so that you could determine if the drug impaired the memory. If you use a weak shock that produces a relatively short crossover latency, you would not be able to see an influence of the drug. This outcome is called a **floor effect** because the performance measure was too low to be further reduced by the drug.

Fear Conditioning

Fear conditioning has become a very popular method for studying the biological basis of memory. The basic methodology is illustrated in Figure 7.9. Some time after a rodent is placed into what is called a conditioning chamber, an auditory stimulus is presented. About 10–15 seconds after the onset of the auditory stimulus, electrical shock is delivered to the rodent's feet. One can administer one or several training trials. An innate defensive response called **freezing** (see Chapter 16) is often used to assess the rodent's memory for the experience. In the presence of a danger signal, such as the sight or sounds of a predator, rodents instinctively become still or immobile. This behavior has survival advantages because a moving animal is more likely to be detected by a predator than a still one.

Experimenters often test the rodent's freezing response to both the context and place where shock occurred and to the tone paired with the shock. Because rodents will freeze in the training context where the shock occurred, the tone is tested in a novel context that has no association with shock. This allows the experimenter to obtain a relatively pure measure of fear of the tone.

Recall that in Chapter 1 you were introduced to what is called the classical or Pavlovian conditioning methodology for studying associative learning. The procedure just described is a modern variation of Pavlovian conditioning. In fear conditioning, the unconditioned stimulus (US) is the foot shock and the conditioned response (CR) is the freezing response. There are two types of conditioned stimuli (CS). One consists of the constantly present features that make up the context–place where shock occurs. It is called the **context CS**, and freezing in that context is called **contextual fear conditioning**. The other type of

Exploration

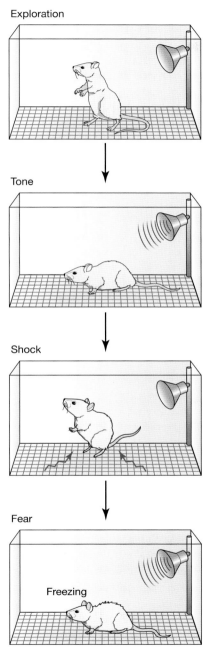

Tone

Shock

Fear

Freezing

Rats have an innate freezing response
to signals associated with danger

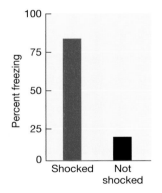

FIGURE 7.9

In fear conditioning, after the rat has explored the conditioning context, an auditory cue (tone) is presented for about 15 seconds. Shock is delivered when the tone terminates. Rats are then tested for their fear of the context–place where shock occurred and later for their fear of the tone. Shocked (S) rats display more freezing than rats that were not shocked (NS).

CS, the **auditory cue**, is not constantly present. It is a phasic event, meaning that it has a distinct onset and termination. Its onset signals or predicts that shock will occur. Conditioning to the tone is referred to as **auditory-cue fear conditioning**. The basic assumption is that the strength of the freezing response is an indicator of the strength of the memory of the training events.

The fear conditioning procedure also has important advantages. It allows the experimenter very precise control over factors that might influence the strength of a memory such as (1) the intensity of the CS and US, (2) the time separating the CS and US, and (3) the number of training trials. The innate freezing response that is the CR is easy to measure. Usually the experimenter will observe the rodent and determine the time it spends freezing. However, there are automated methods available to measure this behavior.

Spatial Learning in a Water-Escape Task

Spatial learning in a water-escape task is a far more complex behavioral test method than the other two described above. The water-escape task was developed by Richard Morris (1981) to allow researchers a method for studying how animals acquire map-like representations of their environments. Essentially, a small platform is located in a large circular pool of water into which rodents are placed and then tested on finding the location of the platform (Figure 7.10). There are two versions of the water-escape task: the **place-learning task** and the **visible-platform task**.

PLACE-LEARNING TASK   To create the place-learning task, the platform is placed in the pool just below the surface of the water but invisible to the rodent. The rodent is placed in the water at the edge of the pool and is released. It can escape from the pool by finding the invisible platform. Note that a special property of this basic task is that the platform remains in the same location of the pool over a block of training trials. The location is specified in relationship to the features of the room in which the pool is located. Typically, the rodent is started randomly from one of several locations inside the side of the pool. This ensures that it has to learn the location of the platform and does not learn just to swim in a particular direction in relationship to some single feature in the room. Rodents are excellent swimmers and, even though the platform is invisible, once the rodent habituates to the surprise of being in the water, it takes very few trials for it to learn to swim quickly and directly to the platform.

Successful performance on this task is measured in several ways. During training, **escape latency** (the time it takes to find the platform) decreases dramatically. The distance the rodent swims before it finds the platform, called

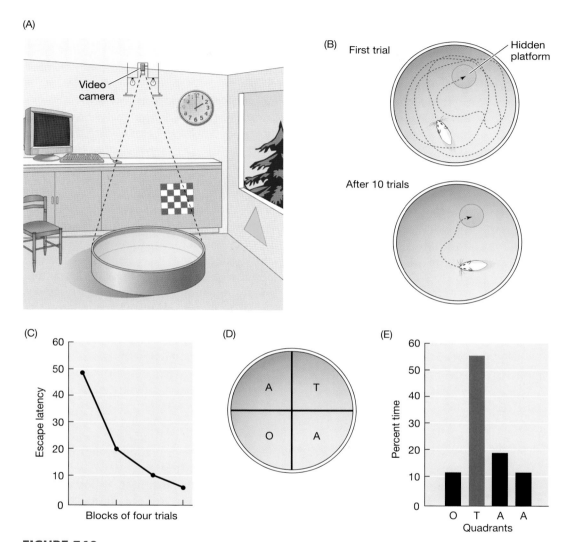

FIGURE 7.10
The place-learning version of the Morris water-escape task. (A) A circular swim-ming pool in the laboratory. (B) On the first trial, the rodent swims a long distance before it locates the platform. After several trials, it learns to swim directly to the platform. (C) Escape latency, the time it takes the rat to find the hidden platform, decreases as a function of training trials. (D) A schematic of the swimming pool that divides it into four quadrants: T, the training quadrant; A, the two adjacent quadrants; O, the quadrant opposite the training quadrant. (E) The results of a probe trial with the platform removed from the pool. Note that the rats spend more time swimming in the training quadrant than in the other quadrants.

path length, also improves. With practice the rodents swim directly to the platform. Usually escape latency and path length are highly connected because, other things being equal, on a trial when the rodent swims a short distance to find the platform the escape latency will be shorter than when it swims a long distance before locating the platform.

Researchers use what is called a **probe trial** to further assess the rodent's memory for the location of the platform. On a probe trial, the platform is removed from the pool and the rodent is placed in the pool and allowed to search for it. The duration of the search can vary (20–60 seconds), depending on the experimenter. The rodent's performance can be videotaped or a special camera that feeds data into a computer for further processing can capture it. In either case the experimenter collects information about where the rodent swims.

One standard measure of performance in this task is called **quadrant search time**. The pool is divided conceptually into four equal quadrants. During training the platform is in one quadrant. A rodent that has stored a memory of the location of the platform will spend more of its search time in the training quadrant than it will in the other quadrants. Another performance measure is called **annulus crossings**. In this case, the measure is how many times during the probe trial the animal actually crosses the exact place where the platform is located compared to how many times it crosses the equivalent area in the other quadrants.

VISIBLE-PLATFORM TASK   The visible-platform task is often used as a control task to evaluate alternative interpretations of the effect of some brain manipulation on performance in the place-learning task. In this task the platform sets above the water surface and usually is painted to make it contrast with the water. The platform location usually varies on each trial. If some drug, genetic manipulation, or lesion disrupts performance on the place-learning version of the task, you would want to know that this treatment did not disrupt sensory, motivational–emotional, or motor systems. If the treatment has no effect on performance on the visible-platform task, then you would be more confident about concluding that the treatment influenced some aspect of memory. If, however, the same treatment disrupted performance on this task you would not want to conclude that the treatment affected memory.

Why These Three Behavioral Test Methods?

These three test methods—inhibitory avoidance conditioning, fear conditioning, and spatial learning in a water-escape task—initially are the center of focus because many researchers who study "memory molecules" have target treatments to two regions of the brain, the **hippocampus** and **amygdala**. The hippocampus is targeted because, as we will later discuss, it makes a critical contribution to what is called episodic memory (see Chapters 13 and 14) and because the bulk of the LTP literature comes from slices taken from the hippocampus. The amygdala is targeted because it is thought to be critically involved in the storage of emotional memories (see Chapter 16). The amygdala is targeted also because it is a region of the brain where LTP is studied.

Given this background, it makes sense to focus on behavioral test methods that depend on the hippocampus and/or the amygdala to store information about the training experiences. Most researchers agree that the hippocampus makes an important contribution to the memory systems supporting inhibitory avoidance learning, contextual fear conditioning, and spatial learning, and that regions of the amygdala make a contribution to emotional memory. Moreover, without some way to constrain our focus it would be almost impossible to provide a reasonably coherent picture of what is known.

Methods for Manipulating Brain Function

Our understanding of how memories are made in the brain requires that the researcher be able to manipulate the brain to determine if a particular region or molecule is critical to creating a memory. This section addresses two general ways this is accomplished. One method, based on damaging or chemically altering neurons in a specific region of the brain, depends on **stereotaxic surgery**. The other method utilizes **genetic engineering** techniques to target specific genes.

Stereotaxic Surgery

Stereotaxic surgery uses a coordinate system to locate specific targets inside the brain to enable some procedure to be carried out on them (for example, a lesion, injection, or implantation). As illustrated in Figure 7.11A, a stereotaxic surgery device allows the researcher to lower a fine wire, called an **electrode**, into a precise region of the brain. By passing electric current through the tip of this wire, the researcher can damage neurons in the region of the electrode tip. The device can also be used to position a small injection needle (often referred to as a **cannula**) into a precise brain region so that the researcher can inject into that region a chemical solution that can also damage neurons. Both of these methods are used to damage a particular brain region.

Stereotaxic surgery can also be used to place what is called a **cannula guide** permanently into the brain (Figure 7.11B), for use after the surgery. The guide allows a drug to be readily injected into an awake and moving animal (an essential state for studies of learning and memory). For example, prior to

(A)

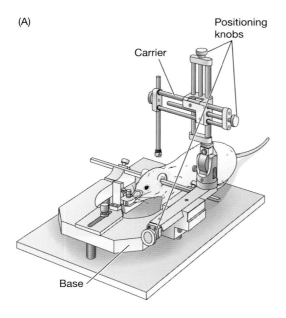

Positioning knobs

Carrier

Base

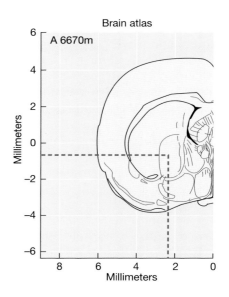

Brain atlas

A 6670m

Millimeters

(B)

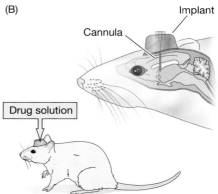

Implant

Cannula

Drug solution

FIGURE 7.11
(A) A stereotaxic device used during surgery for precise placement of a fine wire (electrode) or a small injection needle (cannula) for targeting electrical current or a chemical solution into a specific region of the brain. The base holds the anesthetized animal's head and neck in a stationary position. The carrier portion places the electrode or cannula in a precise location based on the coordinates of the target area identified with a brain atlas. (B) A cannula guide is implanted deep into the rat's brain. Drugs can then be delivered to specific regions of the brain of an awake and moving rat by inserting a cannula into the guide.

providing the animal with a learning experience, the researcher might place the injection needle into the cannula guide and deliver the NMDA-receptor antagonist APV directly into the hippocampus to determine if these receptors play a critical role in memory.

Genetic Engineering

Pharmacological agents have been used with much success in elucidating some of the major molecules that contribute to memory. However, drugs are often "dirty," meaning they are not highly selective to the intended target. This state

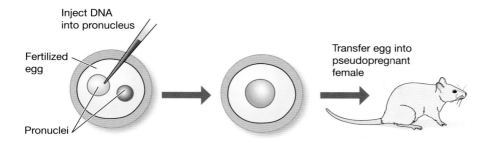

FIGURE 7.12
DNA is injected into a pronucleus from a fertilized egg. This DNA can be designed to replace or knock out a particular gene or it can substitute for another gene.

of affairs can have unintended consequences that can make it difficult to interpret results. Moreover, controlling the spread of the drug to other regions is also difficult and presents other interpretative problems.

Molecular biologists have developed techniques that permit much more precise targeting of specific molecules that might play a role in making memories. These methods have made it possible to alter the DNA in a fertilized egg and thereby alter specific genes. Moreover, because this occurs in the fertilized egg, which is then implanted back into the pseudopregnant animal, this experimentally induced mutation will be carried by the offspring. In general, a particular gene can be removed or "knocked out" or a transgenic animal can be produced, in which case a replacement gene is substituted for the original gene (Figure 7.12).

Researchers often apply genetic engineering methods to mice to study learning and memory. In the so-called first generation of genetically engineered mice, the offspring develop with the mutation and, since a given gene can play an important role in many different functions of the organism, even if the animal survives it might be abnormal in many ways that make it quite difficult to determine the importance of the gene for learning and memory.

Over the years, however, genetic engineering methods have become much more sophisticated. So there now exists what is called a **conditional knock-out methodology**. Under the right conditions, this methodology allows the experimenter to knock out a particular gene in a very well specified region of the brain, such as the CA1 region of the hippocampus, and to do this at different times in development. Moreover, the results of these new techniques can be reversed. Thus, a given gene might be turned off for some period of time and then turned back on, so one can study the same animal with a particular gene knocked out or with that gene functioning.

Summary

This chapter has introduced you to some of the key conceptual and interpretative issues that confront memory researchers seeking to understand how memories are made. Memories cannot be directly observed, so behavior has to be tested in order to infer that a memory has been established. However, behavior is the final product of many different processes. This problem is recognized as the learning–performance distinction. It reminds us that before we can conclude that some brain manipulation influenced memory, we have to make sure that the manipulation did not influence some other process that also was necessary to produce the behavior.

Also introduced in this chapter were (1) the idea that experience can produce memory traces with different properties and (2) the hypothesis that memories tend to consolidate, that is, become more resistant to disruption. Memories can be disrupted either because some agent impacts on the storage of the memory trace or because the event produced a retrieval failure.

Some of the important behavioral test methods (inhibitory avoidance conditioning, fear conditioning, and spatial learning) were described. Methods for manipulating the brain based on stereotaxic surgery and genetic engineering were also presented.

With an understanding of these conceptual issues and the behavioral and brain methodologies in hand, you can now appreciate some of the major findings from research directed at understanding the cellular and molecular basis of memory formation and storage.

References

Cerletti, U. and Bini, L. (1938). Electric shock treatment. *Boll. R. Accad. Med, Roma, 64*, 136–138.

Duncan, C. P. (1949). The retroactive effect of electroshock on learning. *Journal of Comparative and Physiological Psychology, 42*, 332–344.

Korsakoff, S. S. (1897). Disturbance of psychic function in alcoholic paralysis and its relation to the disturbance of the psychic sphere in multiple neuritis of nonalchoholic origins. *Vesin. Psychiatrii 4*: fascicle 2.

McGaugh, J. L. (2003). *Memory and emotion*. New York: Columbia University Press.

Morris, R. G. M. (1981). Spatial localization does not depend on the presence of local cues. *Learning and Motivation, 12*, 239–260.

Müeller, G. E. and Pilzecker, A. (1900). Experimentalle beitrage zur lehre vom gedachtinis. *Zeitschrift für Psychologie und Physiologie der Sinnesorgane, I*, 1–288.

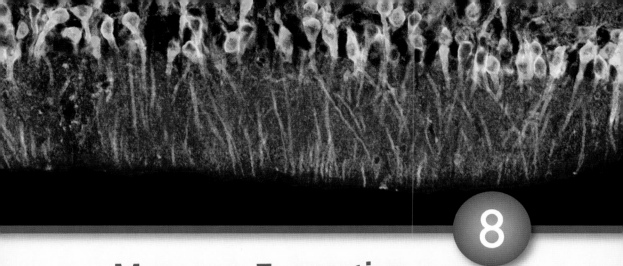

Memory Formation: Post-Translation Processes

Memories are produced by experience. The goal of this and the next chapter is to provide you with an understanding of what is known about some of the important cellular–molecular mechanisms that translate experience into memories. These chapters are organized around the basic ideas presented in Chapters 3 and 4 on synaptic plasticity and how strengthened synapses support LTP. In those chapters, you learned that (1) the strengthened synaptic connections reflected in LTP depend on the intensity of the inducing stimulus, and (2) post-translation processes can support short-lasting LTP but long-lasting LTP requires products that result from transcription and translation processes.

From the perspective of memory formation, these ideas suggest that although experience might initially establish a short-term memory trace that depends primarily on post-translation processes, an enduring long-term memory trace will require the contribution of transcription and translation processes. This chapter examines the contribution of post-translation processes to memory formation, focusing on the role of glutamate receptors and CaMKII. Chapter 9 then considers the contribution of transcription and translation processes to memory storage.

As is the case with synaptic plasticity, the behavioral literature is enormous, so I make no attempt to be comprehensive in my coverage. The goal is to reveal some of the fundamental contributions researchers have made and point out some of the difficulties they have encountered in making the claim that a particular molecule is critical to memory formation.

Glutamate Receptors and Memory Formation

It is generally assumed that the formation of a memory trace begins when a set of neurons that represent a behavioral experience are stimulated. These neurons then release glutamate onto the postsynaptic sites and initiate the cascade of cellular–molecular events that strengthen synaptic connections among the set of co-active neurons (Figure 8.1). Since the cellular–molecular cascade that leads to memory formation begins with the activation of glutamate receptors, this is a good place to start our discussion. We look first at NMDA receptors, then AMPA receptors, and finally at the different contributions NMDA and AMPA receptors make to memory function.

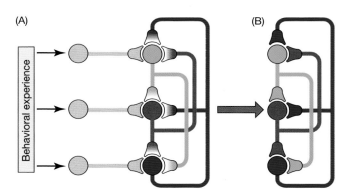

FIGURE 8.1
(A) The formation of a memory trace begins when a behavioral experience activates a set of weakly connected neurons.
(B) The cellular–molecular processes activated in these neurons strengthen their synaptic connections, thereby creating a neural representation of the behavioral experience, called a memory trace.

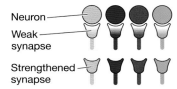

NMDA Receptors and Memory Function

Studies of synaptic plasticity have revealed that changes in synaptic strength are initiated when levels of glutamate are sufficient to occupy NMDA receptors and to depolarize the neuron. Given the critical contribution NMDA receptors play in the initiation of processes that strengthen synapses, one would expect that these receptors are also important for the initiation of memories for behavioral experience. Researchers have used both pharmacological and genetic engineering methodologies to test this hypothesis.

Richard Morris

PHARMACOLOGICALLY ALTERED NMDA RECEPTORS   Richard Morris (Morris, Anderson, Lynch, and Baudry, 1986) was the first researcher to experimentally test the hypothesis that the initial formation of a memory trace depends on the activation of NMDA receptors. To do this he implanted a cannula to deliver the NMDA receptor antagonist APV into the ventricular system of the rat's brain where it would enter the cerebral spinal fluid. Cerebral spinal fluid is the substance that covers your brain and spinal cord and cushions them against impact. It also provides them with oxygen and nutrients and removes waste products.

Morris reasoned that APV injected into this fluid would widely diffuse and occupy NMDA receptors throughout the brain. If NMDA receptors are involved in creating memories for behavioral experiences, then blocking glutamate's access to these receptors at the time of the learning experience should impair memory formation. Morris infused APV dissolved in a vehicle solution into the brain for several days in order to ensure that it occupied NMDA receptors. Control rats were infused with just the vehicle solution. He then trained these rats in the place-learning version of the water-escape task (see Chapter 7).

Morris's experiments revealed that APV prevented the induction of LTP in the dentate gyrus of the hippocampus and, more importantly, dramatically impaired the rat's ability to locate the hidden platform. Morris thus provided the first evidence that the NMDA receptor, which is critical to the induction of LTP, may also participate in the initiation of a memory trace (Figure 8.2). Since Morris et al.'s original publication, there have been a large number of studies using APV to successfully implicate a role for NMDA receptors in memory formation (e.g., Campeau, Miserendino, and Davis, 1992; Fanselow and Kim, 1994; Matus-Amat, Higgins, Sprunger, Wright-Hardesty, and Rudy, 2007; Morris, Davis, and Butcher, 1990; Stote and Fanselow, 2004).

(A)

Cannula

Ventricles

Subarachnoid space

Choroid plexus

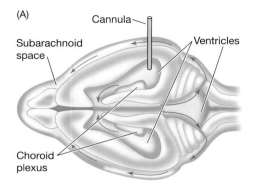

(C) LTP in dentate gyrus

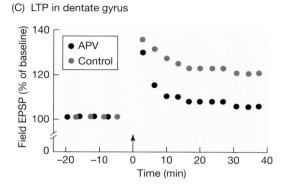

(B)

Computer for image analysis

Video camera

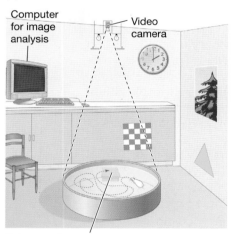

Submerged escape platform

(D)

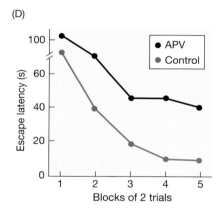

FIGURE 8.2
This figure illustrates the components of the classic Morris experiment. (A) A cannula was implanted into the ventricles of the rat's brain and attached to a time-release pellet that contained the NMDA receptor antagonist, APV. (B) Rats were trained on the place-learning version of the water-escape task. (C) Rats infused with APV could not sustain LTP in the dentate gyrus. (D) Rats injected with APV were impaired in learning the location of the hidden platform. (E) Control rats selectively searched the quadrant that contained the platform during training, but rats injected with APV did not. T = training quadrant; A = adjacent quadrant; O = opposite quadrant.

(E)

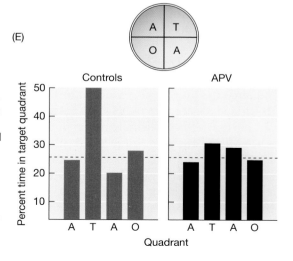

NMDA receptor subtypes

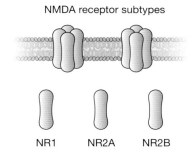

NR1   NR2A   NR2B

FIGURE 8.3
NMDA receptors are composed of four sub-units. All functional NMDA receptors contain NR1 subunits. There are a variety of NR2 subunits. This figure illustrates NMDA-receptor complexes composed of NR1–NR2A and NR1–NR2B subunits.

GENETICALLY ENGINEERED NMDA RECEPTORS   Until fairly recently, the only way a researcher could alter the normal function of some molecule thought to be involved in making memories was to apply a drug that might impair or facilitate the function of that molecule. However, as described in Chapter 7, modern molecular biology has provided genetic engineering methodologies that can be used to manipulate memory molecules. By using these techniques, researchers are able to selectively delete or selectively overexpress the gene for a particular molecule that might be important for making memories. Results provided by the genetic engineering approach have added significantly to the idea that NMDA receptors contribute to memory formation. Before considering some of the key findings, however, the composition of the NMDA receptor needs to be more fully described.

The NMDA receptor is composed of four subunits. The subunits can be divided into two classes: NR1 and NR2. There are several subtypes of NR2 receptors, designated NR2A, NR2B, NR2C, and NR2D. All NMDA-receptor complexes contain the NR1 subunit, but a combination of both NR1 and NR2 subunits are required to form a functional channel that can open to allow Ca^{2+} into the neuron. Researchers interested in the contribution of NMDA receptors to memory have taken advantage of their structure and used genetic engineering methods to selectively delete or overexpress one of these subunits in mice (Figure 8.3).

Susumi Tonegawa and his colleagues (Tsien, Huerta, and Tonegawa, 1996) were able to selectively delete the NR1 subunit in pyramidal cells in the CA1 field of the mouse hippocampus. This mouse is called a CA1 knockout (CA1KO). These researchers then stimulated the Schaffer collateral fibers and recorded field potentials in slices taken from the CA1KO mice. As one would expect, since the NR1 subunit is needed to form a functional NMDA receptor, LTP could not be generated (Figure 8.4). Note in Figure 8.4A that NR1

Susumi Tonegawa

(A)

Normal   CA1KO

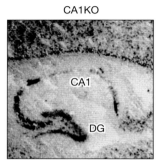

(B) LTP in CA1

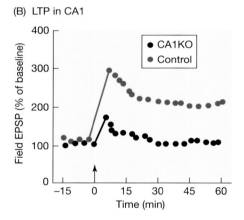

(C) LTP in DG

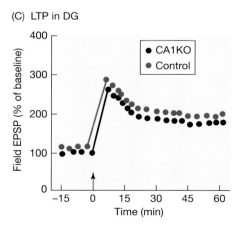

FIGURE 8.4

(A) This photomicrograph shows a section of a normal hippocampus (left section) that has been stained to reveal the presence of the NR1 subunit. Note that the NR1 subunit is absent in the CA1 region of the section taken from the genetically engineered mouse, called a CA1 knockout or CA1KO (right section), but is present in the dentate gyrus (DG). (B) LTP cannot be induced in CA1 in slices taken from mice lacking the NR1 subunit. (C) LTP can be induced in the dentate gyrus in slices taken from the genetically engineered mice because the NR1 subunit is still present. (D) The CA1KO mice are impaired on the place-learning version of the Morris water-escape task. (E) These mice also do not selectively search the training quadrant on the probe trial. (After Tsien et al., 1996.)

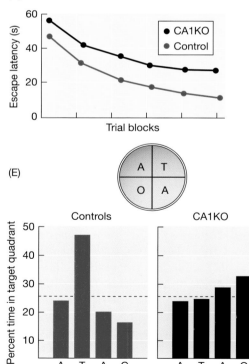

subunits were expressed in neurons in the dentate gyrus. Thus, NMDA receptors in this region should be functional, and it was possible to induce LTP in CA1KO mice by stimulating the perforant pathway and recording field potentials in the dentate gyrus (the location in which LTP was discovered by Bliss and Lomo).

The most important results of these studies, however, were those that demonstrated that the NMDA receptors in CA1 were critical for memory. The researchers tested the CA1KO mice in both the place-learning and visible-platform versions of the Morris water-escape task. These mice were very impaired in acquiring the memory for the location of the hidden platform but were able to learn to swim directly to the visible platform.

Tonegawa and his colleagues (Nakazawa et al., 2003) have also deleted the NR1 receptor, but from the CA3 region of the hippocampus. Mice with this deletion were not impaired on the standard place-learning task. However, these researchers also employed a modified version of this task that required mice to learn the location of the platform in *one trial*. In this study, the rats received four training trials daily, but the platform was moved to a new location each day. Normal mice showed that they acquired the memory for the platform in one trial because their escape latency decreased dramatically between Trial 1 and Trial 2. The escape latency of mice with the NR1 subunit deleted in CA3, however, did not show a change between the two trials. Thus, this experiment implied that the NR1 subunit in CA3 region is necessary for one-trial place learning.

IMPROVING NMDA RECEPTOR FUNCTION MAKES STRONGER MEMORIES   Results of studies discussed thus far indicate that if NMDA receptor function is compromised either by a pharmacological blockade or a genetic deletion of one of its subunits, memory formation can be impaired. Joe Tsien and his colleagues (Tang et al., 1999), however, asked a different question: Can memory formation be *improved* by *enhancing* NMDA function?

During the development of the nervous system, the composition of the NMDA subunits changes. Early in development when the nervous system is being assembled, the NR2B subunits are dominant, but later the NR2B subunits tend to be replaced by NR2A subunits (Figure 8.5). This shift in the ratio of NMDA receptors containing NR2B and NR2A subunits is also associated with different channel opening properties. NMDA receptor complexes that contain NR2B subunits remain open longer than those that contain NR2A subunits and presumably permit more Ca^{2+} to enter the spine. When the NR2B subunits dominate, it is easier to induce LTP than when NR2A subunits dominate.

Based on these findings, Tsien reasoned that if one could genetically modify mice to *overexpress the NR2B subunits*, it might be possible to improve mem-

FIGURE 8.5

The shift in the ratio of NR1–NR2A and NR1–NR2B NMDA receptors that takes place as the brain develops. During the early postnatal period there are relatively more NR1–NR2B receptor complexes (top). With maturation there is a shift in the balance so that there are more NR1–NR2A receptor complexes (bottom).

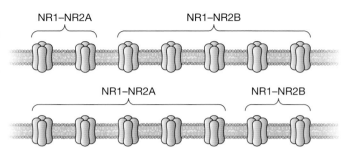

NR1–NR2A   NR1–NR2B

NR1–NR2A   NR1–NR2B

Joe Tsien

ory formation. Tsien was successful in engineering this specific overexpression in the cortex and hippocampus of mice in his study. As expected, these mice showed enhanced LTP compared to control mice. The exciting result, however, was that, in addition to enhanced LTP, these mice also demonstrated enhanced memory formation. Their performance in the place-learning version of the water maze was superior to the control mice. They displayed enhanced place learning as well as stronger contextual and auditory-cue fear conditioning, and their object recognition memory was improved. Tsien called the smart mice Doogie mice after an intellectually precocious teenage character in a once popular television show (Figure 8.6).

NATURAL VARIATION OF NMDA RECEPTOR SUBUNITS   The research just described illustrates the power of modern genetic engineering techniques. Deleting or overexpressing a gene for a subunit of the NMDA receptor can enhance or impair both LTP and memory formation. Memory researchers also have discovered that there is a *natural seasonal variation* in the expression of the NR2B subunits in adult canaries (*Serinus canaries*) (Figure 8.7). During the fall and winter when days are becoming shorter, the songbirds learn a new version of the song they will use to attract a mate. They sing that song during the spring breeding season. Ernest and Kathy Nordeen and their colleagues (Singh et al., 2003) experimentally controlled day length and other variables related to the seasonal changes that control the canary's song learning. Remarkably, they found that in certain regions of the brain that are critical to song learning, the mRNA for NR2B subunits is high in the short daylight period (when the song is being modified) compared to the long daylight periods when the song is stable. A possible interpretation of these results is that

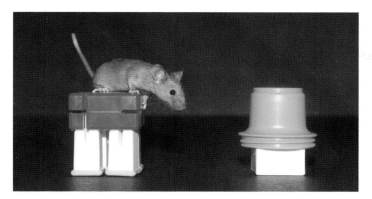

FIGURE 8.6
In the Doogie mouse, the NR1–NR2B NMDA complex is overexpressed in several regions of the brain, including the cortex, hippocampus, and amygdala. (A) Slices from the Doogie mouse show enhanced LTP. (B) The Doogie mouse shows a stable and enhanced memory for a contextual fear-conditioning experience. (Photo provided by J. Z. Tsien.)

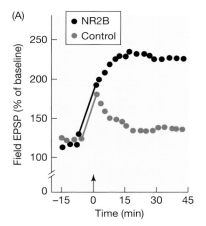

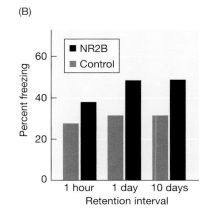

the canary has evolved so that during the period in which it has to learn the complex song, the subunits of the NMDA receptors are adjusted in favor of NR2Bs to facilitate the task.

CAUTIONS AND CAVEATS   Pharmacological, genetic, and natural variation of the NMDA receptor complex provide evidence that the NMDA receptor can make an important contribution to memory function and thus can play an important role in memory formation. However, it is also important to note that: (1) the interpretation of some of these results has been challenged, and (2) there have been reports *that memories can be formed even in the face of a strong pharmacological blockade of NMDA receptors* (e.g., Niewoehner et al., 2007; Saucier and Cain, 1995; Cain, Saucier, and Boon, 1997). The classic Morris et al. (1986) paper reporting that blocking the NMDA receptor with APV impaired the rat's performance on the place-learning task can serve to illustrate this issue. This

FIGURE 8.7
Adult canaries (*Serinus canaries*) experience seasonal variation in the expression of the NR2B subunit of the NMDA receptor. Enhanced expression of this subunit may facilitate learning their mating song. (Photo ©Ene/istockphoto.com)

result is, of course, consistent with the idea that NMDA receptors are important in memory formation.

It is often the case, however, that when important new results are reported, the scientific community greets them with caution and skepticism. A number of researchers challenged the conclusion that APV impaired performance on this task because it interfered with a process critical to memory formation. You will remember that any brain manipulation that alters performance can do so for many reasons. Some researchers believe that APV impaired the processes that support the sensory and motor requirements of the task (Bannerman, Rawlins, and Good, 2006; Keith and Rudy, 1990; Cain, 1997). In fact Saucier and Cain (1995) reported that if you provide rats with the experience of swimming in a pool before you start training on the place-learning task, blocking NMDA receptors and LTP in the dentate gyrus has no effect on performance. Bannerman and his colleagues (2006) have discussed many other examples.

There are several specific lessons to be taken from this discussion.

- Drugs and genetic manipulations can modify behavior without affecting learning and memory.
- These agents can have multiple effects. Even if the targeted molecule or receptor does make a contribution to memory, it might be involved in some other component system that influences behavior.
- Memory formation may take place without the contribution of NMDA receptors.

There is also a more general point that is worth making. As noted, Saucier and Cain (1995) reported that once sensory–motor impairments were reduced, rats easily learned to find the hidden platform even when NMDA receptors were blocked. What should you conclude from this finding? It is tempting to conclude that NMDA receptors do not participate in establishing a memory for the location of the platform. But that would be wrong. Saucier and Cain's observation may mean that there are *other mechanisms that can produce memories* when NMDA receptors are not functional. They do not, however, exclude the possibility that NMDA receptors normally contribute to creating place memories.

The general point is that when a component of the brain is removed and this has no effect on memory formation, one cannot say the component (e.g., brain region, cell, or molecule) is not involved in memory formation when it is normally present. The brain has redundant mechanisms that might substitute for each other. So, *the absence of an effect primarily tells us what the brain can do without the component.* It does not tell us what that component does in the normal brain.

In summary, it is difficult to make a compelling case that a particular component of the brain is involved in memory formation. If it were easy, all of our questions would have been answered by now. Nevertheless, even though the contribution of NMDA receptors to memory formation may be complex and not clearly determined, there is no doubt they are critical to the formation of some memories.

AMPA Receptors and Memory Function

As you know, AMPA receptors play a major role in strengthening synapses. By participating in depolarizing the neuron, they contribute to opening the NMDA calcium channel and thus to initiating intracellular events that strengthen synapses. Moreover, as you have learned, the end product of the biochemical changes that produce LTP is thought to be an increase in AMPA receptor function. Existing receptors may open longer and more of them are present.

Based on these facts one should expect to find evidence that AMPA receptors are involved in both the *formation and retrieval* of a memory. There is evidence that supports this prediction. For example, it is known that object recognition memory critically depends on a cortical region adjacent to the hippocampus called **perirhinal cortex**. Winters and Bussey (2005) infused the AMPA receptor antagonist 6-cyano-7-nitroquinoxaline (CNQX) into the perirhinal cortex of rats to temporarily reduce AMPA receptor function. Infusing this drug before training prevented the rats from forming a memory of the object, while injecting the drug before testing prevented them from retrieving the memory.

Roberto Malinow

FEAR CONDITIONING DRIVES GLUR1 AMPA RECEPTORS INTO SPINES   As discussed in Chapter 3, studies of synaptic plasticity suggest that LTP is in part the result of synaptic activity trafficking GluR1 AMPA receptors into the plasma membrane of dendritic spines. Behavioral procedures that produce fear memories also drive GluR1 receptors into the spines of dendrites located in the amygdala.

In a remarkable set of experiments, Roberto Malinow and his colleagues (Rumpel, LeDoux, Zador, and Malinow, 2005) used genetic engineering methods to create GluR1 AMPA receptors and then injected these receptors into the amygdala. Green fluorescent protein was also expressed by the receptors and allowed neurons that contained these receptors to be visualized (Figure 8.8).

Rats were conditioned by pairing an auditory CS with shock. After the rats were tested for their fear response, they were sacrificed and slices of brain tissue from the basal lateral amygdala were prepared to determine if the behavioral training had driven GluR1 receptors into the spines. Malinow's group was able to detect the presence of these receptors in synapses because when glutamate binds to them a special electrical current can be detected that is slightly different from that produced by endogenous GluR1 receptors. To activate these synapses Malinow's group stimulated the auditory pathway in the thalamus that projects to the amygdala. These experiments revealed that the conditioning experience had driven the GluR1 receptors into the dendritic spines because they were able to detect an increase in the signature response of synapses belonging to the neurons that fluoresced.

PREVENTING AMPA RECEPTOR TRAFFICKING IMPAIRS FEAR CONDITIONING   If the GluR1 AMPA receptor plays a critical role in the support of the fear memory, then it follows that if trafficking this receptor into the spine is prevented, the fear memory should be weak. Malinow's group also used genetic engineering to test this hypothesis. They created and injected a nonfunctional version of the GluR1 subunit receptor that *would compete with the functional receptors for delivery to the membrane*. This nonfunctional unit could be driven into the spine but would not respond properly to glutamate release. You might think of it as a dummy receptor. The experiments revealed that rats with neurons that contained nonfunctional receptors displayed a reduced fear memory (Figure 8.9). This means that the memory for the fear experience as measured by the rat's freezing response depends on trafficking AMPA receptors with functional GluR1 subunits into the membrane.

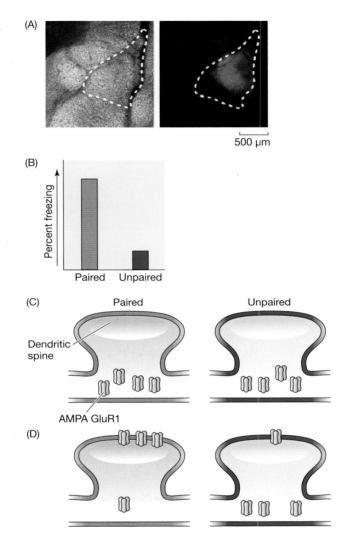

FIGURE 8.8
LTP studies have shown that GluR1 AMPA receptors are inserted into the plasma membrane of dendritic spines in response to synaptic activity. Malinow and his colleagues used a special technique to insert modified glutamate receptors, GluR1, into the lateral amygdala. (A) These receptors were labeled with a fluorescent molecule and could be visualized. (B) Rats with these fluorescent-tag AMPA receptors were tested for fear of a tone paired with shock or tested for fear of a tone unpaired with shock. Rats in the paired condition displayed fear to the tone. The rats were then sacrificed and slices were taken from their brains. An analysis of these slices revealed fear conditioning had driven the GluR1 AMPA receptors into the spines. (C) Schematic representation of the distribution of the GluR1 receptors prior to training. (D) After the training, rats in the paired condition had more GluR1 receptors trafficked into the plasma membrane than rats in the unpaired condition. These results indicate that a behavioral experience that produces fear conditioning also drives AMPA receptors into the synapse. (After Rumpel et al., 2005.)

(A)

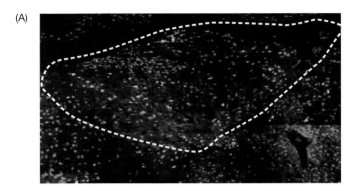

(B)

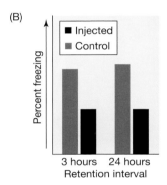

(C)

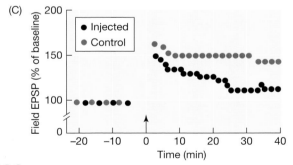

FIGURE 8.9
(A) Modified nonfunctional GluR1 receptors are injected into the lateral amygdala. These modified receptors compete with endogenous functional GluR1 receptors for trafficking into spines. (B) Rats injected with this receptor display impaired fear conditioning to a tone paired with shock. (C) Slices from animals injected with the modified receptor cannot sustain LTP induced in the lateral amygdala. (After Rumpel et al., 2006.)

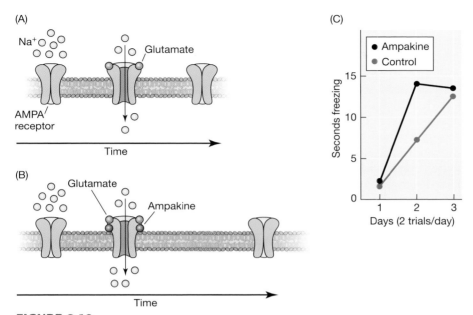

FIGURE 8.10
(A) When glutamate binds to AMPA receptors the conductance channel is briefly opened and this allows positive ions to enter. (B) When ampakines and glutamate both bind to the AMPA receptor, the channel stays open longer and therefore more ions enter and the synaptic response is enhanced. (C) Ampakines enhance the rate of auditory fear conditioning.

AMPAKINES AND COGNITIVE ENHANCEMENT   AMPA receptors play a critical role in initiating the processes that strengthen synapses. The resulting upregulation of these receptors that also occurs is largely responsible for the enhanced synaptic response recorded as LTP (Figure 8.10). The empirical facts behind these conclusions have made AMPA receptors attractive candidates for the development of therapeutics designed to enhance memory and other complex forms of cognition. In this domain, a class of drugs that may enhance cognitive function (called **ampakines**) has been developed by Gary Lynch (Lynch and Gall, 2006).

Ampakines cross the blood–brain barrier and bind to a site on the AMPA receptor. However, they function as neither agonists nor antagonists. Their influence is observed when glutamate binds to the receptor. As you know, when glutamate binds to an AMPA receptor a channel opens and Na^+ enters the cell. Normally this channel rapidly closes. However, when an ampakine also binds to the AMPA receptor it slows down the deactivation or closure of the channel. Functionally, what this means is that when an ampakine is present there will be a prolonged current flow and enhanced synaptic responses. Thus, the neuron will more likely depolarize (which should facilitate the opening of the NMDA-receptor channel) and will also be more likely to release neurotransmitters onto other neurons to which it is connected.

There are a number of reports that ampakines can enhance learning (see Lynch and Gall, 2006, for a review of these). For example, Rogan, Stäubli, and LeDoux (1997) treated rats with an ampakine prior to fear conditioning to a tone paired with very mild shock. They reported that it enhanced the rate at which conditioned fear was established (Figure 8.10C). There is also evidence that ampakines may be used to ameliorate mild memory impairments that develop as we age.

NMDA and AMPA Receptors Make Different Contributions

You will recall that when the NMDA receptor's contribution to LTP was discovered in the hippocampus, researchers found that APV, the NMDA-receptor antagonist, blocked the induction but not the expression of LTP (see Chapter 2). This means that when APV was administered prior to the induction stimulus it prevented LTP, but when it was administered after LTP was established it had no effect. In contrast, AMPA receptors have been shown to be important in both the induction and expression of LTP.

In the context of building memories, these findings suggest that NMDA and AMPA receptors might make different contributions to the acquisition and retrieval of memories. Specifically, as suggested earlier, NMDA receptors should be critical for the acquisition of the memory but not for its retrieval. AMPA receptors, however, should be important for both the acquisition and retrieval of the memory.

Morris and his colleagues (Day, Langston, and Morris, 2003) used a clever one-trial memory task to test this hypothesis. Training occurred in a large open arena that featured two landmarks, a pyramid and a stack of golf balls (Figure 8.11). Rats were first allowed to learn the layout of the arena. The floor of the arena has many small holes that could be filled either with just sand or sand and a food pellet. During the acquisition phase of training, the rat was released into the area twice. Each time it explored the area until it found an uncovered sand well that contained a distinctive food pellet (for example, a banana or cinnamon flavored pellet). The rat's task was to remember the location of the sand wells and the flavor of the pellets they contained.

To determine if the rat remembered the sand-well locations that contained the pellets it was returned to one of four release points and fed one of the pellets (e.g., banana). It was released into the arena, where the two sand wells

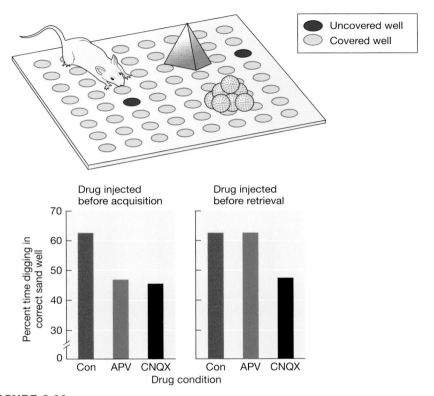

FIGURE 8.11
The top of this figure is a schematic of the arena Morris and his colleagues used to study the role of glutamate receptors in the acquisition and retrieval of a memory for the location of flavored food pellets. On the retrieval test, the two sand wells that contained the flavored pellets on the acquisition trial were uncovered. The rat was fed one of the pellets in the release point. Its task was to remember which sand well contained that pellet during acquisition. When given before acquisition, both APV and CNQX interfered with establishing the food-location memory. However, only CNQX, the AMPA receptor antagonist, interfered with the retrieval of the memory. Con = control group. (After Day et al., 2003.)

that had contained food pellets in the acquisition phase were uncovered. Digging in the sand well that contained banana pellets, it would be rewarded with another banana pellet. However, digging in the other sand well would not yield a food pellet. Each day a new set of flavors was used, and the rats easily learned to dig in the sand well that contained the flavor pellet that they were fed at the release point. About two hours separated the acquisition and retrieval phase of the experiment.

After the rats had learned the task, Morris evaluated the role of NMDA and AMPA receptors in the acquisition and retrieval of the memory of the flavor location. To do this, either the NMDA antagonist (APV) or the AMPA receptor antagonist (CNQX) was injected into the hippocampus. These drugs were injected either before the acquisition phase or before the retrieval phase of the experiment.

Morris found that APV impaired performance when it was injected before the acquisition phase but had no effect when it was injected prior to the retrieval phase. Note that because the rats were not impaired when APV was injected prior to retrieval, we can be confident that the drug did not impair sensory, motor, or motivational processes that are essential to performance. In contrast, CNQX impaired performance when it was injected both prior to the acquisition phase and prior to the retrieval phase. You should recall that Winters and Bussey (2005) reported that AMPA receptors were critical to both the acquisition and retrieval of memories for objects. These results indicate that glutamate receptors (NMDA and AMPA receptors) can play a role in the acquisition and retrieval of a memory similar to the role they play in the induction and expression of LTP. Specifically, NMDA receptors are critical only for acquisition, while AMPA receptors contribute both to acquisition and retrieval.

CaMKII and Memory Formation

Thus far you have learned that NMDA and AMPA receptors can make an important contribution to memory formation. Studies of synaptic plasticity suggest that these receptors are important because opening of the NMDA calcium channel allows a spike of Ca^{2+} to enter the spine. Ca^{2+} is a second messenger and activates another messenger protein, calmodulin, which binds to the kinase CaMKII. This protein plays a critical role in establishing LTP, so one would expect that it also plays an important role in memory formation. Much of what is known about what CaMKII contributes to memory formation comes from studies with genetically engineered mice. The general strategy has been to either remove the CaMKII gene or to overexpress the active form of CaMKII.

It should be noted that the first application of genetic engineering to the study of memory molecules was directed at CaMKII. Alcino Silva and his colleagues successfully deleted the CaMKII gene (Silva, Paylor, Wehner, and Tonegawa, 1992a; Silva, Stevens, Tonegawa, and Wang, 1992b). LTP could not be induced in the CaMKII knockout mice (CaMKII KO) and these mice were severely impaired in both the visible-platform and place-learning versions of the Morris water-escape task (Figure 8.12). These were exciting results. Nevertheless, this pioneering work was also criticized for not completely ruling out the possibility that the mutation caused sensory motor impairments that were responsible for their poor performance.

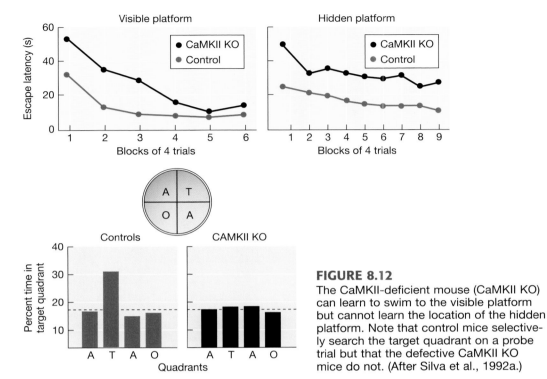

FIGURE 8.12
The CaMKII-deficient mouse (CaMKII KO) can learn to swim to the visible platform but cannot learn the location of the hidden platform. Note that control mice selectively search the target quadrant on a probe trial but that the defective CaMKII KO mice do not. (After Silva et al., 1992a.)

Preventing Autophosphorylation of CaMKII

You will remember that one of the important properties of CaMKII is its capacity to autophosphorylate and remain in an active state. This property is thought to be critical to its role in strengthening synapses. Given the importance of autophosphorylated CaMKII to synaptic plasticity, Giese and his colleagues (Giese, Fedorov, Filipkowski, and Silva, 1998; Irvine, von Hertzen, Plattner, and Giese, 2006) have studied mice that have been genetically engineered to prevent autophosphorylation. Synaptic plasticity studies of these animals indicate that LTP cannot be induced in CA1 by stimulating the Schaffer collateral fibers but that it can be induced in the dentate gyrus by stimulating the mossy fiber pathway (Cooke et al., 2006).

Giese et al. (1998) found that these mice were markedly impaired when trained in the hidden-platform version of the Morris water-escape task. How-

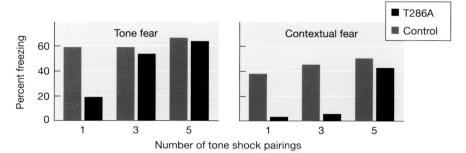

FIGURE 8.13
Autophosphorylation is critical for rapid formation of a fear memory but not essential for memories produced with multiple training trials. In this experiment, mice genetically engineered to impair autophosphorylation of CaMKII (T286A) and control mice received 1, 3, or 5 pairings of a tone and shock. Control mice acquired fear to the context and to the tone after only one pairing; however, the defective mice required several pairings to acquire the fear memory. (After Irvine et al., 2006.)

ever, they were also impaired in learning to swim to the visible platform. Thus, it is difficult to conclude that impaired performance on the place-learning task is a memory formation deficit associated with CaMKII as opposed to a sensory motor impairment.

Under limited training conditions (one trial), these mice also showed a deficit in inhibitory avoidance learning and in contextual and auditory-cue fear conditioning. *However, if they were given only a few extra trials, they were completely normal.* Thus, suppressing the autophosphorylation of CaMKII normally has a significant but limited effect on the formation of memories that support these behaviors (Irvine et al., 2006). However, the finding that with additional training these animals acquired a memory for these tasks suggests that the one-trial impairment is unlikely due to sensory or motor impairment. One important implication of this work is that the autophosphorylation of CaMKII may be critical for the rapid (one-trial) formation of a memory but that other processes can compensate for this contribution when multiple training trials occur (Figure 8.13).

Viral Vector Delivery of CaMKII in Place Learning

There is an interpretation issue that applies to the pioneering Silva study and to Giese's studies. Specifically, the mice in these experiments carried the mutation with them from the time of conception. Thus, it is possible that the muta-tion produced undetected developmental defects in brain function. In this case, poor performance on the memory task could be due to a developmental defect that influenced some other component that contributed to performance and not to some specific memory formation function that depends on CaMKII.

To overcome these interpretative problems one would like to have genetic engineering methodologies that (1) allow alteration of gene expression after the nervous system develops, and (2) restrict the effect to some specific re-gion of the brain thought to support the memory trace. One way this can be accomplished is to use engineering techniques that allow the molecule in question to be directly injected into a particular region of the brain. A rela-tively new technology uses what is called a **viral vector** to deliver a gene to a particular region of the brain of an adult rodent. This technique involves genetically modifying the virus to carry the gene of interest. When the viral vector is then injected into the brain it invades the neurons and delivers the exogenous gene into the genome of the animal where it can then be overex-pressed.

Poulsen and his colleagues (Poulsen et al., 2007) used a viral vector to de-liver CaMKII into the dorsal hippocampus of adult rats to test the hypothesis that an overexpression of this protein enhances memory. Injecting rats with the vector containing CaMKII resulted in a small facilitation of performance on the place-learning version of the Morris water-task. On a probe trial with the plat-form removed, the rats also spent more time searching the quadrant where the platform had been hidden during training. Thus, these results provide additional evidence that CaMKII is involved in the acquisition of new memories.

CaMKII and Fear Memories

Sarina Rodrigues and her colleagues (Rodrigues, Farb, Bauer, LeDoux, and Schafe, 2004) have provided some of the most convincing evidence that CaMKII can play a critical role in the formation of a fear memory. These re-searchers found that CaMKII was present in synapses with NMDA receptors that contained NR2B subunits. They then found that fear conditioning in-creased the presence of phosphorylated CaMKII in dendritic spines, indicat-ing that the conditioning experience activated this kinase. In addition, they observed that a drug (KN-62) that inhibits CaMKII activation blocked the ac-quisition of both contextual and auditory fear conditioning and also prevented LTP in this region of the brain (Figure 8.14). This is exactly the pattern of re-sults one would expect based on the role of CaMKII in synaptic plasticity. You will learn in Chapter 16 that the basolateral region of the amygdala is believed to be a critical memory site for fear conditioning.

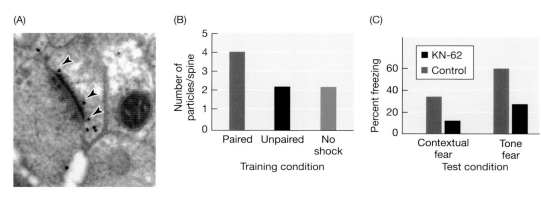

FIGURE 8.14
Fear conditioning produces increased phosphorylated CaMKII in dendritic spines in the amygdala. (A) A micrograph showing particles of phosphorylated CaMKII in a spine. (B) Rats that had received paired presentations of a tone and shock have more particles of phosphorylated CaMKII in spines than control animals that received either no shock or unpaired presentations of the tone and shock. (C) KN-62, which inhibits the phosphorylation of CaMKII, impairs both contextual and tone fear conditioning. (After Rodrigues et al., 2004.)

Summary

Studies of synaptic plasticity have strongly implicated glutamate receptors (NMDA and AMPA receptors) and CaMKII as major components in the chain of events that leads to strengthening of synapses. Both pharmacological and genetic engineering methodologies have been used to determine if these molecules are also critical to memory formation.

There are a large number of reports that NMDA receptors make a critical contribution to the acquisition, but not the retrieval, of some forms of memory. Such studies have revealed that compromising the contribution of these receptors can impair memory formation, while enhancing the NMDA calcium channel function can enhance memory formation.

Studies of AMPA receptors have revealed that they play a critical role in both the acquisition and retrieval of memories. Particularly striking is that just as they can be driven into synapses by high-frequency stimulation used in LTP experiments, they can also be driven into spines by fear conditioning. Moreover, if normal AMPA receptors are not driven into spines, the acquisition of a fear memory is impaired. In addition, delaying the closure of AMPA receptor channels with ampakines appears to provide a potential therapy for enhancing the laying down of memory traces.

Behavioral studies have also provided evidence that CaMKII contributes to translating experience into behavior. The role of CaMKII in fear conditioning is especially compelling.

References

Bannerman, D. M., Rawlins, J. N., and Good, M. A. (2006). The drugs don't work—or do they? Pharmacological and transgenic studies of the contribution of NMDA and GluRA-containing AMPA receptors to hippocampal-dependent memory. *Psychopharmacology, 8,* 533–566.

Cain, D. P. (1997). LTP, NMDA, genes and learning. *Current Opinion in Neurobiology, 7,* 235–242.

Cain, D. P., Saucier, D., and Boon, F. (1997). Testing hypotheses of spatial learning: the role of NMDA receptors and NMDA-mediated long-term potentiation. *Behavioral Brain Research, 84,* 179–193.

Campeau, S., Miserendino, M. J., and Davis, M. (1992). Intra-amygdala infusion of the N-methyl-D-aspartate receptor antagonist AP5 blocks acquisition but not expression of fear-potentiated startle to an auditory conditioned stimulus. *Behavioral Neuroscience, 106,* 569–574.

Cooke, S. F., Wu, J., Plattner, F., Errington, M., Rowan, M., Peters, M., Hirano, A., Bradshaw, K. D., Anwyl, R., Bliss, T. V., and Giese, K. P. (2006). Autophosphorylation of alphaCaMKII is not a general requirement for NMDA receptor-dependent LTP in the adult mouse. *Journal of Physiology, 574,* 805–818.

Day, M., Langston, R., and Morris, R. G. (2003). Glutamate-receptor-mediated encoding and retrieval of paired-associate learning. *Nature, 424,* 205–209.

Fanselow, M. S. and Kim, J. J. (1994). Acquisition of contextual Pavlovian fear conditioning is blocked by application of an NMDA receptor antagonist D,L-2-amino-5-phosphonovaleric acid to the basolateral amygdala. *Behavioral Neuroscience, 108,* 210–212.

Giese, K. P., Fedorov, N. B., Filipkowski, R. K., and Silva, A. J. (1998). Autophosphorylation at Thr286 of the alpha calcium-calmodulin kinase II in LTP and learning. *Science, 279,* 870–873.

Irvine, E. E., von Hertzen, L. S., Plattner, F., and Giese, K. P. (2006). AlphaCaMKII autophosphorylation: A fast track to memory. *Trends in Neurosciences, 8,* 459–65.

Keith, J. R. and Rudy, J. W. (1990). Why NMDA receptor-dependent long-term potentiation may not be a mechanism of learning and memory: reappraisal of the NMDA receptor blockade strategy. *Psychobiology, 18,* 251–257.

Lynch, G. and Gall, C. M. (2006). Ampakines and the threefold path to cognitive enhancement. *Trends in Neurosciences, 10,* 554–562.

Matus-Amat, P., Higgins, E. A., Sprunger, D., Wright-Hardesty, K., and Rudy, J. W. (2007). The role of dorsal hippocampus and basolateral amygdala NMDA receptors in the acquisition and retrieval of context and contextual fear memories. *Behavioral Neuroscience, 12,* 721–731.

Morris, R. G., Anderson E., Lynch, G. S., and Baudry, M. (1986). Selective impairment of learning and blockade of long-term potentiation by an N-methyl-D-aspartate receptor antagonist, AP5. *Nature, 319,* 774–776.

Morris, R. G., Davis, S., and Butcher, S. P. (1990). Hippocampal synaptic plasticity and NMDA receptors: A role in information storage? *Philos Trans R Soc Lond B Biol Sci, 329,* 187–204.

Nakazawa, K., Sun, L. D., Quirk, M. C., Rondi-Reig, L., Wilson, M. A., and Tonegawa, S. (2003.) Hippocampal CA3 NMDA receptors are crucial for memory acquisition of one-time experience. *Neuron, 38,* 305–315.

Niewoehner, B., Single, F. N., Hvalby, O., Jensen, V., Borgloh, S. M., Seeburg, P. H., Rawlins, J. N., Sprengel, R., and Bannerman, D. M. (2007). Impaired spatial working memory but spared spatial reference memory following functional loss of NMDA receptors in the dentate gyrus. *European Journal of Neuroscience, 25,* 837–846.

Poulsen, D. J., Standing, D., Bullshields, K., Spencer, K., Micevych, P. E., and Babcock, A. M. (2007). Overexpression of hippocampal Ca^{2+}/calmodulin-dependent protein kinase II improves spatial memory. *Journal of Neuroscience Research, 85,* 735–739.

Rodrigues, S. M., Farb, C. R., Bauer, E. P., LeDoux, J. E., and Schafe, G. E. (2004). Pavlovian fear conditioning regulates Thr286 autophosphorylation of Ca^{2+}/calmodulin-dependent protein kinase II at lateral amygdala synapses. *Journal of Neuroscience, 24,* 3281–3288.

Rogan, M. T., Stäubli, U. V., and LeDoux, J. E. (1997). AMPA receptor facilitation accelerates fear learning without altering the level of conditioned fear acquired. *Journal of Neuroscience, 17,* 5928–5935.

Rumpel, S., LeDoux, J. E., Zador, A., and Malinow, R. (2005). Postsynaptic receptor trafficking underlying a form of associative learning. *Science, 308,* 83–88.

Saucier, D. and Cain, D. P. (1995). Spatial learning without NMDA receptor-dependent long-term potentiation. *Nature, 378,* 186–184.

Silva, A. J., Paylor, R., Wehner, J. M., and Tonegawa, S. (1992a). Impaired spatial learning in alpha-calcium-calmodulin kinase II mutant mice. *Science, 257,* 206–211.

Silva, A. J., Stevens, C. F., Tonegawa, S., and Wang, Y. (1992b). Deficient hippocampal long-term potentiation in alpha-calcium-calmodulin kinase II mutant mice. *Science, 257,* 201–206.

Singh, T. D., Heinrich, J. E., Wissman, A. M., Brenowitz, E. A., Nordeen, E. J., and Nordeen, K. W. (2003). Seasonal regulation of NMDA receptor NR2B mRNA in the adult canary song system. *Journal of Neurobiology, 54,* 593–603.

Stote, D. L. and Fanselow, M. S. (2004). NMDA receptor modulation of incidental learning in Pavlovian context conditioning. *Behavioral Neuroscience, 118,* 253–257.

Tang, Y. P., Shimizu, E., Dube, G. R., Rampon, C., Kerchner, G. A., Zhuo, M., Liu, G., and Tsien, J. Z. (1999). Genetic enhancement of learning and memory in mice. *Nature, 401,* 63–69.

Tsien, J. Z., Huerta, P. T., and Tonegawa, S. (1996). The essential role of hippocampal CA1 NMDA receptor-dependent synaptic plasticity in spatial memory. *Cell, 87,* 1327–1338.

Winters, B. D. and Bussey, T. J. (2005). Glutamate receptors in perirhinal cortex mediate encoding, retrieval, and consolidation of object recognition memory. *Journal of Neuroscience, 25,* 4243–4251.

Memory Consolidation: Translation and Transcription

As you have learned, many researchers believe that our memory for some particular experience evolves through a succession of memory traces with different properties. The initial short-term memory trace is thought to (1) rapidly emerge, (2) have a rapid decay rate, and (3) be vulnerable to disruption. The long-term memory trace is thought to (1) require time to develop, (2) have a much slower decay rate, and (3) be less vulnerable to disruption (as previously illustrated in Figure 7.3 and reproduced in Figure 9.1A).

One implication of these assumptions is that if you are asked to retrieve a memory very shortly after it has been established, your memory for the event will depend on the rapidly induced short-term memory trace. However, because this trace will decay, if you are tested later, your memory will depend on retrieval of the long-term memory trace. You are not aware of these dynamics because before the short-term trace decays, the long-term trace emerges (Figure 9.1B). Neurobiologists are motivated by another implication, that is, that the molecular requirements for the two traces are different.

FIGURE 9.1
Shortly after an experience, the memory retrieval is supported by the short-term trace. As this trace decays, a more stable, long-term memory trace is generated that can support memory retrieval for a much longer period of time.

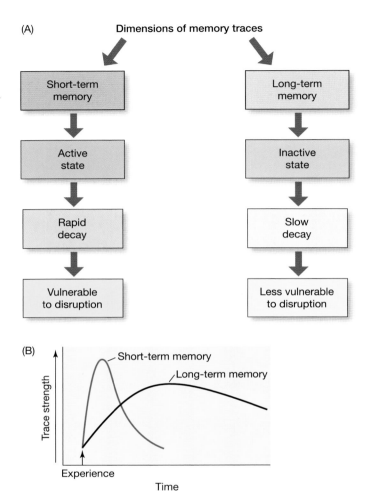

(A) Dimensions of memory traces

Short-term memory → Active state → Rapid decay → Vulnerable to disruption

Long-term memory → Inactive state → Slow decay → Less vulnerable to disruption

(B) Trace strength vs. Time. Short-term memory, Long-term memory. Experience.

More specifically, the construction or consolidation of a stable, long-term memory trace requires different or additional molecular components than does the short-term trace. These behavioral and neurobiological assumptions have determined how neurobiologists have approached the problem of memory consolidation.

The purpose of this chapter is to describe how these ideas have influenced our understanding of how memories are consolidated. First, we present the logic of the research paradigm used to study these issues. We then consider the role of transcription processes in making long-term memories, focusing on the transcription factor CREB. Finally, we discuss translation processes with respect to long-term memories, specifically the *de novo* protein synthesis hypothesis.

The Generic Research Paradigm

The general experimental approach used to pursue issues about memory consolidation is shown in Figure 9.2. The experiment illustrated there begins by providing the subject a training experience, such as fear conditioning. To determine if a particular molecule is critical to consolidation, the effect of a drug or genetic manipulation designed to interfere with that molecule's function is compared to a control condition. The drug or gene treatment is thus one critical variable.

The second important variable is the retention interval, that is, the time between training and testing. At least two retention intervals are sampled. One interval is short, typically about 1–2 hours, while the other is much longer, often around 24 hours. It is assumed that the memory revealed by the short-retention test is supported by the short-term memory trace and the memory revealed at the longer retention interval is supported by the long-term trace.

The logic of this strategy can be further understood by considering a hypothetical experiment in which a drug is used to evaluate the contribution of some particular molecule (M_x) to memory consolidation. The drug is thought to degrade the contribution M_x makes to memory consolidation and, in this case, is infused into the brain prior to training. Figure 9.3 shows two possible outcomes produced by the drug. The pattern of data shown in Figure 9.3A indicates that the drug impaired performance at the long, 24-hour retention interval but had no effect on performance at the short, 1-hour retention interval. These results would be consistent with the hypothesis that M_x contributes to the consolidation of the long-term memory trace. They also support an even stronger conclusion: The short-term memory trace did not depend on a contribution from M_x. This is because retention at the short interval was not impaired by the drug.

The pattern of data in Figure 9.3B shows that the drug impaired performance at both the short and long retention intervals. These data are more difficult to interpret. They could mean that the construction of both the short-term and the long-term memory trace requires a contribution from M_x. However, these data are also consistent with the hypothesis that the drug used to influ-

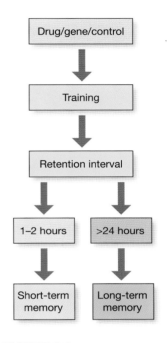

FIGURE 9.2

This figure illustrates the generic research design for determining the contribution of a particular molecule(s) to memory storage. A drug or gene is evaluated by assessing its effect on memory at two retention intervals—a short interval (1–2 hours) designed to assess short-term memory (STM) and a longer interval, usually about 24 hours, designed to assess long-term memory (LTM).

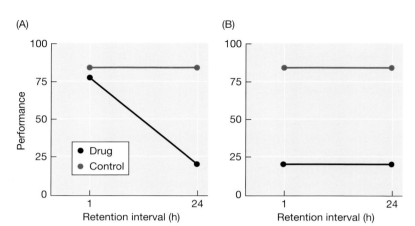

FIGURE 9.3
(A) The drug targeted at M_x impaired performance at the 24-hour retention interval but had no effect at the 1-hour retention interval. This result is consistent with the hypothesis that M_x is important for the consolidation of the long-term memory trace and is not critical for the short-term memory trace. (B) The treatment impaired performance at both the 1-hour and 24-hour retention interval. This result is consistent with the hypothesis that M_x contributes to both short-term memory and long-term memory but is also consistent with other interpretations.

ence M_x interfered with how the animal normally sampled the environment (see Chapter 7). If one repeated the experiment but infused the drug *after training* and got the same result, then this interpretation could be ruled out.

Our survey of the mechanisms involved in producing LTP (see Chapters 2 through 6) suggests that it is possible to induce a short-lasting form of LTP that only requires the post-translation modification of key existing proteins, such as the phosphorylation of CaMKII and AMPA receptors. Longer-lasting forms of LTP, however, appear to require activity-dependent initiation of transcription and translation. It should thus come as no surprise that much of the work on understanding the molecular basis of memory consolidation is guided by the hypothesis that *transcription and translation processes play a critical role in the consolidation of stable memories.* We will first consider some of the research that indicates that transcription processes can play a role in producing stable memories and then discuss the role of protein synthesis.

Transcription Processes

As you know, studies of LTP have supported the idea that enduring synaptic changes can require that the inducing high-frequency stimulus initiate what

FIGURE 9.4
A behavioral experience such as inhibitory avoidance training initiates a genomic signaling cascade that results in new plasticity
products (mRNA and protein) needed to consolidate the memory
for the experience. (Photo courtesy of James McGaugh.)

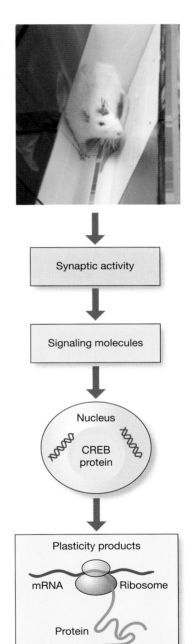

is called a genomic signaling cascade (see Chapter 4). This
cascade results in new transcripts (mRNAs) emerging
from the nucleus and eventually making their way to
synapses, either as mRNAs or new protein.

Some researchers also believe that long-term memories
require new transcripts that are produced by a *behaviorally
induced genomic cascade* (Figure 9.4). This means that the
construction of a stable memory requires that the to-be-
remembered experience initiates a signaling cascade that results in new mRNAs and new protein.

Although we have not focused on the study of invertebrate learning, it is important to remember that the first
evidence that long-term memory might depend on behavior initiating a genomic cascade came from researchers who
embraced the simple-systems approach (see Chapter 2). Eric
Kandel's laboratory demonstrated that transcription inhibitors blocked *Aplysia's* long-term but not short-term
memory for a tail-shock experience, and specifically implicated a role in this process for the transcription factor,
cAMP-responsive element-binding protein, called CREB
(see Chapter 4). (See Kandel, 2001, for a summary of some
of this work.) Genetic and behavioral research using the fruit
fly, *Drosophila melanogaster*, has also played an important
role in these ideas (Yin and Tully, 1996).

A variety of studies have provided evidence that general transcription inhibitors can impair long-term memory
(Matthies, 1989). Much of the research in this field, however, has been driven by the more specific hypothesis that
the transcription factor CREB is especially involved in the
production of **memory genes**. So this protein will be our
primary focus.

CREB and Memory

The idea that long-term memory may depend on the transcription of memory genes regulated by CREB received a

FIGURE 9.5

Mice genetically engineered to repress CREB display fear when tested 3 hours after training but not when tested 24 hours after training. These results are consistent with the hypothesis that long-term memory but not short-term memory requires plasticity products transcribed by CREB. (After Bourtchaladze et al., 1994.)

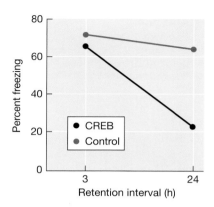

major boost when Rusiko Bourtchaladze and Alcino Silva and their colleagues (Bourtchaladze et al., 1994) reported that mice genetically engineered to repress CREB (CREB knockout mice) displayed normal fear conditioning when the retention interval was short but were impaired when the retention interval was long (Figure 9.5). These mice also were severely impaired when required to learn the place-learning version of the Morris water-escape task.

To complicate matters, however, Kogan et al. (1997) reported that the mutant mice used by Bourtchaladze et al. (1994) had normal long-term memories when the time between training trials was increased. Thus, just a small variation in the training protocol rendered these mice normal. Subsequently, other researchers used a conditional knockout methodology that eliminated CREB in the hippocampus and throughout the brain (Balschun et al., 2003). These mice were not impaired on any of the tasks Bourtchaladze and Silva used. Moreover, enduring LTP could be induced in slices from these brains.

These results with genetically modified CREB are distressingly complex. They could mean that CREB is not involved in transcribing genes needed to make long-term memories. However, it is also possible that there are other transcription factors that can substitute for CREB when it is genetically repressed. Thus, in normal mice CREB might play a role in transcribing memory-making genes, but neurons have redundant mechanisms that can substitute for CREB when it is rendered nonfunctional.

John Guzowski

Other researchers have used a more regional and temporally specific methodology for targeting the disruption of CREB protein levels to study its role in memory storage. John Guzowski and Jim McGaugh (1997) used what is called an **antisense methodology** to disrupt CREB protein level. Antisense oligode-

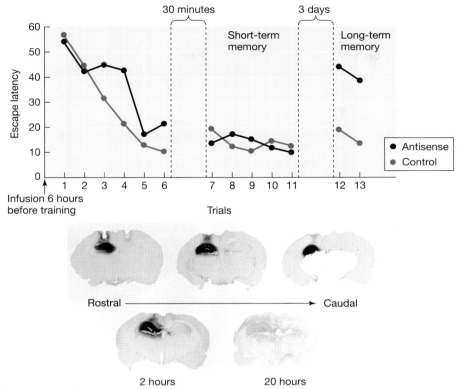

FIGURE 9.6
Infusing an antisense DNA that blocks CREB translation leads to impaired long-term memory for place learning in the Morris water-escape task, but does not affect short-term memory. Note that rats injected with the antisense performed as well as the control rats when the retention interval was only 30 minutes but displayed much longer escape latencies than controls when the retention interval was 3 days. The bottom photograph shows the extent and duration of the antisense. Note that the antisense was no longer present 20 hours after training. (After Guzowski and McGaugh,1997; photo courtesy of John Guzowski.)

oxynucleotides can be made that will interfere with the translation of particular proteins and they can be injected into regions of the brain thought to be memory storage sites. The rationale is that if the antisense is administered long enough before a behavioral experience, no CREB will be available to transcript the new mRNAs needed to produce the enduring memory. Guzowski and McGaugh infused antisense DNA for CREB into the dorsal hippocampus and 6 hours later trained rats on the place-learning version of the Morris water-escape task. They reasoned that if memory genes are transcribed by CREB protein, then reducing available CREB by blocking its translation should

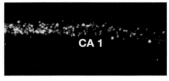

| Naive | Unpaired | Paired |

FIGURE 9.7
A contextual fear conditioning experience activates CREB-mediated transcription in the CA1 region of the hippocampus. Animals in the unpaired condition were housed in the conditioning chamber for 24 hours before they were shocked. Animals in the paired condition received a single shock 2 minutes after being placed into the context. (After Impey et al., 1998; photo courtesy of D. Storm.)

impair long-term memory. Consistent with this reasoning, their rats were normal during training but when tested 3 days later were markedly impaired compared to control rats (Figure 9.6). Unfortunately, the antisense method has not been used to evaluate the role of CREB in other tasks.

If genes transcribed by CREB contribute to making long-term memories, then it follows that a behavioral experience that produces a long-term memory should activate transcription that depends on CREB. Impey et al. (1998) have evaluated this hypothesis. They reported that both fear conditioning and inhibitory avoidance training activate CREB-mediated transcription in both the hippocampus and the amygdala. Figure 9.7 provides an example of the activation of CREB-mediated transcription in hippocampus CA1 neurons produced by contextual fear conditioning.

Studies of LTP have identified kinase-signaling pathways that can lead to the activation of CREB-mediated transcription. Two of these are the PKA kinase and the MAP kinase (see Chapter 4). Drugs targeted to inhibit these kinases have been shown to reduce CREB-mediated transcription (Impey et al., 1998). Given these observations, Glenn Schafe and his colleagues (Schafe, Nadel, Sullivan, Harris, and LeDoux, 1999) injected drugs that inhibited either PKA or MAP kinase into the amygdala and found that in both cases long-term memory for both contextual and auditory-cue fear conditioning were reduced. No evidence was presented that these drugs actually inhibited CREB transcription processes. Nevertheless, these results are consistent with the idea that long-term memory requires CREB-mediated transcription.

Under some conditions of training, normal rats fail to display a long-term fear memory to a visual cue (such as light) that has been paired with shock. This can happen when the **intertrial interval**—the time between the light–shock pairings—is very short (3–15 seconds). When the intertrial interval is short, rats display a short-term but not long-term memory for the conditioning experi-

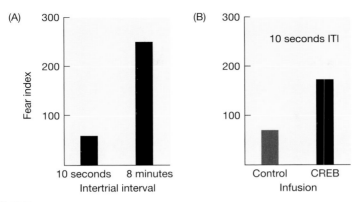

FIGURE 9.8
(A) This graph illustrates the results of a long-term memory test when the intertrial interval (ITI), the time separating light–shock conditioning trials, was either 10 seconds or 8 minutes. Note that long-term memory was poor when the ITI was 10 seconds compared to when the ITI was 8 minutes. (B) This graph shows that the impaired long-term memory normally found when the ITI is only 10 seconds can be eliminated by injecting a virus that contains CREB into the basolateral amygdala prior to the conditioning trials.

ence (Figure 9.8A). Sheena Josselyn and her colleagues (Josselyn et al., 2001), however, were able to prevent the long-term memory impairment associated with the short intertrial interval. They used special methods to inject CREB into the amygdala so that it was overexpressed in the region where the memory is stored. During the period in which the CREB was overexpressed, the mice were able to acquire a long-term memory of the light–shock experience (Figure 9.8B). Moreover, Josselyn and her colleagues (Han et al., 2007) have shown that neurons with increased CREB function are more likely than other neurons to participate in fear conditioning. These results further support the belief that genes transcribed by CREB participate in memory storage.

Critical Activity-Dependent Memory Genes

One of the issues facing the genomic signaling hypothesis is that as yet no one has developed any strong hypothesis about the relevant memory genes that are transcribed in response to memory-producing behavioral events. Are they special or are they just the same ones that generate the proteins that are phosphorylated to produce the short-term trace?

One gene that might be important is an immediate early gene, activity-regulated cytoskeleton-associated protein, called **Arc**. This gene is rapidly transcribed in the hippocampus when rats explore novel environments (Guzowski,

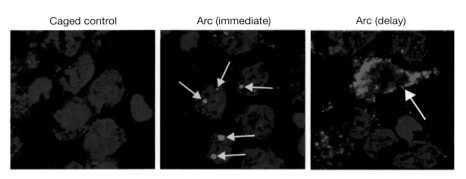

Caged control   Arc (immediate)   Arc (delay)

FIGURE 9.9

Exploring a novel context activates the immediate early gene Arc in the CA1 region of the hippocampus. Note that Arc is initially seen in the nucleus of the cell (immediate) but when rats are sacrificed 20 minutes after exploration (delay), Arc can be seen in the cytoplasm. (Photo provided by John Guzowski et al., 2001.)

McNaughton, Barnes, and Worley, 1999; Huff et al., 2006) or are required to learn the location of the hidden platform in the Morris water-escape task (Guzowski, McNaughton, Barnes, and Worley, 2001). Arc also leaves the nucleus in about 15 or 20 minutes (Figure 9.9). Moreover, when the expression of this gene is inhibited, rats do not show good retention of either inhibitory avoidance learning (McIntyre et al., 2005) or the location of the hidden platform after they have been trained on the Morris water-escape task (Guzowski et al., 2000). These results are promising, and future research will likely focus on the identification of other activity-dependent genes and what they do.

Summary of Transcription Processes

The idea that the construction of long-term memories depends on molecular products resulting from a genomic cascade emerged directly from studies of LTP. Much research has focused on the transcription factor CREB. The repression of this gene has produced somewhat mixed results, suggesting that other transcription factors might substitute for CREB. However, the antisense methodology has revealed a role for CREB in establishing a long-term spatial memory. Moreover, fear conditioning activates CREB-mediated transcription in both the amygdala and hippocampus.

Further evidence that CREB can transcribe genes needed for long-term memory is provided by studies showing that the injection of CREB into the amygdala can prevent a long-term fear memory impairment and that neurons containing excess CREB are more likely to participate in fear memories than neurons that do not. There is very little understanding of just which genes transcribed by CREB are critical for long-term memory. However, one possibility is the immediate early gene Arc, which is rapidly transcribed and the product of which leaves the nucleus within about 20 minutes after its transcription.

The *De Novo* Protein Synthesis Hypothesis

Transcription processes only generate new mRNA. However, as you know, these transcripts must be translated into protein to be functional. The idea that protein synthesis is critical for the consolidation of long-term memories is often referred to as the *de novo* **protein synthesis hypothesis**. According to this view, the consolidation of the memory trace requires that the to-be-remembered experience initiate the synthesis of the new proteins. Flexner, Flexner, and Stellar (1963) put forth this hypothesis long before anything was known about mechanisms of synaptic plasticity, and hundreds of studies were published in the 60s and 70s on this topic (Davis and Squire, 1984).

This hypothesis was tested by using drugs that block protein synthesis—antibiotics such anisomycin, puromycin, and cycloheximine. The rationale for these experiments was that if administering the protein synthesis inhibitor prior to behavioral training impaired long-term retention, then the construction of the memory trace required *de novo* protein synthesis.

These drugs were often injected systemically (into the body cavity), where they temporarily blocked the synthesis of all new proteins. There was never any doubt that these drugs could produce amnesia for the training events. However, because these antibiotics often had major hormonal and neural side effects, including making the animal sick, many researchers were reluctant to conclude that the reason these protein synthesis inhibitors produced a memory impairment was because they blocked protein synthesis (Davis and Squire, 1984; Gold, 2006; Martinez, Jensen, and McGaugh, 1981; Routtenberg and Rekart, 2005). Thus, for some time the idea went into hibernation.

The hypothesis took on new life, however, when Eric Kandel's laboratory (Montarlo et al., 1986) reported that the application of two different protein synthesis inhibitors to the abdominal ganglia of *Aplysia* (see Chapter 2) blocked the long-term retention of its memory for a tail shock but did not have any effect on short-term retention. The effect of these drugs was time dependent. The drugs were only effective if applied at the time of training. Because these drugs were applied directly to the neurons that were believed to support the memory, researchers were encouraged to believe that protein synthesis inhibitors were interfering with activity-dependent, long-term modification of synaptic strength by blocking protein synthesis. This belief has been carried forward in many studies of LTP (see Chapter 4) that have shown that applying protein synthesis inhibitors to the hippocampus slice preparation can block L-LTP but not S-LTP.

Studies of the role of protein synthesis are generally motivated by two hypotheses:

1. Protein synthesis is critical for the formation of the long-term memory trace but not for the induction of the short-term memory trace.

2. It is the synthesis of *new* proteins induced by the training experience, not just some existing level of protein, that is critical for consolidation. This means that the protein synthesis inhibitor must be administered around the time of the behavioral experience that produces the memory. Delaying the administration of the inhibitor for several hours should have no effect on memory retention.

A study by Bourtchaladze and his colleagues (1998) illustrates how these hypotheses are tested. Mice were injected systemically with the protein synthesis inhibitor anisomycin prior to fear conditioning. They were tested at several different times after training. The results for 1-, 6-, and 24-hour retention tests are presented in Figure 9.10A. Note that the drug had no effect at the 1-hour retention interval but impaired retention at the longer, 6- and 24-hour tests. These results are consistent with the idea that a short-term memory trace can be formed that does not depend on protein synthesis, while a long-term memory trace requires new proteins.

This Bourtchaladze study also varied the interval between training and the delivery of anisomycin and found that anisomycin was effective when it was given immediately after training but had no effect when given either 3 or 24 hours later (Figure 9.10B). Their results imply that:

• Memories can be retrieved from a short-term memory trace or a long-term memory trace.

• The two traces have different molecular requirements: the long-term trace but not the short-term trace requires new proteins, synthesized in response to neural activity *induced by the training experience*.

• Blocking protein synthesis per se is not important. It must be blocked shortly after the behavioral experience.

Bourtchaladze's results illustrate some general points. However, they are subject to most of the same criticisms leveled at results based on systemic administration of the anisomycin that were reported when the protein synthesis hypothesis was initially evaluated (Davis and Squire, 1984).

To avoid some of the problems associated with the systemic injection of protein synthesis inhibitors, researchers often inject the drug directly into a region of the brain that is thought to contain the synapses that hold the memory trace.

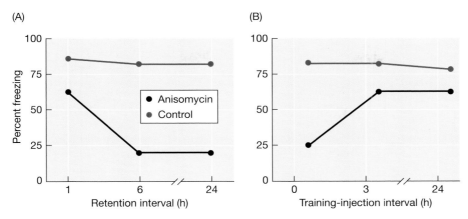

FIGURE 9.10
(A) Anisomycin disrupts retention performance at the 6- and 24-hour retention intervals but not at the 1-hour interval. (B) The effect of anisomycin depends on the interval between training and the injection. It only interfered with memory formation when it was given immediately (0 hour) after training. (After Bourtchaladze et al., 1998.)

For example, Schafe and his colleagues (1999) injected anisomycin directly into the basolateral region of the amygdala where a fear memory trace is believed to be stored (see Chapter 16). Anisomycin was injected into the amygdala just after rats were conditioned to an auditory cue paired with shock. These rats displayed normal freezing at a 1-hour testing interval but very little freezing when they were tested 24 hours later (Figure 9.11). Thus, the pattern of results was consistent with the idea that the long-term memory trace requires the synthesis of new proteins but the short-term memory trace does not.

Methodological Issues in the Use of Drugs

There are many reports that protein synthesis inhibitors can impair the consolidation of the long-term memory trace (e.g., Biedenkapp and Rudy, 2004; Schafe et al., 1999; Barrientos, O'Reilly, and Rudy, 2002; Parsons, Gafford, Baruch, Riedner, and Helmstetter, 2006). However, these studies provide no additional insights about the molecular requirements of long-term memory, so there is no need to discuss them. Instead, we must deal with important methodological issues that cloud the use of protein synthesis inhibitors.

No one doubts that drugs like anisomycin, when given in large amounts, can profoundly block the synthesis of new proteins. Nor does anyone doubt that they can disturb memory storage. However, protein synthesis inhibitors

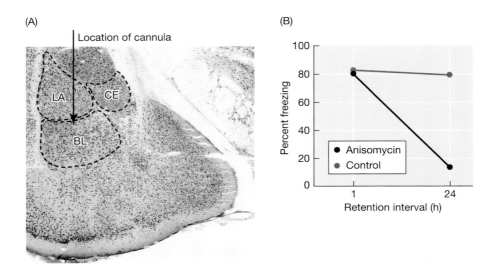

FIGURE 9.11
(A) This figure shows a section of the amygdala and illustrates the location of the cannula in the basolateral (BL) region of the amygdala through which anisomycin was injected. (B) Anisomycin did not impair performance when the retention test was given 1 hour after training but did impair performance when the retention interval was 24 hours. These results are thus consistent with the *de novo* protein synthesis hypothesis. (Photo courtesy of Serge Campeau and Cher Masini; data after Schafe et al., 1999.)

are also toxic and have many side effects (Figure 9.12). In fact, Morris et al. (2006) reported that anisomycin kills neurons around the site of the injection. Moreover, in addition to temporarily blocking protein synthesis, when applied to neurons these drugs initiate a process called **gene superconductance**—a genomic signaling cascade that causes an overproduction of mRNAs (Radulovic and Tronson, 2007). This abnormal production of mRNAs and their subsequent translation into protein can interfere with the normal molecular processes that store the memory trace.

The question still remains, does anisomycin or any other protein synthesis inhibitor produce amnesia because it blocks the synthesis of proteins needed to stabilize the memory, or does it produce amnesia because of *some other effect it has on neurons* (Gold, 2006; Radulovic and Tronson, 2007; Rudy, Biedenkapp, Moineau, and Bolding, 2006; Routtenberg and Rekart, 2005; Rudy, 2007)? Rather than producing amnesia by blocking protein synthesis, such drugs might just disrupt other processes that support the building of an enduring memory trace.

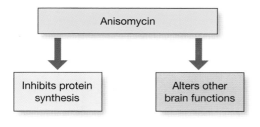

FIGURE 9.12
In addition to blocking protein synthesis, anisomycin has other effects on neurons. The drug is toxic and can kill neurons. It also causes an excessive release of neurotransmitters in the region of the injection and induces genomic signaling cascades in the neuron that result in an overproduction of mRNAs. These additional effects make it difficult to accept the conclusion that the reason anisomycin disrupts memory consolidation is because it inhibits protein synthesis.

Paul Gold and his colleagues (Canal, Chang, and Gold, 2007) have provided a dramatic example of the seriousness of this problem. They injected anisomycin into the amygdala and used microdialyis (see Chapter 10, Figure 10.5, for a description of this methodology) to measure its effect on the release of several neurotransmitters (norepinephrine, dopamine, and serotonin) in the same brain region. They discovered that not only did anisomycin inhibit protein synthesis in the amygdala, it also drastically increased the levels of these transmitters. You will learn in Chapter 10 that norepineprhine itself has an important role in modulating memory storage processes.

Gold's group then asked if the amnesic properties of anisomycin are due to its ability to block protein synthesis or due to its effect on the release of norepinephrine. Some rats were injected with just anisomycin, others were injected with anisomycin and propranolol (which antagonizes the receptors in the brain that are occupied by norepinephrine and thus somewhat negates its effect). Anisomycin blocked protein synthesis, whether injected alone or in combination with propranolol. Anisomycin alone also interfered with the consolidation of the inhibitory avoidance memory. The most important result, however, was that propranolol administered in conjunction with anisomycin markedly reduced the amnesic effect. Thus, the proper interpretation of the effects of anisomycin is that it did not produce amnesia by blocking protein synthesis. Instead, it produced amnesia because of other effects it had on neurons.

Given the serious side effects associated with the use of broad-scale protein synthesis inhibitors, their continued use is no longer warranted and cannot further advance our understanding of the molecular basis of long-term memory. There is, however, a very strong conclusion that can be reached from the observation that protein synthesis inhibitors such as anisomycin do not impair memory when the retention interval is short. Specifically, *there exists a short-term memory trace whose construction does not require the behavioral experience to induce the synthesis of new proteins.*

What Specific Proteins Are Translated?

In addition to the above issues related to the use of drugs, antibiotics like anisomycin are *general* protein synthesis inhibitors—they block the synthesis of *all* proteins. Thus, they tell us nothing about what new proteins need to be synthesized to support long-term memory. Part of the problem in advancing the case that memory storage depends on protein synthesis is that as yet researchers have identified very few specific proteins that might be synthesized in response to a behavioral experience. Nevertheless, some potential players have been proposed.

The so-called mammalian target-of-rapamycin (mTOR) proteins have been shown to be translated locally in dendrites and to contribute to the maintenance of LTP. As noted in Chapter 4, these proteins, such as eukaryotic elongation factor 1A (eEF1A), are important because they control the translation of other proteins. There have been very few reports of the contribution of these proteins to long-term memory. However, Fred Helmstetter's laboratory (Parsons, Gayford, and Helmstetter, 2006) has reported that when rapamycin (a drug that specifically inhibits the expression of these proteins) is injected into the amygdala, it moderately reduces the rat's long-term memory for both contextual and auditory-cue fear conditioning (Figure 9.13).

Fred Helmstetter

The local translation of CaMKII has also been implicated in the development of long-term memory. Mark Mayford and his group (Miller et al., 2002) have genetically engineered mice so that the delivery of CaMKII mRNA to the dendrites is significantly reduced. They found that they could produce a short-

FIGURE 9.13
Proteins called mammalian target-of-rapamycin (mTOR) facilitate the translation of other proteins. Rapamycin is a drug that specifically inhibits the translation of these proteins. When rapamycin is injected into the amygdala before fear conditioning to a tone, it impairs the rat's long-term memory for fear of the tone and of the context in which conditioning occurred. (After Parsons et al., 2006.)

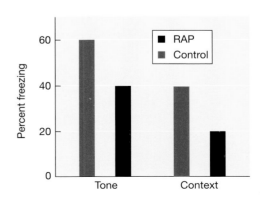

lasting LTP in slices from these mice but could not induce a long-lasting LTP. More importantly, when fear conditioned, these mice were normal at the short retention interval but impaired at the long retention interval. When asked to remember an explored object, these mice were normal when tested shortly after training but impaired when tested at a long retention interval (Figure 9.14). These results imply that sufficient levels of existing CaMKII may traffic into the synapses to support the short-term memory trace, but CaMKII needs to be translated in dendrites in response to a behavioral experience to support long-term memory.

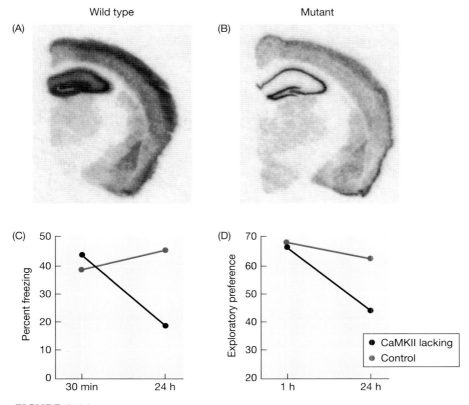

FIGURE 9.14
(A,B) The targeting of CaMKII mRNA to the dendrites was disrupted in the mutant mice compared to wild types. (C) The long-term memory but not short-term memory of contextual fear was impaired in mice lacking CaMKII in the dendrites. (D) These mutant mice also displayed impaired long-term memory for an explored object. (After Miller et al., 2002.)

Summary of the Role of Protein Synthesis

It is currently difficult to make a definitive statement about the contribution that protein synthesis induced by behavioral experience makes to the consolidation of a long-term memory trace. It is clear that a short-term memory trace can be established that does not depend on the synthesis of new proteins. It is less clear that a long-term memory trace depends on new protein synthesis. This is because broad-scale protein synthesis inhibitors have a variety of side effects that could disrupt other molecular processes that contribute to an enduring memory trace.

Additional progress will require a different approach, one that focuses on the synthesis of specific proteins and how they might contribute to memory. The development of methods to target the suppression of specific proteins, such as mTOR proteins and CaMKII, holds some promise for advancing the hypothesis that long-term memories require a behavioral experience to initiate the synthesis of new proteins.

Summary

Memory traces with different properties can support behavior. Researchers believe that short-term memories can be established by the behavioral experience activating post-translation processes that modify and assemble existing proteins. In contrast, the consolidation of enduring long-term memories is thought by some researchers to depend on new proteins produced when the behavioral event initiates both transcription of new mRNA and translation of these transcripts into new protein. This belief is derived largely from evidence that treatments that block transcription and translation impair long-term retention but do not influence short-term retention.

Given the issues (side effects) that are associated with drugs used to block protein synthesis, it is difficult to be sure that the reason they impair long-term retention is because they block protein synthesis. Moreover, very little is known about the specific new mRNAs and proteins that are needed to stabilize the memory. Thus, future research will likely be directed at identifying these molecules and the role they play in securing the memory trace. The strongest conclusion one can draw from the current literature is that short-term memory does not require the transcription and translation of new molecules.

References

Balschun, D., Wolfer, D. P., Gass, P., Mantamadiotis, T., Welzl, H., Schutz, G., Frey, J. U., and Lipp, H. P. (2003). Does cAMP response element-binding protein have a pivotal role in hippocampal synaptic plasticity and hippocampus-dependent memory? *Journal of Neuroscience, 23,* 6304–6314.

Barrientos, R. M., O'Reilly, R. C., and Rudy, J. W. (2002). Memory for context is impaired by injecting anisomycin into dorsal hippocampus following context exploration. *Behavioral Brain Research, 134,* 299–306.

Biedenkapp, J. C. and Rudy, J. W. (2004). Context memories and reactivation: constraints on the reconsolidation hypothesis. *Behavioral Neuroscience, 118,* 956–964.

Bourtchouladze, R., Abel, T., Berman, N., Gordon, R., Lapidus, K., and Kandel, E. R. (1998). Different training procedures recruit either one or two critical periods for contextual memory consolidation, each of which requires protein synthesis and PKA. *Learning and Memory, 5,* 365–367.

Bourtchuladze, R., Frenguelli, B., Blendy, J., Cioffi, D., Schutz, G., and Silva, A. J. (1994). Deficient long-term memory in mice with a targeted mutation of the cAMP-responsive element-binding protein. *Cell, 79,* 59–68.

Canal, C. E., Chang, Q., and Gold, P. E. (2007). Amnesia produced by altered release of neurotransmitters after intra-amygdala injections of a protein synthesis inhibitor. *Proceedings of the National Academy of Sciences, 104,* 12500–12505.

Davis, H. P. and Squire, L. R. (1984). Protein synthesis and memory: a review. *Psychological Bulletin, 96,* 518–559.

Flexner, J. B., Flexner, L. B., and Stellar, E. (1963). Memory in mice as affected by intracerebral puromycin. *Science, 141,* 57–59.

Gold, P. E. (2006). The many faces of amnesia. *Learning and Memory, 13,* 506–514.

Guzowski, J. F., Lyford, G. L., Stevenson, G. D., Houston, F. P., McGaugh, J. L., Worley, P. F., and Barnes, C. A. (2000). Inhibition of activity-dependent arc protein expression in the rat hippocampus impairs the maintenance of long-term potentiation and the consolidation of long-term memory. *Journal of Neuroscience, 20,* 3993–4001.

Guzowski, J. F. and McGaugh, J. L. (1997). Antisense oligodeoxynucleotide-mediated disruption of hippocampal cAMP response element binding protein levels impairs consolidation of memory for water maze training. *Proceedings of the National Academy of Sciences, 18,* 2693–2698.

Guzowski, J. F., McNaughton, B. L., Barnes, C. A., and Worley, P. F. (1999). Environment-specific expression of the immediate early gene Arc in hippocampal neuronal ensembles. *Nature Neuroscience, 2,* 1120–1124.

Guzowski, J. F., McNaughton, B. L., Barnes, C. A., and Worley, P. F. (2001). Imaging neural activity with temporal and cellular resolution using FISH. *Current Opinion in Neurobiology, 5,* 579–584.

Han, J. H., Kushner, S. A., Yiu, A. P., Cole, C. J., Matynia, A., Brown, R. A., Neve, R. L., Guzowski, J. F., Silva, A. J., and Josselyn, S. A. (2007). Neuronal competition and selection during memory formation. *Science, 316*, 457–460.

Huff, N. C., Frank, M., Wright-Hardesty, K., Sprunger, D., Matus-Amat, P., Higgins, E., and Rudy, J. W. (2006). Amygdala regulation of immediate early gene expression in hippocampus induced by contextual fear conditioning. *Journal of Neuroscience, 26*, 1616–1623.

Impey, S., Smith, D. M., Obrietan, K., Donahue, R., Wade, C., and Storm, D. R. (1998). Stimulation of cAMP response element (CRE)-mediated transcription during contextual learning. *Nature Neuroscience, 7*, 595–601.

Josselyn, S. A., Shi, C., Carlezon, W. A. Jr., Neve, R. L., Nestler, E. J., and Davis, M. (2001). Long-term memory is facilitated by cAMP response element-binding protein overexpression in the amygdala. *Journal of Neuroscience, 21*, 2404–2412.

Kandel, E. R. (2001). The molecular biology of memory storage: a dialogue between genes and synapses. *Science, 29*, 1030–1038.

Kogan, J. H., Frankland, P. W., Blendy, J. A., Coblentz, J., Marowitz, Z., Schutz, G., and Silva, A. J. (1997). Spaced training induces normal long-term memory in CREB mutant mice. *Current Biology, 7*, 1–11.

Martinez, J. L. Jr., Jensen, R. A., and McGaugh, J. L. (1981). Attenuation of experimentally-induced amnesia. *Progress in Neurobiology, 16*, 155–186.

Matthies, H. (1989). In search of cellular mechanisms of memory. *Progress in Neurobiology, 32*, 277–349.

McIntyre, C. K., Miyashita, T., Setlow, B., Marjon, K. D., Steward, O., Guzowski, J. F., and McGaugh, J. L. (2005). Memory-influencing intra-basolateral amygdala drug infusions modulate expression of Arc protein in the hippocampus. *Proceedings of the National Academy of Sciences, 102*, 10718–10723.

Miller, S., Yasuda, M., Coats, J. K., Jones, Y., Martone, M. E., and Mayford, M. (2002). Disruption of dendritic translation of CaMKIIalpha impairs stabilization of synaptic plasticity and memory consolidation. *Neuron, 36*, 507–519.

Montarolo, P. G., Goelet, O., Castelluci, V. F., Morgani, J., Kandel, E. R., and Schacter, S. (1986). A critical period for macromolar synthesis in long-term heterosynaptic facilitation in *Aplysia*. *Nature, 234*, 1249–1254.

Morris, R. G., Inglis, J., Ainge, J. A., Olverman, H. J., Tulloch, J., Dudai, Y., and Kelly, P. A. (2006). Memory reconsolidation: sensitivity of spatial memory to inhibition of protein synthesis in dorsal hippocampus during encoding and retrieval. *Neuron, 50*, 479–489.

Parsons, R. G., Gafford, G. M., Baruch, D. E., Riedner, B. A., and Helmstetter, F. J. (2006). Long-term stability of fear memory depends on the synthesis of protein but not mRNA in the amygdala. *European Journal of Neuroscience, 23,* 1853–1859.

Parsons, R. G., Gafford, G. M., and Helmstetter, F. J. (2006). Translational control via the mammalian target of rapamycin pathway is critical for the formation and stability of long-term fear memory in amygdala neurons. *Journal of Neuroscience, 26,* 12977–12983.

Radulovic, J. and Transon, N. C. (2007, in press). Protein synthesis inhibitors, gene superinduction and memory: too little or too much protein? *Neurobiology of Learning and Memory.*

Routtenberg, A. and Rekart, J. (2005). Post-translational protein modifications as the substrate for long-lasting memory. *Trends in Neurosciences, 28,* 12–19.

Rudy, J. W., Biedenkapp, J. C., Moineau, J., and Bolding, K. (2006). Anisomycin and the reconsolidation hypothesis. *Learning and Memory, 13,* 1–3.

Rudy, J. W. (2007, in press). Is there a baby in the bathwater? Maybe: some methodological issues for the *de novo* protein synthesis hypothesis. *Neurobiology of Learning and Memory.*

Schafe, G. E., Nadel, N. V., Sullivan, G. M., Harris, A., and LeDoux, J. E. (1999). Memory consolidation for contextual and auditory fear conditioning is dependent on protein synthesis, PKA, and MAP kinase. *Learning and Memory, 6,* 97–110.

Yin, J. and Tully, T. (1996). CREB and the formation of long-term memory. *Current Opinion in Neurobiology, 2,* 264–268.

Memory Modulation Systems

One of the pioneers of the field, James McGaugh, remarked that there are two general ways in which strong, enduring memories can be created. Common sense and research since Ebbinhaus tell us that one way is *practice or repeated exposure to the to-be-remembered events*. However, strong memories are also created when a *behavioral experience contains highly arousing content*.

I still remember an evening about 10 years ago when my friend Wayne and I were out for a walk with his dogs. Basically, it was like any other walk—uneventful, filled with the usual banter. All that changed when suddenly one of the dogs, Poco, leaped in the air, followed by the sound of a rattlesnake. This was an arousing event for us. I not only vividly remember Poco's reaction but also how we then had to coax the dogs past this point in the road. This is one of the few things that I remember with any detail from our many walks. I am sure you have had similar arousing experiences.

Something about such arousing events makes them memorable. The goal of this chapter is to provide you with a basic understanding of why this is the case. To begin, it will be useful to outline what is called the **memory modulation framework** that organizes this topic and its empirical foundation.

Memory Modulation

The memory modulation framework is the product of James McGaugh, his students, and collaborators. Several key assumptions follow and are also illustrated in Figure 10.1.

1. A behavioral experience can have two independent effects: it can activate specific sets of neurons that represent and store the content of the experience, and it can activate hormonal and other neural systems that can influence the mechanisms that store the memory.

2. These hormonal and other neural systems are called **memory modulators**. They are not part of the storage system, but they can influence the synapses that store the memory.

3. Memory modulators have a time-limited role and influence only the storage of very recently acquired memories. They operate during a period of time shortly after the behavioral experience when the trace is being consolidated.

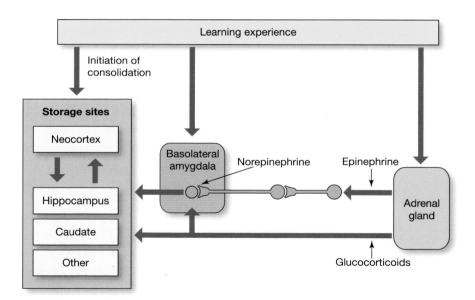

FIGURE 10.1
The memory modulation framework. Experience has two independent effects. It can initiate the acquisition and storage of the memory trace and it can activate the release of adrenal hormones that can modulate the processes that store the memory. (After McGaugh, 2000.)

4. The neural systems that modulate memory strength are not necessary for the retrieval of the memory.

James McGaugh

The factual basis for the memory modulation idea emerged when McGaugh was a graduate student (McGaugh, 1959, 2003; McGaugh and Petrinovich, 1959) and discovered that Karl Lashley (1917) had improved the rate at which rats learned a complicated maze by injecting them with a low dose of strychnine before training. Strychnine, as you may know, can be a lethal poison. However, at a low dose it is a stimulant; it produces a state of arousal. McGaugh's insight was that the state of arousal created by strychnine might influence the processes that consolidate memory traces. To evaluate his idea, he injected the drug *immediately after* the rats had been trained and found improved retention performance. However, when he gave the drug before the retention test, it had no effect on performance.

McGaugh and his colleagues subsequently found that strychnine given after training enhanced memories produced by a variety of behavioral experiences. The effect was quite general. The implication of these finding was unmistakable: There is a brief period of time shortly after the memory-inducing behavioral experience when the strength of a particular memory trace can be modified.

McGaugh's early work was important because it established the idea that events other than the behavioral experience that produces the memory trace can influence the strength of that trace. There is now a wealth of data that indicates that behavioral experiences can generate a state of arousal that influences memory strength. This can happen because naturally arousing stimuli (such as encountering a rattlesnake) can stimulate the adrenal gland to secrete a hormone or molecule into the blood stream called **adrenaline**. One general role of this hormone is to mobilize us for behavioral action. The expression "it gave me an adrenaline rush" relates to this effect. Adrenaline is often called **epinephrine**, and that is the name we will use in our discussion. Epinephrine binds to receptors called **adrenoreceptors**. Drugs that mimic the effects of epinephrine (for example, **norepinephrine**) are called **adrenergics** and they bind to what are called **adrenergic receptors**.

In addition to its energizing effects, epinephrine can have a second effect— *it can influence the strength of a memory trace*. McGaugh (2003) notes that remembering arousing events may be adaptive because the events may be especially important. The release of adrenal hormones helps to ensure that such events will be remembered.

Paul Gold

Paul Gold (Gold and Van Buskirk, 1975) provided the first evidence that adrenal hormones can strengthen memory traces. In this study, rats were given a single trial of inhibitory avoidance training with a low intensity shock that was designed to be minimally arousing. These animals were then injected with epinephrine at different times after training. The basic idea was to inject a dose of epinephrine that would mimic what the adrenal gland would naturally release in response to a stronger, more arousing shock. Remarkably, the avoidance behavior of rats injected with the adrenal hormone was dramatically increased. The effect also was time dependent because the hormone had to be injected shortly after training (Figure 10.2).

Epinephrine also influences the strength of human memories. Larry Cahill, for example, showed people a series of slides containing visual scenes (Cahill and Alkire, 2003). Some of these subjects were injected with epinephrine immediately following exposure to the scenes. A week later, these subjects were able to recall the scenes better than subjects injected with just the vehicle.

(A)

(B)

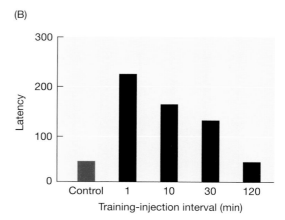

FIGURE 10.2
On the training trial, rats received a mild shock when they crossed to the dark side of the apparatus. Compared to control rats injected with the saline vehicle, rats that were injected with a dose of epinephrine—calculated to mimic the level of epinephrine that would naturally be released from the adrenal gland if the animals had received a strong shock—displayed enhanced inhibitory avoidance. The enhancing effect of epinephrine, however, was time dependent. It was more effective when it was given shortly after the training trial. (After Gold and Van Buskirk, 1975.)

The strength of the memory trace is enhanced when an arousing event causes the adrenal gland to release epinephrine into the blood stream. This result raises two important questions. First, memories are stored in the brain, not in the blood stream, so where in the brain does the hormone exert its effect? Second, epinephrine is a large molecule that does not enter the brain, so if it cannot enter the brain, how does it exert its effects on memory? These two questions are answered in the next sections.

The Great Modulator: The Amygdala

The amygdala is now thought to be the primary mediator of epinephrine's influence on memory (McGaugh, 2002, 2004). This region of the brain has anatomical connections with many other regions of the brain that are thought to be memory storage sites, so it is in a position to influence the memory storage processes in these other regions (Figure 10.3). There is an extensive literature supporting this idea.

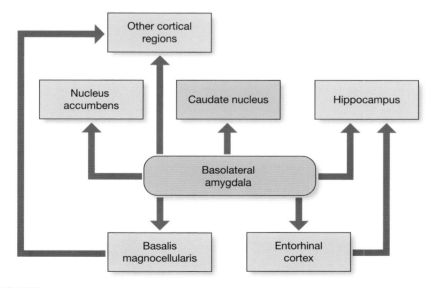

FIGURE 10.3
The amygdala is anatomically connected to many regions of the brain that are likely storage sites for different types of memories. Thus, it is in a position to influence or modulate storage processes in other regions of the brain. (After McGaugh, 2002.)

To clearly establish that the amygdala modulates memory storage in other regions of the brain, it must be shown that the amygdala is not itself a storage site for the memory. This means the animal in the study must be able to learn and remember the behavioral task if the amygdala is removed. For example, both the place-learning and visible-platform versions of the Morris water-escape task can be learned and remembered even when the amygdala is significantly damaged (Sutherland and McDonald, 1990). Thus the amygdala is not a critical storage site for these memories. Instead, the hippocampus (see Chapters 12 and 13) is a key storage area for the place-learning memory, and the caudate (see Chapter 15) is thought to be important for the acquisition and storage of the memory for the visible-platform task. Nevertheless, as shown in Figure 10.4, if D-amphetamine, a stimulant drug, is injected into the amygdala following training, retention performance on both versions of the task is enhanced (Packard, Cahill, and McGaugh, 1994; Packard and Teather, 1998).

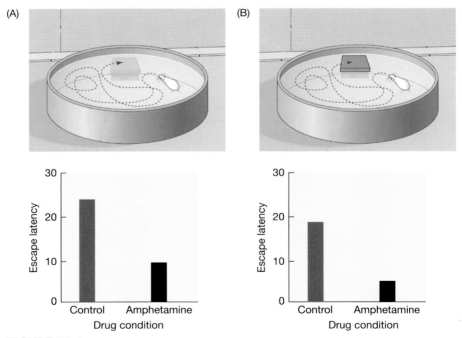

FIGURE 10.4
(A) Injecting the stimulant amphetamine into the amygdala following training on the place-learning version of the Morris water-escape task improved retention performance. (B) Injecting the amphetamine following training on the visible-platform task improved retention performance. The hippocampus is thought to be a critical storage site for place learning and the caudate is thought to be critical for the visible-platform task. (After Packard and Teather, 1998.)

Thus, the amygdala facilitates the storage of these memories but is not needed to retain the memory.

As noted earlier, Gold and Van Buskirk (1975) showed that a peripheral injection of epinephrine, designed to mimic the natural release of that adrenal hormone in response to shock, enhanced avoidance performance. As you might expect, adrenergic drugs like norepinephrine exert their effects by influencing neural processing in the amygdala. This point can be illustrated with results from the place-learning version of the Morris water-escape task and from inhibitory avoidance learning.

In the case of place learning in the Morris water-escape task (Figure 10.5A), injecting norepinephrine into the amygdala following training increases the rat's retention of the location of the hidden platform. In contrast, injecting **propranolol** (a drug that blocks the receptors for norepinephrine) into the amyg-

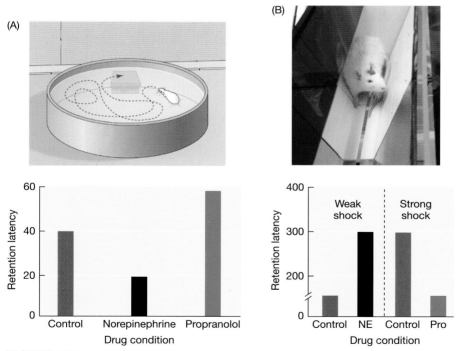

FIGURE 10.5
(A) The injection of norepinephrine into the amygdala following place learning enhanced the rat's retention of the platform location, but when propranolol was injected, retention was impaired. (B) Norepinepherine (NE) injected into the amygdala following inhibitory avoidance training with a weak shock enhanced retention performance. Propranolol (Pro) injected into the amygdala following inhibitory avoidance training with strong shock impaired retention. (After Hatfield and McGaugh, 1999.)

dala following training impairs retention of the platform location (Hatfield and McGaugh, 1999).

In the case of inhibitory avoidance learning (Figure 10.5B), injecting norepinephrine into the amygdala following avoidance training with a weak shock enhances retention of the avoidance response. However, if the antagonist propranolol is injected after avoidance training with a strong shock, the avoidance response is reduced (Gallagher, Kapp, Musty, and Driscoll, 1977; Liang, Juler, and McGaugh, 1986).

It is actually an oversimplification to say that the amygdala modulates memory storage in other regions of the brain. This is because the amygdala is not a unitary structure but consists of many subnuclei (Figure 10.6). Further

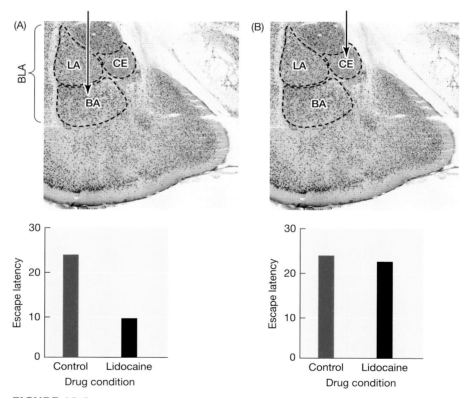

FIGURE 10.6
(A) An injection of lidocaine into the basolateral nucleus of the amygdala (BLA) following avoidance training impaired the retention of the inhibitory avoidance response. (B) Lidocaine had no effect when it was injected into the central nucleus (CE) of the amygdala. LA = lateral nucleus; BA = basal nucleus. (After Parent and McGaugh, 1994.)

research has revealed that it is the **basolateral nucleus of the amygdala (BLA)** that is the critical mediator of the memory modulation properties of this region of the brain. This conclusion is based on experiments in which drugs that influence modulation were injected into specific subnuclei of the amygdala (McGaugh, Roozendaal, and Cahill, 2000).

This point is illustrated in a study by Parent and McGaugh (1994), who injected lidocaine (a drug that temporarily suppresses neuronal activity) into either the basolateral or central nucleus of the amygdala. Note that inactivating the basolateral nucleus impaired retention performance (Figure 10.6A), but inactivating the central nucleus did not (Figure 10.6B).

In closing this discussion, it should be noted that although the BLA has been the most thoroughly studied region of the brain, other regions are also likely to be involved in modulating memory. They include the **nucleus accumbens** (Setlow, Roozendaal, and McGaugh, 2000) and the **anterior cingulate** (Malin and McGaugh, 2006). Just how the amygdala interacts with these other brain regions to modulate memory storage is not yet understood.

Epinephrine and the Vagus Connection

There is no doubt that epinephrine exerts its modulatory effects by its action on the amygdala, but, as noted, this conclusion presents another problem. Epinephrine molecules released as hormones are too large to enter the brain, so how does epinephrine released in the periphery influence amygdala function?

The answer is that when epinephrine is released in the blood stream, it can bind to adrenoreceptors located on a major cranial nerve called the **vagus** or **vagal nerve**. This nerve carries this information about the body into the brain, where it synapses on a brain stem region called the **solitary tract nucleus** (Miyashita and Williams, 2006; Hassert, Miyashita, and Williams, 2004). (The solitary tract nucleus is commonly referred to as the **NTS**, derived from *nucleus tractus solitarius*, translated literally as "nucleus of the solitary tract.") Neurons from this nucleus ultimately project to the BLA and can tell it that an arousing event has occurred. Inactivating this nucleus attenuates the modulation effects of the amygdala (Williams and McGaugh, 1993).

When the information signaled by the release of epinephrine into the blood stream arrives at the amygdala via this vagus-to-NTS pathway, a remarkable coincidence occurs: The related adrenergic molecule norepinephrine is released by neurons terminating within the amygdala (Quirarte, Galvez, Roozendaal, and McGaugh, 1998). Thus, epinephrine released as a hormone into the blood stream ultimately exerts its effect by causing the release of a related adrenergic compound, norepinephrine, in the BLA, which then exerts its effects by binding to adrenergic receptors in the amygdala (Figure 10.7).

FIGURE 10.7
Epinephrine released into the blood stream does not cross the blood-brain barrier. Instead, it binds to receptors on the vagal nerve that carries information into the solitary tract nucleus (NTS). Neurons from the NTS project into the amygdala where they release norepinephrine.

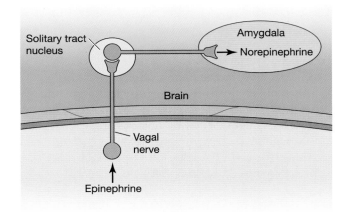

Given this conclusion, one should be able to detect a measurable increase in the level of norepinephrine in the BLA when rats are shocked after crossing to the dark side of the avoidance apparatus. Using a methodology called microdialysis (Figure 10.8), this increase was observed in a study by Quirarte and his colleagues (Quirarte et al., 1998), as shown in Figure 10.9A. However, there is another interesting fact associated with this set of events. By itself, electric shock, the stimulus typically used to produce inhibitory avoidance learning, does not cause epinephrine to be released in the amygdala. Rats have to *both explore the environment and then receive shock* for norepinephrine to be released in the amygdala (McIntyre, Hatfield, and McGaugh, 2002) (Figure 10.9B). It is as if the amygdala is designed to detect the coincidence of a novel behavioral experience and an arousing event.

Glucocorticoids: The Other Adrenal Hormone

Highly arousing behavioral experiences can result in the adrenal gland secreting not only the hormone epinephrine but also the hormone **corticosterone**. Corticosterone is also classified as a **glucocorticoid** because it is involved in the metabolism of glucose. Note that, in contrast to adrenaline, glucocorticoids can directly enter the brain.

It has been known for some time that glucocorticoids can also modulate memory (McEwen and Sapolsky, 1995; Roozendaal, Okuda, Van der Zee, and McGaugh, 2006), and there is evidence that their influence depends on the BLA. If the synthetic glucocorticoid **dexamethasone** is administered system-

(A)

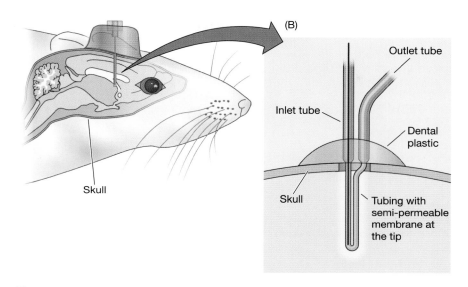

(B)

Outlet tube

Inlet tube

Dental plastic

Skull

Skull

Tubing with semi-permeable membrane at the tip

(C)

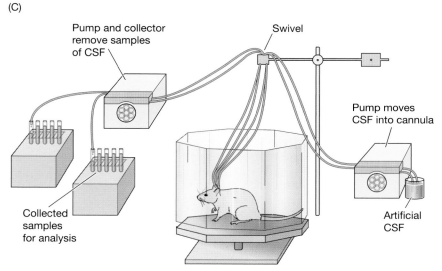

Pump and collector remove samples of CSF

Swivel

Pump moves CSF into cannula

Collected samples for analysis

Artificial CSF

FIGURE 10.8

Microdialysis allows extracellular fluid to be collected from deep within the brain. (A) A rat with a specially designed microdialysis probe implanted in the brain. (B) A detail of the microdialysis probe. (C) A freely moving rat connected to the instrumentation designed to extract a very small quantity of extracellular fluid. The content of this fluid can then be analyzed for its composition. CSF = cerebral spinal fluid.

FIGURE 10.9
The microdialysis methodology was used to extract norepinephrine from the extracellular brain fluid. (A) The level of norepinephrine released into the extracellular fluid in avoidance training is determined by the intensity of the shock. (B) Just shocking a rat or allowing it to explore the avoidance training apparatus does not increase the level of norepinephrine. It requires that the rat both explore the novel apparatus and be shocked. (A after Quirarte et al., 1998; B after McIntyre et al., 2002.)

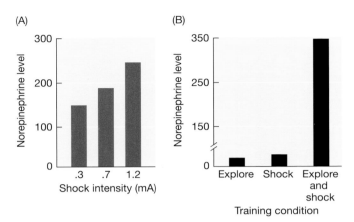

ically after inhibitory avoidance training, retention performance is enhanced. However, if the basolateral nucleus is lesioned, this effect is eliminated. In contrast, similar destruction of the central nucleus of the amygdala has no effect on the ability of dexamethazone to enhance retention. If **RU 28362**, a drug that is a glucocorticoid receptor agonist, is injected into the basolateral nucleus following inhibitory avoidance training, retention performance is enhanced. No enhancement occurs, however, if it is injected into the central nucleus.

It is now clear that memory modulation that depends on the basolateral nucleus is the product of an interaction of the effects of both epinephrine and glucocorticoids. To illustrate this point, consider the experiment by Quirarte, Roozendaal, and McGaugh (1997). They trained rats on the inhibitory avoidance task with weak shock. As expected, rats who were injected systemically with dexamethazone showed enhanced retention performance. However, if propranolol was directly injected into the rats' BLA, dexamethazone did not enhance retention (Figure 10.10). Thus, it appears that the amygdala's ability

FIGURE 10.10
Dexamethazone is a synthetic glucocorticoid. When it is injected systemically following inhibitory avoidance training, it enhances retention. However, the effect of dexamethazone also depends on epinephrine being released in the amygdala, because when injected into the amygdala, propranolol prevents dexamethazone from enhancing retention. (After Quirarte et al., 1997.)

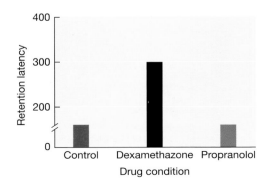

to modulate memory storage depends on a coordinated adrenal gland response to a behavioral experience. Experiences that raise circulating levels of the two adrenal hormones, epinephrine and glucocorticoids, can result in a stronger memory.

The Amygdala Signal

Researchers now have a good understanding of the primary factors involved in initiating amygdala-dependent memory modulation.

1. An arousing behavioral event induces the adrenal gland to release epinephrine and glucocorticoids into the blood stream.
2. Epinephrine binds receptors on the vagal nerve.
3. The vagus transmits a signal into the solitary tract nucleus that is conveyed to the amygdala as the release of norepinephrine.
4. At approximately the same time, glucocorticoids invade the BLA region.

When these conditions are met, the amygdala sends a signal to other regions of the brain that will enable them to better consolidate the memory trace. What does this signal do? Unfortunately, at this time very little is known about what happens when inputs from the amygdala arrive at storage circuits.

Chapter 9 revealed that the consolidation of long-term memories can require both protein synthesis and transcription, so one might suspect that the modulating signal from the amygdala in some way influences these processes. There is some evidence that the amygdala can influence the transcription of plasticity genes (Huff and Rudy, 2004) and their translation into protein. Research by Christa McIntyre and her colleagues, for example, has revealed that inhibitory avoidance training normally leads to the increased translation of the Arc gene in the hippocampus (McIntyre et al., 2005). However, when lidocaine, a drug that inactivates neurons, is injected into the BLA prior to training, the level of Arc protein in the hippocampus is reduced and the memory for the inhibitory avoidance experience is impaired. In contrast, when **clenbuterol**, an adrenergic receptor agonist, is injected into the BLA, the level of Arc protein in the hippocampus is increased and the memory for the training experience is strengthened.

These results (Figure 10.11) indicate that activity in the BLA produced by inhibitory avoidance training modulates the level of Arc protein in another area of

Christa McIntyre

(A)

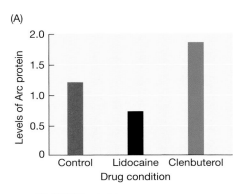

(B)

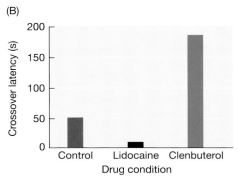

FIGURE 10.11
(A) This graph illustrates the effect of injecting lidocaine and clenbuterol into the BLA on the level of Arc protein in the hippocampus following inhibitory avoidance learning. (B) This graph illustrates the effect of these drugs on inhibitory avoidance. Note that lidocaine reduced the level of Arc protein in the hippocampus and decreased inhibitory avoidance. In contrast, clenbuterol increased the level of Arc protein and enhanced inhibitory avoidance. These results suggest that the BLA might modulate memory by influencing the level of Arc protein in the hippocampus. (After McIntyre et al., 2005.)

the brain, the hippocampus, and that the level of Arc protein correlates with the strength of the memory. Thus McIntyre's research has moved us somewhat closer to understanding how the amygdala influences memory storage processes in at least one region of the brain.

Norepinephrine and AMPA Receptor Trafficking

Thus far we have described the modulation effects of norepinephrine released in the amygdala. However, the amygdala is not the only region of the brain that receives norepinephrine input. As illustrated in Figure 10.12, there is an ascending noradrenergic system that has as its source neurons located in the pons and medulla oblongata. This small region of the brain, called the **locus coeruleus**, contains only about 3,000 neurons. Nevertheless, it projects broadly and provides nearly all the norepinephrine in the cortex, limbic system, thalamus, and hypothalamus.

Central to the topic of memory modulation, there is evidence that norepinephrine in the hippocampus makes an important contribution to LTP (Gelinas and Nguyen, 2005; Katsuki, Izumi, and Zorumski, 1997). Roberto Malinow and his colleagues (Hu et al., 2007) have discovered how norepinephrine

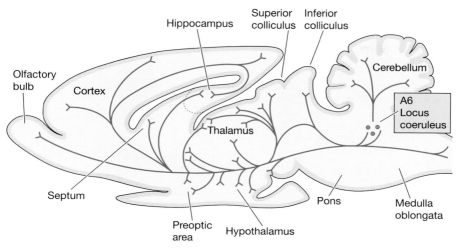

FIGURE 10.12
Arousing stimulation activates a small number of neurons in the locus coeruleus, which provides norephinephrine to many regions of the brain.

facilitates LTP and how it can enhance memory formation. Based on Chapters 3 and 8, you already know that synaptic activity produced by high-frequency stimulation and behavioral experience can traffic AMPA receptors with GluR1 subunits into denditric spines. You also know that GluR1 subunits have several phosphorylation sites (Ser 818, Ser 831, and Ser 845) that participate in this trafficking and in enhancing the function of receptors containing GluR1s. You also know that the Ser 831 site can be phosphorylated by CaMKII and that PKA can phosphorylate the Ser 845 site.

Malinow's group reported that norepinephrine also plays a major role in these processes. In particular, they found that norepinephrine also leads to phosphorylation of GluR1 at the Ser 831 and Ser 845 sites. Moreover, the application of norepinephrine to hippocampus slices facilitated the induction of LTP but much less so in slices obtained from mice in which these phosphorylation sites were genetically deleted. However, norepinephrine itself was not sufficient to induce the trafficking of GluR1. Importantly, they also demonstrated that epinephrine administered systemically facilitated normal mice storing a memory of an explored context, but this did not occur in the genetically modified mice lacking the Ser 845 and 831 phosphorylation sites.

Thus, we have an additional way in which memories for arousing events can be enhanced. Arousing events cause the release of norepinephrine, which in turn results in the phosphorylation of sites on GluR1 receptor subunits that facilitate trafficking and enhance receptor function, thereby ensuring that the memory for the arousing experience is stored (Figure 10.13).

FIGURE 10.13
When norepinephrine is released into the hippocampus, it phosphorylates two sites (Ser 831 and Ser 845) on the GluR1 AMPA receptor subunit. This facilitates the trafficking of GluR1s into the dendritic spine and increases memory strength.

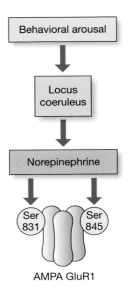

Modulating Hormones and Post-Traumatic Stress Disorder

The experience of strongly aversive events can produce a syndrome called **post-traumatic stress disorder (PTSD)**. Individuals diagnosed with this syndrome have unusually vivid recall of the traumatic events accompanied by severe emotional responses. Individuals report that terrifying experiences are often recalled with intensity, with the traumatic events being re-experienced unchanged over years (van der Kolk and Fisler, 1995). It is estimated that about 8% of the United States population at some time in their lives will experience PTSD. It is much more prevalent among military personnel. Motor vehicle accidents alone result in over three million serious injuries a year and estimates of PTSD in these people vary between 19% and 47%. Interpersonal traumas such as rape or assault may produce even higher rates of PTSD (Pitman and Delahanty, 2005).

Thus, a large number of people present PTSD symptoms. In cases where individuals are hospitalized after the traumatic event, there is an opportunity for what is called **secondary treatment** that might reduce the likelihood that the person will develop the syndrome. One common secondary treatment is called **debriefing**—a brief crisis intervention usually administered within days of a traumatic event in which the trauma-exposed individual is encouraged to talk about his/her feelings and reactions to the event. Unfortunately, it is now clear that debriefing doesn't work (Pitman and Delahanty, 2005).

The need for an effective secondary treatment encouraged Roger Pitman and his colleagues (Pitman et al., 2002) to explore the idea that it might be possible to attenuate PTSD by suppressing the potential memory strengthening effects of epinephrine that would be released by the adrenal gland following the traumatic event. He was led to this hypothesis by the animal research on memory modulation that we have reviewed throughout this chapter.

Although there has not yet been a full-scale test of this hypothesis, the results of some preliminary studies based on a small number of subjects are very encouraging. The patients in these studies were recruited from people brought to the hospital after a traumatic event, usually a motor vehicle accident. Patients who met the criteria for being likely candidates for developing PTSD who agreed to participate were given propranolol orally (to antagonize the effects of epinephrine) or a placebo four times a day over the next few days. Based on objective testing three months later, none of the eight patients who received propranolol were classified as having PTSD, whereas eight of the fourteen patients who did not take propranolol met the criteria for such a classification. If these results hold up with larger sample sizes, then animal work that established the concept of memory modulation and how it works will have made a major contribution to the treatment of a debilitating syndrome.

Summary

The discovery of a memory modulation system and its principal hormonal and neural components is one of the important achievements of biologically driven memory research. This work makes it clear that we should distinguish between neural circuits that store memories and neural circuits that modulate storage circuits. It also brings a whole-organism perspective into the picture.

Memory consolidation is not just the product of the brain; it reflects the integration of behavioral influences on the brain and the adrenal gland component of the endocrine system. Adrenal hormones influence memory by their influence on the BLA, which projects to many other brain regions where the memory is likely stored. Epinephrine released into the blood influences the BLA by binding to receptors on the vagal nerve, which in turn ultimately activates neurons that release norepinephrine in the BLA. Glucocorticoids released by the adrenal gland directly enter the brain and interact in the BLA with norepinephrine to modulate memory storage.

Little is known about how the output of the amygdala influences memory storage in other brain regions; however, one possibility is that it regulates the translation of Arc protein. Future research will likely tell us more precisely just how the modulatory signals coming from the amygdala influence the cellular and molecular processes that change synaptic connections in the regions of the brain where memories are stored.

Norepinephrine released in the amygdala initiates processes that allow the amygdala to strengthen memories in other brain regions. In addition, however, it is becoming clear that norepinephrine itself can more directly initiate processes that strengthen memories. Specifically, in the hippocampus it participates in the phosphorylation of two sites on GluR1 receptors to facilitate trafficking these AMPA receptor subunits into the dendritic spine.

The modulation framework has helped us understand the processes involved in strengthening memories. In addition, the research generated by this framework has provided a scientific basis for potential drug therapies for treating anxiety disorders such as post-traumatic stress disorder.

References

Cahill, L. and Alkire, M. (2003). Epinephrine enhancement of human memory consolidation: interaction with arousal at encoding. *Neurobiology of Learning and Memory, 79,* 194–198.

Gallagher, M., Kapp, B. S., Musty, R. E., and Driscoll, P. A. (1977). Memory formation: evidence for a specific neurochemical system in the amygdala. *Science, 198,* 423–435.

Gelinas, J. N. and Nguyen, P. V. (2005). Beta-adrenergic receptor activation facilitates induction of a protein synthesis-dependent late phase of long-term potentiation. *Journal of Neuroscience, 25,* 3294–3303.

Gold, P. E. and Van Buskirk, R. B. (1975). Facilitation of time-dependent memory processes with posttrial epinephrine injections. *Behavioral Biology, 13,* 145–153.

Hassert, D. L., Miyashita, T., and Williams, C. L. (2004). The effects of peripheral vagal nerve stimulation at a memory-modulating intensity on norepinephrine output in the basolateral amygdala. *Behavioral Neuroscience, 118,* 79–88.

Hatfield, T. and McGaugh, J. L. (1999). Norepinephrine infused into the basolateral amygdala posttraining enhances retention in a spatial water maze task. *Neurobiology of Learning and Memory, 71,* 232–239.

Hu, H., Real, E., Takamiya, K., Kang, M. G., LeDoux, J., Huganir, R. L., and Malinow, R. (2007). Emotion enhances learning via norepinephrine regulation of AMPA-receptor trafficking. *Cell, 131,* 160–173.

Huff, N. C. and Rudy, J. W. (2004). The amygdala modulates hippocampal-dependent context memory formation and stores cue-shock associations. *Behavioral Neuroscience, 118,* 53–62.

Katsuki, H., Izumi, Y., and Zorumski, C. F. (1997). Noradrenergic regulation of synaptic plasticity in the hippocampal CA1 region. *Journal of Neurophysiology, 77,* 3013–3020.

Lashley, K. S. (1917). The effects of strychnine and caffeine upon the rate of learning. *Psychobiology, 1,* 141–170.

Liang, K. C., Juler, R. G., and McGaugh, J. L. (1986). Modulating effects of post-training epinephrine on memory: involvement of the amygdala noradrenergic system. *Brain Research, 368,* 125–133.

Malin, E. L. and McGaugh, J. L. (2006). Differential involvement of the hippocampus, anterior cingulate cortex, and basolateral amygdala in memory for context and footshock. *Proceedings of the National Academy of Sciences, 103,* 1959–1963.

McEwen, B. S. and Sapolsky, R. M. (1995). Stress and cognitive function. *Current Opinion in Neurobiology, 5,* 205–216.

McGaugh, J. L. (1959). *Some neurochemical factors in learning.* Unpublished PhD thesis, University of California, Berkely.

McGaugh, J. L. (2002). Memory consolidation and the amygdala, a systems perspective. *Trends in Neurosciences, 25,* 456–462.

McGaugh, J. L. (2003). *Memory and emotion.* New York: Columbia University Press.

McGaugh, J. L. (2004). The amygdala modulates the consolidation of memories of emotionally arousing experiences. *Annual Review of Neuroscience, 27,* 1–28.

McGaugh, J. L. and Petrinovich, L. (1959). The effect of strychnine sulfate on maze learning. *The American Journal of Psychology, 72,* 99–102.

McGaugh, J. L., Roozendaal, B., and Cahill, L. (2000). Modulation of memory storage by stress hormones and the amygdala complex. In M. S. Gazzaniga (Ed.), *The new cognitive neurosciences* (pp. 1981–1998). Cambridge, MA: MIT Press, pp. 1981–1998.

McIntyre, C. K., Hatfield, T., and McGaugh, J. L. (2002). Amygdala norepinephrine levels after training predict inhibitory avoidance retention performance in rats. *European Journal of Neuroscience, 16,* 1223–1226.

McIntyre, C. K., Miyoshita, T., Setlow, B., Marjon, K. D., Steward, O., Guzowski, J. F., and McGaugh, J. L. (2005). Memory-influencing intra-basolateral amygdala drug infusions modulate expression of Arc protein in the hippocampus. *Proceedings of the National Academy of Sciences, 102,* 10718–10723.

Miyashita, T. and Williams, C. L. (2006). Epinephrine administration increases neural impulses propagated along the vagus nerve: role of peripheral beta-adrenergic receptors. *Neurobiology of Learning and Memory, 85,* 116–24.

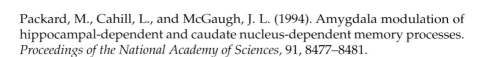

Packard, M., Cahill, L., and McGaugh, J. L. (1994). Amygdala modulation of hippocampal-dependent and caudate nucleus-dependent memory processes. *Proceedings of the National Academy of Sciences, 91,* 8477–8481.

Packard, M. G. and Teather, L. A. (1998). Amygdala modulation of multiple memory systems: hippocampus and caudate-putamen. *Neurobiology of Learning and Memory, 69,* 163–200.

Parent, M. B. and McGaugh, J. L. (1994). Posttraining infusion of lidocaine into the amygdala basolateral complex impairs retention of inhibitory avoidance training. *Brain Research, 66,* 97–103.

Pitman, R. K. and Delahanty, D. L. (2005). Conceptually driven pharmacologic approaches to acute trauma. *CNS Spectrums, 10,* 99–106.

Pitman, R. K., Sanders, K.M., Zusman, R. M., Healy, A. R., Cheema, F., Lasko, N. B., Cahill, L., and Orr, S. P. (2002). Pilot study of secondary prevention of posttraumatic stress disorder with propranolol. *Biological Psychiatry, 51,* 189–192.

Quirarte, G. L., Galvez, R., Roozendaal, B., and McGaugh, J. L. (1998). Norepinephrine release in the amygdala in response to footshock and opioid peptidergic drugs. *Brain Research, 808,*134–140.

Quirarte, G. L., Roozendaal, B., and McGaugh, J. L. (1997). Glucocorticoid enhancement of memory storage involves noradrenergic activation in the basolateral amygdala. *Proceedings of the National Academy of Sciences, 94,* 14048–14053.

Roozendaal, B., Okuda, S., Van der Zee, E. A., and McGaugh, J. L. (2006). Glucocorticoid enhancement of memory requires arousal-induced noradrenergic activation in the basolateral amygdala. *Proceedings of the National Academy of Sciences, 103,* 6741–6746.

Setlow, B., Roozendaal, B., and McGaugh, J. L. (2000). Involvement of a basolateral amygdala complex-nucleus accumbens pathway in glucocorticoid-induced modulation of memory consolidation. *European Journal of Neuroscience, 12,* 367–375.

Sutherland, R. J. and McDonald, R. J. (1990). Hippocampus, amygdala, and memory deficits in rats. *Behavioural Brain Research, 12,* 57–79.

van der Kolk, B. A. and Fisler, R. (1995). Dissociation and the fragmentary nature of traumatic memories: overview and exploratory study. *Journal of Traumatic Stress, 8,* 505–525.

Williams, C. L. and McGaugh, J. L. (1993). Reversible lesions of the nucleus of the solitary tract attenuate the memory-modulating effects of posttraining epinephrine. *Behavioral Neuroscience, 6,* 955–962.

The Fate of Retrieved Memories

A persistent theme in memory research is that memory traces consolidate—they become less vulnerable to disruption as they age.
Much of the research we have previously described has focused on
identifying the cellular–molecular processes that consolidate the
memory trace. Memory traces are especially vulnerable to disruption
immediately following a learning experience. However, you will now
learn that the age of a memory trace is not the only determinant of
its vulnerability. Under some conditions, *retrieving the memory can
make the trace vulnerable to disruption*.

The goal of this chapter is to provide you with an understanding
of the empirical facts and theoretical concepts that are associated
with this observation. First, the basic findings are introduced. We
then examine two theoretical interpretations—active trace theory
and reconsolidation theory. Finally, memory erasure as a potentially
successful treatment for memory-based behavioral disorders is
discussed.

Reactivated Memory Disrupted by ECS

That retrieved memory traces are vulnerable to disruption first came to light about 40 years ago when Don Lewis and his colleagues (Misanin, Miller, and Lewis, 1968) reported that simply retrieving or reactivating a fear memory trace made it vulnerable to the disruptive effects of electroconvulsive shock (ECS).

In the Lewis study, a Pavlovian fear-conditioning procedure was used to establish the fear memory trace. Rats received a single pairing of a noise–conditioned stimulus (CS) and a shock–unconditioned stimulus (US). The next day, after the trace was "consolidated," some rats were brought to the training environment where the noise–CS was presented for 2 seconds. This experience was designed to retrieve or *reactivate* the fear memory trace. In order to determine if the reactivated trace was vulnerable to disruption, some of these rats also received ECS immediately after the reactivation experience. Other rats also received ECS the next day, but without the reactivation experience. Rats that received both the reactivation treatment and ECS were extremely impaired when given a full test the next day, that is, they showed no fear in the presence of the noise (Figure 11.1). ECS had disrupted a fear memory trace that had already had time to consolidate and attain long-term memory status.

FIGURE 11.1
(A) A fear conditioning experiment was used to study the vulnerability of a reactivated memory—a noise CS was paired with a shock US. In one condition, 24 hours after fear conditioning, the CS was presented to reactivate the fear memory. Some animals received electroconvulsive shock (ECS), while others did not. In the second condition, the fear memory was not reactivated, but animals received either ECS or no ECS. All animals were tested for fear of the CS. (B) The results of the experiment. Note that when the memory trace was reactivated by briefly presenting the CS, ECS disrupted the memory for the CS–shock experience. ECS had no effect when it was presented in the absence of shock.

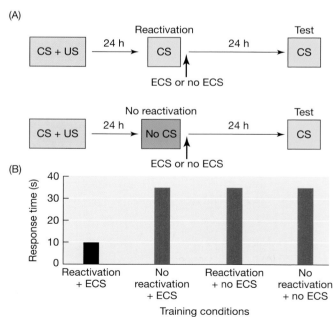

Active Trace Theory

As noted in Chapter 7, consolidation theory assumes that memory traces are vulnerable to disruption shortly after they are first established but, with time, the trace becomes stable and resistant to disrupting events. This relationship is generally true. However, based on the results of the work described above, Lewis (1979) suggested that the age of the memory trace at the time of the disrupting event may not be the only variable that determines its vulnerability.

Recall from previous chapters (see Chapters 7 and 9) that memory traces can be distinguished by their state of activation. Lewis proposed that this dimension might also be a critical determinant of the vulnerability of the trace to disruption. Memories in the active state are more vulnerable to disruption than memories in an inactive state. His theory is called **active trace theory**. The specific assumptions of this framework are as follows (Figure 11.2).

- Memories can exist in either a short-term memory *active state* or long-term memory *inactive state*.

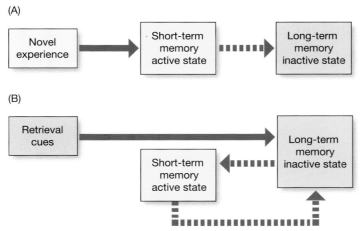

FIGURE 11.2
This figure illustrates the assumptions of active trace theory. Memories exist in either a short-term memory (STM) active state or a long-term memory (LTM) inactive state. (A) Novel experience can create an active STM trace that will decay into the inactive LTM state. (B) Retrieval cues can retrieve an inactive LTM trace and place it in the active state that then will decay into the inactive LTM state. Memories in the active state are more vulnerable to disruption than memories in the inactive state.

- There are two ways a memory trace can be put into the short-term active state:
  1. Novel experiences generate new active memory traces.
  2. Retrieving or reactivating existing long-term memory traces will return these traces to the short-term active state.
- Memories in the active state are vulnerable to disruption.
- Memory traces become inactive with time, and in the inactive state they are less vulnerable to disruption.

The critical point of Lewis's theoretical analysis is that it is not just the age of the memory relative to when a disruptive event occurs that is the critical determinant of its vulnerability—the *state* of the memory trace is also important. Memory traces in the active state are more vulnerable to disruption than traces in the inactive state.

Lewis's results and theory were intriguing but also generated much controversy. Although some researchers replicated these results, others did not, and no one had any ideas as to why this was the case. Thus, the idea that retrieved memories are placed in a state of vulnerability lay dormant for about 25 years. Two findings, however, brought the idea that reactivated memories are vulnerable to disruption out of hibernation.

Reconsolidation Theory

The first important observation was reported by Susan Sara (Przybyslawski and Sara, 1997). Rats were first trained to solve a spatial learning task. The researchers discovered that if an NMDA antagonist was systemically injected following the reactivation of this memory trace, the rats were not able to perform the task the next day. They also reported that memory was disrupted only if the drug was given within 90 minutes of reactivating the memory. This suggested the intriguing possibility that reactivated memories might need to be reconsolidated.

Susan Sara

Shortly thereafter, Karim Nader and his colleagues (Nader, Schafe, and LeDoux, 2000) published their novel findings and the fate of retrieved memories and the concept of reconsolidation entered center stage. Nader's experiments were similiar to the Lewis experiment (Misanin et al., 1968) with two exceptions:

- Instead of using ECS to disrupt memory, he injected the protein synthesis inhibitor anisomycin into the basolateral region of the amygdala (BLA) following the reactivation of a Pavlovian conditioned auditory-cue fear memory.

- The rats were tested twice. One test was designed to measure the effect of anisomcyin on short-term memory. The other test, at a longer retention interval, was designed to test anisomycin's effect on long-term memory.

Anisomycin had no effect on the short-term memory test but produced a large impairment on the long-term memory test (Figure 11.3).

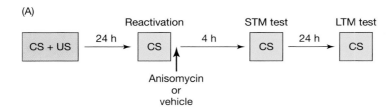

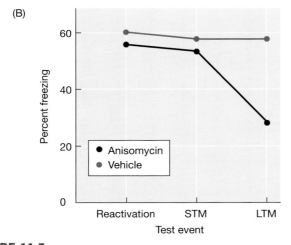

FIGURE 11.3
(A) The design of Nader et al.'s 2000 experiment. Rats were conditioned to an auditory-cue CS paired with a shock US. Following the reactivation of the fear memory, the protein synthesis inhibitor anisomycin or the vehicle solution in which the drug was suspended was injected into the lateral nucleus of the amygdala. Rats were then given either a short-term memory (STM) test or a long-term memory (LTM) test. (B) Anisomycin disrupted the long-term retention of the reactivated fear memory but had no effect on the short-term retention of the memory. (After Nader et al., 2000.)

Karim Nader

As you now know, when Nader and his colleagues published their findings (2000), the idea that active memory traces are vulnerable to disruption was not new. The reason Nader's result captured the interest of neurobiologists was that he proposed a bold new idea called **reconsolidation theory** to explain the result (Nader, 2003). Although it shared Lewis's idea about the importance of the activation state of the memory, in other ways reconsolidation theory was quite different.

Nader's theory, which has two parts, is illustrated in Figure 11.4. First, he proposed that when a memory is retrieved *the synapses underlying the trace become unbound or weakened.* This means that retrieval itself can disrupt an established memory trace *and thereby produce amnesia.* This thought should give you pause. It implies that the

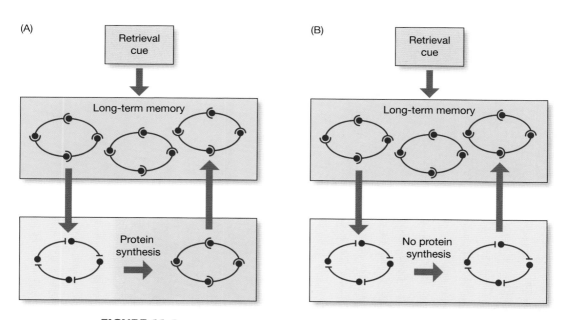

FIGURE 11.4

(A) A retrieval cue activates a well-consolidated but inactive memory trace from long-term memory. The synaptic connections linking the neurons involved in the trace become unbound. However, retrieval also initiates protein synthesis and the memory trace is reconsolidated. Thus, when it returns to the inactive state it will be stable. (B) If protein synthesis is prevented, the memory trace will be weakened or lost when it returns to the inactive state.

	Active trace theory	Reconsolidated theory
Memory retrieval	Makes the trace vulnerable to amnestic agents	A. Initiates processes that degrade the trace B. Initiates a new round of protein synthesis that saves the trace from degradation
Anisomycin	Causes amnesia when the memory trace is in an active state	Blocks protein synthesis needed to rebuild the trace. It does not cause amnesia; it reveals the amnesia produced by retrieval.

FIGURE 11.5
Comparison of Lewis's active trace theory and Nader's reconsolidation theory. For each theory, the role played by memory retrieval and anisomycin is shown.

very act of retrieving a memory can potentially cause you to lose the memory. The reason this does not actually happen is explained by his second assumption—that *retrieval also initiates another round of protein synthesis so that the trace is "reconsolidated."* The new round of protein synthesis rescues the trace weakened by retrieval.

It is valuable to compare Nader's theory with active trace theory (Figure 11.5). The differences are subtle but important. The active trace theory account stipulates that when a memory trace has been retrieved into the active state, it is vulnerable to disruption by amnesic agents such as ECS or anisomycin; *the agent is the cause of the amnesia.* In contrast, reconsolidation theory stipulates that *the act of retrieval itself is the cause of the amnesia* because it uncouples the synapses that contain the trace. Anisomycin itself does not disrupt the memory trace; it blocks the synthesis of the proteins needed to rebuild the trace. Note that, unless the retrieved memory is followed by a protein synthesis inhibitor, one would not know that the synapses holding the trace together had become uncoupled and needed to be restabilized.

Assessing Reconsolidation Theory

Many memory researchers have been attracted to reconsolidation theory because it implies that some of the same mechanisms that contribute to changes in synaptic strength and to the consolidation of the memory trace are activated when the memory trace is retrieved. Consequently, this theory has stimulated a large body of research to evaluate the implications.

Unfortunately, it is not easy to provide a concise summary of the status of reconsolidation theory. Several factors contribute to this problem. Reconsolidation is a theory about the fate of a reactivated memory. However, many researchers confuse the theory of reconsolidation with the empirical fact that a reactivated memory is vulnerable to disruption. To provide a context for this issue, reconsider the Lewis finding that ECS given following a reactivated fear memory disrupts the subsequent retrieval of that memory trace. No one believes that ECS blocks protein synthesis. What this result means is that a reactivated memory trace is vulnerable to disruption—not that it has to be reconsolidated.

A second factor centers on the empirical issue: Are reactivated memories vulnerable to disruption by protein synthesis inhibitors? There is a substantial literature that provides a positive answer to this question (Alberini, Milekic, and Tronel, 2006; Dudai and Eisenberg, 2004; Tronson and Taylor, 2007). Yet many researchers report no evidence that reactivated memories are disrupted by protein synthesis inhibitors (Biedenkapp and Rudy, 2004; Cammarota, Bevilaqua, Medina, and Izquierdo, 2004; Fischer, Sananbenesi, Schrick, Speiss, and Radulovic, 2004; Vianna, Szapiro, McGaugh, Medina, and Izquierdo, 2001).

A third problem that confronts reconsolidation theory is that there are reports that the amnesia produced by protein synthesis inhibitors and other agents is temporary (Lattal and Abel, 2004; Power, Berlau, McGaugh, and Stewart, 2006). Reconsolidation theory supposes that the amnesia is due to the loss of the memory trace. It implies that amnesia should be permanent. However, if the memory can be recovered, then the amnesia is most likely a retrieval failure.

By far the most serious problem for the theory, however, is that it is based on the observation that a protein synthesis inhibitor, anisomycin, disrupts the subsequent retrieval of a reactivated memory trace. As noted in Chapter 9, there is a growing concern that the amnesia produced by broad-scale protein synthesis inhibitors like anisomycin may not be due to their preventing protein synthesis (Gold, 2006; Rudy, Biedenkapp, Moineau, and Bolding, 2006; Rudy, 2007; Radulovic and Tronson, 2007). These drugs are toxic and have many side effects that can directly produce amnesia by disrupting the normal functions of the neural circuits that support the memory trace. If anisomycin produces amnesia by directly disrupting these circuits, as opposed to blocking the synthesis of proteins, then much of the empirical basis of reconsolidation theory largely disappears.

There are problems that prevent an uncritical acceptance of reconsolidation theory as an explanation of all claims in the literature that reactivated memories can be disrupted. Nevertheless, given the wealth of data that now exist, it is reasonable to conclude that the basic assumptions of reconsolidation theory have captured something that is very important. The fact is that reactivated memory traces are not just vulnerable to disruption by protein synthesis inhibitors; they can be influenced by a variety of pharmacological agents targeted at specific molecules that have been shown to be important in memory consolidation (Alberini et al., 2006; Dudai and Eisenberg, 2004; Tronson and Taylor, 2007). Moreover, some reactivated memory traces are *bidirectional labile*, that is, their strength can be increased or decreased by targeting molecules involved in consolidation.

An experiment by Joseph LeDoux and his colleagues (Doyere, Debiec, Monfils, Schafe, and LeDoux, 2007) illustrates that targeting specific molecules can disrupt a reactivated memory. To influence the reactivated memory, they injected a drug called U0126, which inhibits the activity of a kinase called MAPK (pronounced MAP K) into the lateral nucleus of the amygdala of rats (see Chapter 4). This drug has previously been shown to influence the initial storage of an auditory-cue fear memory trace (Schafe, Nader, Blair, and LeDoux, 2001). They conditioned rats to two quite different auditory-cue conditioned stimuli, CS1 and CS2. During the reactivation phase, however, they presented only CS1. Prior to presenting CS1, U0126 was injected into the amygdala. They later tested the rats for fear of both CS1 and CS2. The important finding was that the U0126 disrupted the rats' fear response only to CS1. It did not disrupt the fear response to CS2, presumably because the memory trace associated with CS2 was not in the active state when U0126 was injected (Figure 11.6).

It is clear from these data that the reactivated memory trace is placed into an unstable state and vulnerable to disruption. These results are consistent with the idea that the trace must be reconsolidated, and this process depends on biochemical interactions involving MAPK.

Natalie Tronson and her colleagues (Tronson, Wiseman, Olausson, and Taylor, 2006) have revealed that reactivated memory traces can be bidirectionally modified. They demonstrated that a fear memory trace could be strengthened by using a drug called N6-benzoyladenosine-3',5'-cyclic monophosphate (6-BNZ-cAMP) which activates PKA. They first used a low level of shock to establish a weak fear memory. They then injected 6-BNZ-cAMP into the BLA following presentations of only the CS. As shown in Figure 11.7, the fear response of rats with repeated CS-only presentations followed by the drug injection increased. Injecting the drug without reactivating the fear memory, however, had no effect.

Natalie Tronson

In another set of experiments, Tronson and her colleagues showed that when the PKA inhibitor Rp-adenosine 3',5'-cyclic monophosphorothioate (Rp-cAMPS) was injected into the BLA following reactivation of the

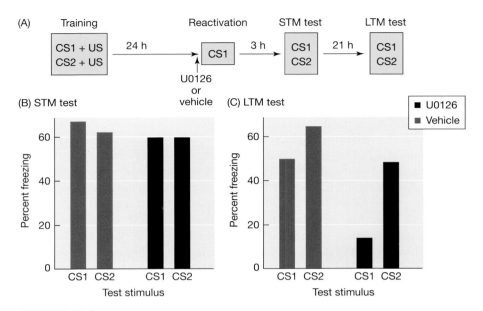

FIGURE 11.6
In Doyere et al.'s experiment (2007) two different auditory stimuli, CS1 and CS2, were paired with a shock US. However, only the fear memory associated with CS1 was reactivated. CS2 was not presented. (B,C) Infusing the MAPK inhibitor U0126 into the amygdala just prior to reactivating the fear memory associated with CS1 had no effect on the short-term memory (STM) test with CS1, but significantly reduced the fear response to CS1 on the long-term memory (LTM) test. Note that U0126 had no effect on the ability of CS2 to retrieve the fear response on either the STM or LTM test. This last outcome indicates that unless the fear memory is reactivated it is not vulnerable to disruption by U0126.

fear memory, it impaired the subsequent retrieval of the memory. Rp-cAMPS also influenced subsequent retrieval of the memory trace only if it was injected immediately after the reactivation of the trace. Thus, not only can a retrieved memory trace be weakened by interfering with biochemical processes that consolidate memories, it can also be strengthened by enhancing these processes. These results support the general assumptions of reconsolidation theory.

Memory Erasure: A Potential Therapy

Reactivated memories are vulnerable to disruption. This fact has encouraged researchers to pursue the possibility that drug treatments given after reacti-

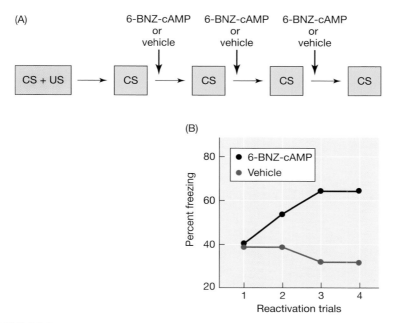

FIGURE 11.7
Injecting the PKA activator 6-BNZ-cAMP, compared to injecting the vehicle alone, into the basolateral amygdala following reactivation trials increased the rat's fear response to a CS paired with shock. (After Tronson et al., 2006.)

vation might be successful in eliminating memories that are the basis of serious behavioral disorders. This strategy has been pursued to develop potential treatments for two important clinical problems: (1) drug addiction and relapse, and (2) debilitating fears such as those associated with post-traumatic stress disorder.

Preventing Drug Addiction Relapse

One of the major problems associated with drug addiction is relapse (Figure 11.8). Even after drug addicts have gone through what appears to be successful treatment, they often relapse into the addictive cycle. Environmental cues associated with drugs are one important contributor to relapse. It is now understood that when a drug such as cocaine is taken, the environmental cues become associated with some properties of the drug. This is another example of Pavlovian conditioning. When these cues are encountered, they in-

FIGURE 11.8
This figure illustrates the drug addiction–relapse cycle. Encountering cues associated with drug use can lead to relapse.

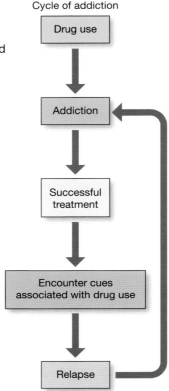

Cycle of addiction

Drug use

Addiction

Successful treatment

Encounter cues associated with drug use

Relapse

duce or create a *craving or urge to take the drug* (Figure 11.9). This state is well documented in people (Childress et al., 1999). In some ways it is similar to the urge you experience when you encounter a bag of potato chips or the sight of chocolate candy. However, the urge associated with drug-related cues is much more potent and difficult to resist.

Imagine that a person with a specific drug addiction has gone through treatment and is now off the drug. Unfortunately, when that individual later encounters cues that were associated with the drug, the urge produced can be so powerful that relapse occurs and the individual reverts back to taking the drug. Given the power of these drug-related cues to evoke memories that produce relapse, it would be of enormous benefit to find treatment methods that could be used to attenuate or erase these memories. Recent studies with rodents suggest that this might eventually be possible.

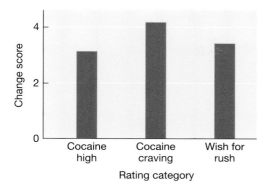

FIGURE 11.9
Cues associated with drug use induce a conditioned cocaine high, a craving for cocaine, and a wish to get high. The graph shows changes in the subjective state of recovering cocaine addicts after viewing a video showing simulated purchase, preparation, and smoking of crack cocaine. The subjects were patients in a treatment center and had not used cocaine for about 14 days. (After Childress et al., 1999.)

Barry Everitt and his colleagues (Lee, DiCiano, Thomas, and Everitt, 2005; Lee, Milton, and Everitt, 2006) have used the reactivation procedure to eliminate the ability of drug-related cues to produce relapse in rats that have learned to self-administer cocaine. The exact procedures for their experiments are complicated but entail training rats to learn a lever-press response that produces an infusion of cocaine (Figure 11.10A). This is the drug-seeking response. During this training the delivery of the cocaine is also paired with a Pavlovian CS, the presentation of a light. The light is thus associated with the drug. Theoretically, the light acquires the ability to evoke an urge to take the drug and its presence can lead to relapse. To demonstrate relapse, rats receive a session of training in which the response no longer produces the drug or the light. This results in the elimination of the drug-seeking response. If these rats then receive presentations of the light CS, they will relapse into drug-seeking behavior.

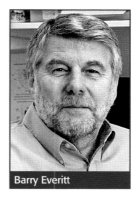

Barry Everitt

Everitt's group asked if the reactivation procedure could be used to eliminate the memory evoked by the CS and thus prevent relapse. To do this they presented rats with multiple presentations of the CS without the drug. They then infused an antisense into the BLA, which was designed to prevent translation of a gene called *Zipf268*. This protein is expressed in the amygdala in response to presentations of the drug-associated CS. Thus, Everitt reasoned that it might be involved in the "reconsolidation" of the reactivated drug memory. Remarkably, preventing the expression of the Zipf268 protein completely eliminated the ability of the CS to induce relapse. The rats behaved as if the light–drug memory had been erased (see Figure 11.10B).

FIGURE 11.10
(A) The experimental methodology used to train a rat to press a lever to self-administer a drug and become drug addicted. A conditioned stimulus (CS) is also presented when the drug is delivered. The presentation of the drug-associated CS can produce drug-seeking behavior (relapse) in rats that have learned that lever pressing no longer produces the drug. (B) Antisense that blocks the translation of the gene *Zipf268* or the vehicle is delivered after repeated CS presentations. (C) This graph shows that during the test for relapse the rats treated with *Zipf268* antisense made fewer bar presses than rats who received the vehicle. This result suggests that *Zipf268* antisense prevented the reconsolidation of the drug memory associated with the CS.

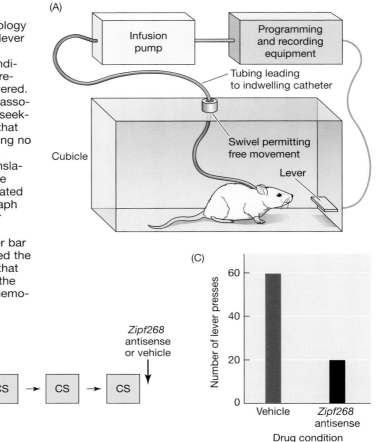

Eliminating Debilitating Fears

Post-traumatic stress disorder was discussed in some detail in Chapter 10. Although the evidence is not yet conclusive, the evidence suggests that giving propranolol (the adrenergic receptor antagonist) during the post-trauma period may retard the development of this syndrome. Even if this treatment proves effective, it may not be applicable to people who have already developed the syndrome. Given the vulnerability of reactivated memories to disruption, there is some hope that it might be possible to develop therapies based on this methodology to treat people with existing debilitating fears.

The possible application of the reactivation procedure to help eliminate fear was explicitly recognized by Przybyslawski, Roullet, and Sara (1999). They reported that the systemic administration of propranolol following the reactivation of an inhibitor avoidance memory greatly attenuated subsequent avoidance responding. Debiec and Nader (2004) also found that systemic injections of propranolol following the reactivation of the auditory-cue fear memory attenuated the rat's subsequent response to that cue.

There is also evidence that midazolam, a benzodiazepine agent, when given after the reactivation of a contextual fear memory, can greatly attenuate subsequent fear responses to that context (Bustos, Maldonado, and Molina 2006). Benzodiazepine agents are well known for their ability to reduce anxiety and for their sedative and muscle-relaxant effects. Thus, their effects on reactivated memories would be through quite different mechanisms than those produced by propranolol.

Such experiments are obviously far removed from clinical application. However, Roger Pitman, an expert in the treatment of post-traumatic stress disorder, and his colleagues (Brunet et al., 2007) have reported that administering propranolol following the retrieval of traumatic memories from patients experiencing post-traumatic stress disorder attenuated their subsequent response to the retrieval cues. These results suggest that one day it may be possible to combine the use of pharmacological agents with reactivation methodology to attenuate debilitating memories produced by a traumatic experience.

Summary

Over 40 years ago, Don Lewis reported that reactivated memories might be vulnerable to disruption. He suggested that it is the state of the memory trace— active versus inactive—that makes it vulnerable to disruption. Interest in the fate of retrieved memory traces increased when Karim Nader proposed the reconsolidation hypothesis—that retrieving a memory has two effects: (1) it unbinds the synapses that hold the trace, and (2) it initiates a new round of protein synthesis that will ensure that the memory trace is restabilized. This idea has become the focal point of a large body of research that has further revealed the labile nature of retrieved memory traces and may have implications for clinical treatments aimed at removing memory traces that produce debilitating behaviors.

References

Alberini, C. M., Milekic, M. H., and Tronel, S. (2006). Mechanisms of memory stabilization and de-stabilization. *Cell Molecular Life Science, 63,* 999–1008.

Biedenkapp, J. C. and Rudy, J. W. (2004). Context memories and reactivation: constraints on the reconsolidation hypothesis. *Behavioral Neuroscience, 118,* 956–964.

Brunet, A., Orr, S. P., Tremblay, J., Robertson, K., Nader, K., and Pitman, R. K. (2007, in press). Effect of post-retrieval propranolol on psychophysiologic responding during subsequent script-driven traumatic imagery in post-traumatic stress disorder. *Journal of Psychiatric Research.*

Bustos, S. G., Maldonado, H., and Molina, V. A. (2006). Midazolam disrupts fear memory reconsolidation. *Neuroscience, 139,* 831–842.

Cammarota, M., Bevilaqua, L. R., Medina, J. H., and Izquierdo, I. (2004). Retrieval does not induce reconsolidation of inhibitory avoidance memory. *Learning and Memory, 11,* 572–578.

Childress, A. R., Mozley, P. D., McElgin, W., Fitzgerald, J., Reivich, M., and O'Brien, C. P. (1999). Limbic activation during cue-induced cocaine craving. *American Journal of Psychiatry, 156,* 11–18.

Debiec, J. and Nader, K. (2004). Disruption of reconsolidation but not consolidation of auditory fear conditioning by noradrenergic blockade in the amygdala. *Neuroscience, 129,* 267–272.

Doyere, V., Debiec, J., Monfils, M. H., Schafe, G. E., and LeDoux, J. E. (2007). Synapse-specific reconsolidation of distinct fear memories in the lateral amygdala. *Nature Neuroscience, 10,* 414–416.

Dudai, Y. and Eisenberg, M. (2004). Rites of passage of the engram: reconsolidation and the lingering consolidation hypothesis. *Neuron, 44,* 93–100.

Fischer, A., Sananbenesi, F., Schrick, C., Speiss, J., and Radulovic, J. (2004). Distinct roles of hippocampal de novo protein synthesis and actin rearrangement in extinction of contextual fear. *Journal of Neuroscience, 24,* 1962–1966.

Gold, P. E. (2006). The many faces of amnesia. *Learning and Memory, 13,* 506–514.

Lattal, K. M. and Abel, T. (2004). Behavioral impairments caused by injections of the protein synthesis inhibitor anisomysin after contextual retrieval reverse with time. *Proceedings of the National Academy of Sciences, 101,* 4667–4672.

Lee, J. L., DiCiano, P., Thomas, K. L., and Everitt, B. J. (2005). Disrupting reconsolidation of drug memories reduces cocaine-seeking behavior. *Neuron, 47,* 795–801.

Lee, J. L., Milton, A. L., and Everitt, B. J. (2006). Cue-induced cocaine seeking and relapse are reduced by disruption of drug memory reconsolidation. *Journal of Neuroscience, 26,* 5881–5887.

Lewis, D. J. (1979). Psychobiology of active and inactive memory. *Psychological Bulletin, 86,* 1054–1083.

Misanin, J. R., Miller, R. R., and Lewis, D. J. (1968). Retrograde amnesia produced by electroconvulsive shock after reactivation of a consolidated memory trace. *Science, 160,* 554–558.

Nader, K. (2003). Memory traces unbound. *Trends in Neurosciences, 26,* 65–72.

Nader, K., Schafe, G. E., and LeDoux, J. E. (2000). Fear memories require protein synthesis in the amygdala for reconsolidation after retrieval. *Nature, 406,* 722–726.

Power, A. E., Berlau, D. J., McGaugh, J. L., and Stewart, O. (2006). Anisomycin infused into the hippocampus fails to block "reconsolidation" but impairs extinction: the role of re-exposure duration. *Learning and Memory, 13,* 27–34.

Przybyslawski, J., Roullet, P., and Sara, S. J. (1999). Attenuation of emotional and nonemotional memories after their reactivation: role of beta adrenergic receptors. *Journal of Neuroscience, 19,* 6623–6238.

Przybyslawski, J. and Sara, S. J. (1997). Reconsolidation of memory after its reactivation. *Behavioural Brain Research, 84,* 241–246.

Radulovic, J. and Tronson, N. C. (2007, in press). Protein synthesis inhibitors, gene superinduction and memory: too little or too much protein? *Neurobiology of Learning and Memory.*

Rudy, J. W. (2007, in press). Is there a baby in the bathwater? Maybe: some methodological issues for the de novo protein synthesis hypothesis. *Neurobiology of Learning and Memory.*

Rudy, J. W., Biedenkapp, J. C., Moineau, J., and Bolding, K. (2006). Anisomycin and the reconsolidation hypothesis. *Learning and Memory, 13(1),* 1–3.

Schafe, G. E., Nader, K., Blair, H. T., and LeDoux, J. E. (2001). Memory consolidation of Pavlovian fear conditioning: a cellular and molecular perspective. *Trends in Neurosciences, 24,* 540–546.

Tronson, N. C. and Taylor, J. R. (2007). Molecular mechanisms of memory reconsolidation. *Nature Review Neuroscience, 8,* 262–275.

Tronson, N. C., Wiseman, S. L., Olausson, P., and Taylor, J. R. (2006). Bidirectional behavioral plasticity of memory reconsolidation depends on amygdalar protein kinase A. *Nature Neuroscience, 2,* 161–169.

Vianna, M. R., Szapiro, G., McGaugh, J. L., Medina, J. H., and Izquierdo, I. (2001). Retrieval of memory for fear-motivated training initiates extinction requiring protein synthesis in the rat hippocampus. *Proceedings of the National Academy of Sciences, 98,* 12251–12254.

PART THREE

Neural Systems and Memory

The Content of Memory: Memory Systems and the Hippocampus

We are our memories. Without a record of our experiences we would be disconnected from our past, have no recognition of our relatives and friends, possess no knowledge of the world, and always be completely lost. We could not anticipate dangerous situations or locate the food and water we need to survive. We would be unable to acquire even the most rudimentary of skills, let alone learn to drive a car or become an expert violinist or tennis player. We could not be left alone.

The activities and functions that our memories support are remarkably varied and should make you ask, "How can the brain do all of this?" A part of the answer is that the brain contains *specialized systems* that are designed to store and utilize the different kinds of information contained in our experiences. Neurobiologists have achieved some basic understanding of how these systems are organized to support different types of memory.

The purpose of this chapter and the remaining ones is to introduce you to some of what we now know about these different systems. We begin with a quick overview of the multiple memory systems perspective, one of the important achievements of modern memory research (see Squire, 2004, for a historical overview).

The Multiple Memory Systems Perspective

The *content* of our experience matters to the brain. It sorts content and assigns its storage to different regions of the brain. This idea is the essence of what is called the **multiple memory systems** perspective (McDonald and White, 1993; White and McDonald, 2002; Squire, 2004). Some examples will help you to understand this concept.

Example 1: Personal Facts and Emotions

Suppose you were in a minor automobile accident and no one was injured. As a consequence of that experience, you will very likely remember many of the details leading up to the accident—whom you were with, where it happened, who you thought was at fault, and so on. Now imagine that you were in a much more serious accident, you suffered facial lacerations and multiple fractures in one leg, and were pinned in the car for some time. It was bad. This second case contains additional content. The experience was quite aversive and frightening. In addition to recording the details of the accident, your brain will record the aversive aspects of the experience in ways that may later alter your behavior. Not only will you be able to recall the cold facts of the experience, you may be afraid to drive or even get into an automobile.

The details that make up an episode and the impact of the experience are stored in different brain regions. Memory researchers have been aware of this possibility for a long time. For example, Édouard Claparède (1951), a French psychologist, reported on a test he performed on an amnesic patient with a brain pathology. He concealed a pin in his hand and then shook hands with the patient, who quickly withdrew her hand in pain. A few minutes later Claparède offered his hand to the patient again. The patient resisted shaking it. When asked why, the patient replied, "Doesn't one have a right to withdraw her hand?" Claparède then insisted on further explanation and the patient said, "Is there, perhaps, a pin hidden in your hand?" However, the patient could not give any reason why she had this suspicion.

Consider how you would react to such an experience. You also would be reluctant to shake hands, but you would be able to recall the content of the experience as an explanation of your behavior. Although Claparède's patient's brain pathology produced amnesia for the episode, it is reasonable to conclude that this pathology spared the system in the brain that was modified to produce a reluctance to shake hands. This example suggests that some aspect of *the aversive content* of the experience, as well as associations with the cues of the doctor, were stored outside of the region of the brain that supported recollection of the experience.

Example 2: Personal Facts and Skills

We ride bikes, drive cars, play musical instruments, ride skateboards, and do many other things quite well. The level of accomplishment obtained by individuals such as concert violinists or professional skateboarders is truly amazing. Obviously, to achieve even a functional level of performance, such as needed to safely drive a car, requires an enormous amount of practice. Once a skill is acquired, it can be performed without your having any sense of awareness. The many hours of practice have left an enduring impression in your brain that now supports the skill. In addition to acquiring a skill, however, you will also remember much about the practice sessions, where they occurred, who your instructors were, and how difficult it was initially to perform. Nevertheless, these aspects of your memory have absolutely nothing to do with your ability to perform the skill. We know this because people who are amnesic in the sense of having no recollection of their training episodes can still perform (Bayley, Frascino, and Squire, 2005). The inescapable conclusion is that the memory system that supports skillful behaviors is outside of the region of the brain that supports our ability to recollect the training episodes.

Such examples and brain research have led memory researchers to believe that: (1) a complete understanding of memory can only be achieved by recognizing that the content of experience is important; and (2) memories are segregated into different brain regions according to their content. The remainder of this chapter explores the episodic memory system, how memory researchers learned that episodic memory depends on a neural system that involves the hippocampus (Figure 12.1), and different models researchers used to study this system. The story begins with patient H.M.

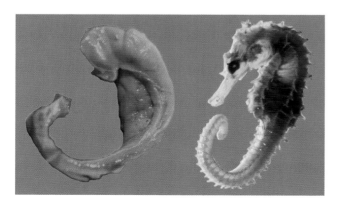

FIGURE 12.1
A hippocampus dissected from a human brain (left) and the tropical fish *Hippocampus leria* or seahorse (right). The striking similarity in shape is undoubtedly why the Bolognese anatomist Giulio Cesare Aranzi named this brain region the hippocampus. (Andersen, Morris, Amaral, Bliss, and O'Keefe, 2007). (Photo courtesy of Professor Laszio Seress, University of Pécs, Hungary.)

Brenda Milner

The Case of H.M.

The two previous examples made the point that brain insults can result in the loss of the ability to recall personal experiences, while sparing memories such as those that support emotional responses, skills, and habits. It was not until Brenda Milner reported her analysis of the anonymous amnesic, Henry M. (H.M.), that memory researchers first gained insight into the regions of the brain that are responsible for our ability to remember our experiences.

H.M. is the most famous and important amnesic in the history of memory research. His personal tragedy revolutionized how we think about the relationship between memory and the brain. The seeds of H.M.'s tragedy were sown when, at the age of nine, he sustained a head injury that eventually led to epilepsy. Over the years his seizures became more frequent, and by the age of 27 they were so disturbing that he was no longer able to function. Because H.M.'s seizures were thought to originate in the temporal lobes, the decision was made to bilaterally remove these regions. This was the first time these regions had been bilaterally removed. The surgery was successful in reducing his epilepsy. Moreover, H.M.'s cognitive abilities were left intact; his IQ actually increased. Unfortunately, however, shortly after the surgery it was discovered that the surgery profoundly and permanently affected his memory.

H.M. was brought to the attention of Brenda Milner, who then tested him in a variety of ways and described her results to the scientific community (Milner, 1970; Scoville and Milner, 1957). The essence of her analysis was that H.M. had severe **anterograde amnesia**; he could not acquire some types of new memories. For example, he never recognized Milner even though they interacted many times. Soon after eating he could not remember what he ate or that he had eaten. His experiences registered initially and could be maintained for a short period of time. However, the memory vanished if he was distracted. Thus, although H.M.'s short-term memory was intact, *his long-term memory was severely disturbed.*

Although H.M. had some preserved childhood memories, he had extensive retrograde amnesia that disconnected him with most of his personal past. Thus, even though other intellectual capacities remained intact, H.M. could not acquire enduring new memories or remember a significant part of his past.

In spite of these severe memory impairments, formal tests revealed that *some of his memory capacities were spared*. For example, he was able to learn and remember the skill of mirror tracing (Figure 12.2), which requires coordinating hand movement with an inverted image of the object being traced,

(A) The mirror-tracing task

FIGURE 12.2
(A) The mirror-tracing task. (B) H.M.'s performance improved with training.

(B) Performance of H.M. on mirror-tracing task

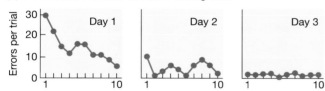

and a rotary pursuit task (Corkin, 1968), which requires acquiring a new motor skill. Remarkably, even though H.M.'s performance improved on these tasks, he never recalled the training experiences that established the skills.

Although H.M. was severely amnesic, he had some understanding of his state. Milner (1970) reports that between tests he would suddenly look up and say rather anxiously: "Right now, I'm wondering. Have I done or said anything amiss. You see at this moment everything looks clear to me, but what happened just before? That's what worries me. It's like waking from a dream; I just don't remember." (p. 37)

It is difficult to overestimate how important H.M.'s tragedy was for memory research. He wasn't the first patient to display amnesia for certain types of information. What was unique was that the location of the brain damage was known because the surgeon, William Scoville, had made a careful record of the surgery. This meant that for the first time researchers had a testable hypothesis about just what regions of the brain may be critical for memory. In addition, that H.M.'s intellectual capacities were intact meant that memory functions could be separated from other cognitive abilities. That his anterograde and retrograde amnesia were restricted to certain kinds of content also provided a foundation for the multiple memory view.

The Episodic Memory System

Today many researchers believe that the removal of H.M.'s medial temporal lobes disrupted what is called the **episodic memory system**. This is the system that supports what most people mean when they use the term memory. It extracts and stores the content from your experiences (episodes), which allows you to answer questions such as, "What did you have for lunch?" "Where did you park your car?" and "Who went with you to the movies?" Thus, it supports your ability to *consciously recollect* and report on facts and events that you experienced. You can declare that you have a memory. The episodic memory system has other properties that are discussed in more detail in Chapter 13.

It is important to emphasize that H.M. had some spared memory capacities. He could learn and retain the skills needed to perform the mirror tracing and rotary pursuit tasks. These abilities and others are supported by memory systems that depend on different regions of the brain. Some of these other systems will be discussed in later chapters.

H.M.'s tragedy revealed that there are regions in the brain that are essential to the episodic memory system. At the time of surgery, Scoville estimated that a large part of what is called the medial temporal lobe was bilaterally removed, including much of the hippocampus, amygdala, and some of the surrounding regions of the underlying neocortex (Figure 12.3). Modern neuroimaging techniques largely confirmed Scoville's estimates. However, it is notable that more of the posterior part of the hippocampus was spared than was originally estimated. Portions of the ventral perirhinal cortex were spared and the parahippocampal cortex was largely intact (Corkin, Amaral, Gonzalez, Johnson, and Hyman, 1997).

Given the extent of H.M.'s brain damage, it is difficult to know if one region was more critical to the episodic memory system than any other. It is interesting, however, that based on her analysis of patients with different combinations of brain damage, Milner (1970) speculated that the hippocampus might be a critical region of the medial temporal lobes that supported the recall of the memories lost by H.M. Much research has been directed at trying to define critical regions of the brain responsible for H.M.'s memory impairment.

There are two ways that one can determine the critical brain regions that support episodic memory. One is by using laboratory animals (rodents and primates) to answer the question. The other is by studying patients that have selective damage to a particular medial temporal lobe structure or structures. Let's first consider the animal model strategy.

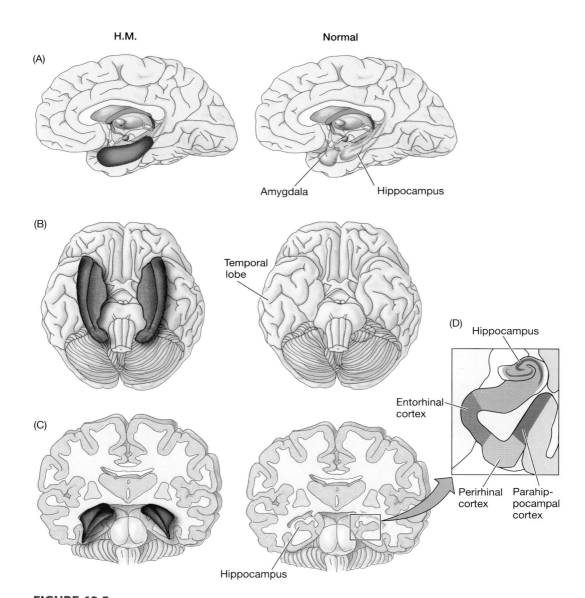

FIGURE 12.3
The tissue removed from H.M.'s brain. (A) Sagittal view of the brain showing that most of the amygdala and hippocampus were removed. (B) This view shows the extent to which underlying cortical tissue was removed. (C) This coronal section illustrates the combined loss of the cortical regions and hippocampus. (D) Another coronal view shows the cortical regions (entorhinal cortex, perirhinal cortex, parahippocampal cortex) and hippocampus in more detail. (B,C from Scoville and Milner, 1957.)

The Animal Model Strategy

The animal model strategy has the advantage that the researcher has some control over the location of the brain damage and can selectively target different regions. However, there is a fundamental problem with this approach that has never been completely solved. Specifically, the most important and easily demonstrated property of the episodic memory system is that *it supports our ability to consciously recall our experiences*. When I ask my wife what she had for lunch and she answers "a McDonald's hamburger and fries," unless she lied, I can be confident that she consciously recalled the experience, and that her response depended on her episodic memory system. In contrast, my cat also might remember what it had for breakfast, but I have no way of knowing that it can consciously recollect this experience. Thus, researchers who use the animal model approach are faced with the problem of trying to convince themselves, and the rest of the scientific community, that the particular task that they use measures episodic memory.

Milner's analysis of H.M. provides a related problem for animal models of episodic memory. H.M.'s primary impairment was relatively selective. He lost the ability to acquire memories that could be consciously recollected. However, some of his other memory capacities, such as his ability to improve on the pursuit of the rotor task, were spared. Since we cannot ask animals to consciously recollect their daily events, it is likely that many of the tasks used to study memory in animals may not depend on the hippocampus because the memory-based performance can be supported by other neural systems that do not include the hippocampus. Given these problems, it is not surprising that it is difficult to develop a consensus on an animal model of episodic memory.

The Delayed Nonmatching-to-Sample Task

The primate brain is anatomically similar to our brain, so in the late 1970's Mortimer Mishkin (1978, 1982) decided to use primates to determine what brain regions contributed to H.M.'s memory loss. To do this he developed a memory testing procedure called **delayed nonmatching to sample (DNMS)**, which is illustrated in Figure 12.4. In the DNMS task each trial consists of two components. First, the monkey is shown a three-dimensional object. It is called the *sample*. Some time later he is presented with a choice between the sample object and a new object. This is called the *choice* component. If the monkey chooses the new object, it will find a reward such as a grape or a peanut. The task is called nonmatching to sample because the correct object on the choice test does not match the sample. There are two important features of this task: (1) new objects are used on every trial; and (2) the experimenter can vary the interval between the sample and the choice trial.

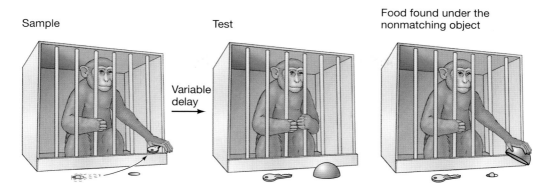

FIGURE 12.4
The delayed nonmatching-to-sample task was invented to study episodic memory in monkeys. The animal's task is to remember the object it sampled and to choose the novel object on the choice trial.

To make the correct choice the monkey must retain information about the sampled object. It is the *to-be-remembered* episode. Implicit in the use of the DNMS task is the assumption that when the monkey chooses the correct object, it is telling the experimenter, "I remember seeing the old object at a particular time and in this particular place." If this assumption is true, then this task depends on the episodic memory system. If one believes that the DNMS task *exclusively measures episodic memory,* then evaluating monkeys with selective damage to medial temporal lobes should reveal which of these regions were responsible for H.M.'s amnesia.

Mortimer Mishkin

Mishkin initially used this task to determine if damage to the hippocampus and/or amygdala caused H.M.'s amnesia. Viewed against Milner's hypothesis, the results of his experiments and others were somewhat surprising. They revealed that damage to either the hippocampus *or* the amygdala had very little effect on DNMS performance; however, *damage to both regions* dramatically impaired performance. Moreover, monkeys with damage to both of these regions were able to acquire motor skills (Squire, 1987). This outcome initially encouraged the belief that it was the combined damage to both the hippocampus and the amygdala that produced H.M.'s amnesia.

Larry Squire

Larry Squire, however, pointed out that the surgical approaches used to remove both the hippocampus and amygdala produced extensive damage to the immediate surrounding cortical tissue compared to when only the hippocampus was surgically removed (Squire, 1987). Subsequent research led to the conclusion that it was the damage to the rhinal cortex, not damage to either the amygdala or hippocampus, that drastically impaired performance on the DNMS task (Zola-Morgan, Squire, Amaral, and Suzuki, 1989; Murray and Mishkin, 1998; Meunier, Bachevalier, Mishkin, and Murray, 1993). An example of these results is presented in Figure 12.5. Thus, researchers now agree that this medial temporal lobe region is critical for performance on the DNMS, and that neither the hippocampus nor the amygdala is critical.

The results of DNMS experiments are both surprising and disconcerting because selective damage to the hippocampus has almost no effect on performance. Baxter and Murray (2001) reviewed all of the relevant studies and concluded that extensive damage to the hippocampus has a smaller effect on DNMS than does limited damage (but see Zola and Squire, 2001). This conclusion runs counter to Milner's hypothesis that it was damage to the hip-

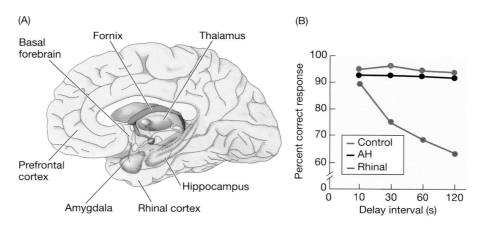

FIGURE 12.5
(A) A saggital view of the human brain. (B) The performance on the delayed nonmatching-to-sample task. Primates with damage to both the amygdala and hippocampus (AH) performed normally. However, removal of the rhinal cortical regions profoundly disrupted performance. (After Murray and Mishkin, 1998; Meunier et al., 1993.)

pocampus that was responsible for H.M.'s selective memory impairments. Given that most of the field still believes that the hippocampus makes a critical contribution to episodic memory, this conclusion is alarming because if the DNMS task exclusively depended on the episodic memory system, one would conclude that the hippocampus is not part of the episodic memory system.

Two Process Theories of Recognition Memory

The DNMS task belongs to a category of tasks called recognition memory tasks. Such tasks require the subject to make a judgment about whether something has previously occurred. Today many theorists believe that two different processes can support recognition. One type is called **familiarity** and the other is called **recollection** (Brown and Aggleton, 2001; Rugg and Yonelinas, 2003; Sutherland and Rudy, 1989). To appreciate this distinction you need only to reflect on how often you have recognized a person as familiar without being able to recall information about the place and time you met her. This would be an example of recognition without recall. It would be based on familiarity and not recollection. Recollection would also include the information about such things as where and when you met the person and her name. Often you will get a sense of familiarity before you recollect the details of past encounters.

Contemporary theorists have proposed that recognition based on recollection depends on the hippocampus, whereas recognition based on familiarity depends on surrounding cortices (Brown and Aggleton, 2000). If two types of memory can support recognition memory, it is possible to explain why extensive damage to the hippocampus can have little or no effect on DNMS performance. The monkeys in the DNMS task were using the familiarity process to make their correct choice (Sutherland and Rudy, 1989) and this does not depend on the episodic memory system that supports recollection. Not everyone agrees with this view, however (Manns, Hopkins, Reed, Kitchener, and Squire, 2003; Squire, Wixted, and Clark, 2007).

Studying Patients with Selective Hippocampus Damage

The above discussion illustrates the difficulties one encounters using the DNMS animal model to define a neural circuit for episodic memory. We don't know when nonverbal animals are actually recollecting events from their past. So ultimately our conclusions about the critical contribution the hippocampus makes to the episodic memory system must be derived from people with brain damage limited to the hippocampus.

Steward Zola-Morgan

Since H.M., a number of people with relatively selective damage to the hippocampus have been discovered. Although there is debate about the recognition memory capacity of these patients, no one doubts that they all are impaired in acquiring new episodic memories.

Steward Zola-Morgan, Larry Squire, and David Amaral (1986) described patient R.B. The onset of R.B.'s amnesia was associated with complications of a second artery bypass surgery. Zola-Morgan and his colleagues tested R.B.'s memory and, at his death, conducted an extensive neuropathological evaluation of R.B.'s brain. Formal memory tests indicate that he had difficulty acquiring new information. For example, after a story was read to him, R.B. could only recall a small fraction of the material. He also could only recall a small percentage of words that were read to him twice. Informally R.B. reported that he had severe memory problems. He reported that if he had talked to his children on the phone he did not remember doing so the next day. Thus, R.B. had significant anterograde amnesia. However, formal tests found no evidence of retrograde amnesia, that is, loss of memory for events that occurred prior to the cardiac episode. There was some speculation based on informal observations that he may have had loss of memory for some events that occurred a few years prior to the event.

Remarkably, the neuropathological assessment of R.B.'s brain indicated that the pathology *was restricted to the CA1 region of the hippocampus* (Figure 12.6). Bilaterally, there was a complete loss of neurons from the CA1 field. The CA1 field is a final stage whereby information processed by other regions is sent out via the subiculum and entorhinal cortex. Thus, although the dam-

FIGURE 12.6
Damage to the hippocampus of patient R.B. was restricted to a massive loss of neurons in the CA1 field, outlined in white in the figure.

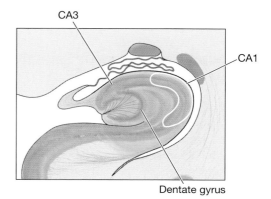

age was restricted, it was in a location that would be expected to significantly diminish the ability of the hippocampus to make its normal contribution to memory.

Cipolotti et al. (2001) described the case of V.C., who became profoundly amnesic at the age of 67, apparently after experiencing an epileptic seizure. Assessment of his brain damage by magnetic resonance imaging indicated that there was significant loss of volume over the entire rostral-caudal length of the hippocampus. However, critical surrounding cortical regions—the entorhinal and parahippocampus cortices—were normal, as were the adjacent temporal lobes. Thus, V.C.'s damage was restricted primarily to the hippocampus. Formal tests revealed that V.C. had profound anterograde amnesia. He was severely impaired on all measures of recall, such as the recall of a story and word associations. V.C. also had extensive retrograde amnesia.

Studies of patients with much more selective damage to the hippocampus, thus, support Brenda Milner's original conjecture that the hippocampus is critically involved in what we now call episodic memory.

Summary

The content of experience matters to the brain. Different attributes are assigned to different regions of the brain for storage. The idea that the brain has multiple memory systems is now central to the neurobiology of memory.

The perspective that different brain regions support different memory systems gained support when Brenda Milner's analysis of patient H.M. revealed that the removal of the medial temporal lobes left him with no long-term episodic memory but did not influence his ability to learn complex motor tasks or perceptual motor adjustments. Milner proposed that it was the damage to the hippocampus that was critical to H.M.'s profound episodic memory impairment.

The delayed nonmatching-to-sample recognition memory task was invented in an attempt to develop an animal model aimed at determining which regions of the medial temporal lobes are critical for episodic memory. This research revealed that the hippocampus is not necessary for animals to perform this task but that the cortical areas surrounding the hippocampus are.

Most researchers believe that recognition is based on both a familiarity process that depends on the cortical areas surrounding the hippocampus, and a recollection process that contains information about where and when the event happens, which depends on the hippocampus. Other human patients with more selective damage to the hippocampus support Milner's hypothesis that the hippocampus is critical for episodic memory. Just how the hippocampus supports episodic memory is the topic of the next chapter.

References

Andersen, P., Morris, R., Amaral, D., Bliss, T., and O'Keefe, J. (2007). Historical perspective: proposed functions, biological characteristics, and neurobiological models of the hippocampus. In P. Anderson, R. Morris, D. Amaral, T. Bliss, and J. O'Keefe (Eds.), *The Hippocampus Book* (pp. 9–36). New York: Oxford University Press.

Baxter, M. G. and Murray, E. A. (2001). Opposite relationship of hippocampal and rhinal cortex damage to delayed nonmatching-to-sample deficits in monkeys. *Hippocampus, 11,* 61–71.

Bayley, P. J., Frascino, J. C., and Squire, L. R. (2005). Robust habit learning in the absence of awareness and independent of the medial temporal lobe. *Nature, 436,* 550–553.

Brown, M. W. and Aggleton, J. P. (2001). Recognition memory: what are the roles of the perirhinal cortex and hippocampus? *Nature Reviews Neuroscience, 2,* 51–61.

Cipolotti, L., Shallice, T., Chan, D., Fox, N., Scahill, R., Harrison, G., Stevens, J., and Rudge, P. (2001). Long-term retrograde amnesia...the crucial role of the hippocampus. *Neuropsychologia, 39,* 151–172.

Claparède, E. (1951). Recognition and me-ness. In D. Rapaport (Ed.), *Organization and Pathology of Thought* (pp. 58–75). New York: Columbia University Press.

Corkin, S. (1968). Acquisition of a motor skill after bilateral medial temporal lobe excision. *Neuropsychologia, 6,* 255–265.

Corkin, S., Amaral, D. G., Gonzalez, R. G., Johnson, K. A., and Hyman, B. T. (1997). H. M.'s medial temporal lobe lesion: findings from magnetic resonance imaging. *Journal of Neuroscience, 17,* 3964–3979.

Manns, J. R., Hopkins, R. O., Reed, J. M., Kitchener, E. G., and Squire, L. R. (2003). Recognition memory and the human hippocampus. *Neuron, 7,* 171–180.

McDonald, R. J. and White, N. M. (1993). A triple dissociation of memory systems: hippocampus, amygdala, and dorsal striatum. *Behavioral Neuroscience, 107,* 3–22.

Meunier, M., Bachevalier, J., Mishkin, M., and Murray, E. A. (1993). Effects on visual recognition of combined and separate ablations of the entorhinal and perirhinal cortex in rhesus monkeys. *Journal of Neuroscience, 13,* 5418–5432.

Milner, B. (1970). Memory and the medial temporal lobe regions of the brain. In K. H. Pribram and D. E. Broadbent (Eds.), *Biology of Memory* (pp. 29–50). New York: Academic Press.

Mishkin, M. (1978). Memory in monkeys severely impaired by combined but not by separate removal of amygdala and hippocampus. *Nature, 273,* 297–298.

Mishkin, M. (1982). A memory system in the monkey. *Philosophical Transactions of the Royal Society London, 298,* 83–95.

Murray, E. A. and Mishkin, M. (1998). Object recognition and location memory in monkeys with excitotoxic lesions of the amygdala and hippocampus. *Journal of Neuroscience, 18,* 6568–6582.

Rugg, M. D. and Yonelinas, A. P. (2003). Human recognition memory: a cognitive neuroscience perspective. *Trends in Cognitive Sciences, 7,* 313–319.

Scoville, W. B. and Milner, B. (1957). Loss of recent memory after bilateral hippocampal lesions. *Journal of Neurology, Neurosurgery, and Psychiatry, 20,* 11–12.

Squire, L. R. (2004). Memory systems of the brain: a brief history and current perspective. *Neurobiology of Learning and Memory, 82,* 171–177.

Squire, L. R. (1987). *Memory and Brain.* New York: Oxford University Press.

Squire, L. R., Wixted, J. T., and Clark, R. E. (2007). Recognition memory and the medial temporal lobe: a new perspective. *Nature Reviews Neuroscience, 8,* 872–883.

Sutherland, R. J. and Rudy, J. W. (1989). Configural association theory: the role of the hippocampal formation in learning, memory, and amnesia. *Psychobiology, 17: 22,* 129–144.

White, N. M. and McDonald, R. J. (2002). Multiple parallel memory systems in the brain of the rat. *Neurobiology of Learning and Memory, 77,* 125–184.

Zola, S. M. and Squire, L. R. (2001) Relationship between magnitude of damage to the hippocampus and impaired recognition memory in monkeys. *Hippocampus, 11,* 92–98.

Zola-Morgan, S., Squire, L. R., Amaral, D. G., and Suzuki, W. A. (1989). Lesions of perirhinal and parahippocampal cortex that spare the amygdala and hippocampal formation produce severe memory impairment. *Journal of Neuroscience, 9,* 4355–4370.

Zola-Morgan, S., Squire, L. R., and Amaral, D. G. (1986). Human amnesia and the medial temporal region: enduring memory impairment following a bilateral lesion limited to field CA1 of the hippocampus. *Journal of Neuroscience, 6,* 2950–2967.

13

The Hippocampus Index and Episodic Memory

As you learned in the previous chapter, the episodic memory system captures the content of our experiences in a form that permits us to recollect or replay them. When the hippocampus is significantly damaged, this capacity is lost and we become disconnected from our past. Thus, there is something special about the hippocampus and its connections with other brain regions that is fundamental to the episodic memory system. How do the hippocampus and its related cortical structures store the content of our personal experiences so that it can be recollected or recalled? The goal of this chapter is to answer this question, by describing:

- the properties of the episodic memory system;
- the neural system in which the hippocampus is situated;
- the indexing theory of episodic memory;
- current evidence supporting the indexing theory; and
- episodic, semantic, and declarative memory distinctions.

Properties of Episodic Memory

Episodic memory has several important properties or attributes, including (1) its support of conscious recollection and storage of temporal–spatial contextual information for later retrieval, (2) its ability to automatically capture episodic and incidental information, and (3) its ability to acquire information about an event that occurs only once, yet protect the representations it stores from interfering with each other.

Conscious Recollection and Contextual Information Storage

The episodic system is most often described as supporting memories that can be consciously recollected or recalled. The term **conscious recollection** has two meanings:

1. It means that you intentionally initiated a search of your memory. This meaning refers to the manner in which retrieval is initiated.
2. It also means that you have an awareness of remembering—a sense that a memory trace has been successfully activated. This meaning refers to a subjective feeling that is a product of the retrieval process (Schacter, 1989).

Our personal experience is consistent with the idea that we can be aware that we have retrieved a memory or had a remembering experience. It also is the case that we can intentionally initiate a memory search that leads to recalling a memory. However, this does not mean that memories retrieved from the episodic system have to evoke a state of conscious awareness to influence behavior. Nor does it mean that our episodic memory system can only be accessed if we intentionally initiate a search.

To appreciate this last point, you also can draw on personal experiences such as encountering a friend whom you haven't seen in a while or visiting an old neighborhood. Such experiences often initiate the recall of many events associated with the friend or neighborhood without any intention on your part to retrieve these memories. Moreover, it is likely that you became aware of having a remembering experience.

The subjective state of conscious awareness that can occur when we have successfully remembered some event may be associated with the content of the memory trace. A number of researchers agree that the feeling of remembering emerges when a retrieved memory trace contains information about the time, place, or context of the experience that established the memory (Squire and Zola-Morgan, 1991; Squire and Kandel, 1999; Nadel and Moscovitch, 1997). Being able to retrieve this contextual information enables a replay of the experience and allows us to declare that we remember. In describing the importance of contextual information for recollection, for example, Squire and Kandel (1999, p. 69) wrote,

> Once the context is reconstructed, it may seem surprising how easy it is to recall the scene and what took place. In this way, one can become immersed in sustained recollection, sometimes accompanied by strong emotions and by a compelling sense of personal familiarity with what is remembered.

Obviously, information about the spatial and temporal context of the experience must be stored if conscious recollection depends on its retrieval. Thus, the episodic memory system must be critically involved in both the storage and retrieval of contextual information.

Automatic Capture of Episodic and Incidental Information

Many theorists believe that the episodic memory system automatically captures information simply as a consequence of our exploring and experiencing the environment (O'Keefe and Nadel, 1978; Teyler and DiScenna, 1986; Morris et al., 2003; O'Reilly and Rudy, 2001; Teyler and Rudy, 2007). The term *automatic* is used to note that the information is captured *without intention* on our part to do so. You can prove this is true by recalling your experiences of the past several days. You will undoubtedly remember a surprising amount of information. Now ask yourself if you intentionally attempted to store any of this information. Your likely answer will be no.

To be sure, you may be able to co-opt this system by instructing yourself to remember a phone number or an address. However, the basic point is that *the hippocampus does not need to be driven by our intentions or goals to capture information.* It contributes to the episodic memory system by automatically capturing the information it receives as we attend to and explore the world. For this reason, some researchers also say that the episodic memory system captures *incidental information*. This means that it will capture information that is incidental to the task at hand. Thus, when you deliberately remember a phone number, it is unlikely that you intend to remember the episode of memorizing the number. Nevertheless, it is likely that you will. Or, if you were trying to learn a new tune on the piano, you did not instruct yourself to remember the practice session. Nevertheless, the episodic memory system likely captured a great deal of this incidental information so that you can later recall much about the practice session.

Single Episode Capture with Protection from Interference

The term episodic memory means that the system captures information about single episodes of our lives. What constitutes the duration of an episode is vague. However, the gist of this idea is that the episodic memory system can acquire information about an event that *occurs only once*. It has been suggested that from the viewpoint of the episodic system, every episode of our lives is unique, even if it contains highly overlapping information (Nadel and Moscovitch, 1997). Thus, we can remember many different instances of practicing the piano or driving our car to the same parking lot.

If the episodic memory system is constantly capturing information about our daily events, then it must be able to store highly similar episodes, such as where you parked your car today versus where you parked it yesterday, so that these memories do not interfere with each other. Our success in keeping memories of similar events separate suggests that an important property of the episodic system is that the representations it stores are somehow protected from interference (O'Keefe and Nadel, 1978; O'Reilly and McClelland, 1994; O'Reilly and Rudy, 2001).

Summary

In summary, many researchers agree about the fundamental attributes of the episodic memory system. It automatically captures information about the single episodes of our lives. The memory trace includes information about the spatial and temporal context of the episode and it is when this contextual information is retrieved that we are consciously aware of the memory and can declare that we remembered some event. The next sections describe how the hippocampus contributes to these properties and supports memories.

A Neural System that Supports Episodic Memory

The hippocampus can support episodic memories because it is embedded in a neural system in which it interacts with other regions of the brain and because both its intrinsic organization and the properties of its synaptic connections are unique. The work of a number of neuroanatomists has led to an understanding of the connectivity of these regions of the brain (Van Hoesen and Pandya, 1975; Amaral and Lavenex, 2007; Lavenex and Amaral, 2000).

The Hierarchy and the Loop

The neural system that supports episodic memory can be organized around two principles (Lavenex and Amaral, 2000) that are illustrated in Figure 13.1.

1. The organization is hierarchical. The level of integration or abstraction of information increases as it flows from the neocortex to the perirhinal and parahippocampal cortices to the entorhinal cortex and through the hippocampus.

2. The circuit is a loop. This means that information carried forward to the hippocampus also is then projected back to the sites lower in the hierarchy that initially brought the information to the hippocampus.

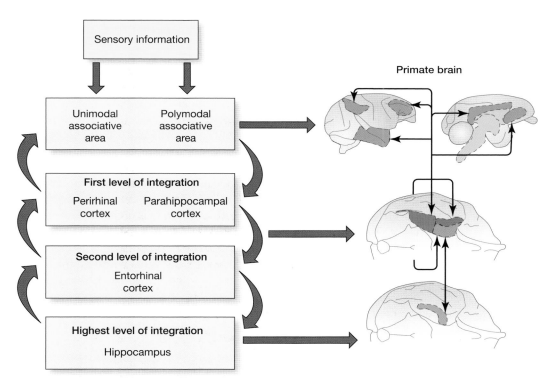

FIGURE 13.1
On the left is a schematic representation of the flow of information from the neocortical unimodal and polymodal associative areas to the medial temporal lobe regions. Information flows to the highest level of integration and then loops back to the neocortical areas. The location of these regions in the primate brain is shown on the right. (After Lavenex and Amaral, 2000 and Eichenbaum, 2000.).

FIGURE 13.2
This figure illustrates the flow of information into and out of the hippocampus, from and to the entorhinal cortex. The combination of hippocampal components and the subiculum is sometimes referred to as the hippocampal formation.

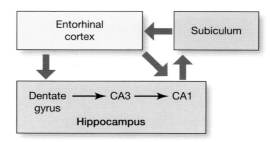

The flow of information to the medial temporal lobes begins when sensory information (e.g., visual, auditory, somatosensory) arrives at different regions of the neocortex (called unimodel associative and polymodal associative areas). Information at this level is not well integrated. However, these regions project to what Lavenex and Amaral call the first level of integration—the perirhinal and parahippocampus cortices. Information from these regions projects forward to the second level of integration in the entorhinal cortex that projects to the highest level of integration—the hippocampus. At each stage the information becomes more compressed or abstract.

Information is processed through the hippocampus and then projects back to the entorhinal cortex. The entorhinal cortex also projects back to the perirhinal and parahippocampal cortices that in turn project back to the neocortical regions. Figure 13.2 provides a more complete representation of the flow of information into and out of the hippocampus. It shows that the entorhinal cortex projects into two regions of the hippocampus, the dentate gyrus and the CA1 region, and that information projects out of the hippocampus to the entorhinal cortex via a region called the **subiculum**. This combination of hippocampal components and the subiculum is sometimes called the **hippocampal formation**.

Most researchers agree that the critical components of this hierarchical system that uniquely contribute to episodic memory are located in the medial temporal lobes. This system is sometimes referred to as the **medial temporal hippocampal (MTH) system**, consisting of the perirhinal, parahippocampal, and entorhinal cortices and the hippocampal formation (see Figure 13.2).

Functional Implications

This MTH system has the following functional implications:

1. Because the hippocampus sits at the top of a hierarchically organized system, it is in a position to receive convergent information from a wide range of cortical regions. In a sense, it sees what is going on in other regions of the brain.

2. The information is so highly processed by the time it reaches the hippocampus that it is described as amodal (Lavenex and Amaral, 2000). This means that hippocampal neurons do not know whether they are receiving auditory, visual, or somatosensory information.

3. The perirhinal, parahippocampal, and entorhinal cortices also have to be considered as part of the episodic memory system because without them the hippocampus receives no information. They are the last stage of information processing before information enters the hippocampus. Thus, whether or not these regions can support other memory functions, such as familiarity-based recognition, they are critical to episodic memory.

Let's now consider a theory of just what the hippocampus contributes to episodic memory.

The Indexing Theory of Episodic Memory

Any theoretical account of how the hippocampus supports episodic memory must be consistent with the anatomy and physiology of the system. Tim Teyler and Pascal DiScenna (1986) provided one such account and called it the **indexing theory of hippocampal memory** (see also Marr, 1971). This theory has been supported by a wealth of data (Teyler and Rudy, 2007) and its basic ideas are shared by a number of theorists (Marr, 1971; McNaughton and Morris, 1987; McNaughton, 1991; O'Reilly and Rudy, 2001; Squire, 1992; Morris et al., 2003).

Figure 13.3 provides a simple illustration of indexing theory. The theory assumes that the individual features that make up a particular episode establish a memory trace by activating patterns of neocortical activity, which then project to the hippocampus (Figure 13.3B). As a consequence, synapses in the hippocampus responding to the neocortical inputs are strengthened by mechanisms that support long-term potentiation (discussed in Chapters 2 through 6). The experience is represented simply as the set of strengthened synapses in the hippocampus that result from the input pattern, that is, there are no modifications among the neocortical activity patterns. Thus, *the memory trace is a representation in the hippocampus of co-occurring patterns of activity in the neocortex.*

Tim Teyler

The "indexing" nature of the memory trace can be illustrated in relationship to memory retrieval. Note in Figure 13.3C that a subset of the original neocortical pattern is received by the hippocampus. The projec-

Memory trace formation

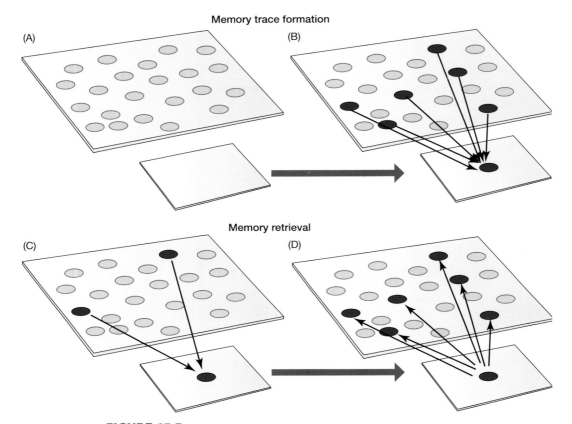

FIGURE 13.3
This figure illustrates the important ideas represented in the indexing theory of the hippocampus. (A) In memory trace formation the top layer represents potential patterns of neocortical activity, while the bottom layer represents the hippocampus. (B) A set of neocortical patterns (purple dots) activated by a particular experience is projected to the hippocampus and activates a unique set of synapses. (C) In memory retrieval, a subset of the initial input pattern can activate the hippocampal representation. (D) When this occurs, output from the hippocampus projects back to the neocortex to activate the entire pattern. Thus the hippocampus stores an index to neocortical patterns that can be used to retrieve the memory.

tions from these input patterns activate the now connected neurons in the hippocampus representing the original experience. The activation of this representation then projects back to the neocortex to activate the pattern representing the entire experience (Figure 13.3D). It is this projection back to the neocortex that conveys the indexing property to the hippocampus representation. This process is called pattern completion and is described more fully below.

The indexing idea can be understood in relationship to a library. A library often contains thousands of books. This creates an obvious problem—how do you find the one you want? Librarians solved the retrieval problem by creating an indexing system that contains information about the location of the book. So you go to the index and find the book's address. Note that the content you are looking for is in the book. The index has no content; it just tells you where to find the book that contains the desired information. Likewise, the episodic memory indexing theory assumes the rich content of our experience is stored in neocortical regions of the brain and all that the hippocampus stores is information about how to retrieve the memories stored in the neocortex. It provides an index to the content represented in the neocortex.

The Hippocampus Does Not Store Content

It is worth reiterating the basic character of the memory trace provided by this system. The content of the memory is contained in the unique patterns of activity in the neocortical regions of the brain activated by the experience. *There is no memory content per se contained in the hippocampus*. All that it contains is the information that a specific pattern of activity in different cortical regions has occurred. This pattern is represented by (1) strengthening the synaptic connections between the input from the neocortex and the neurons activated in the hippocampus and (2) strengthening connections among the neurons that were activated. The only way the full content of the memory experience can be replayed is by outputs from the hippocampus activating the cortical representations of the experience. Thus, the hippocampus simply represents the conjunction of co-occurring input patterns and provides a map to the relevant cortical sites that contain the content of our experiences.

In this context there are two important related concepts that need to be further discussed in relationship to indexing theory—pattern completion and pattern separation. Understanding these concepts is central to understanding how the index retrieves an episodic memory.

Pattern Completion and Pattern Separation

When we encounter a subset or portion of the experience that originally established the memory trace, it can activate or replay the entire experience. The process by which this happens is called **pattern completion**. It is the most fundamental process provided by the index. This process is possible because synapses on neurons in the hippocampus that represent the patterns of activity in the neocortex have been strengthened (this is the index) and because neurons in the hippocampus project back to the same neocortical regions (for example, entorhinal cortex) that projected to it (shown previously in Figures

13.1 and 13.2). Note that this could not happen if there were no return projections back from the hippocampus to the neocortex.

As you learned earlier, one of the remarkable aspects of the episodic memory system is that it has the capacity to maintain distinct representations of similar, but separately occurring, episodes. Many theorists believe that this property of episodic memory derives from the architecture of the hippocampus and its relationship to the neocortex. The basic idea is that outputs from widespread patterns of activity in the neocortex will randomly converge onto and activate a much smaller set of neurons in the hippocampus (O'Reilly and McClelland, 1994; O'Reilly and Rudy, 2001). Because the similar (but different) inputs are likely to converge onto different neurons in the hippocampus, the two similar patterns are likely to create different indices. Thus, the hippocampus is said to support a process called **pattern separation** that keeps representations of similar experiences segregated.

Why Not Just Store the Memory in the Neocortex?

The way in which the memory trace is built by this indexing system might seem overly complex. Why should the brain need an elaborate hierarchical system in which neocortical regions project to the hippocampus and then loop back to the neocortex to store a memory? Why not just directly strengthen the connections between those patterns of activity in the neocortex? There are perhaps two reasons why a hierarchical system has evolved. The first has to do with the associative connectivity problem, while the second is related to the interference problem.

THE ASSOCIATIVE CONNECTIVITY PROBLEM   The associative connectivity problem relates to the potential connections among neurons in the different neocortical regions that support representations of experience. There may not be enough of these connections to support the rapid changes needed to associate patterns of activation distributed widely across the neocortex (Rolls and Treves, 1998). Thus, although there may be on the order of 1010 principle neurons in the cortex, they are not richly interconnected. This makes it difficult to strengthen associative connections among the patterns of activity produced by experience. Without these patterns being strongly connected, pattern completion (the activation of the entire pattern by a subset of the original experience) would be difficult.

In contrast, two regions in the hippocampus, the dentate gyrus and CA3, have high internal connectivity and modifiable synapses. In CA3, in particular, interconnectivity is so high that most of the pyramidal cells are connected within two to three synaptic steps (Rolls and Treves, 1998). Thus, unlike neocortex, the hippocampus is well designed to associate arbitrary input patterns. Moreover, these synapses are easily modified, and mechanisms of synaptic plasticity revealed by studies of LTP (discussed in Chapters 2 through 6) may very well support the changes in synaptic strength needed to maintain new associative connections.

THE INTERFERENCE PROBLEM   The second reason why the hierarchical organization may be favored is related to the interference problem. Many of the episodes that make up our daily experiences occur in similar situations. For these individual episodes to be kept separate, they must be stored so that two similar episodes are not confused. Memory traces composed of directly connected patterns of neocortical activity may not be well suited to solve this problem. Consider what might happen if you have two related experiences such as lunch in the same place with two different friends. As described earlier, the hippocampus index supports pattern separation and thus would keep these two related but different experiences separate (illustrated in Figure 13.4A as ABCD and CDEF). In the neocortex, however, these two similar experiences would be

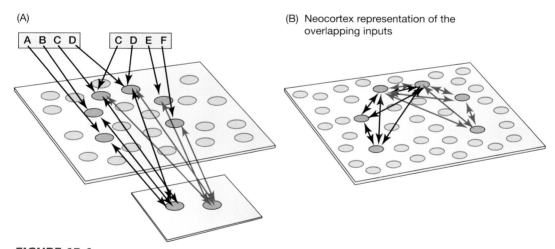

(A)

(B) Neocortex representation of the overlapping inputs

FIGURE 13.4
The hippocampus keeps memories of similar episodes separated. Two similar input patterns (ABCD and CDEF) activate their respective patterns of neocortical activity. Projections from these similar neocortical patterns converge onto different neurons in the hippocampus. The synaptic connections from the cortical projections to and among the hippocampus neurons are strengthened. Thus, the hippocampus provides a separate index for the two similar memories that keeps them separated. Presenting the AC combination selectively activates the ABCD pattern, and the CE combination activates the CDEF pattern. In contrast, the neocortex has difficulty keeping the memories for similar episodes separated. Because the patterns share common features (CD), they are interconnected and the memories for the different episodes lose their identity. Any combination of inputs (e.g., AC, CE, or BD) activates the entire blended network.

integrated into a common representation. The key difference, shown in Figure 13.4B, is that in the neocortex any combination of inputs (AC, CE, or BD) would activate the integrated representation.

Indexing Theory and Properties of Episodic Memory

Indexing theory was developed with the intent of explaining how the neural system in which the hippocampus is situated can support the fundamental features of episodic memory. The properties of episodic memory emerge quite naturally from this theory.

- Conscious recollection and awareness emerge when pattern completion processes activate a representation of the entire event, including the context in which it occurs, sufficiently to replay the memory.

- The automatic or incidental storage property emerges because the synapses that support the memory are automatically strengthened just by the fact that experience generates new patterns of neural activity in the neocortex that project into the hippocampus. Such a mechanism captures the contextual information in which experience occurs because it binds the cortical representations of the entire experience.

- The episodic nature of the memory trace is due to single experiences, each generating unique patterns of neural activity in the neocortex that are captured by the hippocampus index.

- Interference among similar memory traces is reduced because the hippocampus supports pattern separation.

Evidence for Indexing Theory

A wealth of evidence supports the indexing theory of episodic memory. In this section some of the literature that provides support for these ideas is presented. This evidence is intended to be illustrative rather than comprehensive. The experiments were chosen because they comment on some component of the theoretical ideas that have been presented. Two sources of data are described: (1) studies of amnesic people with damage to the hippocampus and (2) studies of animals, primarily rodents, with experimentally induced selective damage to the hippocampus.

People with Damage to the Hippocampus

Patients with significant damage to the hippocampus are selectively impaired in their ability to consciously recall episodes of their personal experiences and events that occurred at specific time and places. Recall that H.M. (see Chapter 12) improved his performance on motor and perceptual reorganization tasks, yet he had no recollection of ever participating in these tasks. Formal tests of other patients with much more selective damage to the hippocampus, such as patients R.B. and V.C., also revealed that their recall of recent experiences was severely impaired (Cipolotti et al., 2001; Zola-Morgan, Squire, and Amaral, 1986).

You have learned that the hippocampus–episodic memory supports conscious recollection. However, you also know that you do not have to intend to remember an episode for the hippocampus to capture aspects about it. The hippocampus automatically captures information and does so even when the information is incidental to some other goal that directs your behavior. Nor do you have to engage in explicit recollection for memories that depend on the hippocampus to be retrieved and influence behavior. Experiments have also revealed these more subtle attributes of memories supported by the hippocampus.

Before describing these experiments, however, it is useful to discuss two ways in which memories can be assessed. They are called *explicit* and *implicit* memory tests (Figure 13.5). Explicit memory tests are based on intentional or conscious recollection of past episodes, whereas implicit memory tests measure the unintentional or unconscious use of previously acquired information (Schacter and Tulving, 1994). To illustrate this distinction, remember Claparède's patient who would not shake hands with him but could not consciously recollect why (specifically, the episode in which Claparède stuck the patient with a sharp object when they shook hands; see Chapter 12). The failure of the patient to shake hands would be an example of an implicit response

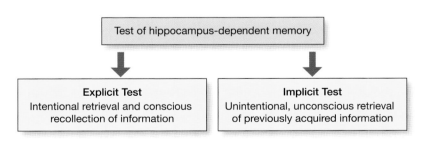

FIGURE 13.5
The kind of information captured by the hippocampus can be revealed by both explicit and implicit memory tests. Explicit memory tests require the subject to intentionally or consciously recollect a past episode. Implicit memory tests use other methods for detecting the effects of experience on memory that do not require the subject to intentionally remember.

Neal Cohen

measure revealing that some information about the hand-shaking experience was stored. The inability to recall the episode would be an instance in which an explicit measure failed to reveal a memory of the experience.

Neal Cohen and his colleagues (Ryan, Althoff, Whitlow, and Cohen, 2000; Ryan and Cohen, 2004) have provided evidence that the episodic memory system automatically captures information that can be revealed by an implicit measure of memory. They did this by tracking how the eye scans visual scenes. Normally people scan novel pictures longer than they scan pictures that they are familiar with, and if the components of a familiar picture are rearranged, they scan the region of the picture that has been altered more than the unaltered region.

Amnesics also scan novel pictures more than they scan familiar pictures; however, rearranging the components of a familiar picture has no effect on their pattern of visual scanning (Ryan et al., 2000; Ryan and Cohen, 2004). Thus, without any explicit instruction or intention, normal people capture and remember the arrangement of the components of pictures and this is revealed without their engaging in intentional or conscious recollection. Amnesics, including one patient with damage to the hippocampus, however, do not store representations of how the components that make up the picture are arranged (Figure 13.6).

These results make the point that memories captured by the hippocampus can be revealed in people by both explicit and implicit measures of memory. Explicit measures reveal that subjects can intentionally or consciously recall the experience. Implicit measures reveal that, without any intention on the person's part, the hippocampus automatically captures information that does not have to be consciously recalled to influence our behavior.

FIGURE 13.6

Control subjects and amnesics scanned two types of visual scenes. All the scenes were repeatedly viewed but occasionally one of the repeated scenes was slightly manipulated by altering some small area of the picture. The eyes of control subjects repeatedly went back to the altered region of the manipulated scene. Amnesics, however, did not alter their scan of the manipulated picture. (After Ryan and Cohen, 2004.)

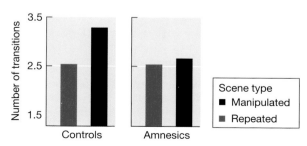

Hippocampus Studies in Rodents

As previously noted, an advantage of studying memory in animals other than people is that the experimenter can precisely damage a particular region of the brain, including the hippocampus or its surrounding cortical regions. The disadvantage of this approach is that non-human animals cannot consciously recollect. Nevertheless, Howard Eichenbaum (2000) has made the point that the anatomical organization of the neural system that contains the hippocampus in primates and rodents is remarkably similar to that system in humans (illustrated previously in Figure 13.1). Thus, even though conscious recollection can be demonstrated only in people, given the anatomy of the rodent brain one should expect that it could support a rudimentary episodic memory system.

Howard Eichenbaum

Indexing theory makes several claims about the role of the hippocampus in episodic memory that can be evaluated even in animals that cannot consciously recollect. These claims are that the hippocampus:

- is critical to forming context representations;
- is the basis for conscious awareness and recollection;
- automatically captures context (incidental) information;
- captures single episodes;
- supports cued recall through pattern completion; and
- keeps separate episodes distinct.

THE HIPPOCAMPUS IS CRITICAL TO CONTEXT REPRESENTATIONS A large number of studies with rodents support the idea that the hippocampus is critical to forming a representation of the context in which events are experienced. The **context preexposure paradigm** developed by Michael Fanselow (1990) provides a powerful tool to study context representations. It is based on a phenomenon called the **immediate shock effect**. If a rat is placed into a fear-conditioning chamber and shocked immediately (within 6 seconds), it will later show little or no fear of the conditioning chamber. However, if the rat is allowed to explore the conditioning chamber for a couple of minutes the day before it receives immediate shock, it will subsequently show substantial fear to that context (Figure 13.7). This result is believed to demonstrate that the rat acquired a representation of the context when it explored it during the preexposure phase. Thus, rats that were not preexposed to the shock–test context failed to show conditioned fear because they did not have time before the shock to acquire a representation of the context.

(A)

Context preexposure

Immediate shock

Fear test

FIGURE 13.7
(A) The top of the figure illustrates the experimental design revealing that the rat acquires a representation of an explored context. It takes advantage of the fact that rats that are simply placed into a particular context and immediately shocked do not later fear that context. However, if they are preexposed to that context the day before the immediate shock experience, they do later show fear. (B) This graph shows that immediate shock itself does produce fear of the context, but that context preexposure markedly increases the fear produced by immediate shock. This result, called the context preexposure effect, indicates that the rat acquires a representation of the explored context. (After Fanselow, 1990.)

(B)

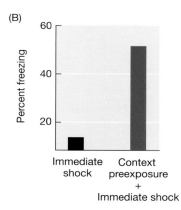

There are a number of reasons to believe that acquiring a representation depends on the hippocampus (Rudy, Huff, and Matus-Amat, 2004). Studies have shown that:

- rats with damage to the dorsal part of the hippocampus do not acquire a representation of an explored context (Rudy, Barrientos, and O'Reilly, 2002), and

- injecting the NMDA receptor antagonist D-APV into the dorsal hippocampus before context preexposure impairs the acquisition of a representation of context (Matus-Amat, Higgins, Sprunger, Wright-Hardesty, and Rudy, 2007).

HIPPOCAMPUS INDEX REPRESENTATIONS SUPPORT CONSCIOUS RECOLLECTION
Indexing theory assumes that conscious recollection derives, in part, from
the index representation that binds components of the episode into a representation of the context. Thus, encountering some component of the episode
activates the index that in turn projects back to the neocortex and activates
the cortical representation of the context. Strong activation of this representation might provide a basis for conscious awareness (see Eichenbaum,
Yonelinas, and Ranganath, 2007, for a similar analysis).

Animals other than people cannot express their subjective feelings. However, it is possible to tell if they have the kind of representation just described.
Studies of object recognition indicate that they do. For example, when given
a choice between exploring a novel object and one previously experienced (a
familiar object), rats spend more time exploring the novel object. Rats with
damage to the hippocampus also explore a novel object more than a familiar one. However, what they apparently can't do is remember the context in
which a particular object was experienced. This point is illustrated in Figure 13.8. A normal rat is first allowed to explore the cube in context A and
the cylinder in context B. In the test phase, the rat is presented with each
object in context A and in context B. A normal rat will explore the object
presented in the different context as if it were novel. This means the representation of the object was bound together with features of the context in
which it was explored. This kind of representation should require an index
and be dependent on the hippocampus. In fact, rats with damage to the
hippocampus treat explored objects as familiar, whether they are tested in
their training context or the other context (Eacott and Norman, 2004; Mumby,
Gaskin, Glenn, Schramek, and Lehmann, 2002; see Eichenbaum et al., 2007,
for a review).

THE HIPPOCAMPUS AUTOMATICALLY CAPTURES INFORMATION   As noted earlier,
the episodic memory system is always online, automatically capturing the
events that make up our daily experiences. The studies just described make
the case that this property also depends on the hippocampus. To appreciate
this point, reconsider the context dependency of the object-recognition study
illustrated in Figure 13.8. There are no explicit demands embedded in an object-recognition task. Nothing forces the animal to remember that the cube occurred in context A and the cylinder occurred in context B, any more than a
normal person must remember where he or she had breakfast. However, this
happens and it depends on an intact hippocampus.

Consider another example based on a different version of object-recognition memory. In this case the rat is allowed to explore two different objects that
occupy different locations in a training arena. For example, object A might be in
the corner of the arena and object B in the center. The normal rat stores a mem-

(A) **Exploration**

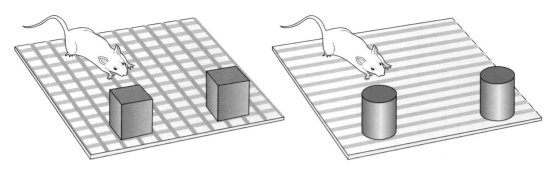

(B) **Test**

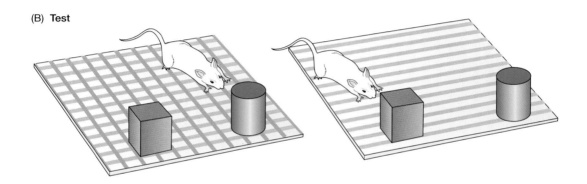

FIGURE 13.8
(A) Rats were allowed to explore two objects, a cube and a cylinder. Each object was explored in a different context. (B) The rats were then tested twice. Both objects were presented in each context. Control rats spent more time exploring the object that had not previously been experienced in the test context. In contrast, rats with damage to the hippocampus explored the objects equally. This means that control animals had a memory of the object and the context in which it occurred, but rats with damage to the hippocampus did not.

ory of the position of these objects because if the position of one of the objects is changed during the test, the rat will explore it as novel. Nothing forces the normal rat to remember the location of the objects (Figure 13.9). Rats with damage to the hippocampus, however, are not sensitive to the location of the objects changing (Eacott and Norman, 2004; Mumby et al., 2002). Thus, the hippocampus supports the processes that automatically capture this information.

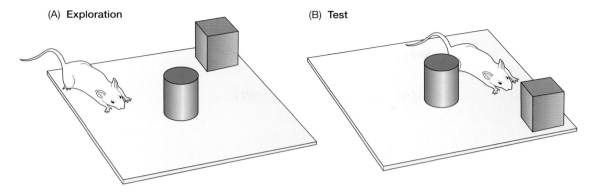

(A) Exploration (B) Test

FIGURE 13.9
(A) Rats were allowed to explore an arena containing two objects. (B) In the test phase the rat was returned to the arena but the location of one of the objects was changed. Control rats explored the moved object much more than they explored the unmoved object. They responded to it as if it were novel. Rats with damage to the hippocampus explored the two objects equally. Thus, automatically capturing information about the location of the objects depended on the hippocampus.

THE HIPPOCAMPUS CAPTURES SINGLE EPISODES There is good evidence that the hippocampus is part of the memory system that captures single episodes. For example, when the location of the hidden platform of the Morris water-escape task is altered on a daily basis, normal rats show dramatic improvement, even on the second trial and even if the intertrial interval is two hours. In contrast, rats with damage to the hippocampus show no improvement. Moreover, an injection of the NMDA-receptor antagonist APV into the dorsal hippocampus prior to the first trial also dramatically impairs performance on the second trial (Steele and Morris, 1999). Morris's group also developed and used a landmark, place-learning task (described in Chapter 8) to make the same point—that the hippocampus is part of the episodic memory system that captures information from a single experience (Bast, da Silva, and Morris, 2005; Day, Langston, and Morris, 2003).

THE HIPPOCAMPUS ENABLES CUED RECALL THROUGH PATTERN COMPLETION An important implication of indexing theory is that when a subset of the features that make up an episode activate the hippocampus, the index activates the entire pattern of neocortical activity generated by the episode. This implies that it should be possible to demonstrate cued recall of a memory in animals. There is good evidence that this occurs (Rudy and O'Reilly, 2001; Rudy et al., 2004).

A compelling example is based on the context preexposure–immediate shock paradigm. My colleagues and I (Rudy and O'Reilly, 2001; Rudy et al. 2002) used this paradigm to demonstrate that a memory of context can be retrieved and associated with shock. Our experiment is illustrated in Figure 13.10. During the preexposure session, rats were transported several times to a particular context (context A). The purpose was to establish a link between the transport (T) cage and a representation of context A. On the immediate shock day, however, the rats were transported to a novel and very different context (context B) and immediately shocked. The rats were later tested in either context A or context B.

Note that the indexing theory makes the unusual prediction that the rats should display fear when tested in context A but no fear in context B, where they were actually shocked. This prediction is unusual because the rats were never shocked in context A. This prediction is made because the transport cue should complete the pattern of activity that represents context A, and this representation should be available for the animals to associate with the shock. They should not display fear when tested in context B, where they were shocked, because they had never experienced it before and they did not have the opportunity to construct a representation of that context before they were shocked.

As you can see in Figure 13.10, this is exactly what we found. Moreover, damage to, or inactivation of, the dorsal hippocampus prevents this result (Matus-Amat, Higgins, Barrientos, and Rudy, 2004; Rudy et al., 2002). Thus, these results indicate that rodents can acquire a representation of a context that can be activated by a subset of the features that make up the episode. In other words, pattern completion supports cued recall in animals other than people, and this depends on the hippocampus.

THE HIPPOCAMPUS INDEX SUPPORTS PATTERN SEPARATION   One of the important properties of the episodic memory system is that it keeps similar episodes somewhat distinct. As noted, an index in the hippocampus provides an advantage over a straight neocortical memory system. There is evidence that pattern separation is better when the hippocampus is intact. One source of such evidence is the study of what is called generalized contextual fear conditioning. In such studies, rats are shocked in one context (context A) and then tested in either that context or a similar but not identical context (context B). To the extent that they show fear to the similar context, they are said to generalize their fear to another context.

Imagine that you were in an automobile accident. You might display fear of being in the specific car involved in the accident and/or generalized fear to other, similar cars. Rats lacking a hippocampus display more generalized fear than normal rats (Antoniadis and McDonald, 2000; Frankland, Cestari, Filip-

(A)

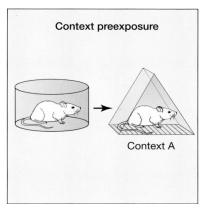
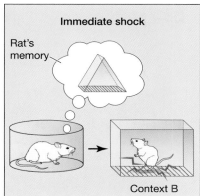
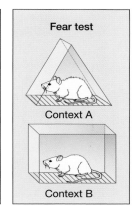

Context preexposure

Context A

Immediate shock

Rat's memory

Context B

Fear test

Context A

Context B

(B)

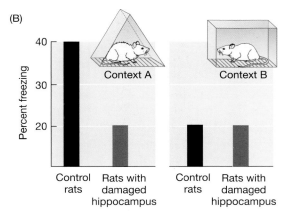

FIGURE 13.10

(A) An experiment demonstrating that rats can retrieve a memory of an explored context. During the context preexposure phase, the rats were transported in a bucket several times to a novel context (context A) and allowed to explore that context. The purpose of this procedure was to allow the transport bucket to become a cue that could retrieve the rat's memory of the explored context. In the immediate-shock phase of the experiment, the rats were transported in the same bucket to a shock chamber (context B), where they received an immediate shock. Note that the shock chamber was quite different from the previously explored context. The rats were then tested in either context A or context B. (B) The control rats displayed no fear in context B, where they were actually shocked, but displayed fear in context A, where they had been allowed to explore and had received no shock. This means that during the immediate-shock phase the control rats recalled the memory of context A (where they thought they were being transported to) and associated it with the shock. Rats with damage to the hippocampus, however, did not show fear to either context A or context B, which means they were not able to acquire or retrieve the memory representation of the preexposed context. (After Rudy et al., 2002.)

kowski, McDonald, and Silva, 1998). This result suggests that the hippocampus provides processes that enable the rat to discriminate the context paired with shock from a similar one that was not paired with shock.

Gilbert and Kesner (2006) have provided another source of evidence that the hippocampus is necessary for pattern separation. They reported that rats with selective neurotoxic damage to the dentate gyrus could discriminate the location of two identical objects (a covered a food well, for example) when the physical distance between them (their spatial separation) was great, but they performed poorly as the distance decreased. In contrast, normal rats were unaffected by the degree of spatial separation. Thus, the hippocampus was necessary for the rats to remember separate, similar spatial locations.

Episodic, Semantic, and Declarative Memory

Our discussion thus far about the role of the hippocampus and memory has been limited to how it contributes to episodic memory. Many memory researchers believe the episodic memory belongs to a broader, long-term memory category called **declarative memory**, which not only includes episodic memory but also **semantic memory**. Semantic memory is believed to support our memory for facts and our ability to extract generalizations from multiple experiences. For example, your past experiences allow you to answer questions like, is a violin a musical instrument or an automobile? You can also answer factual questions such as, what day was your mother born? Note that to answer these questions requires intentional retrieval and explicit recollection. Thus, semantic memory and episodic memory are similar in that people can intentionally retrieve information from them and in some sense declare they have the memory. The content of semantic memory, however, is not tied to the place or context where you acquired it. *It is sometimes said to be context free.* This means that you can know the facts about something without remembering when or where you learned them.

The inclusion of both episodic and semantic memory into a more general category—declarative memory—implies that they are supported by the same neural system. Indeed, some researchers (Manns, Hopkins, and Squire, 2003; Squire and Zola-Morgan, 1991; Squire and Zola, 1996, 1998) have argued that the medial temporal hippocampal system provides support for both types of memory. This is called the **unitary view** (Figure 13.11A). It suggests that damage to any component of this system will produce the same degree of impairment in tests of episodic and semantic memory.

Other researchers, however, do not accept the unitary theory of declarative memory and believe that only episodic memory requires the entire MTH

(A) Unitary view

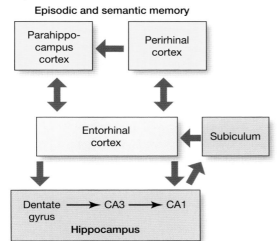

FIGURE 13.11
(A) The unitary view of the medial temporal hippocampal system. Supporters of this view believe that the system is needed to support both episodic and semantic memory. (B). The separatist view. Supporters of this view believe that the entire system, including the hippocampal formation, is required for episodic memory but that semantic memory does not require the hippocampus.

(B) Separatist view

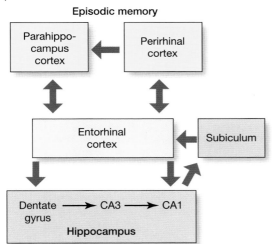

system. This is called the **separatist view**. Researchers who support this view believe that semantic memories can be acquired even when the hippocampus is selectively removed. Thus, while episodic and semantic memory may share some components of the MTH system, these researchers believe that the overlap is not complete and that episodic and semantic memory do not belong to a single declarative memory system (Figure 13.11B).

Farneh Vargha-Khadem

The Vargha-Khadem Findings

The separatist view came to life when Farneh Vargha-Khadem and her colleagues (Vargha-Khadem et al., 1997) reported the results for three patients with amnesia caused by relatively selective damage to the hippocampus sustained very early in life. Each of these patients developed a pronounced memory impairment as a result of an anoxic-ischemic episode, that is, they experienced a reduction in oxygen supply (hypoxia) combined with reduced blood flow (ischemia) to the brain. As revealed by quantitative magnetic resonance imaging, these patients had bilateral damage to approximately 50% of their hippocampus and very little damage to the surrounding cortices. The insult producing the pathology occurred at birth or when the patient was 4 or 9 years old.

These patients were 13, 16, and 19 years old when they received their first neuropsychological examination. The IQ of one of the patients was 109, which is well within the average range, whereas the IQs of the other two were in the low-average range (82 and 86). Their memory for everyday experiences was so poor that none of them could be left alone for any extended period of time. Formal tests of their memory confirmed that they were profoundly amnesic.

The surprising aspect of these patients is that even though they had no episodic memory, they all developed normal language and social skills. Moreover, they were all educated in mainstream schools. They learned to read and write and acquired new factual information at levels consistent with their verbal IQs. In fact, all three patients had fully normal scores on the Vocabulary, Information, and Comprehension subtests of the Weschler Intelligence Scale. Given these findings, Vargha-Khadem and her colleagues concluded that there was a disproportionate sparing of semantic memory compared to episodic memory in these patients who suffered selective damage to the hippocampus early in life.

Is the Medial Temporal Hippocampal System Homogeneous?

The strong implication of the Vargha-Khadem findings is that the MTH system is not a homogeneous system (Mishkin, Suzuki, Gadian, and Vargha-Khadem, 1997; Vargha-Khadem et al., 1997) and that semantic memory may be supported by components of the MTH system that remain after the hippocampus has been removed. Endel Tulving, the psychologist who first strongly argued for the distinction between episodic and semantic memory (Tulving, 1972), proposed that episodic memory be considered as separate from declarative memory (Tulving and Markowitsch, 1998).

Although the separatist position is attractive, it is controversial (Squire and Zola, 1998). Manns and his colleagues, for example, presented data from patients thought to have bilateral damage primarily to the hippocampal region and claimed that their ability to acquire factual knowledge was just as impaired as their memory for episodes. They suggested that the division of labor among the medial structures might not be absolute and that it may not be possible to map psychological categories like episodic and semantic memory precisely onto the hippocampal formation and its adjacent cortical regions because these regions are

Endel Tulving

so interconnected. This is a difficult argument to reject, in part because when damage is inflicted on the hippocampus it is difficult to know the extent to which it spreads and causes damage to the surrounding cortices. Moreover, it is difficult to know exactly how to compare the extent to which semantic memory for facts is impaired relative to episodic memory.

Summary

Our episodic memory system supports our ability to consciously recollect the daily episodes of our lives. The hippocampus is a critical component of the neural system that supports the storage and retrieval of episodic memories. Information flows from the neocortical regions to the hippocampus and then returns to the neocortical projection sites. The indexing theory assumes that the content of experience is stored in the neocortex and that the hippocampus creates indices to memories for different episodes. It does this by binding the inputs it receives from different regions of the neocortex into a neural ensemble that represents the conjunction of their co-occurrence. Because the hippocampus projects back to the projecting areas, when this index is activated it can activate or replay the activity patterns that are the memory of the episode.

The hippocampus is said to support the process called pattern completion—that is, that a subset of the original episode can activate the whole pattern. It also supports pattern separation by creating different indices for similar episodes and thus segregating them. The neocortex is not well suited to rapidly acquire memories for single episodes because potential associative connectivity across neocortical regions is low and patterns of neocortical activity produced by separate but similar experiences may become blended and thus lose their episodic nature. Studies with both people and rodents support this view of the role of the hippocampus in episodic memory.

This chapter also explored the relationship between the medial temporal hippocampal neural system and episodic memories, semantic memories, and the memory category called declarative memory. Studies of patients with selective hippocampus pathology that developed at a young age suggest that episodic memories require the entire medial temporal hippocampal system, but semantic memories can be acquired when the hippocampal formation is removed. However, studies with other patients with damage to the hippocampal formation suggest they are greatly impaired in acquiring semantic memories. Thus, the entire medial temporal hippocampal system may also contribute to the acquisition of semantic memories. While there is some controversy over the role of the entire medial temporal hippocampal system in semantic memory, everyone agrees that it is required for episodic memory.

References

Amaral, D. and Lavenex, P. (2007). Hippocampal anatomy. In P. Anderson, R. Morris, D. Amaral, T. Bliss, and J. O'Keefe (Eds.), *The hippocampus book* (pp. 37–114). New York: Oxford Press.

Antoniadis, E. A. and McDonald, R. J. (2000). Amygdala, hippocampus, and discrimination fear conditioning to context. *Behavioural Brain Research, 108,* 1–19.

Bast, T., da Silva, B. M., and Morris, R. G. (2005). Distinct contributions of hippocampal NMDA and AMPA receptors to encoding and retrieval of one-trial place memory. *Journal of Neuroscience, 25,* 5845–5856.

Cipolotti, L., Shallice, T., Chan, D., Fox, N., Scahill, R., Harrison, G. J., Stevens, J., and Rudge, P. (2001). Long-term retrograde amnesia: the crucial role of the hippocampus. *Neuropsychologia, 39,* 151–172.

Day, M. R., Langston, R., and Morris, R. G. (2003). Glutamate-receptor-mediated encoding and retrieval of paired-associate learning. *Nature, 424,* 205–209.

Eacott, M. J. and Norman, G. (2004). Integrated memory for object, place, and context in rats: a possible model of episodic-like memory? *Journal of Neuroscience, 24,* 1948–1953.

Eichenbaum, H. (2000). A cortical-hippocampal system for declarative memory. *Nature Reviews Neuroscience, 1,* 41–50.

Eichenbaum, H., Yonelinas, A. R., and Ranganath, C. (2007). The medial temporal lobe and recognition memory. *Annual Reviews of Neuroscience, 30,* 123–152.

Fanselow, M. S. (1990). Factors governing one-trial contextual conditioning. *Animal Learning and Behavior, 18,* 264–270.

Frankland, P. W., Cestari, V., Filipkowski, R. K., McDonald, R. J., and Silva, A. J. (1998). The dorsal hippocampus is essential for context discrimination but not for contextual conditioning. *Behavioral Neuroscience, 112,* 863–874.

Gilbert, P. E. and Kesner, R. P. (2006). The role of dorsal CA3 hippocampal subregion in spatial working memory and pattern separation. *Behavioural Brain Research, 169,* 142–149.

Lavenex, P. and Amaral, D. G. (2000). Hippocampal–neocortical interaction: a hierarchy of associativity. *Hippocampus, 10,* 420–430.

Manns, J. R., Hopkins, R. O., and Squire, L. R. (2003). Semantic memory and the human hippocampus. *Neuron, 10,* 127–133.

Marr, D. (1971). Simple memory: A theory for archicortex. *Proceedings of the Royal Society of London B Biological Sciences, 262,* 23–81.

Matus-Amat, P., Higgins, E. A., Barrientos, R. M., and Rudy, J. W. (2004). The role of the dorsal hippocampus in the acquisition and retrieval of context memory representations. *Journal of Neuroscience, 24,* 2431–2439.

Matus-Amat, P., Higgins, E. A., Sprunger, D., Wright-Hardesty, K., and Rudy, J. W. (2007). The role of dorsal hippocampus and basolateral amygdala NMDA receptors in the acquisition and retrieval of context and context fear memories. *Behavioral Neuroscience, 121(4),* 721–731.

McNaughton, B. L. (1991). Associative pattern completion in hippocampal circuits: new evidence and new questions. *Brain Research Review, 16,* 193–220.

McNaughton, B. L. and Morris, R. G. M. (1987). Hippocampal synaptic enhancement and information storage within a distributed memory system. *Trends in Neurosciences, 10,* 408–415.

Mishkin, M., Suzuki, W. A., Gadian, D. G., and Vargha-Khadem, F. (1997). Hierarchical organization of cognitive memory. *Philosophical Transactions of the Royal Society of London B, 352,* 1461–1467.

Morris, R. G., Moser, E. I., Riedel, G., Martin, S. J., Sandin, J., Day, M., and O'Carroll, C. (2003). Elements of a neurobiological theory of the hippocampus: the role of activity-dependent synaptic plasticity in memory. *Philosophical Transactions of the Royal Society of London B Biological Sciences, 358(1432),* 773–786.

Mumby, D. G., Gaskin, S., Glenn, M. J., Schramek, T. E., and Lehmann, H. (2002). Hippocampal damage and exploratory preferences in rats: memory for objects, places, and contexts. *Learning and Memory, 9,* 49–57.

Nadel, L. and Moscovitch, M. (1997). Memory consolidation, retrograde amnesia and the hippocampal complex. *Current Opinion in Neurobiology, 17,* 217–227.

O'Keefe, J. and Nadel, L. (1978). *The hippocampus as a cognitive map*. Oxford: Clarendon Press.

O'Reilly, R. C. and McClelland, J. L. (1994). Hippocampal conjunctive encoding, storage, and recall: avoiding a trade-off. *Hippocampus, 4,* 661–682.

O'Reilly, R. C. and Rudy, J. W. (2001). Conjunctive representations in learning and memory: principles of cortical and hippocampal function. *Psychological Review, 108,* 311–345.

Rolls, E. T. and Treves, A. (1998). *Neural networks and brain function*. Oxford: Oxford University Press.

Rudy, J. W., Barrientos, R. M., and O'Reilly, R. C. (2002). The hippocampal formation supports conditioning to memory of a context. *Behavioral Neuroscience, 116,* 530–538.

Rudy, J. W., Huff, N., and Matus-Amat, P. (2004). Understanding contextual fear conditioning: insights from a two process model. *Neuroscience Biobehavioral Review, 28,* 675–686.

Rudy, J. W. and O'Reilly, R. C. (2001). Conjunctive representations, the hippocampus, and contextual fear conditioning. *Cognitive Affective Behavioral Neuroscience, 1,* 66–82.

Ryan, J. D., Althoff, R. R., Whitlow, S., and Cohen, N. J. (2000). Amnesia is a deficit in relational memory. *Psychological Science, 11,* 454–461.

Ryan, J. D. and Cohen, N. J. (2004). Processing and short-term retention of relational information in amnesia. *Neuropsychologia, 42,* 497–511.

Schacter, D. L. (1989). On the relation between memory and consciousness: dissociable interactions and conscious experience. In H. L. Roediger, III, and F. I. M. Craik (Eds.), *Varieties of memory and consciousness: essays in honor of Endel Tulving* (pp. 355–389). Hillsdale, NJ: Erlbaum Associates.

Schacter, D. L. and Tulving, E. (1994). What are the memory systems of 1994? In D. L. Schacter and E. Tulving (Eds.), *Memory systems 1994* (pp. 1–38). Cambridge, MA: The MIT Press.

Squire, L. R. (1992). Memory and the hippocampus: a synthesis from findings with rats, monkeys and humans. *Psychology Review, 99,* 195–231.

Squire, L. R. and Kandel, E. R. (1999). *Memory: from mind to molecules*. New York: W. H. Freeman and Company.

Squire, L. R. and Zola, S. M. (1996). Structure and function of declarative and nondeclarative memory systems. *Proceedings of the National Academy of Sciences, 93,* 13515–13522.

Squire, L. R. and Zola, S. M. (1998). Episodic memory, semantic memory, and amnesia. *Hippocampus, 8*, 205–211.

Squire, L. R. and Zola-Morgan, S. (1991). The medial temporal lobe memory system. *Science, 253,* 1380–1386.

Steele, R. J. and Morris, R. G. (1999). Delay-dependent impairment of a matching-to-place task with chronic and intrahippocampal infusion of the NMDA-antagonist D-AP5. *Hippocampus, 9,* 118–136.

Teyler, T. J. and DiScenna, P. (1986). The hippocampal memory indexing theory. *Behavioral Neuroscience, 100,* 147–152.

Teyler, T. J. and Rudy, J. W. (2007). The hippocampus indexing theory of episodic memory: updating the index. *Hippocampus, 17,* 1158–1169.

Tulving, E. (1972). Episodic and semantic memory. In E. Tulving and W. Donaldson (Eds.), *Organization of memory.* New York: Academic Press.

Tulving, E. and Markowitsch, H. J. (1998). Episodic and declarative memory: role of the hippocampus. *Hippocampus, 8,* 198–204.

Van Hoesen, G. and Pandya, D. N. (1975). Some connections of the entorhinal (area 28) and perirhinal (area 35) cortices of the rhesus monkey. I. Temporal lobe afferents. *Brain Research, 95,* 1–24.

Vargha-Khadem, F., Gadian, D. G., Watkins, K. E., Connelly, A., Van Paesschen, W., and Mishkin, M. (1997). Differential effects of early hippocampal pathology on episodic and semantic memory. *Science, 277,* 376–380.

Zola-Morgan, S., Squire, L. R., and Amaral, D. G. (1986). Human amnesia and the medial temporal region: enduring memory impairment following a bilateral lesion limited to field CA1 of the hippocampus. *Journal of Neuroscience, 6,* 2950–2967.

14

Ribot's Law, Systems Consolidation, and the Hippocampus

We know from personal experience that, with the passage of time, forgetting takes place. This can result from the decay of the memory trace, in which case some of the information it contained may be lost. Forgetting can also be a retrieval failure—the core memory is still present but is difficult to access. Most of us, however, are unaware that *as memories age they undergo changes that increase their resistance to disruption*. This is the empirical fact called Ribot's law that was introduced in Chapter 1.

In the last 20 years, many researchers have directed their efforts at understanding the neural systems that make old memories resistant to disruption. The purpose of this chapter is to present the major theoretical ideas that have been proposed to explain Ribot's law and some of the evidence that is relevant to evaluating them.

Are Remote Memories Resistant to Disruption?

Before introducing these theoretical issues, it is necessary to discuss why we should believe that older memories are more resistant to disruption. It is not a simple issue and not everyone believes that it is true (Rozin, 1976). Consider people with Korsakoff's disease. They often have better recall and recognition of old events than events that occurred more recently. However, we cannot accept these data as evidence for Ribot's law because Korsakoff's disease is progressive. Its onset is not clearly marked and patients with this disease have difficulty acquiring new memories. Thus, it is possible that the memories for recently experienced events were not stored as well as were memories for more remote experiences (Squire and Cohen, 1984). Consequently, following a disruptive event, recent experiences would be less well remembered than remote ones.

To claim that old memories are more resistant to disruptions one must know when the disruptive event occurred. In fact, the time of some disrupting events such as a stroke, the onset of encephalitis, or a car accident is often known. One must also have confidence that the new and old events were initially stored equally well. This is a difficult criterion because the researcher does not have a record of an individual's past experience. Researchers, however, have developed memory tests that are believed to diminish this problem to some extent.

An experiment by Squire, Slater, and Chance (1975) provides a useful starting point. As you know, electroconvulsive shock (ECS) therapy is sometimes used to treat psychiatric disorders. Squire and his colleagues tested patients who had received five sessions of ECS therapy. These patients were asked questions about television programs that had appeared for only one season. These programs were selected so that the age of the memory at the time of recall varied. A special feature of this experiment was that the same patients were tested both before and after the treatment.

The results of this experiment make two points (Figure 14.1). First, before treatment these patients recalled more about the more recently experienced programs than they did about the older programs. In other words, there was forgetting. Second, following the treatment the patients displayed what is called a **temporally graded retrograde amnesia**. This means that their amnesia was more pronounced for the more recently experienced events than events experienced in their remote past. In this example, amnesia extended only to memories of the shows experienced in the two-year period prior to the treatment. It is this temporal gradient that provides evidence for Ribot's law. As an aside, you should also know that over time the memories disrupted by ECS therapy usually recover. This point is important because it means that the ther-

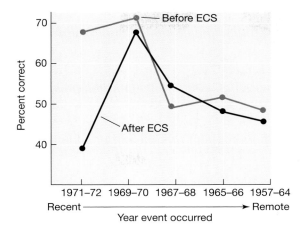

FIGURE 14.1

Patients were tested before and after several treatments of ECS therapy (subjects were tested in 1974). Note that it disrupted recall of the most recently acquired memories but had no effect on their oldest memories. Note also that there was some forgetting because memory for the events experienced within four years of the therapy was better than memories that were at least seven years old. (After Squire et al., 1975.)

apy did not erase the more recently acquired memories. It altered the brain in some way that made the traces temporarily inaccessible. The treatment produced a retrieval failure; apparently it did not damage the storage sites.

Remote Memories and the Hippocampus

Contemporary researchers believe that the hippocampus plays an important role in temporally graded retrograde amnesia. David Marr (1971), a pioneer in the development of theory about the role of the hippocampus and memory, laid the groundwork for linking the hippocampus to the strengthening of remote memories. Relatively speaking, the neocortex is quite large and the hippocampal formation is rather small. So Marr suggested that although the hippocampus can rapidly acquire information, it serves only as a temporary memory store. By temporary Marr meant something on the order of a few days. Memories are permanently stored in the much larger neocortex. However, for a limited time period the hippocampus plays an important role in establishing the permanent neocortical memory trace. Once the memory trace in the neocortex is consolidated, the hippocampus is no longer needed to retrieve the memory.

The Standard Model of Systems Consolidation

Larry Squire, Neal Cohen, and Lynn Nadel (1984) brought these ideas firmly into the modern literature. Their position is called the **standard model of systems consolidation**. They proposed that experience initially lays down a memory trace that depends, for both storage and retrieval, on an interaction between the neocortical areas and the medial temporal hippocampal (MTH) system, described in the previous chapter and shown in Figure 13.11. There are two other critical assumptions associated with their position (p. 202).

The first assumption is that the *critical interaction between the MTH system and other sites is required for only a limited time after learning*. When the memory is originally formed, the MTH system in some way maintains memory coherence, that is, it holds together the components of the trace that are distributed over various regions of the brain. Processes intrinsic to the neocortical storage sites are responsible for consolidating the memory in the brain regions outside of the MTH system. During this period the integrity of the MTH system is also necessary to retrieve the memory. Once this process is sufficiently complete, however, the MTH system is no longer needed for either the storage or retrieval of that memory. Squire and his colleagues never specified what constitutes a limited amount of time. However, based on their discussion of the effects of ECS therapy (as presented in Figure 14.1) and H.M.—the amnesic discussed in Chapter 12 whose retrograde amnesia was thought at that time to be limited to about three years—one might reasonably suppose that they were assuming that consolidation requires about three years.

Their second assumption is that the *MTH system–neocortical interaction is only needed to consolidate declarative memory (episodic and semantic memories)*. It is not involved in what is sometimes called procedural memory—memories that support learned skills such as bike riding or skiing.

According to the standard model, old memories are more resistant to disruption than new memories because they have been consolidated in the neocortex. Newer memories are disrupted because the disruptive event primarily impacts the MTH system; thus, retrieval of new memories requires a functional MTH system (Figure 14.2).

Before further discussing the standard model, it is necessary to briefly digress and distinguish the concept of **systems consolidation** from another concept—**cellular consolidation**. Cellular consolidation refers to the biochemical and molecular events that take place immediately following the behavioral experience that initially forms the memory trace. Several hours may be required for these processes, which were discussed extensively in previous chapters, to consolidate the trace. Systems consolidation refers to changes in the strength of the memory trace brought about by interactions between brain re-

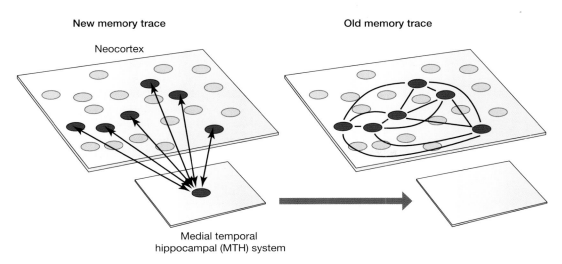

FIGURE 14.2
A schematic representation of the standard model of systems consolidation. Initially the memory trace consists of weakly connected neocortical representations of the features (purple circles) of the experience held together by their temporary connections with the medial temporal hippocampal (MTH) system. New memories require the MTH system for retrieval. As the memory ages, intrinsic processes result in the consolidation or strengthening of the connections among the neocortical representations. Because of the strengthened connections the memory can now be retrieved without the hippocampus.

gions (the MTH system and neocortex) that take place after the memory is initially established. Systems consolidation begins after the trace is initially stored and operates over a much longer time frame—days, months, or years (Figure 14.3).

It is difficult to overestimate the influence that the standard model of systems consolidation has had on the field. It has become repeated so often in textbooks and elsewhere that almost anyone who has heard of the hippocampus believes that it is a temporary memory store and that the neocortex is the permanent site. Thus, you might think that the evidence supporting the theory is overwhelming. If so, then you will be surprised to learn that much controversy now surrounds this idea (Murray and Bussey, 2001; Nadel and Moscovitch, 1997).

The standard model makes only one critical prediction: Damage to the hippocampal formation will spare remote or old episodic and semantic memories, but new episodic and semantic memories will be lost. Experimental results that

FIGURE 14.3
Two types of processes are thought to contribute to the consolidation of long-term stability of memories.

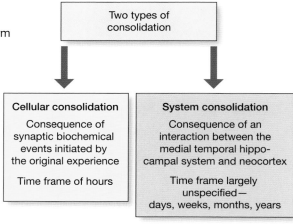

Two types of consolidation

Cellular consolidation

Consequence of synaptic biochemical events initiated by the original experience

Time frame of hours

System consolidation

Consequence of an interaction between the medial temporal hippo-campal system and neocortex

Time frame largely unspecified— days, weeks, months, years

Morris Moscovitch

Lynn Nadel

reveal that damage to the MTH system produces a temporally graded retrograde amnesia (Figure 14.4A) would support this theoretical model. However, if damage to the MTH system produces a flat gradient (Figure14.4B), then the theory would be wrong.

Challenges to the Standard Model

The primary data for evaluating the standard model come from case studies of individuals that are known to have damage to regions in the medial temporal lobes. For many years, H.M. was the only patient available with known bilateral damage to the medial temporal lobes. Over the years, however, a number of patients with damage to the MTH system have been identified and evaluated. When Lynn Nadel and Morris Moscovitch (1997) reviewed this literature, they reached a surprising conclusion: the evidence does not support the standard model. They concluded that when damage to the MTH system is complete there is *no sparing of either new or remote episodic memories*. Spared remote episodic memories are found when damage to the MTH system is incomplete. Thus, they asserted that the MTH system

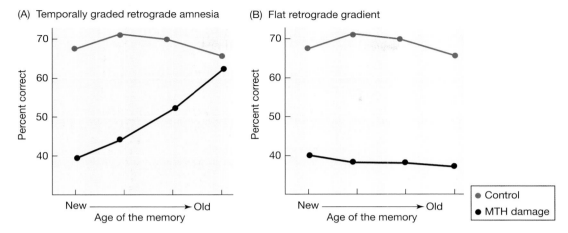

FIGURE 14.4

These graphs illustrate patterns of results that would either support or be evidence against the standard model of systems consolidation. (A) This pattern would support the model because it shows that damage to the hippocampus results in temporally graded retrograde amnesia. (B) This pattern would be evidence against the standard model because damage to the hippocampus produced a flat retrograde amnesia.

continues to be critical to retrieval throughout the life of an episodic memory. Their conclusion regarding the fate of old semantic memories was less clear. They suggested that retrograde damage for general semantic memories is more variable but less severe.

The relevant literature reviewed by Nadel and Moscovitch is complex and controversial; not everyone agrees with their conclusion. For example, some researchers argue that the loss of remote memories reflects the fact that the brain injury extends beyond the MTH system into neocortical areas that would be the storage sites of remote memories (Bayley, Hopkins, and Squire, 2003; Bayley, Gold, Hopkins, and Squire, 2005; Reed and Squire, 1998). Thus, it is useful to consider two relevant case studies as well as to reconsider the case of H.M.

THE CASE OF V.C.   Lisa Cipolotti and her colleagues (2001) describe the case of V.C., who became profoundly amnesic at the age of 67. His performance on general intelligence tests and other measures of cognitive function, however, remained intact. Careful assessment of his brain indicated that there was sig-

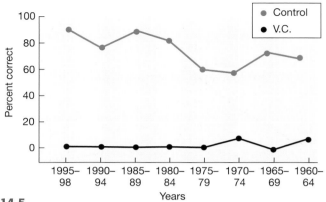

FIGURE 14.5
This figure illustrates V.C.'s flat retrograde amnesia for recall of famous public events. This memory test was conducted in 1998. Control subjects were chosen to match V.C.'s age and educational level.

nificant loss of volume over the entire rostralcaudal length of the hippocampus. However, critical surrounding cortical regions—the entorhinal cortex and parahippocampus—were normal, as were the adjacent temporal lobes. Thus, V.C.'s damage was believed to be restricted primarily to the hippocampus.

If the standard model is correct, then this patient should have displayed a temporally graded retrograde amnesia with remote memories spared. V.C.'s episodic memory was tested in a variety of ways. His retrograde amnesia was extensive and was equally evident for both old and new memories (Figure 14.5). Given that the researchers correctly identified the extent of V.C.'s brain damage, then V.C.'s data should be considered as strong evidence *against* the standard model.

THE CASE OF E.P.   Larry Squire and his colleagues (Stefanacci, Buffalo, Schmolck, and Squire, 2000) described the case of patient E.P. He became amnesic at the age of 70 when viral encephalitis destroyed the medial temporal lobes of his brain. E.P.'s temporal lobe damage was more severe than that of V.C. In addition to significant damage to the hippocampal formation, there was damage to the entorhinal and perirhinal cortices and the rostral parahippocampal cortex. In addition, the cortical volume of the insula, lateral temporal lobes, and left parietal lobe was reduced.

Like V.C., patient E.P.'s retrograde amnesia was also extensive. On tests of information about public events and famous faces, E.P. had no recall regardless of the age of the memory. He also had almost complete amnesia for autobiographical events that extended over the immediate 20-year period before the onset of the disease. The remarkable fact was that his memory for some personal childhood experiences was as good as age-matched controls. He also evidenced remarkable sparing of his spatial memory for the organization of his childhood neighborhood.

Suzanne Corkin

There is no simple explanation for why patient E.P., who had more damage to the medial lobes than patient V.C., displayed pockets of remote memory for adolescent and childhood personal experiences. However, even where there was some sparing of remote memories it was only for events that had been experienced more than 20 years prior to when his medial temporal lobes were damaged. So, unless one is willing to accept an unusual definition of what constitutes a temporary memory storage system, E.P.'s extraordinary memory for childhood and adolescent experiences offers no support for the idea that the MTH system is only temporarily needed for retrieval.

H.M. RECONSIDERED   Suzanne Corkin (2002) has known and worked with H.M. since she was a graduate student in 1962. She and her colleagues (Steinvorth, Levine, and Corkin, 2005) more recently re-evaluated H.M. to determine the extent of his retrograde amnesia. They concluded that H.M.'s episodic memory was severely impaired and that there was no sparing of remote memories. Moreover, his semantic memory was very much in the range of control subjects matched for age, IQ, and level of education. It is interesting that H.M.'s episodic memory impairment was much more severe than was initially believed (Corkin, 1984; Milner, Corkin, and Teuber, 1968). Corkin and her colleagues (2005) believe that the extent of H.M.'s retrograde amnesia was previously underestimated because the early evaluators did not fully appreciate how autobiographical episodic memories differ from semantic memories and thus did not pursue the magnitude of H.M.'s episodic memory impairment.

SUMMARY OF CHALLENGES   What you should appreciate is that based on these clinical data a number of contemporary researchers believe that damage to the MTH system or perhaps even just to the hippocampal formation per se produces a profound retrograde amnesia for both new and old episodic memories. If this is true, then the human clinical literature provides little or no support for the standard model of systems consolidation and its view that for the retrieval of episodic memories the MTH system is needed only for a limited time. The role of the MTH system and semantic memory remains less clear and it is unlikely that the issues that surround clarifying this situation will be resolved by studying patients with medial temporal lobe damage.

Multiple Trace Theory

Faced with their conclusion that even remote episodic memories require the hippocampal formation for retrieval, Nadel and Moscovitch (1997) proposed a new theory called **multiple trace theory** (Figure 14.6) to explain when remote episodic memories will be spared. They assume that:

- Regardless of its age, an episodic memory always requires the hippocampus for retrieval.
- The initial episodic memory trace consists of the patterns of neocortical activity bound together by neurons in the hippocampal formation that serve as an index (as described in Chapter 13).
- Each time the memory trace is reactivated, a new index is established to the original neocortical pattern of activity and to other, new patterns of activity that are present. This results in multiple traces that share information with the original trace.
- Older memories are reactivated more often than newer memories and thus have more copies or indices distributed throughout the hippocampus than do new memories.

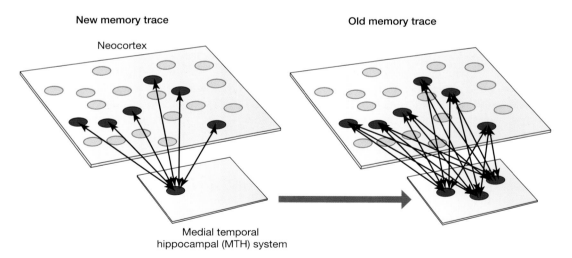

New memory trace

Neocortex

Old memory trace

Medial temporal
hippocampal (MTH) system

FIGURE 14.6

The assumptions of the multiple trace theory of systems consolidation. Old memories still depend on the hippocampus but are more resistant to disruption because they have had more opportunity to be reactivated than new memories, and each reactivation generates another index in the hippocampus. Because these copies are distributed, the memory can survive partial but not complete damage to the hippocampus and will be more resistant to other insults such as a brain concussion.

It is the redundancy of the trace that protects an old episodic memory from disruption. Some of the fidelity of the memory will be lost because the copies are not perfect, but the gist of the experience can still be recalled. Thus, old memories would be more likely to survive some damage to the hippocampus and be more resistant to other disruptive events such as ECS therapy or a brain concussion .

Other Evidence Relevant to the Debate

As noted, the primary evidence for evaluating theories of why old memories may be more resistant to disruption than new memories comes from people with damage to the medial temporal hippocampal system. However, the complexities associated with this literature make it unlikely that data from people with brain damage can resolve the fundamental theoretical debate between the standard model and the multiple trace theory of systems consolidation— whether or not remote memories become independent of the hippocampus. There are, however, other sources of evidence that are potentially relevant to this debate. One source comes from studies that image the brain while people are retrieving new and old episodic memories. Another source comes from studies in which the hippocampus of laboratory animals is damaged at different times following the acquisition of a new memory.

Human Brain Imaging

Modern researchers are now able to image levels of activity in the brain while a person is engaged in cognitive activities such as retrieving memories. The most widely used method is called **functional magnetic resonance imaging** (**fMRI**), illustrated in Figure 14.7. In the context of systems consolidation, this methodology allows researchers to study patterns of brain activity produced when normal subjects are asked to retrieve newly acquired memories compared to when they are asked to retrieve old memories.

If retrieval of old memories becomes independent of the MTH system, as proposed by the standard model, then one would expect much less activity in the MTH system when the subject is asked to retrieve an old memory than when asked to retrieve a new memory. In contrast, the multiple trace theory predicts either no difference or that, if anything, more activity in the hippocampus will be observed when the subject is asked to retrieve old memories than when asked to retrieve new memories (Figure 14.8). This might be expected because the core memory trace of an old memory will have more copies represented in the hippocampus.

Several imaging studies have addressed the theoretical predictions of the standard model and multiple trace theory of systems consolidation. A study

(A)

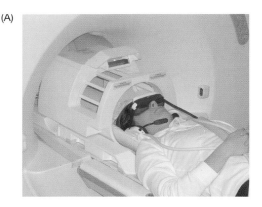

(B)

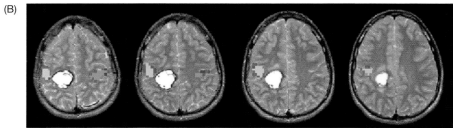

FIGURE 14.7

(A) In functional magnetic resonance imaging (fMRI) the participant's head is placed in the center of a large magnet. A radiofrequency antenna coil is placed around the head for exciting and recording the magnetic resonance signal of hydrogen atoms. Stimuli can be presented to the subject using virtual reality video goggles and stereo headphones. fMRI is based on the fact that hemoglobin in the iron-containing oxygen-transport metalloprotein in the red blood cells slightly distorts the magnetic resonance properties of hydrogen nuclei in the vicinity and the amount of magnetic distortion changes, depending on whether the hemoglobin has oxygen bound to it. When a brain area is activated by a specific task, it begins to use more oxygen and within seconds the brain microvasculature responds by increasing the flow of oxygen rich blood to the active area. These changes in the concentration of oxygen and blood flow lead to what is called a blood oxygenation level-dependent (BOLD) signal—changes in the magnetic resonance signal. (B) fMRI activity during a hand-motion task. Left hand activity is shown in yellow and right hand activity is shown in green. (Photos from Purves et al., 2008.)

by Rekkas and Constable (2005) evaluated these predictions by asking the participants (21-year-old college students) questions designed to facilitate the retrieval of actual episodes from their past. For example, to probe their recall of remote memories they were asked questions such as, "Can you recall the schoolyard of your elementary school?" or "Can you recall a specific high school English teacher?" The mean age of the remote memories being queried was eight years. Recall of remote memories was compared to recent memo-

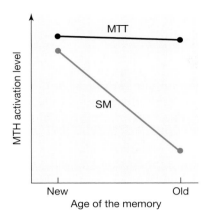

FIGURE 14.8

The predictions that the standard model (SM) and multiple trace theory (MTT) of systems consolidation make about activation in the medial temporal hippocampal (MTH) system. Multiple trace theory predicts that retrieval of both new and old memories should activate the MTH system. The standard model predicts that only the retrieval of new memories should activate the MTH system.

ries established about 2.5 days before the experiment, when the participants were given a tour of the investigator's laboratory. To facilitate recall of the recent episodes, they were asked questions such as, "Can you recall the male researcher who came into the interview room?" or "Can you recall being shown anything specific in the lab?" During the period following such questions, images of the participants' brains were captured. Rekkas and Constable reported that retrieving remote memories produced significantly more activation of the hippocampus proper than retrieving the recently acquired memories. This result provides no support for the standard model but is consistent with multiple trace theory.

Steinvorth, Corkin, and Halgren (2006) used another methodology to determine if the retrieval of new and old memories differentially depend on the MTH system. They developed sentences individually tailored to each participant that asked about salient aspects of specific events that had occurred in their personal past, such as: "Last Thanksgiving, did Jonathan burn the turkey?" (a recent memory probe) or "At a birthday party, who spilled wine on your pants?" (a remote memory probe). They reported that the retrieval of recent and remote memories activated the same constellation of brain regions and that the MTH system was equally activated when either type of memory was retrieved. These data provide support for multiple trace theory but are inconsistent with the prediction of the standard model because the MTH system was equally activated whether new or old memories were being retrieved.

Frédéric Bernard and his colleagues (2004) used an entirely different memory probe—recognition of remote and recent famous faces—to address the issue. They found that recognition of recent and old famous faces equally activated the hippocampus. Again, this report provides no support for the standard model (but see Haist, Gore, and Mao, 2001, for a somewhat similar study that claimed support for the standard model).

Based on this brief overview, fMRI studies appear to support multiple trace theory and provide almost no evidence for the standard model. However, as Cabeza and St. Jacques (2007) noted, there is an important caveat that applies to these studies that may limit their theoretical importance. Specifically, as you know, the indexing theory of the hippocampus (which is at the core of the multiple trace theory) assumes that the MTH system is capturing a continuous record of the patterns of neural activity in the neocortex. Researchers using imaging techniques to evaluate theories of systems consolidation assume that activity in the MTH system is produced by the retrieval cues activating the neurons in that region that represent the index. However, this may not be the case. Suppose, as the standard model assumes, an old memory is retrieved directly from the neocortical sites. Once these sites are activated they will project to the MTH system to cause activation there. If this happens, then the activity in the MTH system will not reflect retrieval but instead will reflect the retrieval experience laying down a new copy of the trace. In fact, multiple trace theory predicts this should happen.

In summary, fMRI studies appear to support multiple trace theory. However, given the above caveat, one should be cautious in concluding that this support is unequivocal.

Remote Memory Animal Studies

There are many problems associated with testing people who have damage to the medial temporal lobes produced by such occurrences as strokes or encephalitis. Two main problems are that (1) the brain damage extends beyond the regions of interest and (2) there is no way to completely control for the initial strength of the memory. For these reasons researchers have used laboratory animals, primarily rodents, to determine the contribution the hippocampus makes to new and old memories. This strategy has the obvious advantage that one can (1) provide animals with a known behavioral experience, (2) vary the exact time between the experience and the occurrence of the brain damage, and (3) vary the extent of the brain damage. One can also hold constant the length of time between when the brain is damaged and when the animals are tested.

Thus, there are substantial reasons to use animals in memory studies. Nevertheless, one should keep in mind that there is no consensus about just what type of memory is being assessed by the tasks used in animal studies. How do we know for certain if these tasks are measuring episodic or semantic memory, or for that matter some other category? Moreover, animal studies have yielded somewhat mixed results on the role of the hippocampus in remote memories.

First, however, let's consider the most consistent results. They come from studies looking at the effect of hippocampus damage on memory for spatial locations. The classic task for studying this kind of memory is the place-learning version of the Morris water-escape task. However, there are other ways to establish the same type of memory (Clark, Broadbent, and Squire, 2005a). No matter what task is used to establish a place memory, removal of the hippocampus produces a flat retrograde amnesia; both new and old memories are lost (Sutherland et al., 2001; Clark, Broadbent, and Squire, 2005b; Martin, de Hoz, and Morris, 2005). These results provide no support for the standard model.

Rats are normally neophobic when it comes to eating, that is, they eat very little of a novel food (as if they want to ensure that it is safe). However, if a rat sniffs the breath of another rat that has recently eaten a food, its neophobia for that food is markedly reduced if it subsequently encounters it. This type of learning, discovered by Barbara Strupp (Strupp and Levitsky, 1984), is called **social transmission of a food preference** (Galef and Whiskin, 2003). There is agreement that damage to the hippocampus disrupts the memory for food odor when it occurs one day following training but not when it occurs a few days later (Clark, Broadbent, Zola, and Squire, 2002; Ross and Eichenbaum, 2006; Winocur, McDonald, and Moscovitch, 2001). These results are consistent with the standard model.

One of the first laboratory studies to reveal a temporally graded retrograde amnesia was reported by Jeansok Kim and Michael Fanselow (1992), who studied the retention of the memory for a contextual fear-conditioning experience. They first conditioned the rats and then damaged the dorsal hippocampus 1, 7, 14, or 28 days later. All rats were tested seven days after surgery. When the lesion was made one day following training, the rats were profoundly amnesic. However, when the lesion was made at least seven days following conditioning, the animals were less amnesic. At the 28-day interval, the rats showed as much fear as the control subjects. The temporal gradient reported by Kim and Fanselow would appear to provide support for the standard model. However, one problem with this experiment is that the damage to the hippocampus was relatively small and limited to the dorsal hippocampus.

Robert Sutherland and his colleagues (Lehman, Lacanilao, and Sutherland, 2007) have compared the effects of partial and complete lesions of the hippocampus on the rat's contextual fear memory. They damaged the hippocampus either one week, three months, or six months following the condi-

(A)

Control

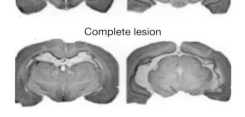

Partial lesion

Complete lesion

(B)

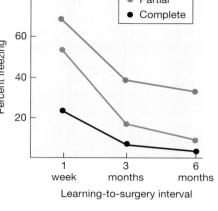

FIGURE 14.9
(A) These images illustrate the extent of the damage to the hippocampus. (B) These data show that over the six-month retention interval control rats showed evidence of forgetting. Note, however, that there was no evidence that the three-month- and six-month-old memories were protected from damage to the hippocampus. (A courtesy of Robert Sutherland.)

tioning session. As illustrated in Figure 14.9, they failed to replicate Kim and Fanselow's results. Partial damage to the hippocampus produced less amnesia than large lesions, but the age of the memory at the time of the lesion did not matter. These results obviously provide no support for the standard model. They also provide no support for multiple trace theory because remote memories were not spared in rats with partial damage to the hippocampus.

Sutherland and his colleagues (Epp et al., in press) have also reported a flat retrograde amnesia gradient when rats were trained to learn a visual discrimination. In this task the rats learned to escape from water by swimming to a platform located beneath one of two visually distinct stimulus patterns. These findings also provide no support for the standard model.

Robert Sutherland

Although there are some inconsistencies in the literature, there now exists a significant number of studies that find no sparing of remote memories when there is significant damage to the hippocampus. Proponents of the standard model can draw no comfort from the increasing number of reports that remote memories are not spared, nor can multiple trace theorists. It may be too early to reach a definitive conclusion but at the very least the animal studies suggest that, as it is currently articulated, the standard model may have limited generality.

Summary

As Ribot proposed, there is evidence that remote memories are more resistant to disruption than newer memories. Theorists have suggested that the MTH system and its interaction with neocortical brain regions is the key to understanding why this is so.

The standard model of systems consolidation proposes that the MTH system is critical for retrieving new episodic and semantic memories while intrinsic processes consolidate these traces in the neocortex. Once the neocortical traces are consolidated, however, the MTH system is no longer necessary to retrieve the trace. This account predicts that removing the MTH system will impair the retrieval of new memories but not the retrieval of old memories.

The multiple trace theory of systems consolidation assumes that the medial temporal regions and the neocortex are necessary for retrieving both new and old memories. Remote memories are resistant to disruption because there are more copies of old memories distributed throughout the relevant medial temporal lobe sites. This theory predicts that remote memories can be spared if damage to the hippocampus is not complete.

In their influential review, Nadel and Moscovitch (1997) concluded that both new and old episodic memories are lost if there is extensive damage to the MTH system. Spared remote episodic memories are found when there is only partial damage to this system. Much of the clinical literature that is relevant to evaluating these theories is controversial. Others have argued that remote memories are lost because these patients also have damage to neocortical sites where the memory is stored.

fMRI studies with normal people suggest that the hippocampus remains involved in the retrieval of both new and old memories and generally support the multiple trace theory. However, interpretive problems limit the theoretical conclusions one can draw from these studies. Studies with laboratory animals are somewhat mixed but many of them provide no support for the standard model of systems consolidation. Many such studies, in fact, challenge the very conclusion contained in Ribot's law and leave one seriously wondering about its generality.

For many years memory researchers accepted the standard model of systems consolidation as an explanation of Ribot's law. As research directed at evaluating this view has accumulated, however, a large number of findings have emerged that challenge this model. Specifically, old memories are often not spared when the MTH system is damaged or even when the damage is restricted to just the hippocampus. Whether or not multiple trace theory will emerge as a better explanation of spared remote memories remains to be seen. You should appreciate that the same data that challenge the standard model also challenge the generality of Ribot's law—that old memories are more resistant to disruption than new memories. Thus, future research will need to uncover the training conditions and the kinds of memory tasks that determine when old memories are spared following damage to the MTH system. Only then will we be able to make progress in understanding the neurobiological basis of Ribot's law.

References

Bayley, P. J., Gold, J. J., Hopkins, R. O., and Squire, L. R. (2005). The neuroanatomy of remote memory. *Neuron, 46,* 799–810.

Bayley, P. J., Hopkins, R. O., and Squire, L. R. (2003). Successful recollection of remote autobiographical memories by amnesic patients with medial temporal lobe lesions. *Neuron, 38,* 135–144.

Bernard, F. A., Bullmore, E. T., Graham, K. S., Thompson, S. A., Hodges, J. R., and Fletcher, P. C. (2004). The hippocampal region is involved in successful recognition of both remote and recent famous faces. *NeuroImage, 22,* 1704–1714.

Cabeza, R., and St. Jacques, P. (2007). Functional neuroimaging of autobiographical memory. *Trends in Cognitive Science, 11,* 219–227.

Cipolotti, L., Shallice, T., Chan, D., Fox, N., Scahill, R., Harrison, G., Stevens, J., and Rudge, P. (2001) Long-term retrograde amnesia: the crucial role of the hippocampus. *Neuropsychologia, 39,* 151–172.

Clark, R. E., Broadbent, N. J., and Squire L. R. (2005a). Hippocampus and remote spatial memory in rats. *Hippocampus, 15,* 260–272.

Clark, R. E., Broadbent, N. J, and Squire, L. R. (2005b). Impaired remote spatial memory after hippocampal lesions despite extensive training beginning early in life. *Hippocampus, 15,* 340–346.

Clark, R. E., Broadbent, N. J., Zola, S. M., and Squire, L. R. (2002). Anterograde amnesia and temporally graded retrograde amnesia for a nonspatial memory task after lesions of hippocampus and subiculum. *Journal of Neuroscience, 22,* 4663–4669.

Corkin, S. (1984). Lasting consequences of bilateral medial temporal lobectomy: clinical course and experimental findings in H.M. *Seminars in Neurology, 4,* 249–259.

Corkin, S. (2002). What's new with the amnesic patient H.M.? *Nature Reviews Neuroscience, 2,* 153–160.

Epp, J., Keith, J. R., Spanswick, S. C., Stone, J. C., Prusky, G. T., and Sutherland, R. J. (in press). Retrograde amnesia for visual memories after hippocampal damage in rats. *Learning and Memory.*

Galef, B. G., Jr., and Whiskin, E. E. (2003). Socially transmitted food preferences can be used to study long-term memory in rats. *Learning and Behavior, 31,* 160–164.

Haist, F., Gore, J. B., and Mao, H. (2001). Consolidation of human memory over decades revealed by functional magnetic resonance imaging. *Nature Neuroscience, 4,* 1139–1145.

Kim, J. J. and Fanselow, M. S. (1992). Modality-specific retrograde amnesia of fear. *Science, 256,* 675–677.

Lehmann, H., Lacanilao, S., and Sutherland, R. J. (2007). Complete or partial hippocampal damage produces equivalent retrograde amnesia for remote contextual fear memories. *European Journal of Neuroscience, 25,* 1278–1286

Marr, D. (1971). Simple memory: a theory for archicortex. *Philosophical Transactions of the Royal Society of London, Series B, 262,* 23–81.

Martin, S. J., de Hoz, L., and Morris, R. G. (2005). Retrograde amnesia: neither partial nor complete hippocampal lesions in rats result in preferential sparing of remote spatial memory, even after reminding. *Neuropsychologia, 43,* 609–624.

Milner, B., Corkin, S., and Teuber, H. L. (1968). Further analysis of the hippocampal amnesic syndrome: 14-year follow-up study of H.M. *Neuropsychologia, 6,* 215–234.

Murray, E. A. and Bussey, T. J. (2001). Consolidation and the medial temporal lobe revisited: methodological considerations. *Hippocampus, 11,* 1–7.

Nadel, L. and Moscovitch, M. (1997). Memory consolidation, retrograde amnesia and the hippocampal complex. *Current Opinion in Neurobiology, 7,* 217–227.

Purves, D., Augustine, G. J., Fitzpatrick, D., Hall, W. C., LaMantia, A.-S., McNamara, J. O., and White, L. E. (2008). *Neuroscience.* Sunderland, MA: Sinauer Associates, Inc.

Reed , J. M. and Squire, L. R. (1998). Retrograde amnesia for facts and events: findings from four new cases. *Journal of Neuroscience, 18,* 3943–3954.

Rekkas, P. V. and Constable, R. T. (2005). Evidence that autobiographic memory retrieval does not become independent of the hippocampus: an fMRI study contrasting very recent with remote events. *Journal of Cognitive Neuroscience, 17,* 1950–1961.

Ross, R. S. and Eichenbaum, H. (2006). Dynamics of hippocampal and cortical activation during consolidation of a nonspatial memory. *Journal of Neuroscience, 26,* 4852–4859.

Rozin, P. (1976). The psychobiology of memory. In M. R. Rosenzweig and E. L. Bennett (Eds.), *Neural mechanisms of learning and memory* (pp. 3–46). Cambridge: The MIT Press.

Squire, L. R. and Cohen, N. J. (1984). Human memory and amnesia. In G. Lynch, J. L. McGaugh, and N. M. Weinberger (Eds.), *Neurobiology of learning and memory* (pp. 3–64). New York: The Guilford Press.

Squire, L. R., Cohen, N. J., and Nadel, L. (1984). The medial temporal region and memory consolidation: a new hypothesis. In H. Weingartner and E. Parker (Eds.), *Memory consolidation* (pp. 185–210). Hillsdale, NJ: Erlbaum and Associates.

Squire, L. R., Slater, P. C., and Chance, P. (1975). Retrograde amnesia: temporal gradient in very long-term memory following electroconvulsive therapy. *Science, 187,* 77–79.

Stefanacci, L., Buffalo, E. A., Schmolck, H., and Squire, L. R. (2000). Profound amnesia after damage to the medial temporal lobe: a neuroanatomical and neuropsychological profile of patient E.P. *Journal of Neuroscience, 20,* 7024–7036.

Steinvorth, S., Corkin, S., and Halgren, E. (2006). Ecphory of autobiographical memories: an fMRI study of recent and remote memory retrieval. *NeuroImage, 30,* 285–298.

Steinvorth, S., Levine, B., and Corkin, S. (2005). Medial temporal lobe structures are needed to re-experience remote autobiographical memories: evidence from H.M. and W.R. *Neuropsychologia, 43,* 479–496.

Strupp, B. J. and Levitsky, D. A. (1984). Social transmssion of food preferences in adult hooded rats (*Rattus norvegicus*). *Journal of Comparative Psychology, 98,* 257–266.

Sutherland, R. J., Weisend, M. P., Mumby, D., Astur, R. S., Hanlon, F. M., Koerner, A., Thomas, M. J., Wu, Y., Moses, S. N., and Cole, C. (2001). Retrograde amnesia after hippocampal damage: recent vs. remote memories in two tasks. *Hippocampus, 11,* 27–42.

Winocur, G., McDonald, R. M., and Moscovitch, M. (2001). Anterograde and retrograde amnesia in rats with large hippocampal lesions. *Hippocampus, 11,* 18–26.

Actions, Habits, and the Cortico-Striatal System

Our brains are sensitive to the outcomes produced by our behaviors. Consequently, we can rapidly adjust our behaviors in response to a changing world and acquire complex behavioral skills. Psychologists have been concerned with how this happens for more than 100 years, and in the last 20 years neurobiologists have also weighed in on this topic. We now understand some of the basic psychological principles that govern the acquisition of new behaviors and how those principles might relate to systems in the brain. This chapter explores that complex relationship, first discussing instrumental behavior and then describing the neural system of the brain that supports two categories of such behavior—actions and habits.

To appreciate the basic problems addressed in this chapter, you might think back to when you initially learned to drive a car. In order to competently drive you had to learn and coordinate many complex behaviors, such as:

- Insert the ignition key
- Turn on the ignition key
- Release the handbrake
- Put the car in gear

- Put your foot on the accelerator
- Generate just the right amount of gas
- Adjust the steering wheel to maintain or change the trajectory
- Make proper fine-grain adjustments to oncoming traffic
- Apply just the right amount of pressure on the brake to stop

Remarkably, once these skills are learned, a competent driver can execute them in a seamless manner and at the same time carry on a conversation and sometimes drive for miles while unaware of even being on the road. However, this was certainly not the case when you were learning to drive. The initial execution of each of these behaviors was *an intentional, goal-driven act* that was motivated by your knowledge or expectancy that it would produce a particular outcome. Only with extensive practice did you acquire and integrate into a well-coordinated process the individual behaviors that comprise the collection of skills needed to drive a car. The initial crude actions you performed while learning to drive later became highly refined motor patterns, liberated from your intentions and conscious control. Driving then became a habit.

The Concept of Instrumental Behavior

Most psychologists use the term instrumental learning or **instrumental behavior** when referring to the study of how behavior is modified by the outcome it produces. This term recognizes that our behaviors can be viewed as instruments that can change or modify our environments. For example, when you turn the ignition key, the engine starts.

As you learned in Chapter 1, the experimental study of instrumental learning emerged when, as a graduate student, E. L. Thorndike (1898) wanted to gain some insight into the "mind" of animals. He was unhappy with the speculation of his contemporaries about what kind of representations of the world existed in the minds of dogs and cats and how these representations were acquired. This was because the speculation was made on the basis of anecdotal accounts of the behavior of animals and, when explaining behavior, psychologists of his era tended to anthropomorphize, that is, attribute to animals human characteristics.

So, as described in Chapter 1, Thorndike developed a novel methodology, called the Thorndike puzzle box, to study how animals solve problems and represent the solution. This methodology was previously illustrated in Figure 1.8. A cat, dog, or chicken was placed into the box and it had to learn a particular behavior to escape—for example, to pull the ring attached by a rope to the door.

(A) Learning curve

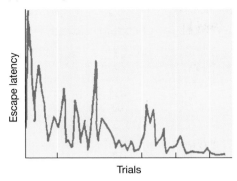

Escape latency

Trials

FIGURE 15.1
Thorndike contributed the puzzle box and learning curves to the study of instrumental learning. (A) These learning curves represented escape latency as a function of trials. (B) He also proposed a theory of instrumental learning known as the Law of Effect. Training experiences: When the animal is placed in the puzzle box, the stimulus situation (S) initiates many responses (R1, R2, R3, R4). The S–R connections linking S to wrong responses (R1, R2, R3) are followed by annoying consequences. The connection linking S to the correct response (R4, ring pull) is followed by a satisfying consequence (the door opens). Resulting changes: Over trials the incorrect S–R connections are weakened and the correct connection is strengthened, as represented by the red arrow.

(B) Law of Effect

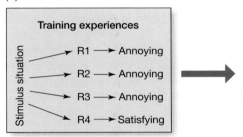
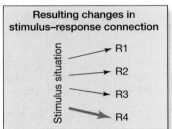

The important feature of this methodology was that it arranged an explicit *contingency* between the animal's behavior and a change in the environment. Specifically, the opening of the escape door was contingent or dependent upon the animal generating a particular behavior—pulling the ring. If the specified response was not made, the door did not open.

More importantly, the animal's behavior was modified by the behavioral contingency Thorndike arranged. In attempting to escape from the box, the animal initially engaged in a wide range of behaviors that had no influence on its situation. However, it gradually learned the behavior that opened the door. Thorndike documented this change in behavior by presenting what may have been the first example of "learning curves." These learning curves represented **escape latency** as a function of trials (Figure 15.1). He found that escape latency gradually decreased as a function of those trials, indicating that the animal had learned to escape.

Two Theories of Instrumental Behavior

Two general ideas about how outcomes change our behavior emerged quite early in the history of experimental psychology and continue to be influential. One idea, called the **Law of Effect** (see Chapter 1), originated with Thorndike. The second idea, called **cognitive expectancy theory**, is associated with Edward C. Tolman (1948; 1949).

Thorndike's Law of Effect

As you learned in Chapter 1, the essence of Thorndike's theory is that outcomes produced by behavior ultimately adapt the animal to the situation by strengthening and weakening existing stimulus–response (S–R) connections. Outcomes that are rewarding strengthen S–R connections, while nonrewarding outcomes weaken connections. His Law of Effect, illustrated in Figure 15.1, is stated as follows:

> If in the presence of a stimulus a response is followed by a satisfying state of affairs, the connection between the stimulus and the response will be strengthened. If the response is followed by an annoying state of affairs, the connection between the stimulus and response will be weakened.

Note that Thorndike described outcomes as resulting in either annoying or satisfying events. The term **reinforcer** or **reward** is often used to represent an outcome that strengthens stimulus–response connections and the term **nonreward** is used to designate an event that weakens such connections.

It is useful to highlight some of the implications of Thorndike's theory. A strengthened S–R connection can produce the appropriate response, but it contains no information about either the behavioral contingency (that is, that the outcome depended on the response) or the nature of the outcome (a reward or nonreward). More generally stated, the instrumental behavior itself should not be considered purposeful or goal directed. Thus, if you asked Thorndike's cat why it pulled the ring every time it was placed in the box, if it could answer it would say something like, "I don't know. It's very strange but when I am placed into the box I get an irresistible urge to pull the ring." A behavior supported by S–R connections is a habit, acquired through frequent repetition.

Tolman's Cognitive Expectancy Theory

Almost no one believes that Thorndike's theory provides a complete description of the processes that control our behavior or how we represent our past experiences. Tolman certainly did not accept this theory. He believed that instrumental behaviors are purposeful and organized around goals. He would say that when the cat solves Thorndike's puzzle box it would learn the relationship between its behavior and the outcome that it produced. The cat acquired an **expectancy** about the relationship between its actions and the outcomes they produced. More generally speaking, Tolman believed that our brains detect and store information about relationships among all the events provided by a particular experience. An expectancy is a three-term association (S1–R–S2) that includes a representation of the stimulus situation (S1) that preceded the response, a representation of the response (R), and a representation of the outcome (S2) produced by the response. The expectancy concept is illustrated in Figure 15.2 in relation to Thorndike's S–R habit.

Edward C. Tolman

Tolman's cognitive expectancy–goal-directed theory of behavior placed a heavy emphasis on the *value of the outcome* produced by an instrumental behavior. The associations that make up an expectancy contain information about relationships between stimuli and relationships between behavior and stimulus outcomes. However, whether or not you act depends on the value of the outcome you expect the behavior to produce. So even though the cat "knows" how to escape from the box, it does not have to automatically initiate the escape response. It does so only if the outcome has value—*if the cat has some motivation to escape.* Similarly, you may know a friend's telephone number, but seeing a telephone does not always result in your dialing the number. You only do so when you want to speak to your friend, that is, when the outcome has value.

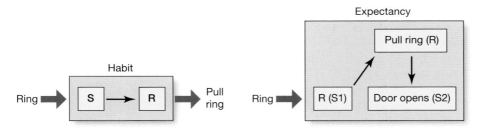

FIGURE 15.2
This figure provides a comparison of the S–R habit versus an expectancy representation of the cat's solution to the puzzle box. Note that the sight of the ring directly evokes a strengthened S–R connection to produce the pull-ring response. In contrast, according to expectancy theory, the sight of the ring activates the representation of the pull-ring response and the consequence it produces—the door opening. Activating the expectancy does not necessarily result in the response. Thus, the expectancy contains information about what would happen, but it does not force a response. This depends on the value of the outcome.

FIGURE 15.3
Instrumental behaviors can be classified as either actions or habits.

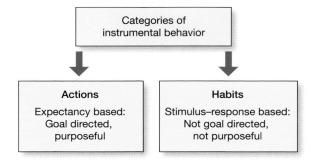

Actions and Habits

Together, the theories of Thorndike and Tolman imply that there are two categories of instrumental behavior (Figure 15.3). One category, supported by expectations, is called a goal-directed **action**. The other category, supported by S–R connections, is called a **habit**. Actions are goal directed, while habits are not. Thus actions are influenced by the value of the outcome, while habits are not.

If you were watching the cat escape from the puzzle box or just watching someone open a door, could you tell if the behavior was an action or a habit? Just observing the behavior would not give you an answer to the underlying basis of the behavior. Thus, researchers have developed an important strategy, called **reward devaluation**, for answering this question. The strategy centers on *changing the value of the outcome* after the animal has solved the problem. The logic of the strategy, which has been used with both primates and rodents, is described as follows.

Since actions are purposeful and generated to produce a specific outcome, when the outcome has value, the animal should produce the appropriate response. But when the outcome has no value, the animal may not give the response. In contrast, since habits are not goal directed, they should be produced regardless of the value of the outcome or reward. Thus, by changing the value of the reward–outcome after an instrumental response has been learned, one can determine if the response is an action or a habit.

An example of the devaluation strategy is illustrated in Figure 15.4. A monkey is trained to solve two discriminations. In the first problem the reward is a grape. If the monkey chooses the pyramid it will find the grape, but it will receive nothing if it chooses the cylinder. In the second problem the reward is a peanut. If it chooses the cube it will find the peanut, but if it chooses the cone it will find nothing. Monkeys easily solve such problems. How can you tell whether the correct response is an action supported by an expectancy or a habit supported by an S–R connection? The answer is, by changing the value of the reward.

Training

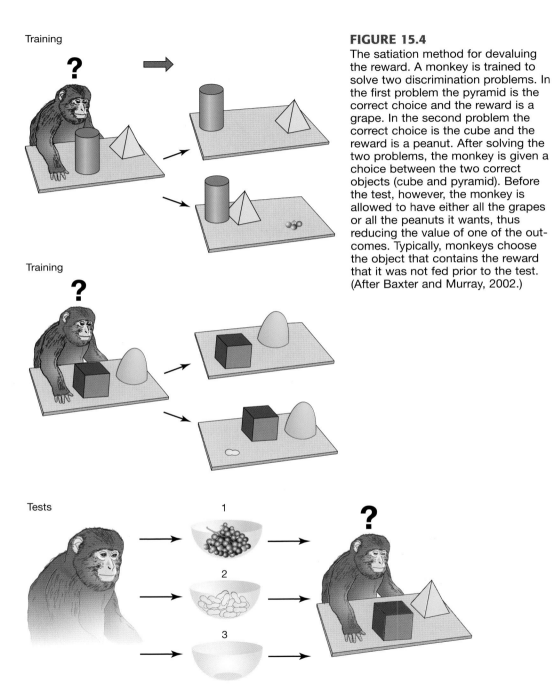

FIGURE 15.4
The satiation method for devaluing the reward. A monkey is trained to solve two discrimination problems. In the first problem the pyramid is the correct choice and the reward is a grape. In the second problem the correct choice is the cube and the reward is a peanut. After solving the two problems, the monkey is given a choice between the two correct objects (cube and pyramid). Before the test, however, the monkey is allowed to have either all the grapes or all the peanuts it wants, thus reducing the value of one of the outcomes. Typically, monkeys choose the object that contains the reward that it was not fed prior to the test. (After Baxter and Murray, 2002.)

Training

Tests

This can easily be done. After the monkey has solved the problem you give it a test in which it must choose between the two correct objects, the pyramid (with the grape) and the cube (with the peanut). Before the test, however, you allow the monkey to have either all the peanuts or all the grapes it wants. By doing this you reduce the value of one of the outcomes. Typically, monkeys choose the object that contains the reward that it was not fed prior to the test (Malkova, Gaffan, and Murray, 1997). Accordingly, the monkey's choice is classified as an action if it chose the pyramid when satiated on peanuts and the cube when satiated on grapes. If the monkey is not sensitive to the value of the outcome, its behavior is classified as a habit.

With Practice, Actions Become Habits

The devaluation methodology has provided evidence for the existence of both actions and habits. In addition, research with animals has revealed a dominance principle. With limited training instrumental behaviors are goal-directed actions, but with practice instrumental behaviors tend to shift from actions to habits, meaning they become insensitive to reward devaluation.

This point is illustrated in Figure 15.5, which presents the results of an experiment in which rats were trained to press a lever to receive food. Thus lever pressing was the instrumental response and food was the outcome–reward. In one condition the rats were given only a limited amount of lever-press training, while in the other they were given extended training. Prior to the test phase, the outcome–reward was devalued for one set of rats. During the test phase, food was no longer delivered in response to lever pressing. Rats that had limited training were sensitive to the value of the reward, making fewer lever-pressing responses than the control rats. In this case, the lever press was considered an action. In contrast, rats that had experienced extended training were insensitive to the value of the reward, pressing the lever as often as the control rats (Adams and Dickinson, 1981). In this case the lever press was considered a habit.

With repetition, an action can become a habit. However, one should not conclude that the expectancy representation of an action is replaced by an S–R representation of a habit. Instead, once established, the two representations co-exist. As you will learn in the next section, what changes with practice is which representation controls behavior (Killcross and Coutureau, 2003).

A Conceptual Model for Actions and Habits

Behavioral neuroscientists have begun to uncover regions in the brain that contribute to the support of actions and habits. The unfolding story is complex and incomplete, so to facilitate your understanding of the concepts, a con-

(A)

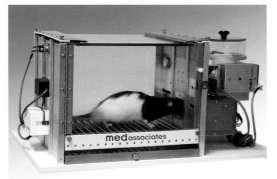

FIGURE 15.5
(A) A rat is collecting food produced by pressing a lever. In this experiment, in one condition the rats were given only a limited amount of lever-press training, while in the other they were given extended training. Prior to the test phase, the food reward was devalued for one set of rats. (B) Rats that had limited training were sensitive to the value of the reward, pressing the lever less than control rats. In this case, the lever press was considered an action. In contrast, rats that had experienced extended training were insensitive to the value of the reward, pressing the lever as often as the control rats. In this case the lever press was considered a habit. (After Adams and Dickinson, 1981.)

(B)

Action — Habit

Limited training — Extended training

■ Control
■ Devalued

ceptual model is provided in Figure 15.6 to illustrate the general idea that instrumental behaviors can be generated by either an action system or a habit system.

In this simple model a stimulus–response–outcome experience is represented at two levels in the brain (Figure 15.6A). The representations of the experience activated in level I are fed forward to level II. The processes operating in level II are responsible for assembling these representations into a goal-directed action, but ultimately processes in level I that associate the stimulus representation and response representation produce habits. The action and habit systems both generate the instrumental behavior (IB) by activating the representation of the response in level I (Figure 15.6B and C).

(A) Initial experience   (B) Action system (after limited training)

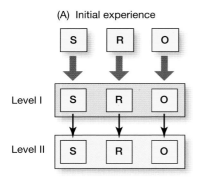

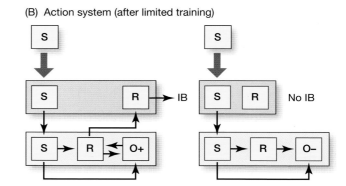

FIGURE 15.6

(A) An animal has an initial experience composed of a sequence of an antecedent stimulus (S), a response (R), and an outcome (O) produced by the response. This experience is represented in two levels of the brain, I and II. (B) With limited training, the representations in level II are associated with and can support an action. The diagram on the left shows that the action system generates an instrumental behavior (IB) if the outcome has value (+). In this case, when S occurs the level-II associations are activated and the output of the action system projects back to the response representation in level I to generate the instrumental behavior. The diagram on the right illustrates the case when the outcome has been devalued (–). In this case the outcome representation does not strongly project onto the response representation in level II. Thus, the response representation in level I is not activated and the instrumental behavior is not produced. (C) With extended training, a habit is formed, that is, connections between the stimulus and response representations in level I become strong enough to support the generation of an instrumental behavior, without projections back from level II.

(C) Habit system (after extended training)

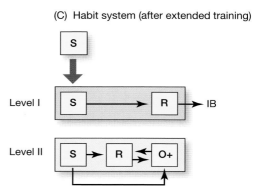

More specifically, the associations that support actions form in level II after limited training (see Figure 15.6B). They link (1) the stimulus representation to both the outcome representation and the response representation, (2) the response representation to the outcome representation, and (3) the outcome representation to the response representation. If the outcome representation has value (+), this association will contribute to activating the response representation in level II. If the response representation in level II is sufficiently activated, its output will project back to the response representation in level I and produce the instrumental behavior. However, if the outcome has no value (–), then the response representation in level II will not be sufficiently activated to activate the response representation in level I and the instrumental behavior will not occur.

With extended training an S–R habit can emerge in level I (see Figure 15.6C). This happens because with repetition the action system repeatedly produces the same response in the presence of the antecedent stimulus, thereby creating the opportunity for it to be directly associated with a representation of the response. After extended training, both the action system and the habit system can produce the instrumental behavior, but the habit system tends to dominate.

A Cortico-Striatal System Supports Instrumental Behavior

The conceptual scheme just described is complex, but even so it is an oversimplification. The reality is that a large number of components of the brain make a contribution to the learning of instrumental behavior, and no one has yet provided a theory that shows how all the relevant components of the brain are integrated to produce such behavior. Nevertheless, there has been some progress in determining which regions of the brain make up the neural system that supports the acquisition and production of instrumental behavior.

One important component of this system, located deep in the center of the brain, is the **basal ganglia**. This region of the brain consists of a number of subcortical nuclei including the caudate nucleus, putamen, globus pallidus, subthalamic nucleus, nucleus accumbens, and substantia nigra. Together, the caudate nucleus, putamen, and nucleus accumbens components of the basal ganglia form a region of the brain called the **striatum**.

The striatum is the basic input segment of the basal ganglia. It receives input from many cortical regions of the brain and projects out through the globus pallidus and substantia nigra to the thalamus and ultimately back to areas of the cortex from which it received input. Thus the striatum is at the center of what is sometimes called the **cortico-striatal system**. You might appreciate that, because the striatum projects back to some of the cortical regions that project to it, the cortico-striatal system has the same sort of return-loop organization that characterizes the medial temporal hippocampal (MTH) system that supports episodic memory, discussed in Chapter 13. Note in particular that the striatum projects back to the motor cortex. This is important because motor cortices are critical for the generation of behaviors.

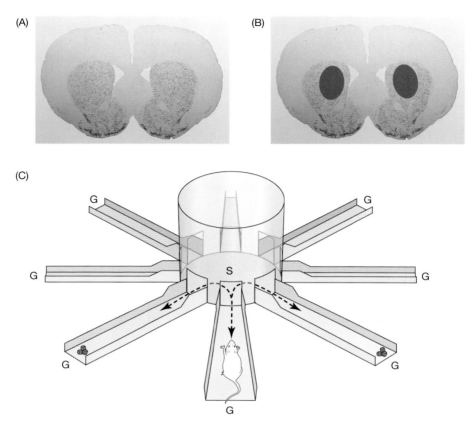

FIGURE 15.7

(A) A photomicrograph of a normal rat brain showing the cortex and striatum. (B) This photomicrograph illustrates the location of the experimentally induced lesion in the dorsal striatum. (C) An illustration of a rat receiving a reward in an eight-arm radial maze after choosing an adjacent arm. On each trial the rat is started randomly from one arm of the maze. In order to receive a reward the rat must leave the start arm and enter an adjacent arm. Rats with damage to the dorsal striatum are greatly impaired on this instrumental learning task (After Cook and Kesner, 1988.)

Many researchers believe that the striatum is the key anatomical region for creating instrumental behaviors (White and McDonald, 2002; Divac, Rosvold, and Szwarcbart, 1967). An experiment by Raymond Kesner (Cook and Kesner, 1988) used a radial maze with eight arms to illustrate this point (Figure 15.7). Each rat was placed randomly into one of these arms and then released. Normally, when released the rat will move out into the arena and enter some distant arm. However, in what is called the **adjacent-arm task**, no matter which

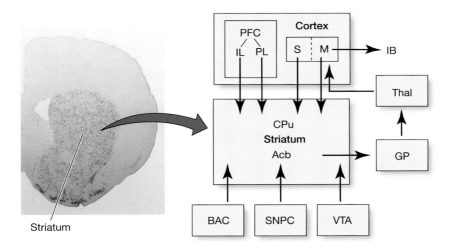

FIGURE 15.8
The rodent striatum and surrounding cortex is displayed on the left. On the right is a highly schematic representation of the rat striatum and some of the important regions of the brain that project to it. Note that information processed by the striatum projects back to the motor (M) cortex via the thalamus (Thal). The striatum of the rat is composed of the caudate putamen (CPu) and the nucleus accumbens (Acb). S = sensory cortex; PFC = prefrontal cortex; PL = prelimbic cortex; IL = infralimbic cortex; BAC = basal amygdala complex; VTA = ventral tegmental area; SNPC = substantia nigra pars compacta; IB = instrumental behavior; GP = globus pallidus.

arm it was placed into to start a trial, the rat was only rewarded if its first choice upon release was to enter one of the two adjacent arms. Normal rats learned this task, but rats with damage to the dorsal striatum were quite impaired. Thus, these animals had difficulty learning what would appear to be the simple task of turning left or right.

Figure 15.8 illustrates the rat's striatum and some of the cortical and other regions in the brain that it interacts with to produce instrumental behavior. This figure provides a framework for discussing some of the key components of the neural system that contribute to assembling and performing action patterns.

Raymond Kesner

You might find it useful to think of the cortico-striatal system as performing the functions of level II in the conceptual model of instrumental behavior described previously and illustrated in Figure 15.6.

Neural Support for Actions and Habits

Much of what is known about the contribution different regions of the brain make to support instrumental behavior comes from the combined use of neurobiological methods to influence the brain and devaluation techniques to determine if the instrumental response is an action or a habit. Researchers use lesions to permanently remove a particular component of the neural system and inactivation methods to temporarily but reversibly prevent a region from contributing to the behavioral outcome. In addition, drugs that influence synaptic plasticity, such as the NMDA receptor antagonist APV, are employed to determine if synapses in a particular region of the brain are modified by experience.

As you have learned, when procedures that reduce the value of the outcome also reduce the production of the instrumental behavior, that behavior is said to be a goal-directed action. Thus, if impairing the normal function of a component of the brain renders the animal insensitive to the value of the reward, one would conclude that that component is part of the action system. Conversely, if impairing the normal function of that component has no effect on the animal's sensitivity to the value of the reward, then one would conclude that it is not part of the action system, but may be part of the habit system.

Support for the Action System

Components of the brain that support the action system play different roles and make different contributions. Components that merit a closer look are the posterior dorsomedial striatum and three regions that provide input to the striatum—the prelimbic and infralimbic regions of the medial prefrontal cortex and the basolateral nucleus of the amygdala.

Bernard Balleine

POSTERIOR DORSOMEDIAL STRIATUM   Bernard Balleine and his colleagues reported several findings that suggest that the **posterior dorsomedial striatum (pDMS)** plays an important role in goal-directed actions. In one study, they damaged this region of the brain either before or after training rats on a two-lever pressing task (Yin, Ostlund, Knowlton, and Balleine, 2005). Pressing each lever produced a different outcome, a food pellet or a sip of a sucrose solution. Prior to the test, they satiated the animals on one or the other of the rewards. During the test no reward was given. When

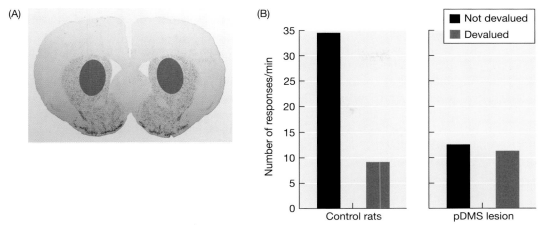

FIGURE 15.9
(A) Illustrates the location of damage to the posterior dorsomedial striatum (pDMS) in rats. In this experiment, the rats were trained to press two levers that each produced a different reward. Following training, one of the rewards was devalued. (B) During the test, when no rewards were delivered, control rats pressed the lever that was associated with the now devalued reward far less than they pressed the other lever. This result indicates that their instrumental behavior was controlled by the action system. In contrast, rats with damage to the pDMS pressed the two levers equally often. This result suggests that the pDMS is part of the neural system that supports actions.

satiated on food pellets, control rats were sensitive to the devaluation treatment and pressed the lever that in the past produced the sucrose. Rats with damage to the pDMS, however, were not sensitive to the devaluation; they pressed the lever as much when the reward was devalued as they did when it was not, and they pressed each lever equally as often. These results (Figure 15.9) suggest that the control rats' behavior was produced by the action system and that the pDMS is part of this system. A different set of experiments, in which the NMDA-receptor antagonist APV was injected into the pDMS, resulted in similar findings, further supporting the idea that neurons in the posterior dorsomedial striatum are important in action learning (Yin, Knowlton, and Balleine, 2005).

MEDIAL PREFRONTAL CORTEX REGIONS Research has also revealed that two regions of the medial prefrontal cortex, the prelimbic and the infralimbic, make separate and quite different contributions to the acquisition and control of instrumental behavior.

The prelimbic region is important during the initial learning of the associations that support an action. However, once these associations are learned, this region of the brain is no longer critical. The evidence for these claims is that if this region of the brain is damaged *before* rats learn an instrumental response, they are insensitive to reward devaluation (Ostlund and Balleine, 2005; Killcross and Coutureau, 2003). So the instrumental response in this case would be called a habit. However, if the prelimbic region is damaged just *after* rats are allowed to learn the associations supporting the action, they remain sensitive to reward devaluation (Ostlund and Balleine, 2005). These results have two implications:

- The prelimbic region is critical in the acquisition of the associations that support an action.
- The prelimbic region is not the site in the brain where these associations are stored.

The infralimbic region plays a quite different role. As you have learned, instrumental behaviors initially start out as actions but with extended training they become habits. Killcross and Coutureau (2003) have reported that the infralimbic region of the prefrontal cortex plays an important role in selecting which system controls behavior. They showed that when the infralimbic region is damaged *prior* to training, the rat's instrumental behavior is always sensitive to the value of the outcome. This is true whether the reward is devalued after very little training or after extensive training, when control animals are insensitive to reward devaluation. This means that an instrumental behavior learned by a rat with damage to the infralimbic region *may never become a habit*.

As you have learned, the instrumental behavior of extensively trained animals is supported by the habit system. So what would happen if the infralimbic region is disabled in extensively trained animals? Coutureau and Killcross (2003) asked this question and found that when the infralimbic region is temporarily inactivated, instrumental behavior again becomes action based, that is, sensitive to reward devaluation. This fact has two important implications:

- The associations that support action-based behavior are still present even after the behavior becomes a habit.
- With extensive training, the infralimbic region exerts inhibitory control over the action system, taking it offline so that it does not influence behavior. Just how the infralimbic region does this is not yet understood.

The results of the experiments examining the role of the prelimbic and infralimbic medial prefrontal cortex are integrated in Figure 15.10. The prelimbic region is required to assemble a particular action but is not important once the action is acquired. The infralimbic region suppresses the output of the

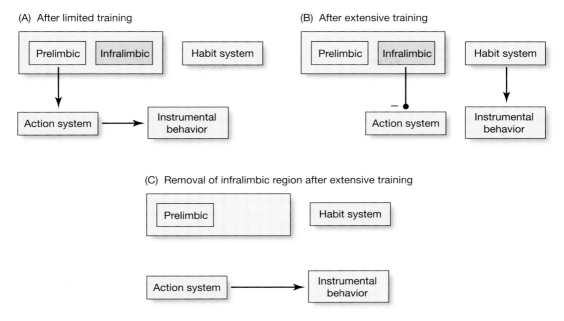

FIGURE 15.10
(A) After limited training, instrumental behavior is controlled by the action system. The prelimbic region is necessary early in training for building the action system that controls a particular instrumental behavior. Note at this stage that the habit system does not contribute to the generation of the instrumental behavior. (B) With extensive training, the prelimbic region is no longer necessary to generate an action. Moreover, the infralimbic region now suppresses the contribution of the action system, and instrumental behavior is produced by the habit system. (C) If the infralimbic region is removed after extensive training, the action system again assumes control over instrumental behavior. This means that after extensive training, associations that can produce instrumental behavior are present in both the action and habit systems.

action system. Instrumental behavior of animals with damage to this region remains under the control of the action system, even if the animal has been extensively trained. Moreover, inactivating the infralimbic region after extensive training, when the animal's behavior is normally generated by the habit system, returns control back to the action system. A general implication of these experiments is that, after extensive training, associations that can produce instrumental behavior are present in both the action and habit systems.

THE AMYGDALA The production of an action depends on the value of the outcome it produces. Outcomes have particular sensory qualities—steak does not taste like oatmeal and peanuts do not taste like raisins. When we experience a particular food, a memory representation of the specific sensory features is established. Moreover, it appears that a particular value also is attached to this representation. So, for example, if you ingest a novel food, not only do you acquire a representation of its sensory properties, an abstract value or rating of your liking (+) or disliking (–) the food is also attached to the representation. Thus, if I asked you to retrieve a representation of an orange, you not only imagine its color, shape, texture, and taste, you could also tell me whether or not you liked it.

Research with both primates and rodents has identified an important role for the **amygdala**, specifically the basolateral nucleus of the amygdala (Balleine and Killcross, 2006), in attaching value to outcomes. Animals with major damage to the amygdala can learn instrumental behaviors. However, these animals are not sensitive to changes in the value of an outcome. For example, monkeys with amygdala damage have no problem learning the visual object discriminations presented in Figure 15.4. However, they are completely insensitive to devaluation of the associated rewards (Malkova et al., 1997). Moreover, monkeys with amygdala damage can learn specific motor patterns when rewarded for making the appropriate response. For example, they can learn to move a lever to the right when the signal is a red light and they can learn to move the lever to the left when the signal is a blue light (Murray and Wise, 1996). Similar results have been obtained when researchers have examined the effect of amygdala damage on instrumental learning in rats (Balleine, Killcross, and Dickinson, 2003; Balleine, 2005). These study results support the idea that the amygdala contributes to learning the value of the outcome and thus plays an important role in the action system.

What about the Habit System?

You have now learned that the construction of an action depends critically on the combined contributions of several regions of the brain, all of which provide input to the striatum, the fundamental locus of the associations that support the action system. But what about the habit system? Is it also supported in the striatum?

Curiously, much less is known about the fundamental neural substrates that support the acquisition and expression of habits. This is in part because it is only recently that behavioral neuroscientists have begun to realize that instrumental behaviors can be supported by both an action and a habit system. Prior to this realization, the striatum had been identified as the locus of the neural system supporting instrumental behaviors because large lesions to this area could profoundly affect their acquisition and expression. Some researchers now believe that the neural system that supports habits is outside of the striatum, most likely located in sensory–motor systems in the neocortex.

Consistent with the conceptual framework provided in Figure 15.6, Earl Miller (Pasupathy and Miller, 2005) has proposed that the striatum is responsible for rapidly assembling associations that support actions and that, once the associations are assembled, regions outside of the striatum that learn more slowly can acquire associations that support habits. Miller arrived at this proposal by simultaneously recording from neurons in both the striatum and the prefrontal cortex in monkeys learning an instrumental response. He found that early in training neural activity in the striatum quickly correlated with correct responding, but neural activity in the prefrontal cortex only gradually associated with the correct response. While these data do not identify the prefrontal cortex as the locus of habit associations, they do indicate that the striatum is rapidly modified by the training experience, which is consistent with the hypothesis that the striatum rapidly assembles the associations that support actions.

The Neural Basis of Rewarding Outcomes

Since Thorndike's original proposal, conceptions of habit formation have been dominated by the idea that the outcome produced by the behavior must have a special property—the ability to strengthen or weaken the associative connection between the stimulus and response. Given the importance of this idea, one might think that the neural basis of strengthening the property of outcomes would be well understood. However, this issue is not yet resolved.

For some time, a number of researchers accepted the **dopamine reinforcement hypothesis**—the idea that the neurotransmitter dopamine is the primary candidate for strengthening the property of outcomes. This source of dopamine is provided by what is called the **mesolimbic dopamine system**. Dopamine in this system comes from neurons located in a region of the brain called the ventral tegmental area (VTA). In particular, the VTA responds to events often used to reinforce instrumental behavior and it has outputs that project into the striatum, specifically the nucleus accumbens (Figure 15.11A). Thus, it is easy to imagine that the outcome produced by behavior first turned on neurons in the VTA that then caused dopamine to be released into the striatum (the nucleus accumbens) and that this dopamine release strengthened the relevant stimulus–response or response–outcome associative connections (Figure 15.11B).

Although this hypothesis is appealing, it is not universally accepted. Kent Berridge (2007) has argued that there is no direct evidence that dopamine released into the striatum strengthens associative connections. He proposed that the response of the mesolimbic dopamine system to a rewarding outcome is to attach motivational significance to stimuli associated with the outcome. This is called the **dopamine-incentive salience hypothesis**. What this means is that the presence of a stimulus associated with a strongly rewarding outcome can

FIGURE 15.11
(A) This sagittal section of the rat brain illustrates the mesolimbic dopamine system. The dopamine neurons are located in the ventral tegmental area (VTA) and their fibers project into the nucleus accumbens of the striatum. (B) The dopamine theory of reinforcement. An outcome–reward has two functions: (1) It generates a representation (O), and (2) it activates dopamine neurons (Dopa) in the VTA that release dopamine into the striatum. This acts to strengthen synaptic connections between the representations of the stimulus complex and the response (R) and perhaps between the representations of the response and the outcome.

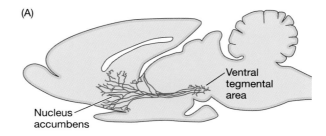

(A)

Ventral tegmental area

Nucleus accumbens

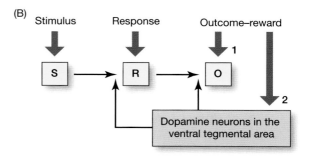

(B)

Stimulus   Response   Outcome–reward

S → R → O

1

2

Dopamine neurons in the ventral tegmental area

evoke an almost irresistible urge for the outcome. It creates a want or motivation for the outcome. The instrumental behavior is produced because it produces the outcome that satisfies the want (Figure 15.12).

Berridge and Terry Robinson (1998) developed the dopamine-incentive salience hypothesis to provide an explanation for drug relapse (see Chapter 11). Their contention is that drug relapse occurs because addictive drugs strongly activate dopamine neurons and neutral cues present at that time acquire the ability to produce the urge to take the drug. Thus the sight of a cigarette or the smell of cigarette smoke might evoke an intense urge to smoke a cigarette because these stimuli were associated with the activation of the dopamine system and acquired extreme incentive properties. These urges motivate the person to engage in instrumental behaviors that produce the outcome that reduces the urge.

Thorndike's concept that the outcome is an event that strengthens or weakens S–R connections has dominated thinking about habits for over 100 years. Yet, at this time, there is no uncontested hypothesis about the neural basis of the strengthening of the property of outcomes. In fact, one might wonder if Thorndike's Law of Effect is now dispensable. There is no doubt that outcomes that reward behavior have properties that influence that behavior. However, most if not all of their effects can be explained as resulting from their influence

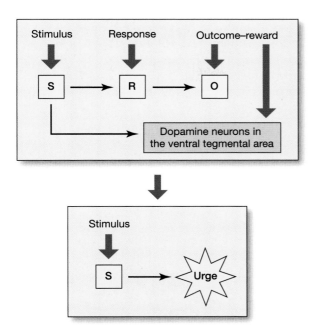

FIGURE 15.12
The incentive salience hypothesis assumes that the reward turns on dopamine neurons in the ventral tegmental area (VTA). Note that in the normal sequence of events that establish instrumental behavior, the stimulus not only can associate with the response, it also can get associated with the incentive properties of the outcome. Subsequently, the stimulus complex itself can elicit strong urges or wants that lead the individual to seek out the reward. Berridge and Robinson (1998) have proposed that these urges play an important role in drug-addiction relapse. Even though an addict might go through drug withdrawal and be "clean," an encounter with stimuli associated with the drug experience can lead to relapse because they can produce irresistible urges to seek the drug.

on motivation processes. Outcomes that have value and stimuli associated with outcomes that activate the dopamine system can create urges. Habits might emerge, then, not because they are strengthened by outcomes but because through repetition of a stimulus–response sequence, the S–R connection is strengthened.

Summary

Our behavior is modified by the consequences it produces and is the instrument by which we change our environment. Instrumental behaviors belong to two categories called actions and habits. Actions are purposeful and goal directed and supported by what are called expectancies. Actions are motivated by the expected outcomes they produce. Habits are not purposeful and thus are thought to be insensitive to the outcomes they produce. Instrumental behaviors begin as actions but, with extensive repetition, they are thought to become S–R habits.

A cortico-striatal neural system linking a variety of cortical and midbrain regions is believed to be the system that integrates the elements of our experience—stimulus inputs, response inputs, and outcomes produced by the response—into an action. S–R habits are thought to emerge once this action system generates a consistent response to a particular antecedent stimulus.

Researchers are beginning to understand the functional contribution of a number of brain regions to the production of actions and habits. These regions of the brain include the striatum, the medial prefrontal cortex, the amygdala, and the dopamine systems.

References

Adams, C. D. and Dickinson, A. (1981). Instrumental responding following reinforcer devaluation. *Quarterly Journal of Experimental Psychology, 33B*, 109–121.

Balleine, B. (2005). Neural bases of food-seeking: affect, arousal and reward in cortico striato limbic circuits. *Physiology and Behavior, 86*, 717–730.

Balleine, B. W. and Killcross, S. (2006). Parallel incentive processing: an integrated view of amygdala function. *Trends in Neurosciences, 29*, 272–279.

Balleine, B. W., Killcross, A. S., and Dickinson, A. (2003). The effect of lesions of the basolateral amygdala on instrumental conditioning. *Journal of Neuroscience, 23*, 666–678.

Baxter, M. G. and Murray, E. A. (2002). The amygdala and reward. *Nature Reviews: Neuroscience, 3*, 563–573.

Berridge, K. C. (2007). The debate over dopamine's role in reward: the case for incentive salience. *Psychopharmacology, 191*, 391–431.

Berridge, K. C. and Robinson, T. E. (1998). What is the role of dopamine in reward: hedonic impact, reward learning, or incentive salience? *Brain Research Review 28*, 309–369.

Cook, D. and Kesner, R. P. (1988). Caudate nucleus and memory for egocentric localization. *Behavioral Neural Biology, 49*, 332–343.

Coutureau, E. and Killcross, S. (2003). Inactivation of the infralimbic prefrontal cortex reinstates goal-directed responding in overtrained rats. *Behavioral Brain Research, 146*, 167–174.

Divac, I., Rosvold, H. E., and Szwarcbart, M. K. (1967). Behavioral effects of selective ablation of the caudate nucleus. *Journal of Comparative and Physiological Psychology, 63*, 183–190.

Killcross, S. and Coutureau, E. (2003). Coordination of actions and habits in the medial prefrontal cortex of rats. *Cerebral Cortex, 13*, 400–408.

Malkova, L. D., Gaffan, D., and Murray, E. (1997). Excitotoxic lesions of the amygdala fail to produce impairment in visual learning for auditory secondary reinforcement but interfere with reinforcer devaluation effects in rhesus monkeys. *Journal of Neuroscience, 17,* 6011–6020.

Murray, E. A. and Wise, S. P. (1996). Role of the hippocampus plus subjacent cortex but not amygdala in visuomotor conditional learning in rhesus monkeys. *Behavioral Neuroscience, 110,* 1261–1270.

Ostlund, S. B. and Balleine, B. W. (2005). Lesions of medial prefrontal cortex disrupt the acquisition but not the expression of goal-directed learning. *Journal of Neuroscience, 25,* 7763–7770.

Pasupathy, A. and Miller, E. K. (2005). Different time courses of learning-related activity in the prefrontal cortex and striatum. *Nature, 433,* 873–876.

Thorndike, E. L. (1898). Animal Intelligence: an experimental study of associative processes in animals. *Psychological Monographs, 2,* Whole No. 8.

Tolman, E. C. (1948). Cognitive maps in rats and men. *Psychological Review, 55,* 189–208.

Tolman, E. C. (1949). There is more than one kind of learning. *Psychological Review, 56,* 144–155.

White, N. M. and McDonald, R. J. (2002). Multiple parallel memory systems in the brain of the rat. *Neurobiology of Learning and Memory, 77,* 125–84.

Yin, H. H., Knowlton, B. J., and Balleine, B. W. (2005). Blockade of NMDA receptors in the dorsomedial striatum prevents action–outcome learning in instrumental conditioning. *European Journal of Neuroscience, 22,* 505–512.

Yin, H. H., Ostlund, S. B., Knowlton, B. J., and Balleine, B. W. (2005). The role of the dorsomedial striatum in instrumental conditioning. *European Journal of Neuroscience, 22,* 513–523.

Learning about Danger: The Neurobiology of Fear Memories

All animals must solve fundamental problems associated with survival and reproduction. Thus, it should not come as a surprise that our evolutionary history has provided us with a brain that is designed to support what are called **behavioral systems** (Timberlake, 1994). A behavioral system is organized specifically to ensure that some particular need is met. There are specialized behavioral systems designed to support our reproductive and feeding-related activities and behavioral systems that allow us to avoid and escape dangerous situations.

According to the behavioral systems view, one major role of the processes that support learning and memory is to properly connect the behavioral infrastructure supported by a particular system to the ever-changing world in which we live. For example, we have the relevant behaviors for finding and ingesting food, but we have to learn the details about where the food is and what is fit to eat. We also have the relevant behaviors needed to avoid and escape from danger. But how do we know what is dangerous?

Some of this information is coded in our genes. However, in a dynamic world we have to adjust to changes in the environment. From a learning and memory perspective, the issue is how experience connects the neural systems that support our survival behaviors with the other features of our world that allow us to anticipate the occurrence of biologically significant events.

Understanding how learning and memory processes interface and tune our behavioral systems to this changing world is a large and complex endeavor because each of the several behavioral systems is specialized and has its own neural components. Rather than attempt a survey of all of these systems, this chapter focuses on just one—the so-called fear system. The importance of this system is obvious and much is known about its fundamental components. We will begin by describing the fear system and its neural basis, then examine how acquired fears motivate and reinforce instrumental behavior, and finally consider dangerous fears and their elimination.

The Fear System

The fear system evolved to allow us to escape from harmful events and to avoid them in the future. Robert Bolles (1970) developed the concept of **species-specific defensive behaviors** to describe the class of innate behaviors that are supported by the fear system. For example, the rat, a subject of hundreds of studies on the fear system, is equipped with several easily observable defensive behaviors, including freezing, flight, and fighting. Freezing is by far the most dominant of these behaviors, and you have already learned that this response—the animal remains essentially motionless, except for breathing—is often used as a measure of fear conditioning. Freezing provides an innate strategy to avoid danger because a motionless animal is less likely to be spotted by a predator than one that is moving. Moreover, flight is not especially effective for rodents because relative to their predators they are very slow.

Michael Fanselow

Michael Fanselow (1991) has argued that these defensive behaviors are organized around what he called a **predatory imminence gradient**, that is, when a potential predator is at a distance the rat will freeze, but as the predator moves within striking distance, the rat might attempt to flee the scene. If caught, it will engage in fighting in an attempt to escape. People respond to danger in much the same way. For example, Caroline and Robert Blanchard (1989), pioneers in research on defensive behaviors, have provided the following description of human defensive behavior:

If something unexpected occurs—a loud noise or sudden movement— people tend to respond immediately … stop what they are doing … orient toward the stimulus, and try to identify its potential for actual danger. This happens very quickly, in a reflex-like sequence in which action precedes any voluntary or consciously intentioned behavior. A poorly localizable or identifiable threat source, such as sound in the night, may elicit an active immobility so profound that the frightened person can hardly speak or even breathe, i.e., freezing. However, if the danger source has been localized and an avenue for flight or conceal- ment is plausible, the person will probably try to flee or hide… Actual contact, particularly painful contact, with the threat source is also likely to elicit thrashing, biting, scratching and other potentially damaging activities by the terrified person.

In addition to activating these easily observed behaviors, a danger signal will engage our autonomic nervous system, causing changes in our internal physi- ology, including increased heart rate and blood pressure and the shunting of blood to the peripheral muscles to prepare for flight or fight. When we are strongly activated by danger signals we also become analgesic—insensitive to pain. Danger signals can also result in the release of adrenal gland hormones that ready us to respond and, as you learned in Chapter 10, can enhance memory. Some stimuli in the rodent's environment such as ferret odor will in- nately activate the fear system. However, learning and memory processes provide the primary way to link stimuli to the neural systems that support fear behav- ior. They allow us to anticipate danger and get out of harm's way. Figure 16.1 provides a schematic of the ba- sic ideas of a defensive behavioral system.

Caroline and Robert Blanchard

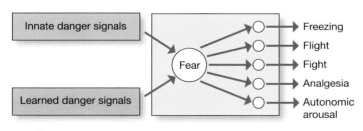

FIGURE 16.1
A defensive behavioral sys- tem. This system organizes the expression of a variety of behaviors that have evolved to protect us from danger. It can be activated by innate danger signals, and experi- ence allows this system to also be activated by learned danger signals.

Experience teaches us to identify dangerous situations. This happens because an experience with an aversive event will modify our response to the otherwise insignificant features of the environment that are also present. Associative learning processes that support Pavlovian conditioning produce this outcome. You already know the basic laboratory procedures used for creating conditioned fear (see Figure 7.9).

You will recall that an aversive stimulus can establish fear to both the place–context where it occurred and the discrete phasic stimulus (a stimulus that has a distinct onset and termination) that preceded the shock. Fear as measured by defensive responses is easy to establish and increases with the intensity of the aversive event. Once established, memories for fear experience endure for a long time. Variations of this basic procedure in combination with methods for altering regions of the brain have been used to reveal much of what has been learned about the neural basis of learned fear.

Joseph LeDoux

Michael Davis

The Neural Basis of Fear

People and other animals display conditioned fear-related behaviors to stimuli that were present when an aversive event was experienced. In the last 20 years, significant progress has been made toward understanding the basic neural circuitry that supports conditioned fear (Davis, 2006; Davis and Shi, 1999; Kapp, Pascoe, and Bixler, 1984; Paré, Quirk, and LeDoux, 2004; Samson and Paré, 2005; Wilensky, Schafe, Kristensen, and LeDoux, 2006). The laboratories of Joseph LeDoux, Michael Davis, and Bruce Kapp, in particular, have made major contributions to different aspects of this problem.

As noted earlier, when confronted with signals of danger, animals display several responses. They freeze, they flee, and they will fight when escape is not possible. They also display autonomic arousal. Subcortical nuclei located in the midbrain are responsible for generating these behaviors. For example, neurons located in what is called the **periaqueductal gray** (**PAG**) are responsible for producing freezing and analgesia, and other neurons in the **lateral hypothalamus** (**LH**) are responsible for the changes in autonomic responses (heart rate and blood pressure) pro-

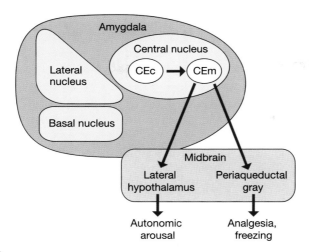

FIGURE 16.2
The important nuclei in the amygdala complex and in the midbrain that play an important role in fear behaviors. Note that the CEm projects to the midbrain nuclei and can generate fear-associated behaviors. CEc = lateral capsule of the central amygdala, CEm = medial nucleus of the central amygdala.

duced by the sympathetic nervous system that prepare us for action (Figure 16.2). Direct electrical stimulation of these brain regions can elicit fear behaviors, and damage to these regions impairs the expression of the behaviors (see Fanselow, 1991, and Kim and Jung, 2006, for reviews).

Midbrain nuclei provide the direct neural basis for specific defensive behaviors that make up the fear system. However, these regions are not directly linked to the sensory–perceptual systems by which we experience the world. Instead, our sensory–perceptual systems interface with the midbrain nuclei by way of a complex region of the brain called the **amygdala** (discussed previously in Chapter 10). This almond shaped structure is composed of many nuclei, but only some are relevant to the understanding of fear.

As illustrated in Figure 16.2, the relevant nuclei are the **lateral nucleus (LA)**, **basal nucleus (BA)**, and **central nucleus (CE)** of the amygdala, as well as two subnuclei of the CE: the **lateral capsule (CEc)** and the **medial nucleus (CEm)** of the central amygdala. You should note that the CEm is the *output region* of the amygdala. When CEm neurons are activated, they in turn activate neurons in the LH and PAG that generate fear behaviors. Thus, the CEm can be thought of as the *command center* for initiating fear-related behaviors. Damage to this nucleus will greatly dampen the ability of animals to express many defensive behaviors.

A Neural System that Supports Learned Fear

Figure 16.3 illustrates how the sensory and perceptual information contained in an aversive experience becomes linked to the fear system. Many regions of the brain converge onto nuclei in the amygdala to provide it with information about an aversive experience. This complex picture can be simplified by describing two routes or pathways out of the sensory thalamus that ultimately project to amygdala nuclei.

One route, called the **subcortical pathway**, goes directly from the sensory thalamus to the LA. It is thought to provide a somewhat impoverished representation of the sensory experience (LeDoux, 1994). The second route, called the **cortical pathway**, is more complex. This pathway carries information from the sensory thalamus to the neocortical regions of the brain, where a richer, more detailed representation of the experience is constructed.

As you know, neocortical regions also project to and interact with the hippocampus (see Chapter 13). Moreover, neocortical regions and the hippocampus also project into the amygdala, primarily to neurons in the LA and CEc. *Synapses connecting these inputs to LA and CEc neurons are believed to be modified by an aversive experience and thus store the experience.* For example, you will recall that Rumpel and his colleagues (2005) found that auditory-cue fear conditioning can drive GluR1 AMPA receptors into synapses located on neurons in the LA and that blocking trafficking of these receptors can impair the acquisition of fear to the tone.

Thus, when a behavioral experience contains an aversive event, synapses linking inputs from the sensory thalamus, neocortex, and hippocampus to neurons in the LA and CEc nuclei are strengthened. A later re-encounter with stimuli that accompanied the aversive event will drive neurons in the LA and CEc to a point where they will activate the CEm and generate defensive behaviors.

The idea that there are both subcortical and cortical projections from the sensory thalamus to the amygdala comes primarily from studies of auditory-cue fear conditioning. Anatomical studies revealed that auditory stimulation projects to the amygdala directly from the sensory thalamus as well as by way of what is called the **auditory cortex**. This organization suggests that both the thalamus and auditory cortex can independently support learned fear to an auditory stimulus. Romanski and LeDoux (1992) tested the implications of this idea. As one might expect, they found that damage to only the relevant thalamic nucleus or damage to only the auditory cortex did not impair the acquisition to the auditory stimulus.

The contribution the hippocampus makes to learned fear comes from studies of contextual fear conditioning. The principle finding is that both small and large lesions of the hippocampus made after a contextual-fear conditioning session produce amnesia in rodents (Lehman, Lacanilao, and Sutherland, 2007;

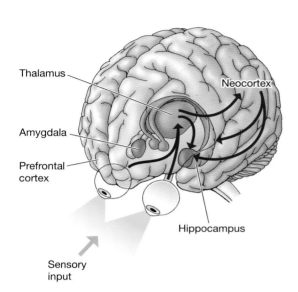

FIGURE 16.3

The elements of the neural system that support learned fear. Sensory information representing an aversive experience comes into the system by way of the sensory thalamus. A subcortical pathway takes unprocessed information directly to the lateral and central nuclei of the amygdala. A cortical pathway brings this information to the neocortex and the hippocampus, where more detailed representations of experience are constructed. Projections from these regions converge on neurons located in the lateral nucleus of the amygdala (LA) and neurons in the lateral capsule of the central amygdala (CEc). Neurons in both the LA and CEc are believed to contain modifiable synapses. Thus, when a behavioral experience contains an aversive event, synapses linking inputs from the sensory thalamus, neocortex, and hippocampus to neurons in these regions are strengthened. After the experience with an aversive event, a re-encounter with the surrounding stimuli will drive neurons in the LA and CEc to a point where they will activate the output region of the central amygdala—the medial nucleus (CEm)—to generate defensive behaviors by activating neurons in the lateral hypothalamus (LH) and the periacqueductal gray (PAG) in the midbrain.

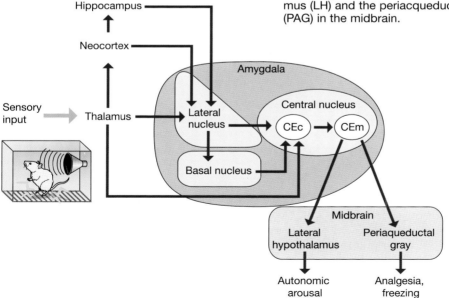

Maren, Aharonov, and Fanselow, 1997; Wiltgen, Sanders, Anagnostaras, Sage, and Fanselow, 2006). In contrast, if the hippocampus is damaged prior to conditioning, even rats with nearly complete damage to the hippocampus will condition to context (Maren et al., 1997; Wiltgen et al., 2006). Two conclusions are implied by this pattern of results. First, in the normal animal the hippocampal system acquires a representation of the context that gets associated with the aversive event. Second, in the absence of the hippocampus, other neocortical regions of the brain can also represent the context and can support conditioning to the context.

Consistent with these conclusions, rats with damage to neocortical regions that project to the hippocampus, perirhinal, and postrhinal cortex also display impaired contextual fear conditioning (Burwell, Bucci, Sanborn, and Jutras, 2004). This happens if the damage occurs either before or after conditioning. Thus, contextual fear conditioning can be supported by either context representations in the hippocampus or by context representations in the neocortices that feed into the hippocampus (Figure 16.4).

Parallel Responses in Humans

The neural system that supports fear has been revealed by research with rodents. However, research on people with damage to similar regions of the brain has yielded results consistent with what one would predict from the work with rodents.

The work of Antoine Bechara and his colleagues (1995) is a good illustration of such parallel responses in humans. In their study, patients with damage to either the amygdala or the hippocampus or to both regions of the brain were conditioned to a very loud noise as the aversive event, preceded by mild tones or flashes of different colored visual stimuli. An autonomic nervous system response called the **galvanic skin response** (GSR) was the measure of defensive fear behavior. Basically, the GSR is a measure of the skin's ability to conduct electricity. Enhanced autonomic activity results in sweaty hands that will conduct more electrical current. As you might expect, patients with damage to the amygdala did not show an enhanced GSR to the conditioned stimuli. However, when asked to describe their experience, they accurately recalled what happened to them (their episodic memory system was still intact). In contrast, people with damage to the hippocampus acquired a conditioned defensive GSR. However, they could not recollect anything about the training experience. In essence, they could display fear but did not know why. People with damage to both the amygdala and hippocampus neither showed a conditioned GSR nor could they recall anything about the training episode.

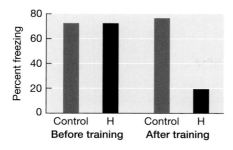
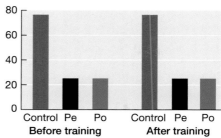

FIGURE 16.4
This figure llustrates the contribution of the hippocampus, perirhinal, and postrhinal cortices to contextual fear conditioning. Note that when the hippocampus is damaged before training, rats learn to fear the context. However, if the hippocampus is removed after conditioning, their context fear is significantly reduced. In contrast, damage to the perirhinal and postrhinal cortices either before or after conditioning significantly reduces fear of the context. H = damage to the hippocampus, Pe = damage to the perirhinal cortex, Po = damage to the postrhinal cortex. (After Burwell et al., 2004.)

There is also evidence that stimuli paired with an aversive outcome activate the amygdala and this activation is correlated with other measures of fear (Cheng, Knight, Smith, and Helmstetter, 2006; LaBar, Gatenby, Gore, LeDoux, and Phelps, 1998). For example, Fred Helmstetter's laboratory (Cheng et al., 2006) has imaged neural activity during fear conditioning in which participants were conditioned to respond to a conditioned stimulus (CS+) that signaled an aversive outcome. In addition, another stimulus (CS–) was presented that was never followed by the aversive outcome. Their important result was that on trials when the CS+ elicited a substantial GSR, there was also substantial neural activity in the amygdala. The CS– rarely elicited an increased GSR or neural activity in the amygdala. On some trials, even the CS+ failed to evoke the conditioned response. On those trials there also was little or no increase in neural activity in the amygdala. This tight coupling between neural activity in the amygdala and the strength of the GSR suggests that the neurons in the amygdala are involved in the expression of defensive behaviors.

Acquired Fears Motivate and Reinforce Instrumental Behavior

Much of our discussion has focused on the fact that the fear system is organized to support innate, observable behaviors like freezing, flight, and fight.

However, psychologists have long believed that, in addition, stimuli associated with the occurrence of strong aversive stimulation can create a subjective psychological state called "fear" that can be described as unpleasant or even aversive. If you are confronted by stimulation that evokes a fear state, it is likely that you will engage in responses calculated to terminate this state. Thus, the state of fear is said to have motivational properties that lead to the initiation of behavior that results in removing this state. Hobart Mowrer (1939, 1947) carried this reasoning a step further and proposed that the termination of the fear state *reinforces the learning of the response that terminated the state.* The idea that people learn behaviors to reduce negatively charged states is pervasive in clinical psychology (Mineka, 1985).

Specifically, Mowrer proposed that (1) by Pavlovian conditioning processes, cues paired with aversive stimulation acquire the ability to elicit a fear state that has motivational properties, and (2) the termination of the fear state itself can reinforce the acquisition of what are called **instrumental responses** (Figure 16.5).

Years ago, Brown and Jacobs (1949) provided support for the general idea that the fear state produced by pairing a stimulus with aversive stimulation can motivate and reinforce the learning of a new behavior (Figure 16.6). They first conditioned rats to fear a conditioned stimulus (CS) by pairing it with an unconditioned stimulus (US), shock. In the critical phase, the rats were placed on one side of an apparatus called a shuttle box. The CS was then presented and if the rat crossed to the other side of the box, the CS was terminated. The rationale for the experiment is that if fear has motivational properties and if terminating this state (by terminating the CS) is a reinforcing event,

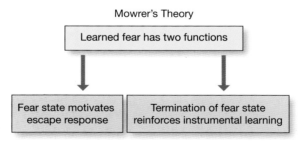

FIGURE 16.5
Hobart Mowrer proposed that stimuli paired with aversive events can evoke a learned fear state. This state motivates instrumental escape behavior, and the termination of the fear state reinforces the instrumental response.

(A) Pavlovian fear conditioning

(B) Learning to escape fear

(C)

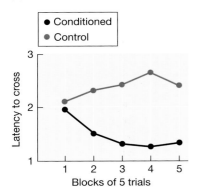

FIGURE 16.6
(A) A rat receives Pavlovian fear conditioning. (B) It is later placed into a shuttle box and the CS is presented. If the animal crosses to the other side, the CS and the fear it produces are terminated. (C) Rats that were conditioned learn the instrumental response that terminates the CS. Their latency to cross to the other side decreases over trials, whereas the latency of the control rats that were not conditioned, if anything, increases. CS = conditioned stimulus, US = unconditioned stimulus. (After Brown and Jacobs 1949.)

then the rats would learn to cross to the other side when the CS was presented. This is just what Brown and Jacobs found.

The question for neurobiologists is, what regions of the brain contribute to the learned-fear state that motivates and reinforces the learning of instrumental behaviors? Very little research has addressed this question; however, Amorapanth, LeDoux, and Nader (2000) have provided some information about the neural substrates of the fear state.

It should come as no surprise that the amygdala also contributes to learned fear. As you can see by looking at Figure 16.7 or by returning to Figure 16.3, the lateral region of the amygdala is the gateway to both the basal region and the central region of the amygdala. Amorapanth and his colleagues determined the role of each of these regions for both the conditioned freezing behavior and the fear state needed to learn a new response. To do this they lesioned the lateral, basal, or central amygdala in different groups of rats to examine the effect on either conditioned freezing or performance in a shuttle-box escape task similar to that used by Brown and Jacobs. As you might expect, damage to either the lateral or central regions of the amygdala dramat-

(A)
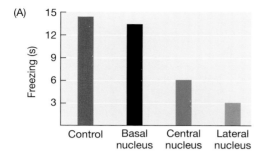

(B)
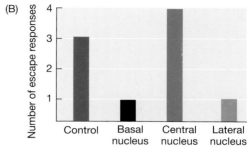

FIGURE 16.7
(A) Compared to control animals, rats with damage to both the central and lateral nuclei of the amygdala, but not to the basal nucleus, exhibit impaired conditioned freezing. (B) Damage to the basal and lateral nuclei, but not to the central nucleus, impairs performance on the instrumental shuttle-box escape task. (C) This figure illustrates the conclusion that synapses in the lateral amygdala that receive input from the CS are strengthened by the CS–US pairings. This allows the CS to activate the freezing response by its projections to the central amygdala and to activate the motivational system that supports instrumental escape behavior by activating the basal nucleus. (After Amorapanth et al., 2000.)

(C)
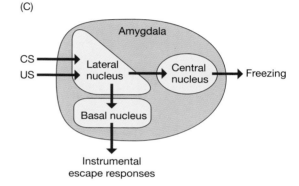

ically reduced conditioned freezing, but damage to the basal region did not. In contrast, the animals with damage to either the lateral or basal nucleus did not learn the escape response, but animals with damage to the central nucleus learned the task.

These results indicate that the lateral region is critical for both types of performance. It integrates the CS and US information and then projects forward to the basal and central regions. The fear state that supports the learned escape response depends on the basal region and the innate freezing response depends on the central amygdala.

Eliminating Dangerous Fears: Psychological Theories of Extinction

The behavioral fear system is designed to produce adaptive behaviors that allow us to stay out of harm's way. However, the properties of this system that enable us to rapidly condition to stimuli surrounding an aversive experience also can be maladaptive and lead to behavioral pathologies. Learned fears and anxieties such as post-traumatic stress disorders that result from intensive aversive experiences and panic attacks that emerge because of our fear of fear itself can be so debilitating that they greatly interfere with our ability to function normally.

For many years, the elimination of learned fears and anxieties has been of great concern to clinical psychologists and psychiatrists. Contemporary psychologists who use Pavlovian conditioning procedures to study how to extinguish conditioned responses have made important contributions to our empirical and theoretical understanding of how to eliminate learned fear. We will now consider some of the facts and ideas that have emerged from this domain that are relevant to eliminating excessive fear responses.

Cues paired with aversive events acquire the ability to evoke a conditioned defensive response. Psychologists called learning theorists generally assume that this occurs because associative connections between representations of these cues and representation of the aversive event are strengthened. The association is thus the critical mediator of the effect of the conditioning experience. Neurobiologists, of course, would substitute the concept of synaptic strength for the concept of association.

As you have learned, in the language of Pavlovian conditioning the cue paired with shock is called the conditioned stimulus (CS) and the aversive event is called the unconditioned stimulus (US). Since Pavlov's work, we have known that a conditioned response (CR) can be eliminated. The method is quite simple. One presents the subject with the CS but the US is not presented. When only the CS is presented, it loses its ability to evoke the conditioned response. This outcome is called **extinction** (Figure 16.8).

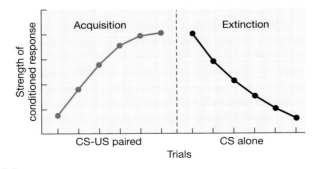

FIGURE 16.8
Paired presentations of the CS and US produce acquisition. The CS acquires the ability to evoke the conditioned response (CR). If the CS is then presented alone, it will lose the ability to evoke the CR. This phenomenon is called extinction.

(A) Associative loss hypothesis

(B) Competing memory hypothesis

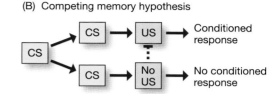

FIGURE 16.9
This figure illustrates two theories of extinction. The associative loss hypothesis assumes that extinction is due to a CS-alone presentation eliminating the original CS–US association. The competing memory hypothesis assumes that extinction produces a new association called a CS–noUS association. The original CS–US association that produced the CR remains intact. If the CS–noUS association occurs, it inhibits (–) the expression of the conditioned response.

Extinction is an empirical fact. Why presenting the CS alone produces extinction, however, is a theoretical question. There are several possible answers to this question. However, we will consider only two hypotheses. One explanation is sometimes called the associative loss hypothesis; the other is called the competing memory hypothesis (Figure 16.9). To put it simply, the **associative loss hypothesis** assumes that extinction is due to the CS-alone presentation eliminating the original CS–US association. The **competing memory hypothesis** assumes that extinction produces a new association called a CS–noUS association, but the original CS–US association that produced the CR remains intact. If the CS–noUS association occurs, it inhibits the expression of the conditioned response. Let's look more closely now at these theories and their implications.

According to the associative loss hypothesis, CS-alone presentations engage mechanisms that essentially *erase or eliminate the associations* that were established and that supported the ability of the CS to produce conditioned responses. This theory has one very important implication. Specifically, if extinction occurs because the underlying association is erased, then unless the CS is again paired with the US, the CS should never again evoke the conditioned response. Extinction training (CS-alone presentations) should permanently eliminate the ability of the CS to evoke a conditioned response.

The associative loss account has intuitive appeal and may be part of the answer. However, at best it only accounts for a small part of the data. The bulk of the evidence indicates that extinction does not eliminate the underlying associative basis of the conditioned response. Instead, *extinction produces new learning*. Pavlov knew this fact. One of his major findings was that after extinction, the conditioned response often would "spontaneously recover." What this means is that with the passage of time the CS would recover the ability to evoke the conditioned response. It did not have to be paired with the US again.

The phenomenon called **spontaneous recovery** has been known for some time. However, it was Mark Bouton's research program that led to a full appreciation of the complexities of extinction (Bouton, 1994; Bouton, 2002). His research revealed other ways to recover the extinguished conditioned response. One way is called the **renewal effect**. In this case rats are given the CS–US pairings in one place or context, but extinction (CS-alone presentations) occurs in a different place. Even though extinction training eliminates

Mark Bouton

the conditioned response, if the animal is returned to the original training environment, the CR recovers. A second example is called **reinstatement**. Just re-presenting the US in the training context can reinstate the ability of the CS to evoke a CR.

Note that in all the cases illustrated in Figure 16.10—spontaneous recovery, renewal, and reinstatement—the CS recovers the ability to evoke the CR even though it is not re-paired with the US. If presenting the CS alone erased the underlying CS–US association, this should not happen.

The general conclusion from these examples is that extinction does not erase the original CS–US association. Instead, as noted, many researchers believe that extinction is the product of new learning. Specifically, when only the CS is presented the subject is thought to learn that the US will no longer occur. For convenience, psychologists say that extinction produces a new association called a **CS–noUS association**.

If extinction does not eliminate or erase the original CS–US association but instead generates a new CS–noUS association, then we have to assume that following acquisition and extinction the CS is involved in two associations: (1) the CS–US association and (2) the CS–noUS association. This state of affairs is called the competing memory trace model of extinction. According to this account, the reason extinction is not permanent is that the original CS–US association is not eliminated. Instead, the CS–noUS association supports a response that competes with the CR generated by the CS–US association for expression (as illustrated previously in Figure 16.9B).

Unfortunately, extinction is not permanent and this has important implications for therapists who want to use extinction-like procedures to eliminate learned fears and anxieties. The problem is how to prevent "extinguished" fears from recovering (Bouton, Westbrook, Corcoran, and Maren, 2006). Before addressing the problem of eliminating human fears, we need to consider the competing memory theory in the context of the neurobiology of the fear system.

FIGURE 16.10

Three findings that indicate that extinction is not permanent. In each example the critical results are from the retention test where the CS is re-presented after extinction has taken place. (A) Spontaneous recovery can occur when there is a long retention interval between extinction and the test. (B) Renewal can occur when the context where extinction trials occur is different from the context in which training occurs, and the test occurs in the training context. (C) Reinstatement occurs if the US is re-presented without the CS. In all cases, recovery from extinction occurs even though the CS and US are never re-paired.

(A) Spontaneous recovery

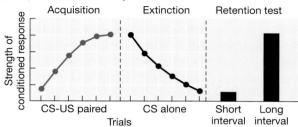

(B) Renewal effect

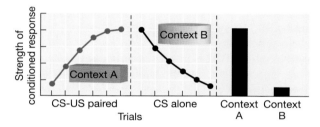

(C) Reinstatement effect

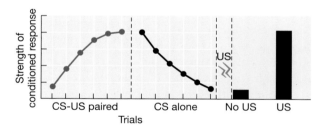

The Neurobiology of Fear Extinction

The basic circuit that supports learned fear was presented in Figure 16.3. This circuit represents the CS–US association as strengthened synaptic connections linking cortical and subcortical representations of experience to neurons in the LA and CEc so that they can then drive the CEm to generate the fear behaviors.

How, then, might a CS–noUS association be represented, and how might this association result in fear extinction? One possible answer to these questions has emerged from the work of Denis Paré (Royer and Paré, 2002). In addition to containing excitatory connections that allow one set of neurons to drive another set, the amygdala contains clusters of cells called **intercalated neurons**. These neurons feed forward to the CE and the output of these neurons is inhibitory, so when they are activated, they prevent excitatory connections on the same receiving neurons from depolarizing. Thus, they can inhibit the output of the neurons in the CEm that generate defensive behavior.

Denis Paré

Paré proposed that at any moment in time the output of the CEm reflects the balance of excitatory versus inhibitory inputs it receives. When the excitatory inputs outweigh the inhibitory inputs, then defensive behaviors will be generated. However, so long as the excitatory and inhibitory inputs are roughly equal, then defensive behaviors will not be generated. The intercalated neurons thus represent a potential way for extinction to reduce the ability of the CS to generate fear behaviors. Perhaps during extinction training, when the CS is presented alone, synapses linking the CS to intercalated neurons get strengthened.

There is also evidence that the extinction procedure recruits the participation of neurons in the **infralimbic region** of the medial prefrontal cortex (Quirk, Garcia, and Gonzalez-Lima, 2006; Quirk, Likhtik, Pelletier, and Paré, 2003; Quirk, Russo, Barron, and Lebron, 2000). For example, Gregory Quirk and his colleagues (Burgos-Robles, Vidal-Gonzalez, Santini, and Quirk; 2007; Sierra-Mercado, Corcoran, Lebron-Milad, and Quirk, 2006) have reported that either inactivating neurons in this region or infusing an NMDA antagonist prior to extinction impairs subsequent extinction test performance. This region of the brain projects onto the inhibitory, intercalated neurons located in the amygdala. So if infralimbic neurons are active during the extinction test, they can also contribute to inhibiting the output of the CEm that generates fear.

Greg Quirk

Thus, there may be two general ways that the CS-alone presentation can produce extinction without eliminating the previously established CS–US association: (1) the CS may associate with the intercalated neurons that reside in the amygdala, and (2) extinction training might recruit the participation of neurons in the infralimbic cortex that project to the intercalated neurons (Figure 16.11). These processes provide an answer to the question of how a CS–noUS association is represented neurologically and how this association

FIGURE 16.11
(A) During fear conditioning, the CS becomes associated with neurons in the basolateral nucleus of the amygdala (BLA) that drive neurons in the medial nucleus of the central amygdala (CEm) to produce fear. Note that, after acquisition, the CS excites (+) the CEm to generate fear. (B) As a consequence of extinction training (CS-alone presentations), the CS also gets associated with the intercalated neurons (IC), and neurons in the infralimbic (IL) medial prefrontal cortex (mPFC) that project to the intercalated neurons are also recruited. So now the excitatory input to the central amygdala is balanced by inhibitory input. Thus, the ability of the CS to evoke fear is reduced.

(A) Acquisition

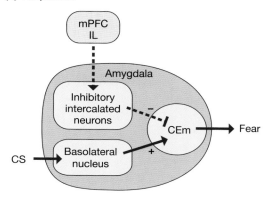

(B) Extinction

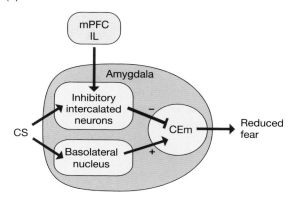

might produce extinction. The CS becomes associated with the inhibitory, intercalated neurons in the amygdala.

Thus, at the completion of both acquisition and extinction, the CS remains associated with the neurons in the basolateral nucleus of the amygdala (BLA) that can excite neurons in the CEm to produce fear responses. In addition, however, the CS also has become linked to the inhibitory, intercalated neurons. Thus, when the CS is presented it would now produce a balanced excitatory and inhibitory input to the CEm and its ability to activate defensive fear behaviors would be reduced. This mechanism would also explain why an "extinguished CS" might recover its ability to evoke fear responses. For fear to recover, all that is required is that the balance shift again to favor the CS placing more excitatory drive onto the CEm.

Extinction Depends on NMDA Receptors

Thus far it has been argued that the new learning that occurs during extinction involves linking the neural representation of the CS to intercalated neurons. This requires that synaptic connections on intercalated neurons be modifiable. Royer and Paré (2002) have provided evidence that supports this assumption. They used a slice preparation taken from the amygdala and applied stimulation to neurons coming from the BLA that synapsed onto intercalated neurons. High-frequency stimulation applied to these neurons resulted in long-term potentiation of the synapses that connect these neurons to intercalated neurons. Moreover, applying the NMDA-receptor antagonist APV to the slice prevented this potentiation. Thus, not only can synapses on intercalated neurons be modified, their modification involves NMDA receptors.

Based on this study, one might expect that the new learning that produces extinction also requires the involvement of NMDA receptors. In support of this idea, several laboratories have reported that the injection of APV into the amygdala prior to CS-alone presentations significantly impairs the acquisition and retention of the learning that supports extinction (see Falls, Miserendino, and Davis, 1992, and Myers and Davis, 2007, for a review). More recently, it has been shown that an antagonist called ifenprodil that selectively blocks glutamates access to the NR2B subunit of the NMDA receptor also blocks the extinction of the fear response (Sotres-Bayon, Bush, and LeDoux, 2007).

In addition to having glutamate-binding sites, the NMDA receptor also has a glycine-binding site (Figure 16.12). The glycine-binding site is important because it contributes to the efficient opening of the NMDA receptor calcium channel. A number of researchers have asked if the glycine-binding site makes a contribution to extinction. They used a partial agonist called **d-cycloserine (DCS)** that binds to the glycine site to enhance the opening of the NMDA receptor. This work has revealed that if DCS is injected either before or after extinction training, the next day the rodents display enhanced extinction (Walker, Ressler, Lu, and Davis, 2002; Ledgerwood, Richardson, and Cranney, 2003; see Davis, Ressler, Rothbaum, and Richardson, 2006, for a review). Given that NMDA receptor antagonists can prevent extinction and the partial agonist DCS can facilitate extinction, it is reasonable to assume that synaptic changes that depend on NMDA receptors play a central role in the new learning that produces extinction.

As noted, it is possible that CS-only presentations produce new learning by strengthening synapses linking CS inputs to intercalated neurons. Thus, one might speculate that it is the NMDA receptors on the intercalated neurons that are being influenced by the NMDA antagonist and agonist to determine the strength of these connections. However, as yet there is no direct evidence that this is the case.

FIGURE 16.12
NMDA receptors have two binding sites, one for glutamate and one for glycine. APV antagonizes the glutamate binding site and interferes with extinction. D-cycloserine (DCS) is an agonist for the glycine site. When it is given before or after extinction training, it facilitates the processes that produce extinction (see Davis et al., 2006, for a review).

(A)

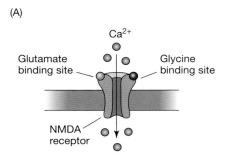

(B)

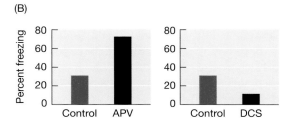

Why Fear Renews: A Role for the Hippocampus

The general picture you should now have is that following extinction of fear, the representation of the CS is involved in two associations. One links the CS to neurons in the amygdala (primarily in the LA and CEc) that can excite the CEm to generate a fear response. The other links the CS to intercalated neurons that can inhibit fear. Given that these two conflicting associations exist, it is not surprising that following extinction training the CS might recover its ability to evoke fear. From a clinical perspective this is a problem, because one would like extinction training to produce a permanent result. Thus, trying to limit fear renewal is a major problem for clinical treatment. Let's consider this problem in more depth.

It is easy to imagine that the context in which CS extinction takes place differs in some important ways from the context in which acquisition takes place. Thus, at the completion of extinction, the person or rodent might have learned that the CS is now safe in a particular context—specifically in the context in which CS-alone presentations were given. Thus, when the CS is re-encountered outside of the extinction context, it again evokes fear. This in essence is what was previously described as the renewal effect (see Figure 16.10). It means that extinction is to some extent *specific to the context* in which it occurred.

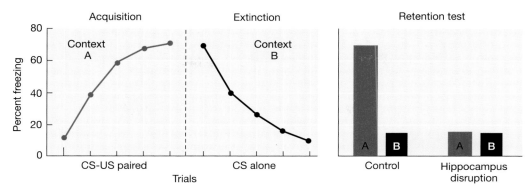

FIGURE 16.13
In this experiment, rats are conditioned to the CS in one context (context A) but extinguished in a different context (context B). Normal rats display renewed fear of the CS if they are tested in context A, but display no fear if tested in context B. In contrast, rats with damage to the hippocampus do not display renewed fear to the CS when tested in context A.

The hippocampus may contribute importantly to this specificity. You will recall that the hippocampus plays a major role in constructing the representation of the context in which we experience events (see Chapter 13). If one could eliminate the contribution of the hippocampus during extinction and thereby eliminate the context representation it supports, then it might be possible to prevent the renewal of extinction when the CS is experienced outside of the extinction context.

Steve Maren and his colleagues (Corcoran and Maren, 2001; Ji and Maren, 2005, 2007) have provided support for this idea. Specifically, if the hippocampus is damaged or inactivated, the rodent does not display renewal of fear when tested in the conditioning context (Figure 16.13).

It is worth noting an implication of this work. Specifically, having a functioning hippocampus (as is the case for healthy people) may limit the effectiveness of extinction as a clinical tool for eliminating conditioned fear. This is because the presence of the hippocampus restricts extinction to the context in which extinction occurs. Ironically, this means that extinction therapy might be more effective if one could inactivate the hippocampus during extinction.

Steve Maren

Eliminating Human Fears

The discovery that DCS facilitates extinction in the laboratory has encouraged researchers to pursue the possibility that DCS, in combination with behavioral theory, might have therapeutic value in eliminating learned fears in people. Kerry Ressler and his colleagues (2004) have tested this hypothesis on people who suffer from acrophobia. People with acrophobia have a debilitating and irrational fear of heights. To test their hypothesis, Ressler's group used what is called **exposure therapy**. In this therapy, patients are forced to experience the stimulus situation that induces the fear response. It is used to treat a number of fear–anxiety disorders. Some participants received exposure therapy and in addition were required to take a pill containing DCS prior to exposure. Other participants received exposure therapy in combination with a placebo (a pill that contained no DCS). The patients had no knowledge of which pill they took. Several measures indicated a significant benefit to combining DCS with exposure therapy. When retested following the treatment, these participants reported a decrease in discomfort produced by exposure. Their autonomic arousal decreased and they were more willing to expose themselves to heights. These benefits persisted for three months after the treatment. These are very promising results and will no doubt stimulate additional work to determine the generality of these effects.

Summary

Our evolutionary history has provided us with neural systems designed to support behaviors that are organized to meet our most fundamental needs. These behavioral systems are finely tuned by our experiences. This chapter focused on the fear system that supports defensive behaviors designed to allow us to anticipate danger and keep out of harm's way.

    The infrastructure for defensive behaviors is provided by midbrain regions that are under the control of neurons in the medial area of the central amygdala. Many brain regions converge onto the neurons in the basolateral nucleus of the amygdala. These inputs provide the amygdala with various levels of detailed information about the environment that is present at the time an aversive event takes place. An aversive experience modifies the strength of these synaptic connections so that when elements of this experience are re-encountered they will drive the CEm to produce defensive behaviors.

    The fear system generally produces adaptive behavior, but intensely aversive experiences can lead to excessive fears that become pathological and debilitating. One way to eliminate learned fears is to use Pavlovian procedures designed to produce extinction. Exposure to just the CS can greatly weaken its capacity to evoke fear. However, this outcome is often not permanent, as extinguished fears can recover. This means that the original associations that produced the fear are not erased but instead CS-alone presentations result in new learning that psychologists call CS–noUS associations.

At the neural systems level, extinction appears to be the result of strengthened synaptic connections to intercalated neurons that have the ability to inhibit the neurons in the CEm so that the CS does not generate fear. Strengthening these synaptic connections also requires the participation of NMDA receptors. Targeting the glycine-binding site with d-cycloserine facilitates extinction and has been used with some success to enhance the extinction of acrophobia.

References

Amorapanth, P., LeDoux, J. E., and Nader, K. (2000). Different lateral amygdala outputs mediate reactions and actions elicited by a fear-arousing stimulus. *Nature Neuroscience, 3,* 74–79.

Bechara, A., Tranel, D., Damasio, H., Adolphs, R., Rockland, C., and Damasio, A. R. (1995). Double dissociation of conditioning and declarative knowledge relative to the amygdala and hippocampus in humans. *Science, 269,* 1115–1118.

Blanchard, C. D. and Blanchard, R. J. (1989). Ethonoexperimental approaches to the biology of emotion. *Annual Review of Psychology, 39,* 43–68.

Bolles, R. C. (1970). Species specific defense reactions and avoidance learning. *Psychological Review, 79,* 32–48.

Bouton, M. E. (1994). Context, ambiguity, and classical conditioning. *Current Directions in Psychological Science, 3,* 49–53.

Bouton, M. E. (2002). Context, ambiguity, and unlearning sources of relapse after behavioral extinction. *Biological Psychiatry, 52,* 976–986.

Bouton, M. E., Westbrook, R. F., Corcoran, K. A., and Maren, S. (2006). Contextual and temporal modulation of extinction: behavioral and biological mechanisms. *Biological Psychiatry, 60,* 352–60.

Brown, J. S. and Jacobs, A. (1949). The role of fear in the motivation and acquisition of responses. *Journal of Experimental Psychology, 39,* 747–749.

Burgos-Robles, A., Vidal-Gonzalez, I., Santini, E., and Quirk, G. J. (2007). Consolidation of fear extinction requires NMDA receptor-dependent bursting in the ventromedial prefrontal cortex. *Neuron, 53,* 871–880.

Burwell, R. D., Bucci, D. J., Sanborn, M. R., and Jutras, M. J. (2004). Perirhinal and postrhinal contributions to remote memory for context. *Journal of Neuroscience, 24,* 11023–11028.

Cheng, D. T., Knight, D. C., Smith, C. N., and Helmstetter, F. J. (2006). Human amygdala activity during the expression of fear responses. *Behavioral Neuroscience, 120,* 1187–1195.

Corcoran, K.A. and Maren, S. (2001). Hippocampal inactivation disrupts contextual retrieval of fear memory after extinction. *Journal of Neuroscience, 2,* 1720–1726.

Davis, M. (2006). Neural systems involved in fear and anxiety measured with fear-potentiated startle. *American Psychologist, 61,* 741–756.

Davis, M., Ressler, K., Rothbaum, B. O., and Richardson, R. (2006). Effects of d-cycloserine on extinction: translation from preclinical to clinical work. *Biological Psychiatry, 60,* 369–375.

Davis, M. and Shi, C. (1999). The extended amygdala: are the central nucleus of the amygdala and the bed nucleus of the stria terminalis differentially involved in fear versus anxiety? *Annals of the New York Academy of Science, 29,* 281–291.

Falls, W. A., Miserendino, M. J. D., and Davis, M. (1992). Extinction of fear-potentiated startle: blockade by infusion of an NMDA antagonist into the amygdala. *Journal of Neuroscience, 12,* 854–863.

Fanselow, M. S. (1991). The midbrain periacqueductal gray as coordinator of action in response to fear and anxiety. In A. Depaulis and R. Bandler (Eds.), *The midbrain periacqueductal gray matter* (pp. 151–171). New York: Plenum Press.

Ji, J. and Maren, S. (2005). Electrolytic lesions of the dorsal hippocampus disrupt renewal of conditional fear after extinction. *Learning and Memory, 12,* 270–276.

Ji, J. and Maren S. (2007). Hippocampal involvement in contextual modulation of fear extinction. *Hippocampus, 17,* 749–758.

Kapp, B. S., Pascoe, J. P., and Bixler, M. A. (1984). The amygdala: a neuroanatomical systems approach to its contribuitions to aversive conditioning. In N. Buttlers and L. R. Squire (Eds.), *Neuropsychology of memory* (pp. 473–488). New York: Guilford.

Kim, J. J. and Jung, M. W. (2006). Neural circuits and mechanisms involved in Pavlovian fear conditioning: a critical review. *Neuroscience and Biobehavioral Review, 30,* 188–202.

LaBar, K. S., Gatenby, J. C., Gore, J. C., LeDoux, J. E., and Phelps, E. A. (1998). Human amygdala activation during conditioned fear acquisition and extinction: a mixed-trial fMRI study. *Neuron, 20,* 937–945.

Ledgerwood, L., Richardson, R., and Cranney, J. (2003). D-cycloserine facilitates extinction of conditioned fear as assessed by freezing in rats. *Behavioral Neuroscience, 117,* 341–349.

LeDoux, J. E. (1994). Emotion, memory and the brain. *Scientific American, 270,* 50–57.

Lehmann, H., Lacanilao, S., and Sutherland, R. J. (2007). Complete or partial hippocampal damage produces equivalent retrograde amnesia for remote contextual fear memories. *European Journal of Neuroscience, 25,* 1278–1286.

Maren, S., Aharonov, G., and Fanselow, M. S. (1997). Neurotoxic lesions of the dorsal hippocampus and Pavlovian fear conditioning in rats. *Behavioural Brain Research, 88,* 261–274.

Mineka, S. (1985). Animal models of anxiety-based disorders: their usefulness and limitations. In A. H. Tuma and J. D. Maser (Eds.), *Anxiety and the anxiety disorders* (pp. 199–244). Hillsdale, NJ: Lawrence Erlbaum Associates, Inc.

Mowrer, O. H. (1939). A stimulus-response analysis of anxiety and its role as a reinforcing agent. *Psychological Review, 46,* 553–565.

Mowrer, O. H. (1947). On the dual nature of learning: a reinterpretation of "conditioning" and "problem solving." *Harvard Educational Review, 17,* 102–150.

Myers, K. M. and Davis, M. (2007). Mechanisms of fear extinction. *Molecular Psychiatry, 12,* 120–150.

Paré, D., Quirk, G. J., and LeDoux, J. E. (2004). New vistas on amygdala networks in conditioned fear. *Journal of Neurophysiology, 92,* 1–9.

Quirk, G. J., Garcia, R., and Gonzalez-Lima, F. (2006). Prefrontal mechanisms in extinction of conditioned fear. *Biological Psychiatry, 60,* 337–343.

Quirk, G. J., Likhtik, E., Pelletier, J. G., and Paré, D. (2003). Stimulation of medial prefrontal cortex decreases the responsiveness of central amygdala output neurons. *Journal of Neuroscience, 23,* 8800–8807.

Quirk, G. J., Russo, G. K., Barron, J. L., and Lebron, K. (2000). The role of ventromedial prefrontal cortex in the recovery of extinguished fear. *Journal of Neuroscience, 20,* 6225–6231.

Ressler, K. J., Rothbaum, B. O., Tannenbaum, L., Anderson, P., Graap, K., Zimand, E., Hodges, L., and Davis, M. (2004). Cognitive enhancers as adjuncts to psychotherapy: use of d-cycloserine in phobic individuals to facilitate extinction of fear. *Archives of General Psychiatry, 61,* 1136–1144.

Romanski, L. M. and LeDoux, J. E. (1992). Equipotentiality of thalamo-amygdala and thalamo-cortico-amygdala circuits in auditory fear conditioning. *Journal of Neuroscience, 12,* 4501–4509.

Royer, S. and Paré, D. (2002). Bidirectional synaptic plasticity in intercalated amygdala neurons and the extinction of conditioned fear responses. *Neuroscience, 115,* 455–462.

Rumpel, S., LeDoux J., Zador, A., and Malinow, R. (2005). Postsynaptic receptor trafficking underlying a form of associative learning. *Science, 308,* 83–88.

Samson, R. D. and Paré, D. (2005). Activity-dependent synaptic plasticity in the central nucleus of the amygdala. *Journal of Neuroscience, 25,* 1847–1855.

Sierra-Mercado, D. Jr., Corcoran, K. A., Lebron-Milad, K., and Quirk, G. J. (2006). Inactivation of the ventromedial prefrontal cortex reduces expression of conditioned fear and impairs subsequent recall of extinction. *European Journal of Neuroscience, 24,* 1751–1758.

Sotres-Bayon, F., Bush, D. E., and LeDoux, J. E. (2007). Acquisition of fear extinction requires activation of NR2B-containing NMDA receptors in the lateral amygdala. *Neuropsychopharmacology, 32,* 1929–1940.

Timberlake, W. (1994). Behavioral systems, associationism, and Pavlovian conditioning. *Psychonomic Bulletin and Review, 1,* 405–420.

Walker, D. L., Ressler, K. J., Lu, K. T., and Davis, M. (2002). Facilitation of conditioned fear extinction by systemic administration or intra-amygdala infusions of d-cycloserine as assessed with fear-potentiated startle. *Journal of Neuroscience, 22,* 2343–2351.

Wilensky, A. E., Schafe, G. E., Kristensen, M. P., and LeDoux, J. E. (2006). Rethinking the fear circuit: the central nucleus of the amygdala is required for the acquisition, consolidation, and expression of Pavlovian fear conditioning. *Journal of Neuroscience, 26,* 12387–12396.

Wiltgen, B. J., Sanders, M. J., Anagnostaras, S. G., Sage, J. R., and Fanselow, M. S. (2006). Context fear learning in the absence of the hippocampus. *Journal of Neuroscience, 17,* 5484–5491.

Photo Credits

The Author would like to thank the following researchers for generously providing the images that appear at the beginning of each chapter.

Chapter 1 Courtesy of Dr. Joseph C. Biedenkapp, University of Colorado

Chapter 2 Courtesy of Dr. Robert J. Sutherland and Neal Melvin, University of Lethbridge

Chapter 3 Courtesy of Dr. Neal J. Waxham, University of Texas Medical School, Austin

Chapter 4 Courtesy of Dr. Robert D. Blitzer, Mount Sinai Medical School

Chapter 5 Courtesy of Dr. Neal J. Waxham, University of Texas Medical School, Austin

Chapter 6 Courtesy of Dr. Gary J. Bassell, Emory University School of Medicine

Chapter 7 Courtesy of Dr. Patricia H. Reggio, University of North Carolina, Greensboro

Chapter 8 Courtesy of Dr. Robert D. Blitzer, Mount Sinai Medical School

Chapter 9 Courtesy of Dr. Gary J. Bassell, Emory University School of Medicine

Chapter 10 Courtesy of Dr. John F. Guzowski, University of California, Irvine

Chapter 11 Courtesy of Dr. Gary J. Bassell, Emory University School of Medicine

Chapter 12 Courtesy of Dr. Michael Babcock, Montana State University

Chapter 13   Courtesy of Dr. Natalie C. Tronson, Northwestern University

Chapter 14   Courtesy of Dr. Sandra T. Bland, University of Colorado

Chapter 15   Courtesy of Dr. Carol A. Seger, Colorado State University

Chapter 16   Courtesy of Dr. Denis A. Paré, Rutgers University

Glossary

A

actin A cytoskeleton protein filament that exists in two states: globular actin (G-actin) and filament actin (F-actin).

actin-depolymerization factor/cofilin (ADF/cof) A protein that depolymerizes F-actin.

action A category of instrumental behavior believed to be supported by expectancies and thought to be goal directed and purposeful.

action potentials The electrical signal conducted along axons by which information is conveyed from one neuron to another in the nervous system.

active trace theory A theory that suggests that both the age of a memory trace and its state of activation at the time of a disrupting event are determinants of the vulnerability of the trace to disruption.

adhesion molecules Proteins located on the cell's surface that bind cells together.

adjacent-arm task A version of the radial arm maze in which a rodent is released from one arm and rewarded for choosing to enter one of the two adjacent arms.

adrenal gland An endocrine gland, located above the kidney, composed of two parts: the adrenal medulla (which secretes epinephrine) and the adrenal cortex (which secretes glucocorticoids).

adrenaline A hormone secreted by the adrenal gland, often as a result of an arousing stimulus; also called epinephrine (EPI).

adrenergic receptors Receptors that bind to adrenergics.

adrenergics Drugs that mimic the effects of epinephrine.

adrenoreceptors Receptors that bind to epinephrine.

after images Briefly lasting sensations; the first of three traces in William James's theory of memory.

agonist A substance that binds to a specific receptor and triggers a response in the cell. It mimics the action of an endogenous ligand (such as a hormone or neurotransmitter) that binds to the same receptor.

AMPA receptor An ionotropic glutamate receptor that is selective for Na^+. AMPA receptors are major contributors to whether or not the sending neuron will depolarize the receiving neuron.

AMPA trafficking The movement of AMPA receptors into and out of the plasma membrane.

ampakines A class of drugs that may enhance cognitive function. Ampakines cross the blood–brain barrier and bind to a site on the AMPA receptor.

amygdala A collection of midbrain nuclei, some of which are involved in supporting fear conditioning and in modulating memory storage in other regions of the brain.

annulus crossings A measure of place learning in the Morris water-escape task based on how many times during the probe trial the animal actually crosses the exact place where the platform was located during training compared to how many times it crosses the equivalent area in the other quadrants.

antagonist A drug that opposes or inhibits the effects of a particular neurotransmitter on the postsynaptic cell.

anterior cingulate The frontal part of the cingulate cortex, believed to be involved in modulating memory formation.

anterograde amnesia The loss of memory for events that occur after a brain insult or experimental treatment.

antisense methodology A methodology that uses an injection of antisense oligodeoxynucleotides to interfere with the translation of particular proteins.

Arc An immediate early gene, activity-regulated, cytoskeleton-associated protein that is rapidly transcribed in the hippocampus when rats explore novel environments.

associative loss hypothesis A hypothesis that assumes extinction is due to the CS–alone presentation eliminating the original CS–US association.

auditory cortex A region of the brain that supports learned fear to an auditory stimulus by projecting the stimulus directly to the amygdala.

auditory cue A type of conditioned stimulus used in fear conditioning, usually a tone.

auditory-cue fear conditioning A conditioning procedure in which an auditory stimulus (tone) is paired with shock.

autoinhibitory–regulatory domain A domain of a kinase protein that keeps the kinase in an inactive state.

autophosphorylation A special property of CaMKII that enables its active subunits to phosphorylate each other.

axon The long fiber of a neuron that extends from the soma and conducts electrical signals away from the cell body.

B

basal ganglia A region of the brain composed of a number of subcortical nuclei including the caudate nucleus, putamen, globus pallidus, subthalamic nucleus, nucleus accumbens, and substantia nigra.

basal nucleus (BA) A nucleus of the amygdala that is thought to be an important part of the neural basis of fear. The BA is a component of the BLA (basolateral nucleus of the amygdala).

basolateral nucleus of the amygdala (BLA) A region of the amygdala that includes the basal and lateral nuclei. It is critically involved in memory modulation and storing fear memories and plays an important role in attaching value to outcomes.

behavioral experience An experience generated by a behaving organism interacting with its environment.

behavioral system A system that is organized specifically to ensure that some particular need is met. For example, there are behavioral systems designed to support our reproductive and feeding-related activities and behavioral systems that allow us to avoid and escape dangerous situations.

C

CA1 A subregion of the hippocampus that receives input from the CA3 region via Schaffer collateral fibers and projects to the entorhinal cortex via the subiculum. It also receives input from the entorhinal cortex.

CA3 A subregion of the hippocampus that receives input from the dentate gyrus via mossy fibers and projects to the CA1 region via Schaffer collateral fibers.

calcium-induced calcium release (CICR) The release of calcium from the endoplasmic reticulum; thought to occur when extracellular calcium enters the dendritic spine through the NMDA receptor and binds to ryanodine receptors.

calmodulin A calcium-binding protein that can regulate a number of protein targets.

CaMKII (calcium-calmodulin-dependent protein kinase II) A kinase protein that, once activated by calmodulin, is able to phosphorylate other proteins in the cell.

CaMKIINtide A noncompetitive inhibitor of CaMKII that can reverse LTP.

cannula A small needle used to inject chemical solutions into precise regions of the brain to damage neurons.

cannula guide A hollow metal tube that is inserted permanently into the brain that allows a drug to be readily injected into an awake and moving animal.

catalytic domain A domain of a kinase that performs the phosphorylation reaction.

ceiling effect A measurement problem that occurs when the value of the performance measure approaches its highest possible level and thus cannot be further increased by some other treatment.

cellular consolidation The biochemical and molecular processes that take place immediately following the behavioral experience and initially stabilize the memory trace. This type of consolidation is thought to take several hours to complete.

central nucleus (CE) A nucleus of the amygdala that is thought to be an important part of the neural basis of fear.

chromosome The part of the nucleus that contains the genetic material DNA (deoxyribonucleic acid).

clenbuterol An adrenergic receptor agonist.

cognitive expectancy theory A theory proposed by Edward C. Tolman that assumes that learning produces representations of behaviors and their resulting outcomes.

competing memory hypothesis A hypothesis that assumes extinction produces a new association called a CS–noUS association, while the original CS–US association that produced the CR remains intact.

conditional knockout methodology A genetic engineering method used to knock out a particular gene in a very well specified region of the brain and to do this at different times in development.

conscious recollection The intentional initiation of a memory with an awareness of remembering; a subjective feeling that is a product of the retrieval process.

constitutive trafficking The routine movement of AMPA receptors in and out of dendritic spines.

context CS The static features of an environment that define the place in which conditioning occurs.

context preexposure paradigm A procedure used to study how rodents acquire a memory of an explored context.

contextual fear conditioning Fear that is produced to the context or place in which the shock US is presented.

cortical pathway A pathway that carries information from the sensory thalamus to the neocortical regions of the brain where a richer, more detailed representation of the experience is constructed.

corticosterone An adrenal hormone that can modulate memory storage; also classified as a glucocorticoid because it is involved in the metabolism of glucose.

cortico-striatal system A brain system composed of the striatum and its afferent and efferent connections.

CREB (cAMP-responsive element binding) protein A transcription factor that is implicated in both synaptic plasticity and behavioral memory; a kind of molecular memory switch that in the on state initiates the production of memory-making messenger ribonucleic acid (mRNA).

CS–noUS association A new association generated when the CS (conditioned stimulus) is no longer presented with the US (unconditioned stimulus). This idea forms the basis of the competing memory theory in extinction studies.

cytoskeleton protein filaments Proteins, consisting of actin, microtubules, and intermediate filaments, that form the internal scaffolding that gives a cell its shape.

cytosol The internal fluid of the neuron.

D

DCS (d-cycloserine) A drug that is a partial agonist and that binds to the glycine site of the NMDA receptor to enhance its opening.

de novo **protein synthesis hypothesis** The hypothesis that the consolidation of the memory trace requires that the to-be-remembered experience initiates the synthesis of new proteins.

debriefing A brief crisis intervention usually administered within days of a traumatic event in which the trauma-exposed individual is encouraged to talk about his or her feelings and reactions to the event.

declarative memory A category of memory that includes both episodic and semantic memory.

delayed nonmatching to sample (DNMS) A memory testing procedure used to study recognition memory in primates.

dendrites Branched projections of a neuron that receive synaptic input from the presynaptic terminal.

dentate gyrus A subregion of the hippocampus that receives input from the entorhinal cortex via the perforant path and projects via mossy fibers to the CA3 region.

depolarization The displacement of a cell's membrane potential toward a less negative value.

dexamethasone A synthetic glucocorticoid.

DHPG   The acronym for (R,S)-3,5-dihydroxyphenylglycine; an agonist that binds to the metabotropic glutamate receptor 1 (mGluR1).

dodecameric holoenzyme   A complex enzyme that forms CaMKII from 12 protein subunits or isoforms.

dopamine   A neurotransmitter, related to norepinephrine and epinephrine, that belongs to a group called catecholamines.

dopamine-incentive salience hypothesis   The theory that the activation of the mesolimbic dopamine system by a rewarding outcome attaches motivational significance to stimuli associated with that outcome.

dopamine reinforcement hypothesis   The theory that the neurotransmitter dopamine is the primary candidate for strengthening the property of outcomes that influence instrumental behavior.

E

electroconvulsive shock (ECS)   A treatment for psychiatric disorders in which seizures are induced with electricity for therapeutic effect; also known as electroconvulsive therapy (ECT).

electrode   A fine wire used to deliver electric current to the brain.

endoplasmic reticulum (ER)   An organelle that is part of the endomembrane system and one of the elements of translation machinery. The ER extends continuously throughout the neuron and works with the plasma membrane to regulate many neuronal processes. It is also a calcium store and it can release calcium when ligands bind to receptors located on its surface.

engram   A sustained neural representation of a behavioral experience; another name for a memory trace.

enzyme   A protein that accelerates the rate of chemical reactions.

epinephrine (EPI)   A hormone produced by the adrenal gland that modulates memory storage; also called adrenaline.

episodic memory system   The memory system that extracts and stores the content of personal experiences.

ERK (extracellular-regulated kinase)   A kinase that participates in many aspects of synaptic plasticity. See ERK–MAPK.

ERK–MAPK   One of several possible signaling pathways or cascades, initiated by neurotrophic factors, that can converge to phosphorylate CREB protein and induce the transcription of plasticity-related mRNAs.

escape latency   The time between when a training trial starts and when the subject completes the trial.

eukaryotic elongation factor 1A (eEF1A)   A translation machinery protein that is synthesized locally, in response to an L-LTP-inducing stimulus, and gets incorporated into the dendritic spine.

excitatory postsynaptic potential (EPSP)   Depolarization of the postsynaptic membrane potential by the action of a synaptically released neurotransmitter.

exocytosis   The process by which AMPA receptors are inserted into the plasma membrane.

expectancy   A three-term association (S1–R–S2) that includes a representation of the stimulus situation (S1) that preceded the response, a representation of the response (R), and a representation of the outcome (S2) produced by the response.

exposure therapy   A therapy in which patients are forced to experience the stimulus situation that induces their fear response; used to treat a number of fear–anxiety disorders.

extinction   In a Pavlovian experiment, the elimination of a conditioned response (CR), achieved by presenting the conditioned stimulus (CS) without the unconditioned stimulus (US).

F

F-actin (filament actin)   A two-stranded helical polymer composed of globular actin.

familiarity   A process that can support recognition memory without recollection of the time or place of the experience.

fiber volley   A measure of action potentials arriving at dendrites in the region of the recording site of an LTP (long-term potentiation) experiment.

field potential (field extracellular excitatory postsynaptic potential)   A measurement of the change in the ion composition of extracellular fluid as positive ions flow away from the extracellular recording and into the surrounding neurons. Also called fEPSP or field EPSP, it is the dependent variable in a long-term potentiation (LTP) experiment.

first messenger   A molecule that carries information from one neuron to another neuron.

floor effect   A measurement problem that occurs when the value of the performance measure is so low that it cannot be further reduced by some other treatment.

freezing   An innate defensive response of rodents in which they become immobile or still. Freezing has survival advantages because a moving animal is more likely to be detected by a predator than a still one.

functional end points   End points of the biochemical processes initiated by the second messenger Ca^{2+} that can strengthen synaptic connections.

functional magnetic resonance imaging (fMRI)   A method for imaging regional activity in the brain while the participant is engaged in cognitive activity.

G

G proteins (guanine nucleotide binding proteins)   Second messenger proteins in the plasma membrane that are activated by glutamate binding to metabotropic glutamate receptors.

G-actin (globular actin)   Subunits of actin that serve as monomer building blocks and that assemble into F-actin.

galvanic skin response (GSR)   An autonomic nervous system response related to the skin's ability to conduct electricity, used to measure defensive fear behavior.

gene superconductance   A genomic signaling cascade that causes an overproduction of mRNAs.

genetic engineering   A collection of methods used by scientists to alter the DNA of living organisms and thereby alter specific genes.

genomic signaling   Processes initiated by synaptic activity that lead to the production of new proteins through transcription and translation.

gill withdrawal reflex   A defensive behavior displayed by *Aplysia californica* when its skin is stimulated.

glucocorticoid   A hormone involved in the metabolism of glucose. In contrast to adrenaline, glucocorticoids can directly enter the brain.

glutamate   An excitatory amino acid neurotransmitter that is the primary neurotransmitter in the induction of long-term potentiation.

H

habit   A category of instrumental behavior believed to be the product of strengthening

S–R connections and believed not to be goal directed or purposeful.

habituation   The idea that the magnitude of the response to an eliciting stimulus decreases with repeated stimulation.

high-frequency stimulus (HFS)   Another name for the inducing stimulus in an LTP experiment.

hippocampal formation   A region of the brain composed of the dentate gyrus (a subregion of the hippocampus), the hippocampus proper (CA1–CA3 fields), and the subiculum.

hippocampus   A region of the brain composed of the hippocampus proper (CA1–CA3 fields) and the dentate gyrus subregion. The hippocampus is believed to make a critical contribution to episodic memory.

hyperpolarization   The displacement of a cell's membrane potential toward a more negative value.

I

immediate shock effect   The display of no fear to a context after rodents have been shocked without being allowed to first explore that context.

in vitro preparation   A method of performing an experiment in a controlled environment outside of a living organism. For example, a slice of hippocampus tissue is often used to conduct long-term potentiation (LTP) experiments.

indexing theory of hippocampal memory   A theory that assumes that the hippocampus stores an index to cortical patterns of neural activity that were generated by an episode.

inducing stimulus   The low-intensity, high-frequency stimulus used to induce LTP.

infralimbic region (infralimbic medial prefrontal cortex)   A cortical region that is believed to suppress the action system and thus to play an important role in selecting which system—the action or habit system—controls instrumental behavior.

instrumental behavior (instrumental responses)   Behavior that can change or modify the environment. Instrumental behaviors can be modified by the consequences they produce.

intercalated neurons   Clusters of cells in the amygdala that produce inhibitory output that, when fed forward to the central nucleus of the amygdala, can reduce the output of the neurons in the CEm that generate defensive behavior.

intertrial interval   The time between pairings of light and shock in fear conditioning.

ion   An atom or a group of atoms that has acquired a net electric charge by gaining or losing one or more electrons.

ion-gated channel   A specific ion channel that opens and closes to allow the cell to alter its membrane potential.

ionotropic receptors   Receptors comprised of several subunits that come together in the cell membrane to form a potential channel or pore which, when open, allows ions such as Na^+ or Ca^{2+} to enter; also called ion-gated channels or ligand-gated ion channels.

IP3 (inositol 1,4,5-triphosphate)   A second messenger that is synthesized when glutamate binds to the metabotropic glutamate receptor 1 (mGluR1).

IP3R (inositol 1,4,5-triphosphate receptor)   A receptor that binds to the second messenger IP3, located on the endoplasmic reticulum in the dendritic compartment near the spines.

K

kinase   An enzyme that, once activated, catalyzes the transfer of a phosphate group from a donor to an acceptor.

L

lateral capsule (CEc) A subnucleus of the central nucleus (CE) of the amygdala that is thought to be an important part of the neural basis of fear.

lateral hypothalamus A region of the brain responsible for changes in the autonomic responses (heart rate and blood pressure, for example) produced by the sympathetic nervous system that prepare an animal for action.

lateral nucleus (LA) A nucleus of the amygdala that is thought to be an important part of the neural basis of fear. The LA is a component of the BLA (basolateral nucleus of the amygdala).

Law of Effect A theory of learning proposed by E. L. Thorndike that assumes that reinforcing events strengthen or weaken stimulus–response connections.

learning–performance distinction A principle that recognizes that performance is influenced by a number of processes in addition to those of learning and memory.

ligand Any chemical compound that binds to a specific site on a receptor.

LIMK1 A kinase that phosphorylates the actin-depolymerization factor / cofilin site.

local protein synthesis The translation of existing mRNA into protein that occurs in the dendrites.

locus coeruleus A small region of the brain that contains only about 3,000 neurons, yet projects broadly and provides nearly all the norepinephrine to the cortex, limbic system, thalamus, and hypothalamus.

long-lasting LTP (L-LTP) An enduring form of long-term potentiation thought to require the synthesis of new proteins.

long-term habituation A long-lasting form of habituation that is produced by many sessions of repeated stimulation.

long-term memory trace A relatively enduring memory trace that is resistant to disruption.

long-term potentiation (LTP) A persistent strengthening of synapses produced by low-frequency, intense electrical stimulation.

M

MAPK (mitogen-activated protein kinase) A kinase that participates in many aspects of synaptic plasticity. See ERK–MAPK.

medial nucleus (CEm) A subnucleus of the central nucleus (CE) of the amygdala thought to be an important part of the neural basis of fear. Note that the CEm is the output region of the amygdala; when CEm neurons are activated, they in turn activate neurons in the PAG and lateral hypothalamus that generate fear behaviors.

medial temporal hippocampal (MTH) system The region of the brain composed of the perirhinal, parahippocampal, and entorhinal cortices and the hippocampal formation.

membrane potential The difference in the electrical charge inside the neuron's cell body compared to the charge outside the cell body.

memory consolidation A process that stabilizes the memory and renders it resistant to disruption.

memory modulation framework A theory that assumes that experience activates both the neurons that store the memory and other modulating neural–hormonal events that can influence the neurons that store the memory.

memory modulators The hormonal and other neural systems that are not part of the storage system but can nonetheless influence the synapses that store the memory.

memory trace A sustained neural representation of a behavioral experience; also called an engram.

mesolimbic dopamine system   A small number of neurons located in a region of the brain called the ventral tegmental area (VTA) that provide dopamine to other regions of the brain.

messenger   A molecule that conveys information from a sending neuron to a receiving neuron.

messenger ribonucleic acid (mRNA)   A molecule of RNA that carries a chemical blueprint for a protein product.

metabotropic receptor   A G-protein receptor that stimulates or inhibits intracellular biochemical reactions. In contrast to ionotropic receptors, metabotropic receptors do not form an ion channel pore; rather, they are indirectly linked with ion channels on the plasma membrane of the cell through signal transduction mechanisms.

mGluR1 (metabotropic glutamate receptor 1)   A subtype of metabotropic receptor located in the plasma membrane near dendritic spines.

molecular memory switch   A way of thinking about CREB protein that describes its role in the production of memory-making mRNAs. In its *on* state it initiates their production, when it is in the *off* state these products are not transcribed.

molecular switch   A molecule that can shift between two or more states in response to one or more stimuli.

mossy fibers   Axons that connect the dentate gyrus to the CA3 region of the hippocampus.

multiple memory systems   A theory that different kinds of information are acquired and stored in different parts of the brain.

multiple trace theory   A theory of systems consolidation that assumes that the medial temporal hippocampal system is always required to retrieve episodic memories but that semantic memories can become independent of this system.

N

neural cadherins   Calcium-dependent cell adhesion molecules; strands of proteins held together by Ca^{2+} ions. Cadherins can exist as either monomers or cis-stranded dimers.

neurobiology of learning and memory   An important scientific field that seeks to understand how the brain stores and retrieves information about our experiences.

neuron doctrine   The idea that the brain is made up of discrete cells, called neurons or nerve cells, that are the elemental signal units of the brain.

neurotransmitter   A substance released by synaptic terminals for the purpose of transmitting information from one neuron to another.

neurotrophic factors   Molecules that promote survival of neural tissues and play a critical role in neural development and differentiation. Neurotrophic factors bind to trk receptors.

NMDA receptor   An ionotropic glutamate receptor selective for the agonist NMDA that plays a critical role in the induction of long-term potentiation (LTP).

nonreward   A term used to represent an outcome produced by an instrumental behavior that decreases the strength of that behavior.

nonsense syllables   Meaningless non-words created by placing a vowel between two consonants, for example, nuh, vag, or boc.

norepinephrine (NE)   An adrenergic neurotransmitter.

nucleus accumbens   A collection of neurons within the striatum that contribute to learning instrumental behaviors and may also modulate memory formation.

P

path length   A measure of place learning in the Morris water-escape task; the distance a rodent swims before finding the hidden platform.

pattern completion   A process assumed to be supported by the hippocampus by which a subset or portion of an experience that originally established a memory trace can activate or replay the entire experience.

pattern separation   A process assumed to be supported by the hippocampus that enables very similar experiences to be segregated in memory.

perforant path   Fibers that connect the entorhinal cortex to the dentate gyrus.

periaqueductal gray (PAG)   A midbrain region responsible for producing freezing and analgesia (loss of sensation of pain) responses to fear in rodents.

perirhinal cortex   A cortical region adjacent to the hippocampus that is critically involved in object recognition memory.

phosphatases (PP1 and PP2)   A class of enzymes whose function is to dephosphorylate proteins.

phosphorylation   The chemical addition of a phosphate group (phosphate and oxygen) to a protein or another compound that causes it to become active.

PKA (cyclic AMP-dependent protein kinase or protein kinase A)   A kinase that is activated by the second messenger, cyclic adenosine monophosphate protein (cAMP), that participates in the process of exocytosis.

PKC (protein kinase C)   A kinase activated by calcium that participates in the process of exocytosis.

place-learning task   A version of the Morris water-escape task in which a rat is required to find a platform hidden below the surface of the water; also called the hidden-platform task.

plasticity   The property of the brain that allows it to be modified by experience.

plasticity products (PPs)   Another name for mRNAs and proteins that are thought to be critical to the production of long-lasting changes in synaptic strength.

polymerization   The process of combining many smaller molecules (monomers) into a large organic module called a polymer.

posterior dorsomedial striatum (pDMS)   A region of the striatum that supports goal-directed actions.

postsynaptic dendrite   The component of a neuron specialized for transmitter reception.

postsynaptic density zone (PSDZ)   A region at the tip of the dendritic spine that is the site of neurotransmitter receptors.

postsynaptic depolarization   The flow of positive ions into the postsynaptic neuron.

postsynaptic potential   A brief electrical event that is generated in the postsynaptic neuron when the synapse is activated.

post-translation modification   The chemical modification of a protein after its translation.

post-traumatic stress disorder (PTSD)   A syndrome in which individuals with this diagnosis have unusually vivid recall of the traumatic events they experienced, accompanied by severe emotional responses.

predatory imminence gradient   A measure of fear response in rodents that is dependent on the distance of a predator, that is, when a potential predator is at a distance a rat will freeze, but when the predator moves within striking distance, a rat might attempt to flee.

prelimbic region (prelimbic medial pre-frontal cortex)   A region of the medial prefrontal cortex believed to be needed to acquire an action. However, once the associations that support an action are learned, this region is believed to no longer be critical.

presynaptic terminal   The component of a neuron that is specialized to release the transmitter.

primary memory   The persisting representation of an experience that forms part of a stream of consciousness; the second of three traces in William James's theory of memory.

probe trial   The stage in the Morris water-escape task in which the platform is removed to assess a rodent's memory of the platform location.

protein synthesis   The assembly of protein molecules from messenger ribonucleic acid (mRNA); also called translation.

Q

quadrant search time   A measure of place learning in the Morris water-escape task. A rodent that has stored a memory of the location of the platform will spend more of its search time in the training quadrant than it will in the other quadrants.

R

receptor   A protein located on the surface of or within cells that is responsible for binding to an active ligand.

recollection   A retrieval process that produces information about the time and place of an experience.

reconsolidation theory   A theory that assumes that the retrieval of a memory itself can disrupt an established memory trace but that the retrieval also initiates another round of protein synthesis so that the trace is "reconsolidated."

reinforcer or reward   Terms used interchangeably to represent an outcome produced by an instrumental behavior that increases the strength of that behavior.

reinstatement   One of several ways to recover an extinguished conditioned response (CR), in which simply re-presenting the unconditioned stimulus (US) in the training context can reinstate the ability of the conditioned stimulus (CS) to evoke the CR.

renewal effect   One of several ways to recover an extinguished conditioned response (CR); achieved by changing the context for extinction but later returning an animal to the training context to recover the CR.

resting membrane potential   The membrane potential or membrane voltage (about –70 mV) maintained by a neuron when it is not generating action potentials.

retrieval failure   Amnesia that is the result of an inability to retrieve an existing memory.

retrograde amnesia   The loss of memory for events that occurred prior to a brain insult or experimental treatment.

reward or reinforcer   Terms used interchangeably to represent an outcome produced by an instrumental behavior that increases the strength of that behavior.

reward devaluation   A method used to determine if an instrumental behavior is an action or a habit.

ribosomes   Dense globular structures that take raw material in the form of amino acids and manufacture proteins using the blueprint provided by the mRNA.

RU 28362   A drug that is a glucocorticoid receptor agonist.

ryanodine receptor (RyR)   A calcium-binding receptor located on the endoplasmic reticulum that extends into dendritic spines.

S

Schaffer collateral fibers   Fibers that connect CA3 to CA1 pyramidal cells in the hippocampus.

second messenger   A molecule that relays the signal received by receptors located in the plasma membrane (such as NMDA and AMPA receptors) to target molecules in the cells.

secondary memory   The record of experiences that have receded from the stream of consciousness but can be later retrieved or recollected; the third of three traces in William James's theory of memory; also called memory proper.

secondary treatment   A method used to decrease the likelihood that the person who experienced a trauma will develop post-traumatic stress disorder.

semantic memory   A category of memory that is believed to support memory for facts and the ability to extract generalizations across experiences.

separatist view   The theory that only episodic memory depends on the entire medial temporal hippocampal system and that semantic memory does not require a contribution of the hippocampus.

Ser-3   The phosphorylation site of ADF/cofilin that regulates its ability to depolymerize F-actin.

short-lasting LTP (S-LTP)   Long-term potentiation with a limited duration, supported by post-translation processes.

short-term habituation   A form of habituation that does not endure.

short-term memory trace   A relatively short-lasting trace that is vulnerable to disruption.

silent synapse   A synapse with no AMPA receptors.

simple system approach   A strategy used to reduce the complexity of studying the neural basis of memory by studying an animal with the simplest nervous system that can support a modifiable behavior.

social transmission of a food preference   A method for studying how rodents acquire food preferences from other rodents.

solitary tract nucleus (NTS)   A brain stem region that receives information from the vagal nerve; also referred to as the NTS (derived from the Latin *nucleus tractus solitarius*).

soma-to-nucleus signaling   A genomic signaling process that occurs when Ca^{2+} enters the soma through voltage-dependent calcium channels opening as a result of action potentials.

spontaneous recovery   The recovery of an habituated response that occurs "spontaneously," with the passage of time.

standard model of systems consolidation   A theory that assumes that as episodic and semantic memories age they no longer require the medial temporal hippocampal system for retrieval.

stereotaxic surgery   A surgery that uses a coordinate system to locate specific targets inside the brain to enable some procedure to be carried out on them (for example, a lesion, injection, or cannula implantation).

storage failure   Amnesia that is the result of a failure to store the memory.

striatum   A subregion of the basal ganglia, composed of the caudate nucleus, putamen, and nucleus accumbens; the basic input segment of the basal ganglia.

subcortical pathway   A pathway that carries information from the sensory thalamus to the lateral nucleus of the amygdala (LA). It is thought to carry a somewhat impoverished representation of the sensory experience.

subiculum   The output component of the hippocampal formation.

synapse   The point of contact between the presynaptic sending neuron and the postsynaptic receiving neuron.

synapse-to-nucleus signaling   A genomic signaling process that begins at the synapse and results in transcription.

synaptic-activity-regulated trafficking   Movement of AMPA receptors in and out of the dendritic spines that is regulated by synaptic activity generated when glutamate binds to postsynaptic receptors.

synaptic cleft   The space that separates the presynaptic terminal and the postsynaptic dendrite.

synaptic plasticity hypothesis   The hypothesis that the strength of synaptic connections—

the ease with which an action potential in one cell excites (or inhibits) its target cell—is not fixed but is plastic and modifiable.

synaptic tagging theory   A theory that assumes that an LTP-inducing stimulus changes a dendritic spine so that it can capture plasticity products generated by strongly stimulated synapses.

synaptic vesicles   Spherical membrane-bound organelles in presynaptic terminals that store neurotransmitters.

systems consolidation   A theory that assumes that a change in the strength of the memory trace is brought about by interactions between brain regions (the medial temporal hippocampal system and neocortex). Systems consolidation is assumed to take place over a long period of time, after the memory is initially established.

T

tag   A biological marking of a synapse in the dendritic spine that has been stimulated so that it will have the capacity to capture new plasticity products.

temporally graded retrograde amnesia
Amnesia that is more pronounced for recently experienced events than for more remotely experienced events.

test stimulus   The stimulus used to establish a baseline in an LTP experiment. It is also the stimulus used to determine that LTP has been established.

theta-burst stimulation (TBS)   A different stimulus protocol for inducing long-term potentiation and the forms of LTP it induces, modeled after an increased rate of pyramidal neuronal firing that occurs when a rodent is exploring a novel environment.

Thr286   A phosphorylation site on the regulatory domain of CaMKII.

transcription   The process of converting genetic material from DNA to messenger RNA (mRNA). The resulting mRNA is called a transcript.

transcription factors   Proteins that interact with DNA to produce mRNA.

translation   The process by which mRNA is converted to protein; also called protein synthesis.

translation machinery   The molecules that participate in translating mRNA into protein.

trk receptors   A class of plasma membrane receptors in the tyrosine kinase family that bind to neurotrophic factors.

U

unitary view   The theory that both semantic and episodic memory depend on the entire medial temporal hippocampal system.

V

vagus or vagal nerve   Cranial nerve X, arising from the medulla and innervating the viscera of the thoracic and abdominal cavities, that carries information about the body into the brain.

viral vector   A new technique for delivering a gene to a particular region of the brain that involves genetically modifying a virus to carry the gene of interest.

visible-platform task   A version of the Morris water-escape task in which a rat is required to find a platform that is visible above the surface of the water.

voltage-dependent calcium channel (vdcc)
A membrane protein that forms a pore, which is permeable to calcium gated by depolarization of the membrane.

Author Index

Subject Index